Lecture Notes in Computer Science 14586

Founding Editors

Gerhard Goos
Juris Hartmanis

Editorial Board Members

The series Lecture Notes in Computer Science (LNCS), including its subseries Lecture Notes in Artificial Intelligence (LNAI) and Lecture Notes in Bioinformatics (LNBI), has established itself as a medium for the publication of new developments in computer science and information technology research, teaching, and education.

LNCS enjoys close cooperation with the computer science R & D community, the series counts many renowned academics among its volume editors and paper authors, and collaborates with prestigious societies. Its mission is to serve this international community by providing an invaluable service, mainly focused on the publication of conference and workshop proceedings and postproceedings. LNCS commenced publication in 1973.

Martin Andreoni
Editor

Applied Cryptography and Network Security Workshops

ACNS 2024 Satellite Workshops
AIBlock, AIHWS, AIoTS, SCI, AAC, SiMLA, LLE, and CIMSS
Abu Dhabi, United Arab Emirates, March 5–8, 2024
Proceedings, Part I

 Springer

Editor
Martin Andreoni
Technology Innovation Institute
Abu Dhabi, United Arab Emirates

ISSN 0302-9743   ISSN 1611-3349 (electronic)
Lecture Notes in Computer Science
ISBN 978-3-031-61485-9   ISBN 978-3-031-61486-6 (eBook)
https://doi.org/10.1007/978-3-031-61486-6

This Springer imprint is published by the registered company Springer Nature Switzerland AG
The registered company address is: Gewerbestrasse 11, 6330 Cham, Switzerland

Preface

These proceedings contain the papers selected for presentation at the ACNS 2024 satellite workshops and the poster session, which were held in parallel with the main conference (the 22nd International Conference on Applied Cryptography and Network Security) from 5 to 8 March 2024.

Eight satellite workshops, two of which were new, were held in response to this year's call for workshop proposals. Each workshop provided a forum to address a specific topic at the forefront of cybersecurity research.

- 6th ACNS Workshop on Application Intelligence and Blockchain Security (AIBlock 2024), chaired by Weizhi Meng and Chunhua Su
- 5th ACNS Workshop on Artificial Intelligence in Hardware Security (AIHWS 2024), chaired by Stjepan Picek and Shivam Bhasin
- 6th ACNS Workshop on Artificial Intelligence and Industrial IoT Security (AIoTS 2024), chaired by Neetesh Saxena and Bong Jun Choi
- 5th ACNS Workshop on Secure Cryptographic Implementation (SCI 2024), chaired by Jingqiang Lin and Bo Luo
- 1st Workshop on Advances in Asymmetric Cryptanalysis (AAC 2024), chaired by Elena Kirshanova and Andre Esser
- 6th ACNS Workshop on Security in Machine Learning and its Applications (SiMLA 2024), chaired by Ezekiel Soremekun
- 1st Workshop on Low-Latency Encryption (LLE 2024), chaired by Shahram Rasoolzadeh and Santosh Ghosh
- 4th International Workshop on Critical Infrastructure and Manufacturing System Security (CIMSS 2024), chaired by Chuadhry Mujeeb Ahmed and; Rajib Ranian Maiti

This year, we received a total of 61 submissions. Each workshop had its own Program Committee (PC) in charge of the review process. These papers were evaluated based on their significance, novelty, and technical quality. The review process was double-blind. Ultimately, 33 papers were selected for presentation at the eight workshops, with an acceptance rate of 54%.

ACNS also awarded the best workshop paper to Marina Krček and Thomas Ordas, *"Diversity Algorithms for Laser Fault Injection"* from the AIHWS workshop. The winning paper was selected from among the nominated candidate papers from each workshop. The authors also received the monetary prize sponsored by Springer.

Besides the regular papers presented at the workshops, there were 12 invited talks.

- "Hard-Hat Cryptanalysis - Drilling Down into Real-world TLS Protocol Failures" by Robert Merget (TII, UAE) and "Attacks Against the CPA-D Security of Exact FHE Schemes, and Threshold-FHE schemes" by Damien Stehlé (Cryptolab, South Korea) at the AAC workshop

- "Building a Low-Latency Pseudorandom Function" by Joan Daemen (Radboud University, The Netherlands), "Designing Low-Latency Primitives and Modes" by Gregor Leander (Ruhr University Bochum, Germany), and "Automated Security Analysis of Symmetric-Key Primitives Using Tools" by Yu Sasaki (Nagoya University, Japan) at the LLE workshop
- "Attacking Machine Learning Models" by Yang Zhang (CISPA, Germany) at the SiMLA workshop
- "Searchable Symmetric Encryption and its attacks" by Kaitai Liang (TU Delft, The Netherlands) at the SCI workshop
- "Hardware Security through the Lens of Dr AI" by Debdeep Mukhopadhyay (IIT Kharagpur, India), and "Touching Points of AI and Cryptography" by Moti Yung (Columbia University & Google, USA) at AIHWS workshop
- "Cybersecurity in the 3D and IoT Era of Power Systems: Load Altering Attacks Unleashed!" by Charalambos (Harrys) Konstantinou (King Abdullah University of Science and Technology, Saudi Arabia) and "The Future of IoT Security: AI/ML and Lightweight Cryptography countering emerging threats" by Hoda Alkhzaimi (NYU Abu Dhabi, UAE) at the AIoTS workshop
- "Securing the Future: Advanced Safety and Resilience in Autonomous and Autonomic Systems" by Shreekant (Ticky) Thakkar (TII, UAE) and "Security of Advanced Machine Learning Features in Autonomous Systems" by Muhammad Shafique (NYU Abu Dhabi, UAE) at the CIMSS workshop

Charalambos Konstantinou also chaired a poster session, and 11 posters are included in the proceedings as extended abstracts. The following poster was recognised with the ACNS 2024 Best Poster Award.

- Francesco Antognazza, Alessandro Barenghi, Gerardo Pelosi, Ruggero Susella, "A Versatile and Unified HQC Hardware Accelerator"

The ACNS 2024 workshops were made possible by the joint efforts of many individuals and organizations. We sincerely thank the authors of all submissions. We thank each workshop's program chairs and PC members for their great effort in providing professional reviews and interesting feedback to authors on a tight schedule. We thank all the external reviewers for assisting the PC in their particular areas of expertise. We are grateful to Springer for sponsoring the best workshop paper award and the local organizing team for sponsoring the best poster award. We also thank the General Chairs, Michail Maniatakos and Ozgur Sinanoglu, and the organizing team members of the main conference and each workshop for their help in various aspects. A special acknowledgment goes to Jianying Zhou for his guidance and suggestions on the workshop organization.

Last but not least, we thank everyone else, speakers, session chairs, and attendees, for their contribution to the success of the ACNS 2024 workshops.

Martin Andreoni

AIBlock 2024

Sixth Workshop on Application Intelligence and Blockchain Security

08 March 2024

General Chair

Robert Deng   Singapore Management University, Singapore

Program Chairs

Chunhua Su	University of Aizu, Japan
Weizhi Meng	Technical University of Denmark, Denmark

Program Committee

Alessandro Brighente	University of Padova, Italy
Jintai Ding	University of Cincinnati, USA
Dieter Gollmann	Hamburg University of Technology, Germany
Cheng Huang	University of Waterloo, Canada
Claudio Juan	Universität Zürich, Switzerland
Georgios Kambourakis	University of the Aegean, Greece
Mario Larangeira	Tokyo Institute of Technology/IOHK, Japan
Wenjuan Li	Education University of Hong Kong, China
Mahmoud Nabil Mahmoud	North Carolina A&T University, USA
Zhe Xia	Wuhan University of Technology, China
Peng Xu	Huazhong University of Science and Technology, China
Haiyang Xue	Hong Kong Polytechnic University, China
Jianfeng Wang	Xidian University, China
Ding Wang	Nankai University, China
Qianhong Wu	Beihang University, China
Chunhua Su	University of Aizu, Japan
Andreas Veneris	University of Toronto, Canada
Cong Zuo	Beijing Institute of Technology, China

Steering Committee

Robert Deng	Singapore Management University, Singapore
Georgios Kambourakis	University of the Aegean, Greece
Sokratis Katsikas	Norwegian University of Science and Technology, Norway
Man Ho Au	Hong Kong Polytechnic University, China
Weizhi Meng	Technical University of Denmark, Denmark (Chair)
Chunhua Su	University of Aizu, Japan

Additional Reviewer

Fuyang Deng	Beihang University, China

AIHWS 2024

Fifth Workshop on Artificial Intelligence in Hardware Security

05 March 2024

Program Chairs

Shivam Bhasin   Radboud University, The Netherlands
Stjepan Picek   Radboud University, The Netherlands

Program Committee

Kashif Nawaz   Technology Innovation Institute, UAE
Liran Lerman   SWIFT/Université libre de Bruxelles, Belgium
Vincent Verneuil   NXP Semiconductors, Germany
Lukasz Chmielewski   Masaryk University, Czech Republic
Luca Mariot   University of Twente, The Netherlands
Zhuoran Liu   Radboud University, The Netherlands
Lejla Batina   Radboud University, The Netherlands
Guilherme Perin   Leiden University, The Netherlands
Kostas Papagiannopoulos   University of Amsterdam, The Netherlands
Ileana Buhan   Radboud University, The Netherlands
Lichao Wu   Radboud University, The Netherlands
David Gerault   Technology Innovation Institute, UAE
Naofumi Homma   Tohoku University, Japan
Dirmanto Jap   Nanyang Technological University, Singapore
Alan Jovic   University of Zagreb, Croatia
Fatemeh Ganji   Worcester Polytechnic Institute, USA

Web Chair

Marina Krcek   Delft University of Technology, The Netherlands

AIoTS 2024

Fifth Workshop on Artificial Intelligence and Industrial IoT Security

05 March 2024

Program Chairs

Neetesh Saxena	Cardiff University, UK
Bong Jun (David) Cho	Soongsil University, South Korea

Web Chair

Mayank Swarnkar	Indian Institute of Technology Varanasi (BHU), India

Publicity Chairs

Daisuke Mashima	Illinois Advanced Research Center, Singapore

Program Committee

Sridhar Adepu	University of Bristol, UK
Ajit Kumar	Soongsil University, South Korea
Daisuke Mashima	Illinois Advanced Research Center, Singapore
Nikhil Tripathi	IIIT Sri City, India
Chuadhry Mujeeb Ahmed	Newcastle University, UK
Vishal Sharma	Queen's University Belfast, UK
Charalambos Konstantinou	KAUST, Saudi Arabia
Mayank Swarnkar	IIT Varanasi (BHU), India
Sangram Ray	NIT Sikkim, India
Ali Ismail Awad	UAE University, UAE
Chaminda Thushara Hewage	Cardiff Metropolitan University, UK
Pradeep Kumar	Swansea University, UK
Rohit Verma	National College of Ireland, Ireland

SCI 2024

Fifth Workshop on Secure Cryptographic Implementation

06 March 2024

Program Chairs

Jingqiang Lin	University of Science and Technology of China, China
Bo Luo	University of Kansas, USA

Publication Chair

Jun Shao	Zhejiang Gongshang University, China

Publicity Chair

An Wang	Beijing Institute of Technology, China

Web Chair

Fangyu Zheng	Chinese Academy of Sciences, China

Program Committee

Sebastian Berndt	University of Lübeck, Germany
Florian Caullery	HENSOLDT Cyber GmbH, Germany
Bo Chen	Michigan Technological University, USA
Jiankuo Dong	Nanjing University of Posts and Telecommunications, China
Haixin Duan	Tsinghua University, China
Shanqing Guo	Shandong University, China

Contents – Part I

AIoTS – Artificial Intelligence and Industrial IoT Security

SCI – Secure Cryptographic Implementation

Contents – Part II

AIBlock – Application Intelligence and Blockchain Security

An End-to-End Secure Solution for IoMT Data Exchange

Saad El Jaouhari(✉)(iD) and Nouredine Tamani(iD)

Institut Supérieur d'Electronique de Paris (Isep), Issy-les-Moulinaux, France
{saad.el-jaouhari,nouredine.tamani}@isep.fr

Abstract. In the field of healthcare, the emerging concept of the Internet of Medical Things (IoMT) plays a crucial role in enhancing the efficiency of medical services and introducing innovative solutions. Traditional healthcare services are no longer adequate to meet the growing medical needs, particularly in countries with an aging population. Remote medical consultations have emerged as a viable solution, especially in rural areas facing the challenge of medical deserts. In such scenarios, instead of physically visiting a hospital, patients can opt for remote medical consultations, particularly for simple cases like medical follow-ups. The patient's health data is collected, monitored, and processed in real-time, subsequently shared with remote doctors or hospitals. IoMT devices, which easily measure vital signs, facilitate the seamless collection of health data. However, ensuring the security and privacy of sensitive IoMT data poses a significant challenge. In this context, one potential solution to ensure the confidentiality and integrity of medical data is the utilization of Blockchain technology. This paper explores the potential of Blockchain in IoMT networks, specifically focusing on guaranteeing privacy, confidentiality, integrity, authentication, and non-repudiation of medical data collected through medical IoT devices. Additionally, a proof of concept is provided to demonstrate how Blockchain can be effectively employed to secure the sharing and storage of IoMT data among connected nodes/devices and authorized users, particularly medical entities.

Keywords: IoT · IoMT · Blockchain · Healthcare · Security and Privacy · Confidentiality · Integrity · Authentication

1 Introduction

Modern medical systems have progressed from traditional electronic medical records, where patient clinical information resides digitally within a single medical center (typically a hospital), to the era of Electronic Health Records (EHR). In EHR systems, patient medical information is distributed across the healthcare system, enabling access and sharing among various entities. This evolution coincides with the integration of an expanding array of Internet of Medical Things (IoMT) devices that collect patient-related medical and environmental

M. Andreoni (Ed.): ACNS 2024 Workshops, LNCS 14586, pp. 3–15, 2024.
https://doi.org/10.1007/978-3-031-61486-6_1

data. IoMT devices serve the primary purpose of furnishing additional medical information to the medical corps, aiming to enhance the assessment of a patient's health condition and potentially improve medical treatment and services. Notably, IoMT devices have proven efficient in remote monitoring and medical follow-ups, eliminating the necessity for the physical presence of the patient. The IoMT market in the United States reached US$30.56 billion in 2022 and is projected to exceed US$327.08 billion by 2032, reflecting a compound annual growth rate (CAGR) of 26.80% from 2023 to 2032, according to a report by [1]. However, this technological advancement has introduced complexities, particularly in the management of data, similar to Electronic Health Records (EHR). Ensuring security and privacy in handling this data is paramount due to the unique nature of the healthcare environment, where security threats can have life-threatening consequences for patients, making it more critical than in any other domain.

For highly sensitive data, ensuring properties such as data integrity, confidentiality, authentication, and non-repudiation becomes imperative. However, in distributed environments, and considering the constraints associated with IoT, maintaining these properties becomes challenging. Specifically, for IoMT data, we must: 1) Ensure that only authorized entities and devices can interact with the medical system, ensuring confidentiality. 2) Guarantee that collected medical data remains unaltered, both accidentally and intentionally, preserving integrity. 3) Ensure the traceability and authentication of data, addressing both authentication and non-repudiation concerns."

In order to solve some of these issues, the Blockchain emerged as a disruptive solution to add a security and privacy layer to the IoMT environment. Blockchain is proven to be a tamper-proof digital ledger that enables secure peer-to-peer exchange of data. It enables data exchange even between unreliable endpoints without a third party. In this paper, we discuss the potential of Blockchain, and in particular the private ones, in IoMT networks and propose a solution to guarantee the privacy, confidentiality, and integrity of medical data collected through medical IoT devices. The solution uses the Hyperledger Fabric (HLF) developed by IBM [9] as a core in order to build a private blockchain. The latter is used to manage our IoMT data between the different entities involved in the process. In this case, only the authorized and registered peers (hospitals for instance) can check and read the data from the private ledger.

The rest of the paper is organized as follows: Sect. 2 provides a summary of related works. In Sect. 3, we present our proposed architecture, including a discussion of use cases. Section 4 provides details about the implementation of our proposal as a proof of concept, and the various interactions among the components of our system. The paper concludes in Sect. 5, where we also draw some lines for future work.

2 Related Work

In [13] and in [14], the authors designed a Blockchain architecture, based on the Hyperledger Fabric, to secure IoT-based health monitoring systems. The proposed architecture consists of two Blockchain networks: a) a Local one that is a single-node Blockchain embedded in the Perception Domain (i.e., IoT edge network), and b) a Global one that connects each Perception Domain to a Blockchain. The authors in [12] used the IoT and Blockchain to improve drug traceability in the pharmaceutical supply chain. The solution relies on the distributed ledger (DLT) to keep an immutable record of all transaction data. In [2], and for mesh-based IoT networks, the authors introduced DAGSec, a secure version of directed acyclic graphs (DAG), for IoT environments with high throughput and low latency. They used directed acyclic graphs and local transaction validation instead of global transaction validation to attain a high transaction rate. Also, they developed a Blockchain-based witness system to approximate the chronological order of independent transactions. In [10], the authors developed a novel decentralized Blockchain-based IoMT framework named Electronic Medical Record Infrastructure (EMRI), where all the clinical reports and IoT data are added. EMRI is an immutable and secure platform for the transaction of healthcare data. However, it is still to be implemented in a healthcare organization. In [3], the authors presented a solution for a collaborative healthcare management system, surgical process management, using IoT and Blockchain integration architecture, ERTCA, which relies on Ethereum. They also solve the issues related to constrained IoT resources when adopting the Blockchain mining process by using a rich-thin IoT client categorization approach. In [5], the authors proposed a model based on Blockchain for the remote patient monitoring scenario, where the patient is equipped with wearable IoT devices. Their model consists of five key parts: a Blockchain Network using Proof of Authority (PoA), Cloud Storage, Healthcare Providers, Smart Contracts, and Patients equipped with healthcare wearable IoT devices. Moreover, in [4], the authors developed a platform for combining IoT-based smart healthcare systems and Blockchain. The proposed system is based on HLF and it consists of five components: an IoT gatway devices, HTTP-based API gateway as device-to-Blockchain interface, membership service provider (MSP), peers, and orderers. Finally, the authors in [15] introduced a permissioned Blockchain-based architecture, built in HLF, to manage access control to medical data and to preserve patient data privacy. The data are collected via an IoT Fog Gateway connected to wearable health devices. The ledgers and transactions are stored in the cloud. The proposed architecture is designed for remote patient monitoring.

However, compared to our solution, most of these works do not take into account contextual IoT data along with users' immediate environment of in order to enhance medical services such as teleconsultation, remote monitoring, or medical follow-up. Moreover, most of them do not take into account the security inside their perception layer (i.e., between the sensors and the gateway) before even sending the data to the blockchain, which can be exploited by an adversary to meddle with such sensitive data. Finally, we propose to use a permissioned

Blockchain, which allows only selected and verified participants to interact with the Blockchain, which we believe is more suitable in the medical domain to protect data confidentiality and integrity, and hence the privacy of the patients.

3   Permissioned Blockchain for IoMT Medical Data

In this paper, a solution based on Hyperledger Fabric (HLF) Blockchain [9], a private and permissioned blockchain, is developed to secure sensitive incoming data from an IoMT sensors network. To do so, Node-RED [7] is used to manage and interact with the different IoMT devices possessed by the patient to collect health data. The data are then sent to the permission Blockchain. Moreover, a User Interface (UI) is also provided to view the history of transactions committed to the ledger. The Blockchain secures the IoMT data with an identity Membership Service Provider (MSP) encapsulated in an X.509 digital certificate and data encryption. The transactions are available and verifiable in the immutable Blockchain ledger ensuring privacy, confidentiality, and integrity to secure the IoMT data. Figure 1 illustrates the functional architecture of the introduced solution along with its main components.

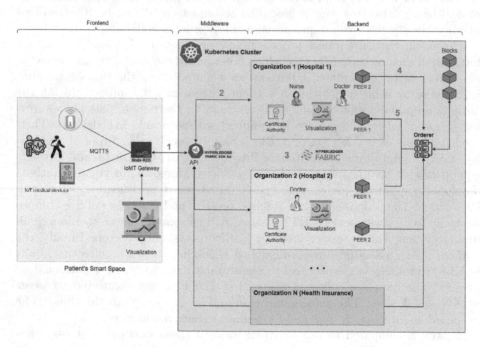

Fig. 1. Blockchain-based architecture for securing IoT health data from the patient's smart space

In what follows, we first present what is a patient's smart space. Then, we illustrate our solution with some use cases and we explain in detail the interaction between the main components. Next, we introduce the HLF chaincode lifecycle together with how Node-RED interacts with the ledger. Finally, we focus on the dashboard representing the Visualization part.

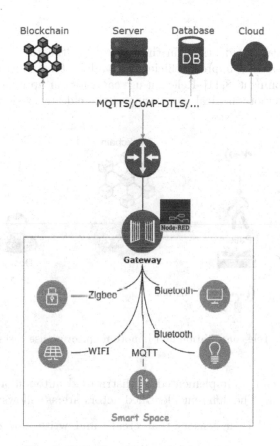

Fig. 2. Definition of a patient's smart space

3.1 Patient's Smart Space

The medical IoT devices are located in the immediate environment of the patient, or in what is called the patient's smart space, as shown in Fig. 2. The goal is to use such medical data, which is considered contextual data, to assist/help the remote medical entity in making decisions.

In this context, a Smart Space (SS) [6] is defined as a user-centric set of heterogeneous Smart Objects (SO)s (i.e., medical IoT devices) communicating using different communication protocols, such as BLE, WIFI, Zigbee, MQTT and so on, and which are accessible through a gateway, in our case via Node-RED, which acts as a manager of all these SOs and an aggregator to all of their data. The latter will be responsible for exchanging and securing the data with the Blockchain, as it will be explained later. For instance, the smart home of a patient can be considered a smart space.

3.2   Use Cases

Several use cases can be identified in the field of healthcare where Blockchain can be a great asset to improve efficiency, availability, and trust within an IoMT-based environment [8,11]. Relevant use cases for our approach can be tele-consultation and remote medical monitoring of the elderly, as shown in Fig. 3.

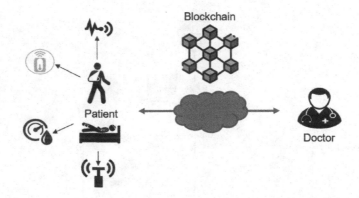

Fig. 3. Tele-consultation and remote monitoring use cases

The use cases can be implemented as distributed autonomous application based on Blockchain. The different identified actors are as follows:

- **Patients** with all their sensors that create and write new data into the Blockchain.
- **Doctors** who consume data and create new data as diagnoses and prescriptions.
- **Pharmacists** who consume data and execute contracts delivering the medication to the patients.
- **Heath insurers** who consume data and execute contracts related to health expenses (related to doctors, hospitals, etc.).
- **Hospital emergency** where nurses and doctors can have access to the historical data of a given patient and can also generate data.
- **Nurses** who need to have access to data in case of ambulatory health service.
- **Researchers** who need to have access to the historical data for research purposes

Sensors perform measurements and save the data into the blockchain. The doctor analyses the data, makes a diagnosis, and creates the prescription. The prescription is accessible to the pharmacist and to the health insurers. The pharmacist serves the patient and validates the prescription and the insurer processes the prescription for the check out. When sensors generate alarming data, a contract can be executed: call the emergency services, call a nurse, schedule an appointment, etc. All these services generate transactions for payments such as a transaction refers to executing a contract. For privacy concerns, the contract can include clauses for the pharmacists who need only to know the prescription content and basic patient information (Social Security Number), and for the insurers who need only to know the client identifier, and the amount of money to pay to a given doctor or hospital.

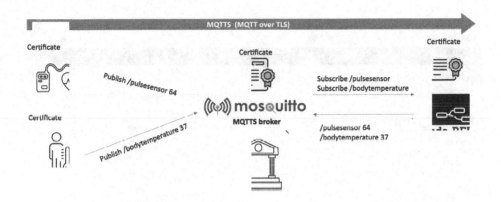

Fig. 4. IoMT devices - gateway communication using MQTTS

4 Implementation of a Proof of Concept

The initial step involves establishing an environment conducive to deploy and implement our solution. To do so, we have used an HPC with a CPU 12th generation intel® core(tm) i9-12900k, 32 GB RAM and a GPU Nvidia GP102 Titan XP. As for the software, the Hyperledger Fabric (HLF), an open source enterprise-grade permissioned distributed ledger technology (DLT) platform, Node-RED, Docker, and Kubernetes were deployed.

4.1 Component Interactions

Before delving into details, we first outline the three types of peers offered by HLF. Each peer is a docker container that is managed by Kubernetes in the Cloud as shown in Fig. 5.

- Endorser peers: with installed chaincode, simulate transaction execution in isolated containers upon receiving a proposal. Using this simulation, they generate a transaction proposal sent to the orderer peer, avoiding the need for sequential transaction execution by all peers.

– Orderer peers: they receive endorsed transactions and organize them into blocks. After grouping transactions, orderers ensure consensus by distributing these blocks to Endorsing peers, where validation occurs before committing the transactions to the shared ledger. Orderer peers maintain records of both valid and invalid transactions, while other peers only store valid transactions.
– Anchor peers: they act as intermediaries between peers within their organization and those belonging to an external one. For instance, an anchor peer is used when a legitimate peer from one organization needs to communicate with a given peer in another organization.

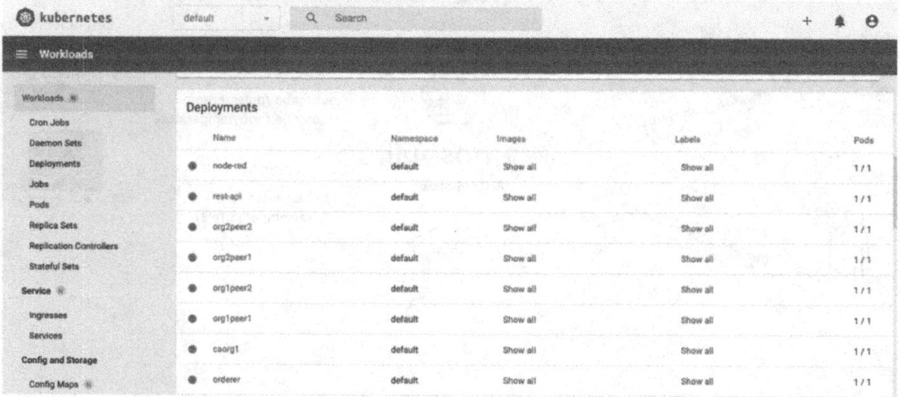

Fig. 5. Kubernetes Dashboard (Cloud)

Next, the main interactions between the different components of Fig. 1 are as follows.

1. First, Node-RED is used as a gateway to collect medical data from the patient's smart space using the lightweight MQTT protocol, as shown in Fig. 4. Moreover, to enhance security, MQTT over TLS (MQTTS) has been used in order to guarantee end-to-end security from the IoT device to Node-RED. It relies on certificates issued by a Certification Authority (CA) to both encrypt the data and guarantee the identity of the communicating parties, hence, guaranteeing the confidentiality, integrity (by using SHA-256 as a hash function), authentication, and non-repudiation in this part of the architecture. The Node-RED, which represents the front end in this case, interacts directly with the Hyperledger Fabric Client SDK APIs.
2. In order to invoke the chaincode (i.e. read, update, and write data to the blockchain), nodes inside the Node-RED are configured to perform HTTPS requests and return the response to the APIs defined by the Hyperledger Fabric Client SDK. The chaincode invocation/lifecycle is explained below.

3. The APIs in HLF Client SDK can directly interact with the chaincode inside the HLF Network (composed of multiple health organizations contributing to the ledger) and can also update and read from the ledger.
4. Endorser Peer "**PEER 2**" executes the functions that are defined in the chaincode in accordance with the request received from the API and then sends the results to the Ordering Service.
5. The Ordering Service (or **Orderer**) creates the corresponding blocks and sends them to "**PEER 1**", representing the Anchor Peers, which will then broadcast the blocks to the Endorser Peers. Anchor peers are only configured to broadcast blocks for our application. Such functionalities provide a private environment for different use cases and applications using private Blockchain.
6. Finally, the Endorser Peers broadcast the message to the API defined by the Hyperledger Fabric SDK and the response can be verified by a debugger on Node-RED.

The transaction history of IoMT data can be verified by checking the history of data coming from the Ledger where it is stored securely and immutably in the Blockchain. Moreover, the data received by the blockchain from the IoMT sensor is encrypted (using the AES256 algorithm) and then packaged onto the chaincode. The chaincode is invoked and data is processed through the ledger. Each input data from the sensor is packed into blocks of immutable datasets. This packaging of data into blocks is performed when the HTTPS request initiates the chaincode lifecycle and invokes the chaincode in the blockchain to commit key-value pairs to the ledger.

4.2 Hyperledger Fabric Chaincode Lifecycle

The HLF chaincode lifecycle is a sequence of actions performed by organizations to agree on the parameters that define a chaincode (such as name, version, endorsement policy, etc.) and deploy the chaincode to a channel for collaborative use. Channel members come to an agreement via the steps below:

1. Package a chaincode: Every organization (e.g., healthcare organizations such as hospitals in our use case) that wants to call chaincode functions obtains the source code of a chaincode and packages it into an appropriate format.
2. Install the chaincode package: The chaincode should be installed on every organization's peer that is supposed to execute or endorse chaincode transactions.
3. Approve a chaincode definition: Every organization that is going to use the chaincode composes and submits a chaincode definition—a set of configuration parameters considered to be acceptable by an organization.
4. Commit the chaincode definition to a channel: Once a required number of channel participants have approved the same chaincode definition, this definition can be then committed to a channel. The commit transaction is performed once and can be triggered by any organization.

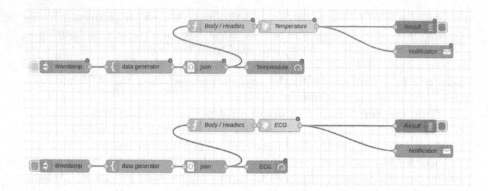

Fig. 6. IoMT sensors network simulated using Node-RED

4.3   Node-RED Interactions with the Ledger

Figure 6 provides views from the IoMT nodes simulated using Node-RED. The real sensors were replaced by simulated sensors in Node-RED for simplicity's sake. In our testbed, the medical sensors (blood pressure sensor, pulse sensor, oxygen level sensor, and temperature sensor) were connected to an MQTT broker, and the generated data is then published in the "MQTT subscribe (input)" node, as shown previously in Fig. 4.

4.4   Visualization

Following the implementation of previous interactions in HLF with medical data from simulated IoMT sensors using Node-RED, Fig. 7 illustrates the digital representation of the value generated by the IoMT pulse sensor.

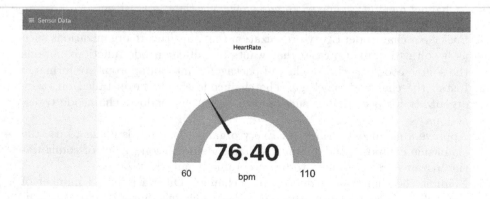

Fig. 7. IoMT data fetching and visualization

Fig. 8. Sensors data transaction history table

Moreover, Fig. 8 shows the history of the ledger, which contains transaction Identities (T×Id), Sensor number, timestamp data, and the value of the data generated by the sensor and fetched from the Hyperledger Fabric API. For instance, in the last transaction details, we can confirm that it is identical to the sensor data generated in Fig. 7. The history is fetched from the Ledger where the data is stored immutably in the Blockchain.

5   Conclusion

In this paper, a permissioned Blockchain solution based on HLF is used to enhance the security and privacy of the IoMT environment. In this environment, the involved parties are well-known and trusted since X.509 certificates are used to identify each stakeholder. The solution encrypts IoMT data to ensure its privacy and integrity. Moreover, the IoMT data stored in the Blockchain is tamper-proof and cannot be modified. Furthermore, transaction hashes and the history of the ledger are verifiable, ensuring, hence, accountability and traceability of the IoMT data. A proof-of-concept using Node-RED, HLF, and IoMT sensors, has also been developed and showed the successful configuration and the real-time deployment of our solution. In future work, we plan to extend our approach to execute smart contracts among the stakeholders involved in healthcare ecosystems, including insurers, practitioners, nurses, pharmacists, etc. to implement a secure end-to-end distributed application. Furthermore, we plan to conduct extensive experiments to validate and assess the performance of our approach.

References

1. Internet of medical things market (2023). https://www.precedenceresearch.com/internet-of-medical-things-market
2. Alvarenga, I.D., Camilo, G.F., De Souza, L.A.C., Duarte, O.C.M.B.: Dagsec: a hybrid distributed ledger architecture for the secure management of the internet of things. In: 2021 IEEE International Conference on Blockchain (Blockchain), pp. 266–271 (2021). https://doi.org/10.1109/Blockchain53845.2021.00043
3. Bataineh, M.R., Mardini, W., Khamayseh, Y.M., Yassein, M.M.B.: Novel and secure blockchain framework for health applications in IoT. IEEE Access **10**, 14914–14926 (2022). https://doi.org/10.1109/ACCESS.2022.3147795
4. Bhawiyuga, A., Wardhana, A., Amron, K., Kirana, A.P.: Platform for integrating internet of things based smart healthcare system and blockchain network. In: 2019 6th NAFOSTED Conference on Information and Computer Science (NICS), pp. 55–60 (2019). https://doi.org/10.1109/NICS48868.2019.9023797
5. Dwivedi, A.D., Malina, L., Dzurenda, P., Srivastava, G.: Optimized blockchain model for internet of things based healthcare applications. In: 2019 42nd International Conference on Telecommunications and Signal Processing (TSP), pp. 135–139 (2019). https://doi.org/10.1109/TSP.2019.8769060
6. El Jaouhari, S., Bouabdallah, A., Corici, A.A.: SDN-based security management of multiple wot smart spaces. J. Ambient. Intell. Humaniz. Comput. **12**, 9081–9096 (2021)
7. Foundation, O.: Node-red - low-code programming for event-driven applications. https://nodered.org/. Accessed 13 Sept 2022
8. Haleem, A., Javaid, M., Singh, R.P., Suman, R., Rab, S.: Blockchain technology applications in healthcare: an overview. Int. J. Intell. Netw. **2**, 130–139 (2021). https://doi.org/10.1016/j.ijin.2021.09.005. https://www.sciencedirect.com/science/article/pii/S266660302100021X
9. IBM: Getting started with iot blockchain service (2021). https://www.ibm.com/docs/en/wip-bs?topic=SSCG66/iot-blockchain/developing/generic_connect.html. Accessed 13 Sept 2022
10. Mallick, S.R., Sharma, S.: EMRI: a scalable and secure blockchain-based iomt framework for healthcare data transaction. In: 2021 19th OITS International Conference on Information Technology (OCIT), pp. 261–266 (2021).https://doi.org/10.1109/OCIT53463.2021.00060
11. Mamun, Q.: Blockchain technology in the future of healthcare. Smart Health **23**, 100223 (2022). https://doi.org/10.1016/j.smhl.2021.100223. https://www.sciencedirect.com/science/article/pii/S2352648321000453
12. Nawale, S.D., Konapure, R.R.: Blockchain & iot based drugs traceability for pharma industry. In: 2021 IEEE International Conference on Engineering, Technology and Innovation (ICE/ITMC), pp. 1–4 (2021).https://doi.org/10.1109/ICE/ITMC52061.2021.9570251
13. Oikonomou, F.P., Mantas, G., Cox, P., Bashashi, F., Gil-Castiñeira, F., Gonzalez, J.: A blockchain-based architecture for secure iot-based health monitoring systems. In: 2021 IEEE 26th International Workshop on Computer Aided Modeling and Design of Communication Links and Networks (CAMAD), pp. 1–6 (2021). https://doi.org/10.1109/CAMAD52502.2021.9617803
14. Oikonomou, F.P., Ribeiro, J., Mantas, G., Bastos, J.M.C., Rodriguez, J.: A hyperledger fabric-based blockchain architecture to secure iot-based health monitoring

systems. In: 2021 IEEE International Mediterranean Conference on Communications and Networking (MeditCom), pp. 186–190 (2021).https://doi.org/10.1109/MeditCom49071.2021.9647521

15. Zaabar, B., Cheikhrouhou, O., Ammi, M., Awad, A.I., Abid, M.: Secure and privacy-aware blockchain-based remote patient monitoring system for internet of healthcare things. In: 2021 17th International Conference on Wireless and Mobile Computing, Networking and Communications (WiMob), pp. 200–205 (2021).https://doi.org/10.1109/WiMob52687.2021.9606362

EasyLog: An Efficient Kernel Logging Service for Machine Learning

Xundi Yang, Kefan Qiu, and Quanxin Zhang$^{(\boxtimes)}$

Beijing Institute of Technology University, Beijing 100081, China
{kfqiu,zhangqx}@bit.edu.cn

Abstract. Recently, logs serves as a crucial tool to monitor system's real-time state for experiments and generate data for machine learning. However, the existing Linux logging system faces challenges such as excessive log output and a high rate of important log message loss. To tackle these issues, we propose the EasyLog solution, which effectively mitigates these problems. EasyLog draws inspiration from the design principles of log-related functions like `pr_xx`, `dev_xx`, and the `Devkmsg` service. EasyLog extracts and records logs with special identifier suffixes by introducing a ring buffer. In terms of interface utilization, EasyLog offers the `easy_xx` interface for kernel developers and the reading interface for user-space applications.

Keywords: Machine learning systems · Linux logging service · Log message loss · Ring buffer · Interface utilization · Server kernel development

1 Introduction

In recent years, there has been a growing deployment of machine learning systems on Linux Operating Systems. Within the Linux environment, numerous runtime problems and potential threats necessitate resolution through security monitoring and analysis, which includes the examination of logs to identify causes [1]. Log information serves as an immediate reflection of a system's operational status. Developers utilize logs for diagnosing system malfunctions, recording experimental results, and generating data for training security analysis models.

In this paper, we focus on the logging service in the Linux server kernel and aim to assist programmers in designing kernel drivers and generating data for machine learning. Generally, developers strive to capture system state dumps, execute tracing, and communicate events through log data. Within the 13,390,104 lines of source code in the Linux kernel, there are 498,897 lines (approximately 3.79%) dedicated to logging code [2]. Logging functions in the Linux kernel write messages into the log buffer. Commonly used logging functions include the `printk` function, which is similar to the `printf` function. The distinction lies in `printk`'s specification of the log level for event recording. Subsequent Linux kernel versions have introduced variations of the `printk` function such as `pr_info`, and `dev_warn`, which incorporate log levels into their nomenclature.

However, the existing kernel logging services are unreliable due to several factors. Firstly, the Linux kernel generates a substantial volume of continuous log output from numerous programs. When Shiqing et al. [3] tested the overhead of the Linux audit system, they found that servers generate approximately 130GB of log data per day, while client machines generate about 5GB of log data per day. Nevertheless, developers often focus on specific Linux kernel modules. For instance, Tan Y et al. [4] employ authorization lists recorded in the logs as the basis for comparison. In the RootAgency [5], the logs document the time consumption from the test app initiating the request until the end user receives the reply for the root privilege request. Neither of them pays attention to logs related to unrelated modules. The excessive volume of irrelevant logs has caused interference in their experiments. Furthermore, the kernel logging service also faces the issue of log loss. The kernel log buffer is a ring buffer, which operates on a first-in, first-out (FIFO) basis. The default size of the Linux kernel log buffer is 128KB. As data accumulates beyond the capacity of the ring buffer, the oldest data is overwritten to accommodate new information.

In this paper, we introduce a kernel logging service solution, EasyLog, which effectively mitigates the above issues. In terms of interface utilization, EasyLog provides write interfaces such as `easy_xx` for log writing at the kernel layer and system call interfaces such as `open`, `read`, and `close` for log reading at the application layer. Besides, regarding log simplification, the design of the `easy_xx` functions is influenced by kernel functions like `dev_info`, appending specific identifiers to the end of each log. When our write interfaces append to record logs, EasyLog extracts logs using the identifier and stores them in our new ring log buffer, which can be expanded to 2 MB. This approach significantly reduces the volume of logs. It also elongates the time required to fill the circular buffer and decreases the likelihood of log loss. Furthermore, developers can utilize the `easy_xx` functions in their experimental kernel, subsequently compile and execute the code, and directly get logs from the new log buffer. To sum up, EasyLog reduces log volume, enhances effective log density, diminishes the probability of log loss, and facilitates the development of new modules for programmers.

The rest of the paper is structured as follows. Section 2 describes recent application of logs, the principles underlying the `printk` mechanism, and recent advancements in kernel-level logging service. In Sect. 3, the comprehensive architectural design is presented. Section 4 describes the details of the implementation and the interface design of EasyLog. In Sect. 5, we validate the effectiveness of EasyLog in mitigating the loss rate of important logs. Section 6 elucidates the utilization of the EasyLog service to assist in the development of new modules for the Linux kernel. Section 7 concludes.

2 Background

2.1 The Applications of Logs

When the kernel crashes, developers can solve bugs by analyzing the preserved system log files. In recent years, logs aid developers in diagnosing system errors, training security models, and documenting experimental results. In 2015, the EASEAndroid platform [6], the inaugural audit log analytic system for SEAndroid, employed semi-supervised learning to autonomously enhance the SEAndroid policy. In 2018, Xue B et al. [7] obtain the encryption rate and data processing size of the baseband processor through log information. In 2021, Li Y et al. [1] proposes a host security analysis method based on D-S evidence theory, which involves extracting information from monitoring logs and subsequently training a security analysis model. The model can be applied to host security analysis in different operating systems with minimal or almost no modification.

2.2   The Analysis of Printk

The kernel log module resides in `./kernel/printk/`. Figure 1 illustrates the read-write framework of the kernel log module. As depicted in the figure, its core component is the ring buffer, denoted as the "log buffer". The `printk` function and the `devkmsg_write` function, acting as producers, store messages in the log buffer. On the other hand, the log service modules on the right side of the figure function as a consumer, reading messages from the log buffer.

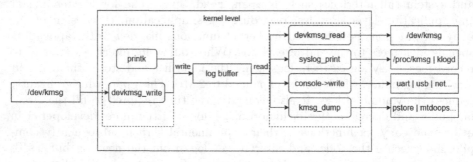

Fig. 1. The Read-Write Framework of the kernel log module

Log Buffer: The size of the kernel log buffer is determined jointly by the configuration parameters `CONFIG_LOG_BUF_SHIFT` and the number of CPU cores in the SMP system. During the kernel boot, information regarding the system's memory layout and the number of CPU cores is unknown before device tree parsing. To support the utilization of the `printk` function, the kernel defines a static global log buffer with a size of (1 << `CONFIG_LOG_BUF_SHIFT`). After CPU initialization, an additional global log buffer is dynamically allocated with a size of (1 << `CONFIG_LOG_BUF_SHIFT` + 1 << `LOG_CPU_MAX_BUF_LEN`), and the log data from the original static buffer is copied into it.

The log buffer is managed through the data structure `printk_ringbuffer`. Figure 2 presents the data structures of `printk_ringbuffer`. As depicted, it comprises three main components: 1) a ring buffer for data storage, managed using head and tail pointers to track the buffer's status. When data needs to be written, the head pointer is updated based on the length of the data being written. If the free space in the ring buffer is insufficient, the oldest data is purged starting from the tail pointer. Additionally, each piece of written data is assigned an ID, which is used to indicate the index in the `prb_desc` array and the `printk_info` array. 2) An array of `prb_desc` structures, with each element maintaining the position information of a log within the ring buffer, along with its status. 3) An array of `printk_info` structures, with each element responsible for managing additional information associated with a log, such as its sequence number(seq), timestamp, length, log level, and more.

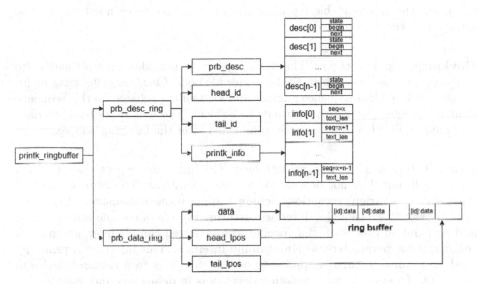

Fig. 2. Principal Members and Data Structures of printk_ringbuffer

Log Stoarge Process: We use the `printk` interface as an example for explaining the log storage process. 1) Allocate an entry and increment the sequence number: The `desc_reserve` function retrieves an available entry from the `prb_desc` structure array. If no free entry is available; it overwrites the oldest log. Upon successful allocation, the descriptor's status is set to `desc_reserved`. Subsequently, the sequence number for that log is set. 2) Allocate space and copy the log: The `data_alloc` function allocates a segment of space from the ring buffer to store the new log data. The `log_data_copy` function copies the data to be written into the allocated space within the ring buffer. 3) Update the status: The `_prb_commit` function updates the status of the new element in the `prb_desc` array to `desc_committed`, and then the `desc_make_final` function updates the status to `desc_finalized`. After this operation, the log is written and ready for reading.

Log Retrieval Process: When reading logs, a sequence number (`seq`) is provided as a parameter, and the `prb_read` function is called to retrieve the log corresponding to that sequence number. 1) Retrieve a valid status log: The `desc_read_finalized_seq` function reads the status of the log corresponding to the provided sequence number. If the status is valid, the subsequent log data and information retrieval operations are executed. After completion, the status of that log is rechecked. If it remains valid and the sequence number has not changed, it signifies that during the reading process, the data was not modified by write operations. Otherwise, the reading process fails. 2) Handling of Reading Failures: In case of reading failures, the `prb_first_seq` function is called to obtain the first readable log after the provided sequence number, and the retrieval process is restarted.

Devkmsg Log Interface: The `devkmsg` service provides log read and write operations to user space through the device file node `/dev/kmsg`. Devkmsg maintains an independent sequence number and log reading is based on this sequence number to determine which log needs to be read. The user space read interface provided by EasyLog in this paper is modeled after the `Devkmsg` service.

Other Interfaces: 1) `syslog` interface: This interface exports logs through system calls but does not provide log writing operations. The `syslog` interface finds utility in various scenarios, including applications like `dmesg`, `klogd`, and `/proc/kmsg`. 2) Console log interface: It primarily offers console initialization, and registration processes, and specifies the preferred console interface through command-line parameters. 3) Kmsg dump interface: This interface is primarily used by `pstore`. `pstore` is applied to save system logs to a backend device in the event of a system crash, assisting developers in debugging and analysis.

2.3   Recent Work About Logging

Linux manages storage devices, networks, man-machine interfaces, CPUs, and more through software layers such as device drivers, file systems, and communication protocols. These intricate modules are maintained by hundreds of programmers. As Linux grows in complexity, an increasing number of system analysis tools have been proposed to help developers in analyzing system behavior. The simplest logging tool in Linux is the `printk` function, as mentioned earlier. In Linux kernel v1.3.983 [2], a set of additional logging functions was introduced to enhance the conciseness of log statement recording. These functions incorporate log levels in their names. Consequently, programmers are no longer required to use `printk` function with log-level parameters such as `KERN_DEBUG` and `KERN_INFO`. Another set of logging functions specifically designed for device drivers, such as `dev_dbg` and `dev_info`, automatically embed the device name in their outputs, thereby facilitating the identification of the source of log messages.

Both `dev_xx` functions and `pr_xx` functions are variants of the `printk` function, and the underlying issues with `printk` remain unresolved. The `printk` function uses an asynchronous daemon to read and write a ring buffer, making the buffer vulnerable to overwriting and event loss. The Linux Trace Toolkit (LTT) [8] logs around 45 predefined events, including interrupts, system calls, and network packet arrivals. The tool is advantageous due to its relatively low overhead and the presence of a visualization tool to aid in analyzing logged data. However, it lacks flexibility and scalability. Relayfs [9] is proposed, which divides logs into different subsystem/client channels, effectively addressing the fundamental overhead caused by locking during logging. KLogger [10] is presented as a software tool for logging operating system kernel events. Developers can insert new log events into the kernel using this tool. Furthermore, an alternative approach to logging all events is sampling. OProfile [11] adopts a sampling approach, serving as the underlying infrastructure for HP's Prospect tool. OProfile uses Intel's hardware performance counters to generate traps for every N occurrence of specific hardware events. However, since OProfile is based on periodic sampling, it may miss events with finer granularity than the sampling rate.

3   Architecture

Figure 3 illustrates the architecture of EasyLog. 1) The server kernel subsystem utilizes the `easy_xx` functions to record log entries. 2) EasyLog service filters logs with specific suffixes and directs them into a newly created ring buffer. 3) User-space applications access the new log buffer through the character device node `/dev/easylog`.

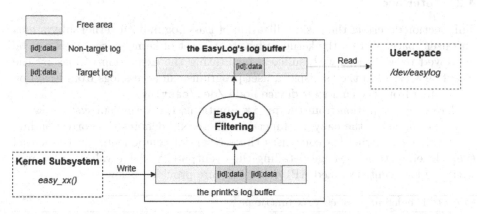

Fig. 3. The architecture of EasyLog

4   Implementation

4.1   Channel and Data Management Schemes

The EasyLog module maintains a ring buffer as its log buffer. Its structure, initialization, and read-write processes resemble the `printk`'s log buffer.

Initialization: During the early stages of kernel startup, the original static log buffer is still employed. Subsequently, in the `start_kernel` function, an initialization function is called to dynamically allocate a global log buffer of size (1>>CONFIG_EASYLOG_BUF_SHIFT).

Log Storage: The kernel subsystem uses the `easy_xx` functions to record log entries, with each log appended with a special identifier suffix.

Log Filtering: The `log_store` function is responsible for appending logs generated by other modules to the original log buffer. Within the `log_store` function, the EasyLog service performs a hook-like operation. The service filters logs generated by other modules, extracts logs with suffixes, removes the suffixes, and subsequently stores them in our log buffer following the writing procedure described in Sect. 2.1. This process ensures that the log buffer's read and write operations do not conflict through spin locks and local interrupt disabling. During this filtering step, both our log buffer and the `printk`'s log buffer need to be locked for protection.

Log Retrieval: EasyLog maps our ring buffer to a pseudo-file, namely the character device file `/dev/easylog`, which can be accessed by userspace for reading or process memory mapping.

4.2 Interface

This section describes the basic utilization of EasyLog in both kernel subsystems and user space. Within the kernel subsystem, a set of kernel-space APIs can be employed to write logs with suffixes, facilitating the extraction of logs by the EasyLog service. In the user space, user programs can access logs from EasyLog by reading from the character device node `/dev/easylog`.

Drawing inspiration from the `pr_xx` functions, the kernel subsystems write a special log using the `easy_xx` function, where 'xx' denotes the corresponding log level. Each kernel log comprises three essential components [2]: the kernel event level, a static message detailing the event, and variable values associated with the log event. Detailed API definitions are provided below.

Code 1: The definition of easy_xx functions

```
1: __printf(2, 3) void easy_suffix_printk(const char *, const char *,
      ...);
2:
3: #define easy_emerg(fmt, ...) \
4:     easy_suffix_printk(KERN_EMERG, fmt, ##__VA_ARGS__)
5: #define easy_crit(fmt, ...) \
6:     easy_suffix_printk(KERN_CRIT, fmt, ##__VA_ARGS__)
7: #define easy_alert(fmt, ...) \
8:     easy_suffix_printk(KERN_ALERT, fmt, ##__VA_ARGS__)
```

```
 9: #define easy_err(fmt, ...) \
10:     easy_suffix_printk(KERN_ERR, fmt, ##__VA_ARGS__)
11: #define easy_warn(fmt, ...) \
12:     easy_suffix_printk(KERN_WARNING, fmt, ##__VA_ARGS__)
13: #define easy_notice(fmt, ...) \
14:     easy_suffix_printk(KERN_NOTICE, fmt, ##__VA_ARGS__)
15: #define easy_info(fmt, ...) \
16:     easy_suffix_printk(KERN_INFO, fmt, ##__VA_ARGS__)
```

In this context, the `easy_suffix_printk` function, inspired by the `dev_xx` functions, appends the "–easylog–" identifier to the end of each log. Subsequently, it invokes the `vprintk_emit` function, passing the kernel event level and the newly generated log with the suffix.

The reading operation of user programs in EasyLog draws inspiration from the reading operation of the `devkmsg` service. `/dev/easylog` is a readable character device file, permitting multiple user processes to access log records. Each process can obtain a complete set of log entries from EasyLog.

The collection of user-space file operations provided by EasyLog is as follows: 1) The open function, responsible for opening the character device file node `/dev/easylog` and creating a `deveasylog_user` structure object (as detailed later) named `user`, corresponding to the `deceasylog_open` function in the kernel. 2) The read function, which reads log entries from the log buffer, corresponds to the `deceasylog_read` function in the kernel. 3) The release function, responsible for releasing all resources acquired by the open function, corresponding to the `deceasylog_release` function in the kernel.

Code 2: The collection of user-space file operations provided by EasyLog

```
1: const struct file_operations easylog_fops = {
2:       .open = deveasylog_open,
3:       .read = deveasylog_read,
4:       .release = deveasylog_release,
5: };
```

Each process that opens `/dev/EasyLog` is associated with an independent `deveasylog_user` structure object, as described below. The `deveasylog_user` structure maintains a unique sequence number for each reading process, denoted as `seq`, which represents the sequence number of the log currently being read by the process. The mutex lock, denoted as `lock`, ensures that only one thread within each process can perform write operations on the `text_buf`. The `rs` variable is used for rate limiting. Following the Log Retrieval Process in Sect. 2.1, logs are read from EasyLog's log buffer, recorded in the `text_buf`, and subsequently returned to user space by invoking the `copy_to_user` function.

Code 3: The structure of deveasylog_user

```
1: struct deveasylog_user {
2:        u64 seq;
3:        struct ratelimit_state rs;
4:        struct mutex lock;
5:        char buf[CONSOLE_EXT_LOG_MAX];
6:        struct printk_info info;
7:        char text_buf[CONSOLE_EXT_LOG_MAX];
8:        struct printk_record record;
9: };
```

5   Experiment

This section of experiments aims to demonstrate the significant reduction in the loss rate of important logs achieved by EasyLog. Important logs refer to the logs associated with the development modules during server kernel development. Within the developing server kernel subsystems, developers invoke the easy_xx functions and append specific identifiers to the end of each log. This experiment considers such logs as important logs, defined as label logs. EasyLog extracts the logs with specific identifiers and stores them in a new ring log buffer.

In our experiments, it was essential to simulate real-world log generation scenarios as closely as possible, ensuring that normal logs and label logs terminated their output as synchronously as feasible. The original printk and EasyLog log buffer were set to 256 KB. We designed two kernel modules: one module invokes pr_info to write N normal log entries, while the other module invokes easy_info to write N*0.1 label log entries, ensuring a ratio of 100 normal logs to 10 label logs. The values of N range from 2048, 4096, 6144...20480. Additionally, normal logs were generated at intervals of 0.1 s, whereas the generation intervals for label logs were a random number between [0.5, 1.5] (with a mean of 1). These two modules were executed concurrently, writing normal logs and label logs in parallel. We consider the logs recorded in /dev/kmsg as the logs logged by the original logging system, while the logs in /dev/easylog are the logs recorded by EasyLog. The loss rate of label logs was tested separately. The formula for calculating the loss rate of label logs is provided in Eq. 1. Table 1 presents the experimental results.

$$Label\ Logs\ Loss\ Rate = \frac{Label\ Logs\ Loss\ Count}{Label\ Logs\ Count} \times 100\% \qquad (1)$$

Table 1. The loss rate of label logs

NO	Label Logs Count[a]	Normal Logs Count[b]	Total Logs Count	Label Logs Loss Rate	
				/dev/kmsg[c]	/dev/easylog[d]
1	205	2,048	2,253	0	0
2	410	4,096	4,506	0	0
3	614	6,144	6,758	0	0
4	819	8,192	9,011	8.91%	0
5	1,024	10,240	11,264	26.86%	0
6	1,229	12,288	13,517	39.71%	0
7	1,434	14,336	15,770	48.12%	0
8	1,638	16,384	18,022	54.46%	0
9	1,843	18,432	20,275	59.31%	0
10	2,048	20,480	22,528	62.79%	0

[a] The generation intervals for label logs were a random number between $[0.5, 1.5]$.
[b] Normal logs were generated at intervals of 0.1 s.
[c] The logs in /dev/kmsg are the logs logged by the original logging system.
[d] The logs in /dev/easylog are the logs recorded by EasyLog.

The Table 1 shows that: 1) When the log volume is relatively small, there is no significant difference in the loss rate of label logs and it remains at 0. 2) As the log volume gradually increases, the loss rate of label logs in the /dev/kmsg increases progressively. 3) Due to the constraint of ensuring that normal and label logs terminate their outputs concurrently, the growth in the loss rate of label logs in the /dev/kmsg slows down as the log volume increases, and it will not reach 100%. 4) Because the total size of label logs is less than 256 KB, the loss rate of label logs consistently remains at 0. In summary, EasyLog reduces the volume of logs that need to be recorded by extracting important logs, allowing the system sufficient time to store the logs from the buffer into files, thus effectively reducing the probability of log loss.

6 Application

EasyLog aims to assist programmers in designing kernel drivers and generating data for machine learning. In this section, we demonstrate how EasyLog aids developers in kernel driver development. Some hardware devices, such as GPUs, have old versions phased out and new versions released, necessitating corresponding driver updates. Besides, the driver subsystems are significantly larger than other subsystems. From Linux versions v4.3 to v5.3, there were a total of 211,437 modifications to log statements, with the driver subsystem accounting for 86.60% of the overall log code changes [2]. Therefore, optimizing the logging system is of paramount importance for Linux server kernel driver development.

In this chapter, we take USB storage device-related drivers as an example. We output logs when USB flash drives are inserted and removed. The log content includes relevant information about the USB flash drive, such as product, vendor, manufacturer, serial number, as well as the time of insertion and removal. The

```
[   70.293517] usb 6-1: new SuperSpeed Gen 1 USB device number 2 using xhci-hcd
[   70.324543] usb 6-1: New USB device found, idVendor=174c, idProduct=55aa, bcdDevice= 1.00
[   70.324573] usb 6-1: New USB device strings: Mfr=2, Product=3, SerialNumber=1
[   70.324581] usb 6-1: Product: KS-CUTS25W
[   70.324588] usb 6-1: Manufacturer: KINGSHARE
[   70.324595] usb 6-1: SerialNumber: 123456789010
[   70.331128] scsi host0: uas
[   70.334830] ---------INSERT USB STORAGE: TIME IS 2023-09-18 17:34:08-----------easylog--
[   70.334859] scsi 0:0:0:0: Direct-Access     KINGSHAR KS-CUTS25W     0    PQ: 0 ANSI: 6
[   70.334894] product:KS-CUTS25W--easylog--
[   70.334899] manufacturer:KINGSHARE--easylog--
[   70.334907] serial:123456789010--easylog--
[   70.334914] Vendor:KINGSHAR--easylog--
[   70.334922] Model:KS-CUTS25W     --easylog--
[   70.334929] Rev:0   --easylog--
[   70.334935] Type:Direct-Access   --easylog--
[   70.334943] ANSI  SCSI revision: 06--easylog--
[   70.342949] sd 0:0:0:0: [sda] 234441648 512-byte logical blocks: (120 GB/112 GiB)
[   70.343111] sd 0:0:0:0: [sda] Write Protect is off
[   70.343124] sd 0:0:0:0: [sda] Mode Sense: 43 00 00 00
[   70.343335] sd 0:0:0:0: [sda] Disabling FUA
[   70.343347] sd 0:0:0:0: [sda] Write cache: enabled, read cache: enabled, doesn't support DPO or FUA
[   70.343476] sd 0:0:0:0: [sda] Optimal transfer size 33553920 bytes
[   70.423948]  sda: sda1
[   70.425658] sd 0:0:0:0: [sda] Attached SCSI disk
[   76.956610] ------------- USB DISCONNECT, DEVICE NUMBER 2 ----------------easylog--
[   76.956622] log_usb:product:LOGUSB--easylog--
[   76.956645] log_usb:manufacturer:BIT--easylog--
[   76.956653] log_usb:serial:FC142F1200DA6--easylog--
[   76.956660] log_usb:Vendor:BIT--easylog--
[   76.956666] log_usb:Model:LOG--easylog--
[   76.957991] sd 0:0:0:0: [sda] Synchronizing SCSI cache
[   76.958020] sd_shutdown
[   77.563502] sd 0:0:0:0: [sda] Synchronize Cache(10) failed: Result: hostbyte=DID_ERROR driverbyte=DRIVER_OK
[   77.563538] sd_sync_cache finished
[   78.033525] usb 6-1: new SuperSpeed Gen 1 USB device number 3 using xhci-hcd
[   78.064466] usb 6-1: New USB device found, idVendor=174c, idProduct=55aa, bcdDevice= 1.00
[   78.064493] usb 6-1: New USB device strings: Mfr=2, Product=3, SerialNumber=1
[   78.064501] usb 6-1: Product: KS-CUTS25W
[   78.064508] usb 6-1: Manufacturer: KINGSHARE
[   78.064515] usb 6-1: SerialNumber: 123456789010
[   78.067736] scsi host0: uas
[   78.069638] ---------INSERT USB STORAGE: TIME IS 2023-09-18 17:34:15-----------easylog--
[   78.069657] scsi 0:0:0:0: Direct-Access     KINGSHAR KS-CUTS25W     0    PQ: 0 ANSI: 6
[   78.069684] product:KS-CUTS25W--easylog--
[   78.069689] manufacturer:KINGSHARE--easylog--
[   78.069696] serial:123456789010--easylog--
[   78.069702] Vendor:KINGSHAR--easylog--
[   78.069709] Model:KS-CUTS25W     --easylog--
```

Fig. 4. The output of "dmesg". The figure indicates the original kernel logs include too much unrelated information.

```
<6>[   70.334836] ---------INSERT USB STORAGE: TIME IS 2023-09-18 17:34:08---------
<6>[   70.334896] product:KS-CUTS25W
<6>[   70.334900] manufacturer:KINGSHARE
<6>[   70.334908] serial:123456789010
<6>[   70.334915] Vendor:KINGSHAR
<6>[   70.334923] Model:KS-CUTS25W
<6>[   70.334930] Rev:0
<6>[   70.334936] Type:Direct-Access
<6>[   70.334944] ANSI  SCSI revision: 06
<6>[   76.956614] ------------- USB DISCONNECT, DEVICE NUMBER 2 --------------
<6>[   76.956623] log_usb:product:LOGUSB
<6>[   76.956646] log_usb:manufacturer:BIT
<6>[   76.956654] log_usb:serial:FC142F1200DA6
<6>[   76.956661] log_usb:Vendor:BIT
<6>[   76.956667] log_usb:Model:LOG
<6>[   78.069642] ---------INSERT USB STORAGE: TIME IS 2023-09-18 17:34:15---------
<6>[   78.069686] product:KS-CUTS25W
<6>[   78.069689] manufacturer:KINGSHARE
<6>[   78.069696] serial:123456789010
<6>[   78.069703] Vendor:KINGSHAR
<6>[   78.069710] Model:KS-CUTS25W
<6>[   78.069716] Rev:0
<6>[   78.069722] Type:Direct-Access
<6>[   78.069729] ANSI  SCSI revision: 06
<6>[   78.139236] ------------- USB DISCONNECT, DEVICE NUMBER 3 --------------
<6>[   78.139253] log_usb:product:LOGUSB
<6>[   78.139289] log_usb:manufacturer:BIT
<6>[   78.139298] log_usb:serial:FC142F1200DA6
<6>[   78.139312] log_usb:Vendor:BIT
<6>[   78.139320] log_usb:Model:LOG
<6>[   84.994382] ---------INSERT USB STORAGE: TIME IS 2023-09-18 17:34:22---------
<6>[   84.994496] product:SSK Storage
<6>[   84.994508] manufacturer:SSK
<6>[   84.994529] serial:DD56419883935
<6>[   84.994547] Vendor:SSK
<6>[   84.994565] Model:
<6>[   84.994582] Rev:0212
<6>[   84.994600] Type:Direct-Access
<6>[   84.994619] ANSI  SCSI revision: 06
```

Fig. 5. The output of "cat /dev/easylog". The figure indicates the EasyLog's logs are clearer and more coherent.

driver functions involved in this process include the `scsi_add_lun` function in `scsi/scsi_scan.c` and the `usb_disconnect` function in `usb/core/core.c`. In these respective locations within the functions, the `easy_info` function is called to write the relevant log content. Repeatedly inserting and removing different USB flash drives or hard drives, Fig. 4 and Fig. 5 depict screenshots of the `dmesg` output and the `cat /dev/easylog` output. The Fig. 5 is clearer and more coherent, devoid of interference in the logs, which is advantageous for programmers working on new modules.

7 Conclusion

To address issues such as log loss and excessive log volume in the Linux logging service, this paper proposes the EasyLog service. EasyLog maintains a ring buffer as the log buffer. EasyLog extracts logs with special identifiers from the logs written to the original log buffer and stores them in our new log buffer. Furthermore, EasyLog provides `write` functions such as `easy_xx` for kernel modules to write logs and `read` functions for applications to read logs.

In the fifth section, experimental results demonstrate that when the total log volume is relatively low, both EasyLog and the original Linux logging module have a log loss rate of 0 for critical logs. However, when the proportion of critical logs remains constant but the total log volume increases, the log loss rate of critical logs in the original Linux logging system gradually rises. In contrast, the EasyLog module en sures that these critical logs are not overwritten by unrelated logs by extracting critical logs and storing them in our new ring buffer. As a result, the log loss rate of critical logs in EasyLog is significantly lower than in the original Linux logging system. When the total size of critical logs does not exceed the log buffer capacity, the loss rate of critical logs is 0.

In conclusion, EasyLog proficiently mitigates log loss concerns and facilitates the creation of kernel drivers as well as the generation of data for machine learning applications.

Acknowledgements. This work was supported by the National Key Research and Development Program of China under Grant 2022YFB2701501 the National Natural Science Foundation of China (no. U2336201).

References

1. Li, Y., Yao, S., Zhang, R., et al.: Analyzing host security using D-S evidence theory and multisource information fusion. Int. J. Intell. Syst. **36**(2), 1053–1068 (2021)
2. Patel, K., Faccin, J., Hamou-Lhadj, A., et al.: The sense of logging in the linux kernel. Empir. Softw. Eng. **27**(6), 153 (2022)
3. Ma, S., Zhai, J., Kwon, Y., et al.: Kernel-supported cost-effective audit logging for causality tracking. In: 2018 USENIX Annual Technical Conference (USENIX ATC 18), pp. 241–254 (2018)

4. Tan, Y., Xue, Y., Liang, C., et al.: A root privilege management scheme with revocable authorization for Android devices[J]. J. Netw. Comput. Appl. **107**, 69–82 (2018)
5. Xue, Y., Tan, Y., Liang, C., et al.: RootAgency: a digital signature-based root privilege management agency for cloud terminal devices. Inf. Sci. **444**, 36–50 (2018)
6. Wang, R., Enck, W., Reeves, D., et al.: EASEAndroid: automatic policy analysis and refinement for security enhanced android via large-scale semi-supervised learning. In: 24th USENIX Security Symposium (USENIX Security 15), pp. 351–366 (2015)
7. Xue, B., Lu, L., Sikang, H., et al.: An isolated data encryption experiment method by utilizing baseband processors. In: Proceedings of the 2018 2nd International Conference on Management Engineering, Software Engineering and Service Sciences, pp. 176–181 (2018)
8. Yaghmour, K., Dagenais, M.R.: Measuring and characterizing system behavior using kernel-level event logging. In: 2000 USENIX Annual Technical Conference (USENIX ATC 2000) (2000)
9. Zanussi, T., Yaghmour, K., Wisniewski, R., et al.: relayfs: an efficient unified approach for transmitting data from kernel to user space. In: Linux Symposium, vol. 494 (2003)
10. Etsion, Y., Tsafrir, D., Kirkpatrick, S., et al.: Fine grained kernel logging with klogger: experience and insights. In: Proceedings of the 2nd ACM SIGOPS/EuroSys European Conference on Computer Systems 2007, pp. 259–272 (2007)
11. Cohen, W.E.: Tuning programs with OProfile. Wide Open Maga. **1**, 53–62 (2004)

LM-cAPI:A Lite Model Based on API Core Semantic Information for Malware Classification

Yifan Zhou, Zhenyan Liu$^{(\boxtimes)}$, Jingfeng Xue, Yong Wang, and Ji Zhang

School of Computer Science and Technology, Beijing Institute of Technology,
Beijing 100081, China
zhenyanliu@bit.edu.cn

Abstract. Currently, malware is continually evolving and growing in complexity, posing a significant threat to network security. With the constant emergence of new types and quantities of malware coupled with the continuous updating of dissemination methods, the rapid and accurate identification of malware as well as providing precise support for corresponding warning and defense measures have become a crucial challenge in maintaining network security. This article focuses on API call sequences in malware that can characterize the behavioral characteristics of malware as text and then uses the latest text classification-related technologies to achieve the classification of malware. This article proposes a flexible and lightweight malicious code classification model based on API core semantic information. To address the issues of prolonged training time and low accuracy caused by excessive noise and redundant data in API call sequences, this model adopts an intimacy analysis method based on a self-attention mechanism for key information extraction. To enhance the capture of semantic information within malware API call sequences, a feature extraction model based on a self-attention mechanism is used to transform unstructured key API sequences into vector representations, extract core features, and finally connect to the TextCNN model for multi classification. In the dataset of the "Alibaba Cloud Security Malicious Program Detection" competition, the F1 value reached 90% in eight category classification tasks. The experimental results show that the model proposed in this article can achieve better results in malware detection and multi-classification.

Keywords: Network Security · Malware Classification · API call sequence

1 Introduction

Malware is one of the most serious threats to network security, serving as a key attack carrier in various network security events. When malware is executed, it

Supported by Major Scientific and Technological Innovation Projects of Shandong Province (2020CXGC010116) and the National Natural Science Foundation of China (No. 62172042).

poses a risk to the confidentiality, availability, and integrity of sensitive information and data in the target system. Moreover, in order to avoid traditional malware detection and eradication mechanisms (such as firewalls, antivirus software, and other signature-based defense methods) and improve their own survivability, malware programmers employ sophisticated techniques. These involve modifying and confounding malicious samples within the same family using diverse strategies to alter code structures and generate various different code variants while maintaining semantic equivalence. There are certain similarities in structure and behavior among variant samples from the same family. As malware spreads, it utilizes various deformation engines to automatically generate new variants. Simultaneously, the development of the malware industry chain is also continuously collectivized and organized. Overall, the above phenomenon has resulted in the proliferation of malware not only in terms of quantity but also in the diversification of defense evasion methods. Consequently, the need for automated detection, elimination, and tracing of malware has become increasingly urgent.

Over the past few years, the volume of malware data has grown rapidly. Within the realm of artificial intelligence, natural language processing (NLP) has emerged as a mature subfield, with machine learning [1] and neural network methods of natural language processing gradually reaching maturity in the domain of malware detection. Machine-learning-based malware detection methods [2,3] can automatically analyze a large amount of data through inductive reasoning, enabling the detection and classification of malware into families. The essence of machine-learning-based methods lies in feature extraction and model building. The feature extraction process can be achieved through both static and dynamic analysis methods. Commonly used features include opcode sequences, API call sequences, byte sequences, etc. [4–6]. The model classifies samples by analyzing features and using algorithms such as classification or clustering. An API serves as the interface between an application program and a system. Its call sequence encapsulates the behavioral information of the code during actual runtime, providing an accurate characterization of the program's purpose. Through the analysis of API call sequences, it becomes evident that malware typically calls fixed API sequences to perform destructive behavior. With the continuous development of technology in the field of natural language processing, API sequences can be regarded as a form of semantic text, exhibiting temporal relationships between APIs. The relevant technologies of natural language processing can be applied to analyze API sequences [5,7].

We present a versatile and lite malware classification model based on the key semantic information of API call sequences. To address the issue of long training time and low accuracy resulting from excessive noise and redundant data in API call sequences, this model employs keyword extraction technology for key information extraction. To enhance the extraction of semantic information from API call sequences, this article extensively employs language-training language models to obtain rich semantic representations. Moreover, neural network models are employed to address the multi-classification challenge posed by malware. In this experiment, we used the dataset provided by the "Alibaba Cloud Tianchi Competition Security malware Detection;; competition question and conducted the necessary data processing. The experimental findings demonstrate the superiority of our proposed method in comparison to the general classification methods using API call sequences as features. The proposed method is more effective in multi classification of malware, with an accuracy rate of 90%.

2 Related Work

Malware technology has caused significant harm to users, enterprises, and even countries due to its continuous development. Numerous information security researchers both domestically and internationally are dedicated to the research of malware.

The core of machine-learning-based malware detection methods lies in feature extraction and modeling. The model classifies samples by analyzing features and using algorithms such as classification or clustering. An API serves as the crucial interface between an application program and a system, and its call sequence can substantially reflect the program's behavior. Therefore, numerous malware analyses are based on API sequences. Darshan [8] et al. extracted API call sequences from JSON files obtained from sandbox operations. They then applied the N Gram method to process the sequences and used machine learning algorithms to construct classifiers with high detection accuracy. However, a drawback of this method is its consideration of only a small subset of features from a larger pool, necessitating further improvement in accuracy. Fang Yong [9] et al. addressed this limitation by mixing dynamic and static API features through weight ratios to compensate for the shortcomings of a single feature. They also proposed a new semi-supervised clustering algorithm based on the unsupervised DBSCAN algorithm, significantly improving the accuracy of clustering.

The above methods all require a large amount of data and labor to ensure accurate classification. Furthermore, some models require the use of manual design feature extraction, resulting in serious limitations in generalization issues. The use of neural networks based on deep learning methods to solve text classification problems is currently a hot research topic. Deep learning [10] is a branch of machine learning based on multi-layer neural networks to learn deeper features in samples. It is a complex machine learning algorithm capable of automatically extracting the features of malware through multi-layer neural networks, simplifying the feature extraction process and enhancing detection accuracy. Lu Xiaofeng [11] et al. proposed a model assembly method. They introduced a correlation analysis algorithm for API calls to mine features of API sequences. Machine learning algorithms were then employed to learn these features. Subsequently, a recurrent neural network was utilized to detect malware, and finally, a model combination was conducted, resulting in improved outcomes. However, its drawback is that recurrent neural networks are unstable when dealing with long sequences, potentially leading to extended model training time and poor detection performance. Cui [12] et al. used grayscale images to represent disassembly files of malware. They leveraged the advantages of convolutional neural networks in image processing to recognize and classify grayscale images and used bat algorithms to address the problem of data imbalance between different malicious software families. Nevertheless, a drawback is that the model exhibits low flexibility and requires setting the input images of all samples to a uniform size.

The malware classification method based on deep learning does not require the use of manually designed feature extraction and has high classification accuracy. However, the training time of neural networks is long, and they may generate a large number of parameters, resulting in excessive hardware costs. Currently, it is impossible to avoid the problem of using deep learning for prediction. To address the issue of a large number of malware variants while also considering detection efficiency and effectiveness, this article combines the characteristics of the target task and the data used, takes API call sequences as the research object, and regards them as a piece of text with semantic information. Additionally, it implements a lightweight model based on API core semantic information using the self-attention mechanism, which enhances the accuracy of multi-classification.

3   A Lite Model Based on API Core Semantic Information

Figure 1 illustrates process of malware classification based on deep learning using API call sequences as the research object. Firstly, collect executable programs on the Windows platform, encompassing both malicious and benign samples. Subsequently, utilize the Cuckoo sandbox environment for simulation execution. After certain data processing, obtain API sequences. Then, classify them using a classification model. Finally, process the text data for classification and input it into the trained model to obtain the malware classification results. The lightweight nature of the model proposed in this article is evident in two aspects. Firstly, the model's input consists of API call sequences containing only key information. Secondly, while ensuring the model's effectiveness, the number of parameters in the model is greatly reduced.

3.1   API Call Sequence

The malware classification task based on API call sequences utilizes API call log files as analysis objects. It extracts features from the collected files using text analysis methods, preprocesses the data, and incorporates other techniques for feature selection. However, there are significant differences between API call log files and real-world text files. The first distinction lies in the fact that data in text files is often in common languages such as Chinese or English, encompassing Chinese and English words, etc. In contrast, data in API call log files represents API functions, serving as the interface between the application program and the Windows system, with a specific nature. Therefore, when classifying malware using a pre-trained model with good training results, such as the powerful BERT, it is necessary to extract API functions from the API sequence and establish a special API vocabulary to retrain the language model. The second difference arises

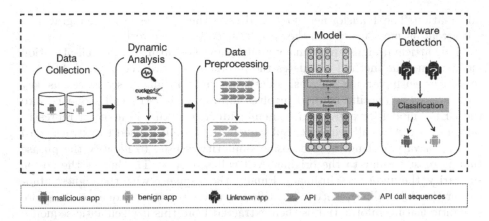

Fig. 1. Malware Classification Process.

from the fact that, to avoid analysis, malware often inserts a significant amount of redundant behavior into normal behavior. This results in excessively long API sequences that interfere with analysis and conceal the malicious intent of the code. Therefore, before extracting the core semantic information of API call sequences, it is necessary to perform data preprocessing operations to remove redundant and noisy data from the original sequence. This article reprocesses API call sequences to reduce their complexity. However, the data preprocessing method only removes multiple duplicate sequences, solving the redundancy problem in file format. At this point, a substantial amount of information in the API call sequence still has little impact on the classification results. Therefore, this article proposes an operational method for extracting core semantic information from the noise information in the API call sequence after deduplication. Considering that the classification process of malware often relies on a few key information points to obtain the classification results, it is necessary to perform key information extraction and feature selection operations on the API call sequence after preprocessing the extensive data and ultimately extracting its core semantic information.

3.2 A Lite Method for Extracting Key Semantic Information Based on BERT

Since API call sequences fall into the category of a special text sequence, they can be considered unstructured data. When classifying malware, it is essential to convert these sequences into vector form. Therefore, a word embedding layer is needed for vector representation.

The advent of the Transformer model has overcome the shortcomings of using convolutional neural networks and recurrent neural networks in malware classification. These traditional models, being sequence-dependent, are constrained to unidirectional semantics and lack the ability to simultaneously utilize contextual information. The Transformer model addresses these challenges by integrating a self-attention mechanism into the encoder-decoder framework.

This article designs an intimacy analysis method utilizing the self-attention mechanism. The method calculates the intimacy of word vectors and API call sequences with varying lengths, identifying high intimacy sequences as key sequences. The specific method involves inputting the API call sequence into the BERT model for extraction and embedding, resulting in a vector representation of the API call sequence. Subsequently, N-gram is used to extract word vectors of varying lengths, and cosine similarity is used to identify the phrase that is most similar to the original API call sequence. The higher the cosine similarity, the higher the intimacy. Finally, the sequence with the highest affinity for the API call sequence is identified as a key semantic sequence. The core semantic feature information is then extracted from this key semantic sequence as input.

3.3 A Lite Method for Core Semantic Information Based on BERT

API call sequences are considered unstructured data due to the fact that they belong to a distinct category of text sequences. When classifying malware, it is necessary to convert it into vector form, which necessitates the use of a word embedding layer for vector representation. The Transformer model, by bypassing the limitations associated with autoregressive models in feature extraction, has the capability to comprehensively learn any dependency relationships mentioned in the previous text. This article uses a simplified and improved ALBERT model as a feature extractor and then uses a classification model to achieve multi-classification of malware. There are several explanations for the feature extraction model:

Model Input: The model converts each word into a vector as input, establishing a word vector table. The original text is tokenized, and [CLS] is inserted at the beginning to indicate that the feature is used for the classification model. In the model's final layer, the corresponding vector of this bit can serve as the semantic representation of the entire sentence. This is because compared to other words already in the text, this symbol without obvious semantic information will more "fairly" integrate the semantic information of each word in the text. As a result, it adeptly represents the semantics of the entire sentence. The key semantic sequences are input into the Embedding and Encoder layers of the BERT model to obtain an embedded representation containing the core semantic information.

Word Embedding: The vector of word embedding relies on word mapping, and it learns contextually independent representations. The output value from the feature extractor not only encompasses the word's own semantics but also incorporates contextual semantics. It learns contextual representations and should contain more semantic information. Consequently, the BERT model's Encoder should yield a larger vector dimension to accommodate more semantic information. In this article, the word embedding dimension E (API) of the model is 128 dimensions, while the vector dimension T (API) output by the Encoder encoder of the BERT model is 384 dimensions. E (API) is much smaller than T (API). When processing API call sequences, there are a total of 295 categories of API functions, resulting in a vocabulary size V (API) of 295. The specific operation of the word embedding layer is to input a vector with dimension V (API) into a low-dimensional word embedding matrix, map it to a low-dimensional space with dimension E (API), and then input a low-dimensional word embedding matrix with dimension E (API) into a high-dimensional word embedding matrix, and finally map it to a T (API) dimensional word embedding. Dimensionality reduction operations significantly reduce the number of parameters in the model. The Eqs. (1) and (2) show the change in time complexity after word embedding matrix decomposition.

$$O = V(API) * T(API) \tag{1}$$

$$O = V(API) * E(API) + E(API) * T(API) \tag{2}$$

Layer Parameters: In the BERT model, the sharing of parameters is limited to either the fully connected layer or the attention layer. This article incorporates parameter sharing between several layers to further minimize training parameters and enhance training time. Specifically, the multi-head attention layer and the fully connected feedforward neural network layer share parameters. The parameter size of the feature extractor can be greatly reduced by using an improved self-attention mechanism-based core semantic extraction method, the overall computational speed of the model can be accelerated, the hardware memory overhead can be reduced, the training speed can be accelerated, and the risk of model degradation can be reduced. The feature extractor presented in this paper is more flexible and lightweight when compared to the steps of extracting features in a large pre-trained language model.

3.4   TextCNN Classification Model

Extract the features of the sentence by inputting the embedded representation containing sufficient semantic information into the convolutional layer of the TextCNN model.

The feature maps are then input into the TextCNN model's maximum pooling layer, where they are concatenated to form a vector representation, resulting in a one-dimensional vector. Subsequently, the ReLU activation function is used to output, and a dropout layer is added to prevent overfitting. The fully connected layer is responsible for establishing the relationship between feature information and category information. Finally, all fully connected layer output values are connected to the softmax layer, and multi-classification results are output.

Finally, the overall structure of the model is shown in Fig. 2, which is mainly composed of an input layer, an extraction core sequence layer, a feature extraction layer, a TextCNN layer, and an output layer. Initially, the API call sequence is input from the input layer to the core sequence layer for extracting key information, shortening the data length, and reducing the data volume. The feature extraction layers are then connected to extract sufficient semantic representation while significantly reducing the training time. After encoding, the text of the API call sequence, similar to text, is converted into serialized data, which is then fed into the Transformer encoder. The final feature vector representation of the output text is obtained after training with a self-supervised multi-layer bidirectional Transformer encoder. It then enters TextCNN's convolutional layer to extract the feature representation of the sentence, obtain the feature map, and connect the maximum pooling layer. The one-dimensional vector input is a fully connected layer after the pooling procedure. Finally, all fully connected layer output values are connected to the softmax layer, and multi-classification results are output.

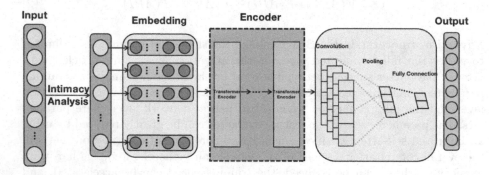

Fig. 2. A Lite Malware Classification Model Based on API Core Semantic Information.

The model incorporates key information extraction mechanisms, self-supervised learning mechanisms, and a simple convolutional neural network to form an overall model. Through the above improvement techniques, the model greatly reduces the large number of parameters generated during the self-supervised learning process and significantly accelerates its training speed. After conducting numerous experiments, it was discovered that the above enhancements effectively improve the accuracy of model predictions. This indicates that relevant improvements are very necessary.

4   Experimental Validation and Result Analysis

4.1   Dataset

The dataset is provided by the Alibaba Cloud Tianchi Competition Security Malicious Program Detection Challenge, which is derived from the API instruction sequence of a Windows binary executable program simulated by a sandbox program. The sample data provided in the question was obtained from the internet. The types of malicious files include infectious viruses, Trojan programs, mining programs, DDOS Trojan horses, ransomware, etc., totaling 600 million pieces of data. In consideration of the experiment's utilization of call sequences distinguished by file numbers, there are a total of 13887 files. The training set was divided into 11110 and 2777 pieces, with a total of 295 API functions counted, according to the 8:2 ratio. Table 1 illustrates the distribution of sample types and specific quantities.

Table 1. Types and quantity of Malware samples.

Label	Type	Quantity
0	**Benign sample**	4978
1	**Ransomware virus**	502
2	**Mining procedures**	1196
3	**DDoS Trojan**	820
4	**worm-type virus**	100
5	**Infectious virus**	4289
6	**Backdoor program**	515
7	**Trojan program**	1487

4.2 Data Preprocessing

To elude analysis, malware frequently injects a significant amount of redundant behavior into normal operations, resulting in the presence of multiple consecutive identical APIs or API sequence fragments in the sequence. This redundancy in information causes the resulting API sequence to become overly lengthy. This not only hampers analysis and conceals the malicious intent of the code but also extends the training time. Therefore, this article aims to reprocess API call sequences, diminishing their complexity and yielding API call sequences that genuinely reflect program behavior.

Additionally, manage APIs that convey the same meaning but have distinct function names within Windows APIs. For instance, LoadLibraryA and LoadLibraryW are both library loading functions that end with A and W, respectively. The reason is that the system provides different APIs for different encodings, with the W ending mainly for UNICODE encoding and the A ending mainly for ASCII encoding format. For such functions, consider the approach of eliminating the suffix, presenting both LoadLibraryA and LoadLibraryW as LoadLibrary.

We analyzed the distribution of data length before and after data preprocessing. Among these, 4,806 samples exhibit API sequence lengths within 500, while 2,769 samples have API lengths exceeding 10000, accounting for 19.9 of the total samples. There are 6216 API sequences with a length less than 500, and only 827 with a length greater than 10000, accounting for 5.9 of the total. Through statistical analysis, it is evident that the deduplication operation effectively reduces the length of API sequences, which helps to improve subsequent analysis efficiency.

4.3   Evaluation Indicators

According to the statistics of different categories of malware in the dataset used, it can be seen that the data distribution is uneven. There are over 4000 benign samples in the training set, although the minimum number is less than 100. Therefore, the text adopts accuracy P, recall R, f1 value, and weighted average value as evaluation indicators for the malware classification model, which are all calculated based on TP, TN, FP, and FN. TP denotes predicting positive cases as positive cases; FN denotes predicting positive cases as negative cases; FP denotes predicting negative cases as positive cases; and TN denotes predicting negative cases as negative cases.

Based on the values of the above indicators, calculate the accuracy, recall, and value of the i-th Malware category using formulas (3), (4), and (5). Set the number of data items for the i-th Malware category as, and the total number of data items as N. Then, calculate the weighted average P, weighted average R, and weighted average value using Eq. (6) (7) (8):

$$P_i = \frac{TP_i}{TP_i + FP_i} \tag{3}$$

$$R_i = \frac{TP_i}{TP_i + FN_i} \tag{4}$$

$$F_i = \frac{2 \times P_i \times R_i}{P_i + R_i} \tag{5}$$

$$P = \sum P_i \times \frac{N_i}{N} \tag{6}$$

$$R = \sum R_i \times \frac{N_i}{N} \tag{7}$$

$$F = \sum F_i \times \frac{N_i}{N} \tag{8}$$

4.4   Experimental Results

Parameter Settings. The key to handling sequence problems with TextCNN is to use convolution to express sequence information. It is a one-dimensional convolution, and using a single-length convolution kernel may lose some feature information. Therefore, this article sets up a TextCNN model to extract features from various angles using several convolution kernels of varying sizes, thereby increasing the comprehensiveness of the features. This article conducts experimental comparisons and designs convolutional kernels with sizes of 4, 5, 6, and

7. Each convolutional kernel contains 128 neurons, and ReLU is used as the activation function. A maximum pooling approach is utilized to reduce dimensionality after each convolutional layer. The concatenate function is then applied to combine numerous convolutional and pooling layers. The cross-entropy loss function is utilized to calculate the loss value during model training, and the Adamw optimization method is used to achieve gradient descent and update the model parameters. Setting the batch size to 32 when using the batch training method, which divides the entire dataset into several small datasets, helps the model converge and alleviates the problem of falling into local optima. Set the number of iterations for training, i.e., the epoch value, to 10 and save the optimal model for comparative analysis. Finally, it was determined that the best classification performance was achieved when the improved convolutional neural network parameters were taken from Table 2.

Table 2. LM-cAPI Parameter settings

Label	Type
$embedding_size$	128
$hidden_size$	384
$learning_rate$	5e−5
$filter_sizes$	[4,5,6,7]
$num_filters$	128
$classifier_dropout_prob$	0.1
num_train_epochs	10
$batch_size$	32

Experimental Results and Analysis. According to the comparative experimental results in Table 3, it can be seen that this article established a dictionary based on API call functions and retrained the language model, achieving good multi-classification results. Furthermore, the model introduces and optimizes key information extraction and self-supervised learning methods. From a technical perspective, it is beneficial to learn as much semantic information as possible from the API sequence. This will significantly reduce the problem of parameter explosion caused by self-supervised learning while ensuring the accuracy of model classification.

We draws the loss index and accuracy change curves of the model on the training and validation sets, as shown in Fig. 3. In the training process of malicious code multi classification, when the loss is generally between 0.1 and 0.2, the model has basically converged.

Table 3. Comparison of experimental results

model	precision	recall	f1-score
textcnn	0.80	0.79	0.81
bert	0.70	0.69	0.69
lm-capi	0.93	0.88	0.90

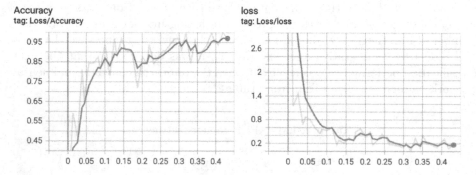

Fig. 3. The loss index and accuracy change curve of the model on the training and validation sets.

Ablation Experiment. This section will split each module and conduct a series of ablation experiments on the AAPD dataset to verify Verify the effectiveness of each module of LSGG. It is mainly divided into the following five parts:

(1) TextCNN: Remove the word embedding part of the LM-cAPI to directly interact with the label text in TextCNN.
(2) B-TCNN: Only BERT and TextCNN are used, excluding the shared parameter mechanism and word embedding layering mechanism of LM-cAPI. In the neural network part, the English BERT pre training model is used.
(3) Pre B TCNN: Only BERT and TextCNN are used, excluding the shared parameter mechanism and word embedding layering mechanism of LM-cAPI. In the neural network part, in order to ensure fairness, the BERT model is retrained for special datasets to obtain a pre trained language model based on API call sequence vocabulary.
(4) M-cAPI: does not perform core semantic extraction, removes the core semantic extraction part of LM-cAPI, and directly classifies based on the cleaned dataset.
(5) LM cAPI: The standard LM cAPI. As shown in Fig. 4, it can be concluded that pre-B-TCNN, M-cAPI, and LM cAPI perform better than B-TCNN in multiple indicators. This implies that when employing pre-trained language models for API call sequences, a new vocabulary needs to be used to re-train the model.

Moreover, the performance of pre-B-TCNN has seen a slight decline when compared to TextCNN. This suggests that the BERT model is limited to handling text data with a length of 512. The truncated text loses some key data,

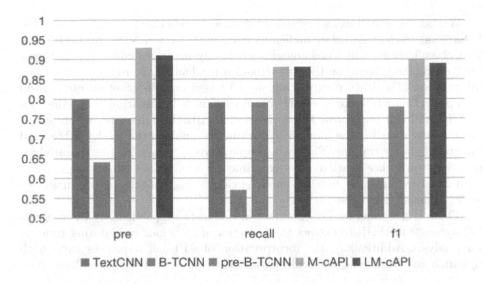

Fig. 4. Schematic diagram of LM-cAPI ablation experiment.

potentially leading to a decrease in results. In addition, the training of pretrained language models is more time-consuming, necessitating the use of a lightweight model.

5 Conclusion

In the face of the rapid proliferation of malicious code types and quantities, coupled with the continuous updating of dissemination methods, the challenge of promptly and accurately identifying malicious code stands as a critical aspect of maintaining network security. Machine learning, a hot topic in artificial intelligence research, has found applications across multiple fields. Therefore, machine learning can be used for malicious code detection to achieve automation and intelligence in detection. This article takes dynamic API call sequences as the research object and extracts and processes API sequences from two perspectives. It then uses machine learning and deep learning algorithms for model training. Through the modification of model parameters and optimization of the network structure, the detection accuracy of the model is improved, fully leveraging the advantages of using machine learning algorithms for malicious program detection.

API call sequences are one of the most important features in malicious code detection. This article analyzes the current research status of existing malicious code detection methods, especially those based on API sequences. In response to the limitations of existing research, enhancements are made in both feature extraction and model training. From different perspectives, two malicious code detection methods were implemented. The experimental results show that both methods can effectively detect malicious code, highlighting their important research significance. The main achievements of this article are as follows:

We examined API call sequences in malicious code that can characterize the behavioral characteristics of malicious code as text, and then used advanced text classification-related technologies to classify malicious code. The intimacy analysis method, based on the self-attention mechanism, is used to extract key information. The feature extraction model based on self-attention mechanism uses pre-training to more efficiently obtain semantic information about the context in API call sequences. In comparison to BERT, it has the advantage of significantly reducing the number of parameters, making the model lighter and facilitating faster training. Finally, a simple TextCNN model is incorporated for malicious code classification. The experimental results show that the proposed model outperforms the baseline model in detecting and classifying malicious code, achieving good results.

There is still room for improvement in this method, particularly by integrating dynamic methods to extract the behavior of malicious code during runtime for analysis. Additionally, the incorporation of API call sequences from both dynamic and static analyses could potentially enhance detection results.

References

1. Wadkar, M., Troia, F.D., Stamp, M.: Detecting malware evolution using support vector machines. Expert Syst. Appl. **143**, 113022.1-113022.10 (2020)
2. Natani, P., Vidyarthi, D.: Malware detection using API function frequency with ensemble based classifier. In: International Symposium on Security in Computing & Communication, pp. 378–388 (2013)
3. Han, W., Xue, J., Wang, Y., et al.: MalDAE: detecting and explaining malware based on correlation and fusion of static and dynamic characteristics. Comput. Secur. **83**, 208–233 (2019)
4. Cha, S.K., Moraru, I., Jang, J., et al.: SplitScreen: enabling efficient, distributed malware detection. J. Commun. Netw. **13**(2), 187–200 (2011)
5. Malhotra, A., Bajaj, K.: A hybrid pattern based text mining approach for malware detection using DBScan. CSI Trans. ICT **4**(2–4), 1–9 (2016)
6. Karnik, A., Goswami, S., Guha, R.: Detecting obfuscated viruses using cosine similarity analysis. In: Asia International Conference on Modelling & Simulation, pp. 165–170. IEEE Computer Society (2007)
7. Kinable, J., Kostakis, O.: Malware classification based on call graph clustering. J. Comput. Virol. **7**(4), 233–245 (2011)
8. Darshan, S., Kumara, M., Jaidhar, C.D.: Windows malware detection based on cuckoo sandbox generated report using machine learning algorithm. In: 2016 11th International Conference on Industrial and Information Systems (ICIIS), pp. 534–549 (2016)
9. Fang, Y., Zhang, W., Li, B., et al.: Semi-supervised malware clustering based on the weight of bytecode and API. IEEE Access **8**, 2313–2326 (2019)
10. Lecun, Y., Bengio, Y., Hinton, G.: Deep learning. Nature **521**(7553), 436 (2015)
11. Xiaofeng, L., Fangshuo, J., Xiao, Z., Baojiang, C., Shengwei, Y., Jing, S.: A malicious sample detection framework based on the combination of API sequence features and statistical features. J. Tsinghua Univ. (Nat. Sci. Ed.) **58**(05), 500–508 (2018)
12. Cui, Z., Xue, F., Cai, X., et al.: Detection of malicious code variants based on deep learning. IEEE Trans. Ind. Inf. **14**, 3187–3196 (2018)

Acki Nacki: A Probabilistic Proof-of-Stake Consensus Protocol with Fast Finality and Parallelisation

Mitja Goroshevsky[✉], Nikita Sattarov, and Alina Trepacheva

GOSH, 919 North Market Street, Suite 950, Wilmington, Delaware 19801, USA
{mitja,nikita,alina.t}@gosh.sh

Abstract. We propose an asynchronous, highly effective proof-of-stake protocol optimized for fast finality, while allowing for high throughputs via execution parallelization. It is a probabilistic protocol that achieves higher Byzantine fault tolerance than Nakamoto, BFT (including Hotstuff and AptosBFT), Solana, and other modern consensus protocols. Our protocol reaches consensus in two communication steps and has a total number of messages that are subquadratic to the number of nodes, with probabilistic, dynamically adjusted safety guarantees. We trade off deterministic consensus with theoretical constraints on message complexity and the number of Byzantine agreements, with probabilistic algorithms overtaking these boundaries. We further claim that because of the use of randomness and socioeconomics in blockchain designs, no real trade-off is actually present. One of the key ingredients of our approach is separating the verification of execution by a consensus committee from the attestation of block propagation by network participants. Our consensus committee is randomly selected for each block and is not predetermined, while the Leader is deterministic.

Keywords: blockchain · consensus · BLS signature · DDoS attack

1 Introduction

Current public blockchains are almost exclusively used for financial applications, be it for the store and transfer of value or decentralized finance. Users are ready to pay gas and transaction fees when transacting in value. Blockchains do not achieve mass adoption because they cannot support the quality of user experience expected from modern computer software. For one, it is almost impossible to support free transactions to be able to offer a freemium business model for developers. Secondly, the blockchain user interfaces suffer from long delays for task completion related to block finalization times. The primary reason for this user experience inefficiency is the inherent lack of performance in both transaction execution throughput and time to finality, due to strict requirements on state validation. Private blockchains have also failed to achieve mass production

© The Author(s), under exclusive license to Springer Nature Switzerland AG 2024
M. Andreoni (Ed.): ACNS 2024 Workshops, LNCS 14586, pp. 43–62, 2024.
https://doi.org/10.1007/978-3-031-61486-6_4

in enterprise use cases due to their maintenance complexity and high computing costs.

In this paper, we present a highly efficient, scalable, and practical blockchain protocol optimized for heavy parallelization and extremely fast finality times. The goal of the protocol is to produce performance comparable to cluster cloud databases without compromising security.

Our paper has the following structure: in the next section, we give some background on assumptions and a survey of related works. The third section describes our protocol, the fourth and fifth sections analyze our protocol's security, the sixth section analyzes the performance of our protocol, and the last section concludes.

2   Background

Usually, computer science consensus protocols are classified into two groups: probabilistic and deterministic. The deterministic protocols, under different safety conditions, were developed from 1978 [11,19] to the present day for various applications [5], and with different safety properties, culminating in the development of pBFT [9]. However, they were not used for solving the double-spending problem of decentralized money use cases[1].

2.1   Bitcoin

The first protocol that addressed this use case was introduced by Nakamoto on Oct 31, 2008 [20]. Bitcoin uses a probabilistic consensus protocol based on *Proof-of-Work*, where miners compete to win a slot to propose the new block and be rewarded by expending computing resources to solve cryptographic puzzles.

In Bitcoin, economic incentives play a vital role in network safety and are embedded into the matrix of the protocol's safety guarantees.

The subsequent formula for the probability of a successful Double-Spend attack in the Bitcoin network is based on the article by A. Pinar Ozisik and Brian Neil Levine [21].

$$p_{bitcoin}\left(z, \delta\right) = 1 - \sum_{k=0}^{z+1}\left(\frac{(z \cdot \delta)^k \cdot e^{-z \cdot \delta}}{k!} \cdot \left(1 - \delta^{z+1-k}\right)\right),$$

where z - number of blocks till probabilistic "finality", $0 < \mu < 1$ – fraction of malicious miners, $\delta = \frac{\mu}{1-\mu}$.

The downside of the Bitcoin protocol is its performance limitations. Bitcoin is known to produce just 7 transactions per second, and its transaction finalization time can exceed an hour. As we will see below, its security assumptions are

---

[1] A double-spend attack, in the context of blockchain and digital currencies, refers to a situation where a single set of digital tokens or currency is spent more than once. This type of attack exploits the digital nature of the currency, as digital information can be replicated.

quite weak as well. All of this did not prevent Bitcoin from being the largest cryptocurrency by value to date. However, it did prevent Bitcoin from being used for much more than a store and transfer of value.

Ethereum [31], introduced in 2014 as a smart contract platform [8], initially also used PoW consensus. Its TPS was about 17 per second, but even this was far from sufficient to meet the growing demand for Decentralized Applications (dApps), primarily in the Decentralized Finance (DeFi) sector.

This unsatisfactory performance of PoW forced researchers to look for alternatives.

2.2 BFT

Notably, even before Ethereum, back in 2012, S. King and S. Nadal proposed a protocol they called Proof-of-Stake [15] (PoS), where instead of committing computing resources and electricity, network participants would commit a valuable stake, which they could subsequently lose if proven to act maliciously. This opened a way to use deterministic consensus protocols such as pBFT-based and others [10,14] in cryptocurrency settings, in combination with PoW and later PoS protocols. Many protocols have been proposed since then, and some have been implemented in working systems, improving on the original pBFT messaging requirements and such [2,3,24].

All BFT-based protocols [30,34] generally have two states (faulty or not, 0 or 1) under the protocol assumption. However, in the PoS environment, the decision to act maliciously or not depends not on the properties of the protocol but on the economic realities of the PoS system. In addition, most blockchains rely on probabilistic encryption [13] for their cryptography. Therefore, the BFT consensus algorithms used in the settings of PoS consensus protocols somewhat lose their deterministic properties, as we can no longer prove that non-malicious participants will not turn Byzantine based on the content of the message they are registering, and their determinism will always be bound by cryptographic probability. Thus, if we have a probabilistic consensus protocol with safety guarantees comparable to modern cryptography and/or game theory, it will have practically the same safety as BFT. Yet the penalty we pay in performance for having a presumably deterministic protocol is limiting.

An upper bound on the number of malicious nodes for breaking BFT consensus protocols is $\frac{2}{3} \cdot N + 1$, where N is the total number of nodes in the network. From this, a formula for the successful probability of an attack for BFT consensus protocols is easily derived:

$$p_{BFT}(M, N) = \mathbb{I}_{[\lceil \frac{2}{3} \cdot N \rceil + 1,\, N]}(M),$$

where N is the number of network participants, M is the number of malicious network participants, and $\mathbb{I}_F(x)$ is an indicator function that takes the value 1 if $x \in F$, and 0 otherwise.

2.3 Fast Byzantine Paxos

In [16,17], fast asynchronous Byzantine consensus was proposed. The authors state that this protocol can reach consensus in two communication steps in the common case. However, the cost of such fast finality is that the total number of nodes must be $\geq 5 \cdot f + 1$, where f is the number of Byzantine nodes [18]. Consequently, it can handle a much smaller number of malicious nodes than pBFT. Moreover, it's proven that this bound is tight for deterministic protocols, i.e., for the total number of nodes equal to $5f$, it's impossible to construct a Byzantine consensus that works in two steps.

2.4 Modern Blockchains

Recognizing the performance problems of Nakamoto and BFT consensus protocols, recently a few other approaches have surfaced. We will compare with the three most performant among them: Solana, Avalanche, and Aptos.

Solana. Solana is a blockchain platform engineered for hosting decentralized applications, emphasizing scalability and efficiency. It exhibits a higher transaction processing capacity, with an ability to handle a greater number of transactions per second, coupled with reduced transaction fees. Distinctively, Solana operates on a Proof-of-Stake (PoS) blockchain architecture, but it augments this with an additional mechanism called Proof-of-History (PoH). Yakovenko published a white paper [32] describing the Proof-of-History (PoH) concept. PoH allows the blockchain to reach consensus by verifying the passage of time between events, and it is used to encode the passage of time into a ledger. Instead of individual validator nodes, Solana uses validator clusters, where groups of validators work together to process transactions. Although the PoH-based network has shown some improvements in blockchain throughput, it has been criticized for lacking a sound scientific foundation for its claims [23].

Avalanche. In the Avalanche consensus mechanism [1], nodes decide on transaction acceptance by conducting repeated voting among a small, randomly selected group of validator nodes. When a node needs to determine the status of a transaction, it inquires of a subset of validators for their opinion. These chosen validators respond with their preferred transaction. If a significant majority of the sampled validators agree on a specific transaction, that transaction becomes the choice of the inquiring node. Over time, this node will also favor the transaction that most validators support. This process of sampling and gathering responses continues until there is consistent agreement among the validators over several consecutive rounds.

The threshold for what constitutes a significant majority, and the 'Confidence Threshold,' which is the required number of consecutive rounds for achieving consensus, are both adjustable parameters.

In Avalanche, subsampling has low message overhead. It doesn't matter whether there are twenty validators or two thousand; the number of consensus messages a node sends during a query remains constant. Transitive voting, where a vote for a block is a vote for all its ancestors, helps with transaction throughput. Each vote is effectively many votes in one.

A notable issue arises when multiple blocks are proposed at the same height. In such scenarios, the Avalanche protocol may face delays in determining the correct block to accept, even though all proposed blocks could potentially be valid. This delay is primarily due to the requirement that each block must be executed and assessed by the subset of validators.

As described in the Avalanche white paper [26], the attack probability dynamically changes based on the algorithm's input parameters, such as the number of nodes in the network, the number of malicious nodes, the size of the query sample sent to another node for knowledge about a transaction, and the number of rounds of these queries. Reducing the attack probability directly leads to an increase in finalization time and message complexity. The asymptotic message complexity is $O(k \cdot n \cdot \log n)$ [25], where n is the number of nodes in the network, and k is the size of the sample in a single query, with the constraint $1 \leq k \leq n - 1$.

AptosBFT. Aptos [27] improves on advanced variants of pBFT, namely Hotstuff [33]. In this respect, a comparison with Aptos in general is already described in the BFT section above.

Like many other protocols, Aptos places a lot of emphasis on randomly choosing the Leader and rotating it with every block. The main performance weakness of such an approach is that often, leader rotation necessitates replicating external messages, which users send to the blockchain, to all nodes in the network. This represents an additional quadratic complexity growth overhead, usually excluded when calculating the protocol's messaging complexity.

Sharding. In search of further performance improvements, researchers came up with the concept of sharding, which was first introduced in the Zilliqa blockchain [29] and later developed in Ethereum for state sharding [6,7].

Additionally, several sharded protocols were proposed. These protocols attempted to overcome the performance problem by sharding data and/or execution, introducing parallel leader selection, and state synchronization mechanisms, notably in TON [12], Near [22], Elrond [28], and others. We do not compare these protocols in our analysis because most of them use BFT as their basic consensus algorithm and, therefore, may be considered as belonging to the previously discussed groups.

Although the concepts of parallel execution of contracts and sharded states are important advances in consensus algorithms and have improved network scaling, these concepts alone have not overcome a certain barrier, approximately 100K TPS, even in laboratory environments.

3   Construction of Acki Nacki

Now we present the Acki Nacki probabilistic consensus protocol, with the goal of pushing the performance of fault-tolerant consensus protocols as far as possible.

In Acki Nacki, participants can perform three roles: Block Producer, Block Keeper, and Verifier (which we call an Acki-Nacki entity). All these roles could be performed by any network participant in parallel. Thus, many Acki Nacki chains (called Threads) can exist simultaneously, but since their security and functionality do not depend on each other, we will proceed below with a description of an isolated chain[2].

3.1   Definitions

Definition 1. *Account (contract) is a record in a distributed database.*

Definition 2. *Thread is a subset of nodes serving a particular subset of Accounts.*

Definition 3. *Block Producer (BP) is a leader of a particular Thread, responsible for block production.*

Definition 4. *Block Keeper (BK) is an entity with two functions:*

- *Receives blocks from BP and sends an Attestation with the block hash and other metadata back to BP. BK does not check the validity of block transactions, nor does it attempt to execute the block, only applies it to its local state with a mark 'Not Final'.*
- *Performs a self-check to determine if it needs to become a Verifier for this block as described below. If so, BK will verify the Block and broadcast the result: Ack if the Block is okay, and Nack if the block is invalid.*

Definition 5. *Verifier (Acki-Nacki) is a BK responsible for block validation and notifying all network participants about their verdict: whether the block is valid or not.*

Definition 6. *Attestation is a message sent to BP by any BK after receiving the block. Attestation is a BLS signature performed on BK's private key. The BP of the next block must aggregate all received Attestations for the previous block into one BLS signature and include it in the Common section of the new block.*

Definition 7. *Ack is a message broadcasted to all network participants by Acki-Nacki if the block is verified and valid.*

Definition 8. *Nack is a message broadcasted to all network participants by Acki-Nacki if the block is verified and not valid.*

Attestations and Verifier's messages must contain the block hash, its BLS signature [4] on BK's private key, and some extra data. For example, Nack contains the reason for block rejection.

---

[2] Because of this multithreaded property, Acki Nacki uses an Asynchronous Virtual Machine to execute transactions. This is beyond the scope of this paper, so we mention it here for future references.

3.2   Security Assumptions

We follow standard assumptions of Safety and Liveness [23] properties for Acki Nacki protocol. These properties ensure that the network operation resembles that of a monolithic, valid server, i.e., a linearizably consistent block ledger.

- **Safety**: No two honest BKs accept different blocks of the same height, and no block with an incorrect transaction is finalized.
- **Liveness**: If an honest BP receives a transaction, it will eventually be included in every honest node's ledger.

In accordance with these properties, we classify attacks that violate them:

Safety Attacks. Such attacks include dissemblance and private chain attacks. Dissemblance means that the adversary maintains Byzantine nodes to send different messages to different nodes, potentially leading to nodes' disagreement. Private chain attacks occur when the adversary controls Byzantine nodes to work on a separate blockchain privately while ostensibly following the protocol.

Liveness Attacks. These types of attacks include the aforementioned dissemblance and withholding attacks. Apart from affecting safety, dissemblance may prevent honest nodes from making decisions indefinitely, thereby breaking liveness. Withholding means that the adversary controlling Byzantine nodes refrains from sending messages to particular nodes, potentially causing them to be unable to make decisions indefinitely.

3.3   Block Producer Selection Algorithm

BP selection in Acki Nacki is not random, as the security assumptions of the protocol allow for BPs to be potentially malicious. The following deterministic algorithm is used: the hash of the block with a shard split (or any other Thread rotation demand) message is taken as a seed, and random sampling of one key from the sorted list of BKs' public keys is performed. The current list of BPs is always presented in the Common Section of any Block.

Note: In Acki Nacki, a Block, besides containing TRXs, has a Common Section for collecting block-related data like Attestations, Verifier's messages, BPs list, slashing/reward conditions, etc.

3.4   Acki-Nacki Selection Algorithm

After receiving a block, BK checks whether they are Acki-Nacki for this block. To do this, they calculate $a = \mathsf{sign}(\mathsf{hash}(B), sk)$, where sk is the secret BLS key of BK, B is the current block. They then calculate the remainder of $r = a\%b$, where $b = N/v$, N—the total number of network participants, v—the desired average number of Acki-Nacki, with v such that N is divisible by v without a remainder. Both a and b are integers. If the remainder r equals 0, then it is Acki-Nacki; otherwise, it's not.

Thus, any BK can randomly become Acki-Nacki with a probability of v/N. The selection of each Acki-Nacki is an independent event.

This allows for controlling the average number of Acki-Nacki per block. More details are described in the section "Expected Number of Acki-Nacki per Block" 4.5.

3.5   Block Production and Broadcast

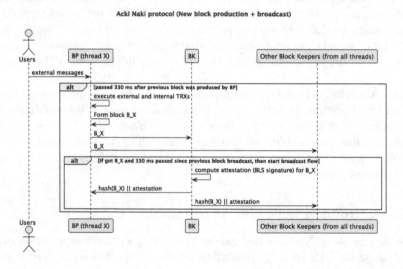

Fig. 1. The Acki-Nacki protocol (Block production and broadcast).

BP releases a new block every 330 ms. As soon as the time arrives, it collects the unprocessed messages, executes transactions, and creates a block (the block is limited by the maximum computed operations and time). Once the block is created, BP signs it with its BLS private key and broadcasts it to all BKs (Fig. 1).

Upon receiving the block from BP, BK checks if the min. block timeout since the previous Attestation (at least 330 ms) is satisfied, computes an Attestation for the block (BLS signature), and sends it back to the BP.

The min. block timeout from the previous Attestation is necessary to prevent a 'too many blocks' safety attack, where a malicious BP generates so many blocks that verifying them and producing Ack/Nacks in time becomes impossible. The attacking BP can spam the network with valid blocks until it produces a malicious one, which may lead to the acceptance of a block with an incorrect transaction.

3.6   Block Verification

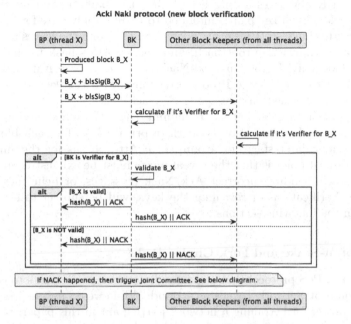

Fig. 2. The Acki Nacki protocol (Block verification).

Block verification is carried out solely by Acki-Nacki entities that are chosen based on the Acki-Nacki Selection Algorithm, as described above. Acki-Nacki must validate a block and send an Ack/Nack message to the network (Fig. 2). Otherwise, they will be subject to slashing (see 'Slashing' 3.11). While any third party may also validate the block and send acknowledgments, provided they put up a bond, they are not obliged to do so and thus are not part of the security assumptions of the protocol.

If a BP creates a block with overly complex execution, it may attempt to cause Acki-Nacki to delay block verification for more than the max., verification, time, preventing Ack/Nack transmission within the required timeframe. This could result in a block with an incorrect transaction being accepted.

To mitigate the 'Block with too complex execution' safety attack, an Acki-Nacki that executes such a block will stop after 330 ms and send a special Nack with the message 'too complex'. The committee will then check the block and penalize the BP if necessary.

3.7   Acki-Nacki Selection Proof

Periodically, BK generates a long list of BLS key pairs, sorted by sequential number (SeqNo). Each key pair is intended to be used only once for each block. BK then inserts the hash (BLS private key || SeqNo) into the leaves of a Merkle Tree, computes the Merkle root hash, and commits this hash to the network. After each block, if BK was an Acki-Nacki, it reveals its private key and its SeqNo, along with the Merkle Proof corresponding to this key and the block hash, within the Verification message (Ack/Nack).

It is important to note that the remaining BKs (those not serving as Acki-Nacki for this block) must also reveal their private keys for each block. This can be done at a later stage, for example, in Attestations for the subsequent block. The crucial point is that the reveal phase must be exhaustive in the end. Both Acki-Nacki sending incorrect Ack/Nack messages, or being negligent in not sending Verifications or revealing the keys, will be subject to slashing, as described in the following sections.

3.8   Proof-of-Stake and Fork Choice Rule

Acki Nacki is a PoS protocol that requires all network participants to commit a certain amount of Network Tokens as a Bond. While we do not discuss the economic motivation for becoming a network participant in this paper, we assume that the Tokens have a finite supply, as this plays a role in probability calculations, as will be shown below. In connection with the Fork Choice Rule, we provide an algorithm based on the weight of stakes (Fig. 3).

Sometimes, a situation may arise where the network has two valid blocks at the same height, without any malicious intent. To address this, we have developed the Fork Choice Rule algorithm, which deterministically selects one of the valid blocks for finalization by all BKs.

Key definitions and notations used throughout this section are as follows:

1. N—number of BKs;
2. A— number of Attestations till probabilistic "finality";
3. b_j—block with index j;
4. $\mathcal{K} = \{k_1, k_2, \ldots, k_N\}$—BK set;
5. $\mathcal{S} = \{s_1, s_2, \ldots, s_N\}$—BK's stake set where s_i is stake of Block Keeper k_i;
6. $\mathcal{A}_j = \{k_i \mid k_i$ has attested $b_j\}$—set of BKs that have attested block b_j
7. $\mathsf{hash}\,(b_j)$—hash of the block b_j header;
8. $\mathsf{height}\,(b_j)$—height of the block b_j;
9. $\mathsf{KeySignBP}\,(b_j)$ — key of the BP proposed block b_j;
10. $\mathcal{F}_h = \{b_j \mid \mathsf{height}(b_j) = h\}$—conflicting blocks set at the height h;
11. $\mathcal{A} = \{\mathcal{A}_j \mid b_j \in \mathcal{F}_h\}$—set of $\mathcal{A}_j$ containing Block Keepers $k_i \in \mathcal{K}$ that have attested block $b_j \in \mathcal{F}_h$.

Each BK can attest to only one block at a certain height. In other words, if a BK attests to two blocks at the same height, they will be subject to slashing.

Each BK executes the Acki-Nacki Selection Algorithm only for the block that has more than A Attestations; otherwise, it is executed only for the block that currently has the highest stake amount. For instance, if after verifying block B_i, another block B_j appears at the same height with a greater stake amount, the BK executes the Acki-Nacki Selection Algorithm for block B_j. After applying the Fork Choice Rule, the BK sends to other BKs either the block with Attestations, or the block with Attestations and Ack/Nack, depending on whether they became Acki-Nacki for that block.

Algorithm 1 Acki-Nacki Fork Choice Rule

1: **procedure** $FCR(\mathcal{K}, \mathcal{S}, \mathcal{F}_h, \mathcal{A}, A)$
2: **repeat**
3:    update $(\mathcal{F}_h)$ ▷ Checking for the receipt of new blocks
4:    update $(\mathcal{A})$ ▷ Checking for the receipt of new attestations
5:    BPFailure $\leftarrow \exists b_i, b_j \in \mathcal{F}_h : \mathsf{KeySignBP}(b_i) = \mathsf{KeySignBP}(b_j)$ ▷ Checking for the several blocks by one BP
6:    BKFailure $\leftarrow \left| \bigcap_{A_j \in \mathcal{A}} A_j \right| \neq \varnothing$ ▷ Attestation of several blocks by one BK
7:    **if** BKFailure or BPFailure **then**
8:      JOINT COMMITTEE
9:    **else**
10:      **if** $\exists! \, b_j \in \mathcal{F}_h : |A_j| \geq A$ **then**   ▷ Checking for the absence of forks
11:        **return** b_j
12:      **else**
13:        $\mathcal{U} \leftarrow \left\{ u_j \,\middle|\, b_j \in \mathcal{F}_h, A_j \in \mathcal{A}, u_j = \sum_{s_i \subset \mathcal{S} : h_i \subset A_j} s_i \right\}$ ▷ Set of stake amounts having confirmed blocks
14:        $\mathcal{M} \leftarrow \{ u_j \mid \forall u_k \in \mathcal{U} : u_j \geq u_k \}$ ▷ Set of maximum stake amounts
15:        $\mathcal{D} \leftarrow \{ d_j \mid u_j \subset \mathcal{U} \backslash \mathcal{M}, \, u_m \in \mathcal{M}, \, d_i = u_m - u_j \}$
16:        $d' \leftarrow \min \mathcal{D}$ ▷ Min add stake amount for condition change
17:        $\mathcal{C} \leftarrow \left\{ s_i \,\middle|\, s_i \in \mathcal{S}, k_i \in \bigcup_{A_j \in \mathcal{A}} A_j \right\}$ ▷ Set of stakes having already confirmed blocks
18:        $r \leftarrow \sum_{s_i \in \mathcal{S} \backslash \mathcal{C}} s_i$ ▷ Stake amount having not yet confirmed blocks
19:      **until** $r \geq d'$ **or** $\sum_{A_j \in \mathcal{A}} |A_j| < A$
20:      **if** $|\mathcal{M}| = 1$ **then**   ▷ Checking for several maximum stakes
21:        $b' \leftarrow b_j \subset \mathcal{F}_h : u_j \in \mathcal{M}$
22:        **return** b'
23:      **else**   ▷ If there are multiple maxima, check hashes
24:        $\mathcal{H} \leftarrow \{ h_j \mid u_j \in \mathcal{M}, h_j = \mathsf{hash}(b_j) \}$ ▷ Set of hashes of block headers having
25:        $b' \leftarrow b_j \in \mathcal{F}_h : h_j \in \mathcal{H}, \forall h_k \in \mathcal{H} : h_j \leq h_k$ ▷ the maximum amount of stake
26:        **return** b'

Fig. 3. Pseudocode of the Fork Choice Rule algorithm.

3.9 Block Finalization

Each BK obtains a new block, mutates the state, and marks the mutations as not final. They then wait for Attestations for this block, sent by BP in the Common section of subsequent blocks, until the minimum Attestation Threshold is reached. The Minimum Attestation Threshold percentage is specified in the network configuration.

After receiving the block and while collecting the necessary amount of block Attestations, BK also waits for T ms as specified in the min. finality time for block B_X. If T ms pass and no Nacks have been received, then BK marks this block as final (Fig. 4).

If there are not enough block attestations, the block won't be finalized. In this case, network participants can decide on the course of action: whether to allow continuous, not finalized block production; to halt the network after a certain number of blocks; to slash or not to slash BKs for not providing attestations, etc.

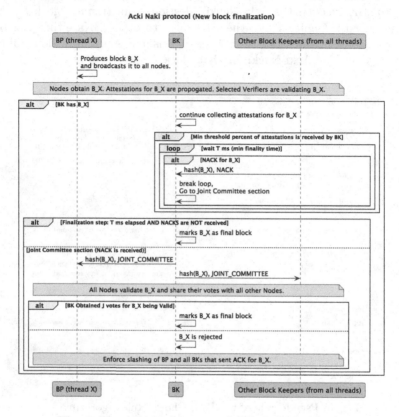

Fig. 4. The Acki Nacki protocol (Block finalization).

3.10   Joint Committee

If at least one BK receives a Nack, or if they receive an Attestation for the same height on more than one block from a single BK, or detect any other malicious action as described in the 'Slashing' section, they invoke the Joint Committee function. This requires each BK to vote on whether to slash malicious BKs, malicious BPs, and/or to reject a malicious block. In response, each BK either verifies the block, checks Attestations, or performs any other necessary action to ascertain whether someone is acting maliciously or otherwise falls under one of the Slashing conditions. To confirm or reject that an action is a result of malicious activity, the network must gather J votes, where J is a parameter set by the network participants.

3.11   Slashing

The following are slashing conditions which can lead network participants to either lose their entire stake or a portion of it (bleeding). When we say 'lose,' we mean that the stake will be burned and not transferred to any other party. Burning plays a role in security assumptions, as discussed in a separate section below.

- An accepted Nack will slash the BP and every Acki-Nacki which sent an Ack for their entire stake.
- Attesting to more than one block at the same height will result in the slashing of the entire stake of the BK.
- Producing two blocks at the same height from the same BP will result in the slashing of the BP's entire stake.
- A non-performing Acki-Nacki will result in the bleeding of its stake.
- A non-performing BK will result in the bleeding of its stake.
- Non-randomized BK keys will result in the bleeding of the stake.
- Non-sequential Acki-Nacki Keys in the Acki-Nacki Merkle Tree will result in the bleeding of the BK's stake.
- Too complex execution of a block by BP will result in the bleeding of its stake.

3.12   Dynamically Adjustable Parameters

One of the main advantages of the Acki Nacki consensus protocol is the presence of several dynamically adjustable parameters. These include the number of Attestations needed for block finalization, the average expected number of Acki-Nacki per block, the number of votes required for the Joint Committee, and the probability of a successful attack given a certain percentage of malicious BKs. All these parameters can be changed by network participants through voting, according to their preferences. For instance, participants can input the number of BKs and the desired attack probability with a certain number of malicious BKs. Based on this, Acki Nacki will then automatically adjust the parameters for the number of Attestations and Acki-Nacki, ensuring that the network achieves the highest throughput with the shortest finality.

4   Attack Analysis

4.1   Input Parameters

Notations, types and domains of the terms used in this section:

Name	Notation	Type	Domain
Number of BKs	N	$\mathbb{Z}_+$	$[3; +\infty]$
Number of malicious BKs	M	$\mathbb{Z}$	$[0; N-1]$
Number of spammed BKs	d	$\mathbb{Z}$	$[0; N-M]$
Number of Attestations	A	$\mathbb{Z}_+$	$[1; N]$
Successful attack probability	p	$\mathbb{R}$	$(0; 1)$
Expected number of Acki-Nacki per block	v	$\mathbb{Z}$	$[0; N]$
Number of votes for Joint Committiee	J	$\mathbb{Z}_+$	$[1; N]$

4.2   Combined Double-Spend and DDoS Attack

There are N BKs, of which M are malicious. The malicious BKs, using a distributed denial-of-service (DDoS) attack[3], disconnect d honest BKs from the network and perform a Double-Spend attack (Fig. 5). Verification prevents attacks on consensus. If at least one of the honest BKs, which have survived the DDoS attack, becomes an Acki-Nacki, the attack is deemed unsuccessful.

4.3   Constraints on the Number of Malicious Block Keepers

A malicious block will always be finalized if none of the honest BKs survive after a DDoS attack. Additionally, malicious blocks will always be finalized if, in the Joint Committee, the number of malicious BKs exceeds the number of honest BKs. Thus, to determine the number of malicious BKs at which the attack will be successful, or, in other words, the number of malicious BKs at which the Safety property is violated:

$$M \geq min(A, J) \tag{1}$$

At the same time, if all malicious BKs disconnect and stop sending messages, the network will halt, as it will not be able to collect enough Attestations. A similar situation may occur if all malicious BKs disconnect or reject Nacks for a malicious block during the execution of the Joint Committee function. Thus, to determine the number of malicious BKs at which the network will stop, or, in other words, the number of malicious BKs at which the Liveness property is violated, we have:

$$M \geq min(N - A + 1, N - J + 1) = N + 1 - max(A, J) \tag{2}$$

As the constraints on the number of malicious BKs depend on the number of Attestations needed for block finalization and the number of votes for the Joint Committee, the Acki Nacki Security Assumptions are dynamically adjustable. This allows the network to maintain the probabilistic safety property even when the number of malicious BKs exceeds 50% of the network participants, and

---

[3] A distributed denial-of-service (DDoS) attack is a malicious attempt to disrupt the normal traffic of a targeted server, service, or network by overwhelming the target or its surrounding infrastructure with a flood of Internet traffic.

furthermore, even when it exceeds 66% of the network participants. This holds true for any assumption regarding the number of malicious BKs agreed upon by network participants through voting.

4.4 Constraints on the Number of Spammed Block Keepers

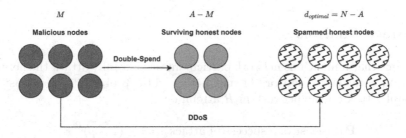

Fig. 5. Scheme of the optimal DDoS Attack

Since consensus requires A Attestations, among the $(N - d)$ BKs that continue to function after the DDoS attack, at least A BKs must be capable of gathering the required Attestations. Therefore $N - d \geq A$.

In order for malicious BKs to launch a successful attack, they aim to spam as many honest BKs as possible.

From this understanding, we conclude that $d_{optimal} = N - A$.

4.5 Expected Number of Acki-Nacki per Block

The probability of becoming an Acki-Nacki per block for each BK is expressed as v/N.

Let the random variable ξ denote the number of BKs that become an Acki-Nacki. Then, the probability that k BKs become Acki-Nacki is described by the following probability:

$$\mathbf{P}\left(\xi = k\right) = C_N^k \cdot \left(\frac{v}{N}\right)^k \cdot \left(1 - \frac{v}{N}\right)^{N-k} \tag{3}$$

We find that the random variable ξ follows a Binomial distribution, and its expected value is $\mathbb{E}(\xi) = v$. In other words, v is precisely the mathematical expectation of the number of BKs that become an Acki-Nacki per block.

4.6 Successful Attack Probability in the Acki Nacki Consensus

Since honest BKs only collect A number of Attestations to finalize the block and check for the absence of Nacks, the successful attack probability on the block will be equal to the probability that no honest surviving BK has become Acki-Nacki:

$$p(N, M, d, v) = \left(1 - \frac{v}{N}\right)^{N-M-d}. \tag{4}$$

Since malicious BKs DDoS the maximum possible number of honest BKs, then the resulting successful attack probability on the block is expressed as:

$$p(N, M, A, v) = \left(1 - \frac{v}{N}\right)^{A-M}. \tag{5}$$

5 Safety Analysis

We assume that if malicious network participants successfully attack the network at least once, the entire network breaks. Let's find the probability of at least one successful attack on the network in R attempts:

$$\mathbf{P}\,(\text{at least one successful attack}) = 1 - (1 - p)^R. \tag{6}$$

Since, in the Acki Nacki consensus protocol, the probability of breaking the network at least once increases more rapidly when colluding with more malicious BKs than when attempting more times, it is more advantageous to attempt once with the maximum possible number of malicious BKs. The number of malicious BKs may be at a maximum of $A - 1$. If $A > N/2$, then it is almost impossible to place stakes for so many malicious BKs, so let's assume that attempts to break the network will be made about once every year. We say 'a year' rather than 'a day' because if the attacker had easy enough access to that much money, why wouldn't they buy the whole network at once?

Even if the attacker attempts to attack our network once a year, they have a limited number of attempts since all stakes of the network participants that were slashed are burned.

Figure 6 and Fig. 7 are illustrating the successful attack probability from a number of malicious network participants for Bitcoin, pBFT, and Acki Nacki protocols with a total of 1000 network participants. To calculate the successful attack probability in Bitcoin, we use the commonly accepted number of blocks for probabilistic 'finality', which is 6. For calculating the successful attack probability in Acki Nacki, we use the number of Acki-Nacki set to 40 and the number of Attestations set to 800.

As observed, Acki Nacki provides significantly higher security guarantees compared to Bitcoin. Furthermore, this holds true when compared to pBFT, especially in scenarios where the number of malicious network participants exceeds 2/3 of the total network participants. To further illustrate this point, we compared the probability of at least one successful attack on our network in the coming years with the probability of a comet hitting the planet Earth, leading to a global catastrophe. Assume that such a comet falls once every 10^6 years.

As we can see in Fig. 8, it is more likely that a comet will fall in the coming years and destroy life as we know it than for malicious BKs to successfully attack the network.

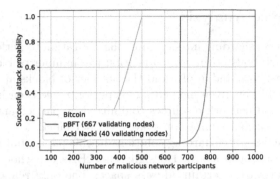

Fig. 6. Comparison of successful attack probabilities in Bitcoin, pBFT and Acki Nacki

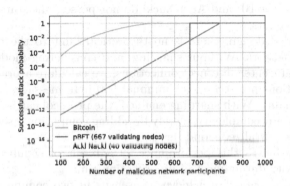

Fig. 7. Fig. 6 with log-scaled y-axis

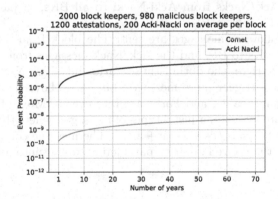

Fig. 8. Comparison plot of the successful attack probability in the Acki Nacki consensus protocol with the global catastrophe probability

6   Performance Analysis

Without taking state sharding into account, the limitation to performance in the Acki Nacki network boils down to two factors: the number of blocks a BK can receive over the network and apply, and the number of blocks all network Acki-Nacki can process at any given moment. This performance is entirely dependent on the computer and network resources committed by participants, the number of BKs, and the expected number of Acki-Nacki per block.

We do not discuss state sharding solutions in this paper, but it is quite easy to envision an Acki Nacki sharded design: some BKs can choose not to store a state that belongs to a certain address space. The only remaining practical limitation in an asynchronous system would be how messages passed from one Account to another, residing in two different shards, would be executed by the BP and verified if the BP and Acki-Nacki do not possess the state of one of the participating Accounts.

With a sharded design, there is no theoretical limit to the throughput of the Acki Nacki network. Without sharding, and considering modern computer hardware and datacenter internet connections, we calculate a practical limit of $250,000$ transactions per second for minimal 500-byte messages, achieving less than 1-second finality. With sharding enabled, the protocol can scale to millions of transactions of any complexity, merely by adding computing resources, making it comparable to centralized cloud services.

Acki Nacki achieves this performance as a result of significantly reduced message complexity during most of its operation time.

The Acki Nacki algorithm achieves consensus in two communication steps. The first step involves sending the block from BP to BKs. The second step involves sending Ack/Nacks from Acki-Nacki to all BKs, in parallel with the sending of Attestations from BKs to BP.

In total, the following messages are sent: The block from BP to BKs, the Attestations from BKs to BP, and the Ack/Nack messages from several chosen Acki-Nacki to BKs. Here, the optimistic scenario ends. The Nack message and accidental Forks will trigger more messages, but as we have shown, Nack messages are highly improbable, and Forks are rare events. Most of the time, the network will operate by sending just 3 types of messages, where the total number of all messages sent equals $(N-1) \cdot v + 2 \cdot N$. The message complexity of Acki Nacki depends on the desired security parameters, taking into account that, in practice, $v \ll N$.

7   Conclusion

We have demonstrated an efficient probabilistic consensus protocol with reduced message complexity and high parallelism in transaction execution, leading to fast finality times and scalability improvements. Our security assumptions are dynamic and can change during network operations, demonstrating the protocol's flexibility. Our safety analysis shows high adaptability to network parameters while maintaining desired safety guarantees.

References

1. Ava Labs, Inc.: The avalanche documentation. avalanche consensus (2024). https://docs.avax.network/learn/avalanche/avalanche-consensus
2. Bach, L.M., Mihaljevic, B., Zagar, M.: Comparative analysis of blockchain consensus algorithms. In: 2018 41st International Convention on Information and Communication Technology, Electronics and Microelectronics (MIPRO), pp. 1545–1550. IEEE (2018). https://doi.org/10.23919/MIPRO.2018.8400278
3. Berrang, P., von Styp-Rekowsky, P., Wissfeld, M., França, B., Trinkler, R.: Albatross - an optimistic consensus algorithm. In: 2019 Crypto Valley Conference on Blockchain Technology (CVCBT), pp. 39–42. IEEE (2019). https://doi.org/10.1109/CVCBT.2019.000-1
4. Boneh, D., Drijvers, M., Neven, G.: Bls multi-signatures with public-key aggregation. In: ASIACRYPT (2018). https://crypto.stanford.edu/~dabo/pubs/papers/BLSmultisig.html
5. Boneh, D., Shoup, V.: A graduate course in applied cryptography (2020). https://dlib.hust.edu.vn/bitstream/HUST/18098/3/OER000000253.pdf. draft 0.5
6. Buterin, V., et al.: Ethereum roadmap, what about sharding? (2022). https://ethereum.org/en/roadmap/#what-about-sharding
7. Buterin, V., et al.: Combining ghost and casper (2020). https://doi.org/10.48550/arXiv.2003.03052
8. Buterin, V., Wood, G.: A next generation smart contract and decentralized application platform. White Paper (2014). https://static.peng37.com/ethereum_whitepaper_laptop_3.pdf
9. Castro, M., Liskov, B.: Practical byzantine fault tolerance. In: Proceedings of the 3rd Symposium on Operating Systems Design and Implementation (OSDI 1999), New Orleans, Louisiana, pp. 173–186. (1999). https://pmg.csail.mit.edu/papers/osdi99.pdf
10. Danezis, G., Kokoris-Kogias, L., Sonnino, A., Spiegelman, A.: Narwhal and tusk: a dag-based mempool and efficient bft consensus. In: Proceedings of the Seventeenth European Conference on Computer Systems, pp. 34–50 (2022). https://doi.org/10.5281/zenodo.6353717
11. Diffie, W., Hellman, M.: New directions in cryptography. IEEE Trans. Inf. Theory 22(6), 644–654 (1976). https://doi.org/10.1109/TIT.1976.1055638
12. Durov, N.: Telegram open network blockchain (2020). https://ton.org/tblkch.pdf. white Paper
13. Goldwasser, S., Micali, S.: Probabilistic encryption. J. Comput. Syst. Sci. 28(2), 270–299 (1984). https://mit6875.github.io/PAPERS/probabilistic_encryption.pdf
14. Grigg, I.: Eos-an introduction (2017). https://iang.org/papers/EOS_An_Introduction.pdf. white paper
15. King, S., Nadal, S.: Ppcoin: peer-to-peer crypto-currency with proof-of-stake (2012). https://decred.org/research/king2012.pdf
16. Ku, T.W., Chen, K.: No need for recovery: a simple two-step byzantine consensus (2019). https://doi.org/10.48550/arXiv.1911.10361
17. Martin, J.P., Alvisi, L.: Fast byzantine consensus. In: 2005 International Conference on Dependable Systems and Networks, DSN 2005, pp. 402–411 (2005). https://doi.org/10.1109/DSN.2005.48
18. Martin, J.P., Alvisi, L.: Fast byzantine consensus. IEEE Trans. Depend. Secure Comput. 3(3), 202–215 (2006). https://doi.org/10.1109/TDSC.2006.35

19. Merkle, R.C.: Secure communications over insecure channels. Commun. ACM **21**(4), 294–299 (1978). https://doi.org/10.1145/359460.359473
20. Nakamoto, S.: Bitcoin: a peer-to-peer electronic cash system (2008). https://bitcoin.org/bitcoin.pdf
21. Ozisik, A.P., Levine, B.N.: An explanation of nakamoto's analysis of double-spend attacks. CoRR abs/1701.03977 (2017). https://doi.org/10.48550/arXiv.1701.03977
22. The NEAR White Paper (2021). https://near.org/papers/the-official-near-white-paper
23. Shoup, V.: Proof of history: what is it good for? (2022). https://www.shoup.net/papers/poh.pdf
24. Sun, Z., Chang, J., Zhu, N., et al.: Rangers protocol 2.0 (2022). https://rangersprotocol.obs.ap-southeast-1.myhuaweicloud.com/Navigation/RangersProtocolWhitepaper.pdf
25. Team Rocket: Snowflake to avalanche: a novel metastable consensus protocol family for cryptocurrencies (2018). https://knowen-production.s3.amazonaws.com/uploads/attachment/file/1922/Snowflake%2Bto%2BAvalanche%2B-%2BA%2BNovel%2BMetastable%2BConsensus%2BProtocol%2BFamily.pdf
26. Team Rocket, Yin, M., Sekniqi, K., van Renesse, R., Sirer, E.: Scalable and probabilistic leaderless bft consensus through metastability (2020). https://doi.org/10.48550/arXiv.1906.08936. Cornell University
27. The Diem Team: Diembft v4: State machine replication in the diem blockchain (2021). https://developers.diem.com/papers/diem-consensus-state-machine-replication-in-the-diem-blockchain/2021-08-17.pdf
28. The MultiversX Team: Multiversx, a highly scalable public blockchain via adaptive state sharding and secure proof of stake (2019). https://files.multiversx.com/multiversx-whitepaper.pdf. Technical whitepaper - release 2 - revision 2
29. The Zilliqa Team: The zilliqa technical whitepaper (2017). https://docs.zilliqa.com/whitepaper.pdf
30. Tse, S., Liu, M., et al.: Harmony technical whitepaper-version 2.0 (2023). https://harmony.one/whitepaper.pdf
31. Wood, G.: Ethereum: a secure decentralised generalised transaction ledger (2014), p. 32. https://ethereum.github.io/yellowpaper/paper.pdf. Ethereum project yellow paper 151.2014
32. Yakovenko, A.: Solana: a new architecture for a high performance blockchain v0 8.13 (2018). https://solana.com/solana-whitepaper.pdf
33. Yin, M., Malkhi, D., Reiter, M., Gueta, G., Ittai, A.: Hotstuff: bft consensus with linearity and responsiveness. In: 38th ACM Symposium on Principles of Distributed Computing (PODC 2019), Toronto, ON, Canada, 29 July–2 August 2019 (2019). https://doi.org/10.1145/3293611.3331591
34. Zhong, W., et al.: Byzantine fault-tolerant consensus algorithms: a survey. Electronics **12**(18), 3801 (2023). https://doi.org/10.3390/electronics12183801

AIHWS – Artificial Intelligence in Hardware Security

FPGA Implementation of Physically Unclonable Functions Based on Multi-threshold Delay Time Measurement Method to Mitigate Modeling Attacks

Tatsuya Oyama[1]($^{\boxtimes}$), Mika Sakai[1], Yohei Hori[2], Toshihiro Katashita[2],
and Takeshi Fujino[1]

[1] Ritsumeikan University, Kyoto, Shiga, Japan
{ri0068hi,ri0101xh}@ed.ritsumei.ac.jp, fujino@se.ritsumei.ac.jp
[2] National Institute of Advanced Industrial Science and Technology,
Tsukuba, Ibaraki, Japan
{hori.y,t-katashita}@aist.go.jp

Abstract. Physically Unclonable Functions (PUFs) are security primitives that generate chip-specific responses by exploiting the subtle manufacturing variations in semiconductor devices. Arbiter PUF is a typical extensive PUF that has a large space for challenge response pairs (CPRs); however, it is vulnerable to deep learning (DL) attacks predicting unknown CRPs. One of the approaches to mitigate DL attacks is the RG-DTM PUF, which utilizes the delay time measurement (DTM) method with a multi-offset sense amplifier; however, this technique is difficult to implement on FPGAs. In this paper, we propose a DTM method for FPGAs (fDTM) by placing multiple DFFs at unbalanced positions from the output of the delay paths. We implement the fDTM PUF on Xilinx Artix-7 and in a simulation and demonstrate its attack resistance against DL attacks. The experimental results show that the fDTM PUF achieves much higher attack resistance than the conventional Arbiter PUF with the equivalent area and achieves equivalent attack resistance to previous PUFs with areas around several to dozens of times smaller.

Keywords: Physically Unclonable Function (PUF) · Arbiter PUF · RG-DTM PUF · Field-programmable Gate Array (FPGA) · Modeling attacks · Deep neural networks (DNN)

1 Introduction

In recent years, many electronic devices, including sensor nodes, home appliances, and automobiles, have become connected to the so-called Internet of Things (IoT). Since IoT devices exchange vast amounts of information, often deployed within attackers' reach, the security of IoT devices is of great significance. However, implementing security in IoT devices is difficult in many cases because the hardware resources of such devices are limited.

M. Andreoni (Ed.): ACNS 2024 Workshops, LNCS 14586, pp. 65–83, 2024.
https://doi.org/10.1007/978-3-031-61486-6_5

For the security of resource-limited IoT devices, Physically Unclonable Functions (PUFs) [1] have been actively studied for the past few decades. A PUF is a security primitive generating chip-specific identifications (IDs) exploiting subtle variations in semiconductor devices. Given the same input (challenge), no two PUFs generate the same output (response) due to this device variation. The challenge–response pairs (CRPs) of PUFs are different from each other, and thus, PUFs can be used for security purposes, e.g., identification, authentication, and secret key generation. The international standard ISO/IEC 20897 [2] defines two types of PUFs: extensive PUFs (strong PUFs), which provide huge challenge–response space, and confined PUFs (weak PUFs), which provide only a limited space for CRPs. Examples of extensive PUFs are Arbiter PUF [3] and Loop PUF [4]; examples of confined PUFs are Ring Oscillator PUF [5] and SRAM PUF [6].

On another front, the market of Field-Programmable Gate Arrays (FPGAs) has recently been expanding due to their short time-to-market and low development cost compared to Application-Specific Integrated Circuits (ASICs) [7, 8]. Several reports have mentioned that vendors integrate IoT services into FPGAs [9]. Therefore, the usage of FPGAs is expected to expand into security-critical applications.

Considering the above backgrounds, implementing PUFs on FPGAs would be a promising approach to secure FPGA-based IoT devices. This paper focuses on the arbiter-based extensive PUF, which can be used for simple challenge–response authentication and updatable secret key generation. However, there are two major problems with implementing arbiter-based PUFs on FPGAs. First, Arbiter PUFs are vulnerable to modeling attacks using machine learning (ML) [10–12]. To improve modeling attack resistance, variants of Arbiter PUFs have been proposed such as XOR PUFs [5], lightweight secure PUFs (LSPUFs) [13], multiplexer PUFs (MPUFs) [14], and interpose PUFs (IPUFs) [15]. Nevertheless, the physical size of these PUFs are several to dozens of times larger than the Arbiter PUF.

Secondly, implementing a PUF on an FPGA is difficult because the logic and wiring resources in FPGAs are fixed. When implementing the Arbiter PUF, manual place-and-routing is necessary to achieve equal-delay wiring, which is impractical in the FPGA design flow. Consequently, responses of Arbiter PUFs on FPGA are prone to bias, resulting in low uniqueness, which also leads to a high success rate of modeling attacks. To improve the uniqueness of the Arbiter PUF on FPGAs, Double Arbiter PUFs [16], FF-APUFs [17], and Response Generation according to Delay Time Measurement (RG-DTM) PUFs [18] have been proposed. However, the resource utilization of the Double Arbiter PUF and the FF-APUF significantly increases compared to the Arbiter PUF. The size of the RG-DTM PUF is almost equivalent to the Arbiter PUF, but it requires a multi-offset sense amplifier, which usually cannot be implemented on FPGAs.

To improve both ML attack resistance and the uniqueness of an FPGA-implemented PUF with only a small resource overhead, we propose the multi-threshold delay time measurement method for FPGAs (fDTM) and an fDTM

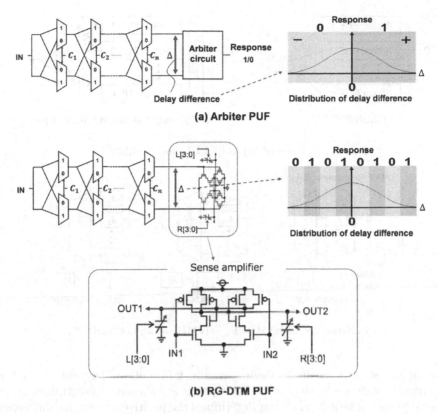

(a) Arbiter PUF

(b) RG-DTM PUF

Fig. 1. Structure of (a) Arbiter PUF and (b) RG-DTM PUF.

PUF that has a sophisticated delay arbitration scheme. The proposed PUF requires only several flip-flops and XOR gates in addition to the Arbiter PUF.

The contributions of this study are summarized as follows:

- Realizes the fDTM method that has the equivalent functionality to a multi-offset sense amplifier, which is previously considered difficult to implement on FPGAs.
- Develops and implements the modeling-attack-resistant fDTM PUF on FPGAs.
- Mounts deep learning (DL) attacks on the fDTM PUF and demonstrates its attack resistance in FPGA implementation and simulation.

2   Preliminaries

2.1   Arbiter PUF

The Arbiter PUF [3] comprises a multi-stage selector and an arbiter circuit (Fig. 1(a)). The Arbiter PUF uses the delay difference between two equal-length

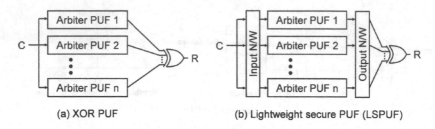

(a) XOR PUF   (b) Lightweight secure PUF (LSPUF)

Fig. 2. Structure of (a) XOR PUF and (b) LSPUF.

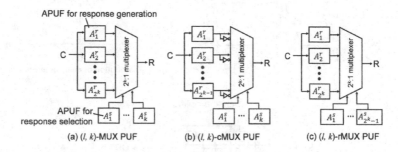

(a) (l, k)-MUX PUF   (b) (l, k)-cMUX PUF   (c) (l, k)-rMUX PUF

Fig. 3. Structure of (a) MPUF, (b) cMPUF, and (c) rMPUF.

paths in the selector chain as device-specific information. Depending on the challenge input to each selector, the two paths are chosen to go straight or to cross each other. The arbiter circuit determines the positive or negative difference in delay time at the final stage of the two paths and outputs a 1-bit response of 0 or 1. The Arbiter PUF is characterized by a vast CRP space, such that the number of CRPs doubles when the number of selector stages is increased by one. However, there is a problem in that the response and challenge are correlated, and the CRPs can be predicted by ML-based modeling attacks.

2.2   Variants of Arbiter PUF

To mitigate ML attacks, variants of the Arbiter PUF, for example, XOR PUF [5], LSPUF [13], MPUF [14], and IPUF [15], have been introduced in the previous studies.

The n-XOR PUF consists of n Arbiter PUFs and an XOR gate as shown in Fig. 2(a). The outputs from the n PUFs are XORed to generate a one-bit response. The LSPUF also consists of n Arbiter PUFs (Fig. 2(b)). In the output network, m bits out of n outputs are chosen and XORed to generate a response. The length of response in the LSPUF generated at once is up to the number of different m-bit outputs chosen from n.

As Fig. 3(a) depicts, the (l, k)-MPUF comprises 2^k Arbiter PUFs for response generation (denoted as A_i^r), k Arbiter PUFs for response selection (denoted as A_i^s), and a 2^k-to-1 multiplexer, where l denotes the length of the selector chain. The 2^k-to-1 multiplexer has k multiplexer stages, which are broken down into

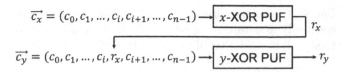

Fig. 4. Structure of IPUF.

$2^k - 1$ of 2-to-1 multiplexers in total. The 1-bit response of the MPUF is selected from the 2^k outputs of A_i^r according to the k-bit select signal from A_i^s. In the cMPUF, the number of Arbiter PUFs for response generation (A_i^r) is 2^{k-1}, half the number of the MPUF (Fig. 3(b)). In the rMPUF, the number of Arbiter PUFs for response selection (A_i^s) is $2^k - 1$ since each 2-to-1 multiplexer has a different selection signal (Fig. 3(c)).

(x, y)-IPUF consists of two XOR PUFs in which the number of Arbiter PUFs is x and y, respectively (Fig. 4). The response of the upper XOR PUF, r_x, is interposed to the challenge of the lower XOR PUF.

The above PUFs are composed of multiple Arbiter PUFs. Thus, the area of these PUFs is several to dozens of times larger than the Arbiter PUF.

2.3   RG-DTM PUF

The RG-DTM PUF is proposed to improve the uniqueness and the resistance against ML-based modeling attacks. The RG-DTM PUF has a similar structure to the Arbiter PUF, except that it has a multi-offset sense amplifier as an arbiter circuit (Fig. 1(b)). The offset sense amplifier can switch the number of small capacitors added to the sense node by control signals L[3:0] and R[3:0]. It enables multiple thresholds of the signal propagation delay in the arbiter circuit. Consequently, the RG-DTM PUF outputs 0/1 responses according to the delay distribution divided into multiple segments, as shown in Fig. 1(b).

The RG-DTM PUF can achieve high uniqueness and attack resistance to modeling attacks with only a small resource overhead. However, FPGAs cannot implement the offset sense amplifier.

2.4   Evaluation Metrics

The evaluation metrics of PUF performance in this study are the steadiness and uniqueness defined in the international standard ISO/IEC 20897 [2].

Steadiness. The steadiness is the property that indicates whether the same challenge to the same PUF returns the same response. High steadiness ensures that the PUF responses are reproducible and that a genuine device is correctly authenticated; low steadiness can result in the false rejection of a genuine device. The PUF responses are noise-prone as they are generated from the subtle difference in the signal propagation delay. Therefore, it is difficult to obtain the same responses every time the same challenges are input.

The steadiness is evaluated using the intra-Hamming distance (intra-HD) among the repeatedly generated responses [2]. μ^{intra} (the mean of intra-HD) and σ^{intra} (the standard deviation of the intra-HD) should ideally both be zero.

Uniqueness. The uniqueness is the property indicating that different PUFs generate different responses when the same challenge is input. High uniqueness ensures that different devices are distinguished from each other; low uniqueness can result in a fake device can impersonating a genuine device.

The uniqueness is evaluated using the inter-Hamming distance (inter-HD) among the responses from different PUFs [2]. Since all responses are ideally independent of each other, the distribution of the inter-HD follows a binomial distribution. μ^{inter} (the mean of the inter-HD) should ideally be $N_{res}/2$, and σ^{inter} (the standard division of inter-HD) should be $\sqrt{N_{res} \cdot p^1 \cdot (1 - p^1)} = \sqrt{N_{res}}/2$, where p^1 is the probability of the response being 1 and N_{res} is the length of the response block for evaluation.

2.5 PUF Model

We use the Arbiter PUF model introduced in [10] for simulation and DL attacks. Let w^i be the delay difference of the i-th stage of the selector chain, and $\Phi^i \in \{-1, 1\}$ be the parity of the i-th stage ($1 \leq i \leq n+1$). The $(n+1)$-th parameter is for the arbiter circuit. The parity Φ^i determines if the delay difference w^i has a positive or negative impact eventually at the arbiter circuit. The parity is calculated from challenge bits $c_i \in \{0, 1\}$ as follows:

$$\Phi^i = \begin{cases} \prod_{k=i}^{n}(1 - 2c_k) & (i = 1, \cdots, n) \\ 1 & (i = n+1). \end{cases} \tag{1}$$

Then, the total delay difference Δ of the Arbiter PUF is given by

$$\Delta = \vec{w}^T \vec{\Phi}, \tag{2}$$

where

$$\vec{w} = (w^1, w^2, \cdots, w^n, w^{n+1})^T, \tag{3}$$

$$\vec{\Phi} = (\Phi^1, \Phi^2, \cdots, \Phi^n, \Phi^{n+1})^T. \tag{4}$$

Finally, the response of the Arbiter PUF r is obtained by

$$r = \begin{cases} 1 & (\Delta \geq 0) \\ 0 & (\Delta < 0). \end{cases} \tag{5}$$

3 Proposed Method

We propose the fDTM method to detect the delay difference between two paths by using multiple DFFs and XOR gates, which has the equivalent functionality

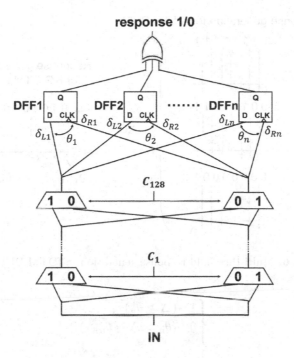

Fig. 5. Structure of the proposed fDTM PUF.

to a multi-offset sense amplifier. This technique enables the modeling-attack-resistant fDTM PUF. The concept of the fDTM method is illustrated in Fig. 5. The structure of the fDTM PUF is similar to that of the Arbiter PUF except that is has the DTM circuit for signal arbitration. Two selector chains are separately placed at the left and right side with sufficient distance. The key idea is to place the DFFs at unbalanced locations from the output of the two selectors and XOR the outputs from the DFFs (Fig. 5).

Let δ_{L_i} and δ_{R_i} be the delay from the output of the left/right selector to the i-th DFF, respectively. If the DFF is located at the unbalanced position, $\delta_{L_i} - \delta_{R_i}$ will be some non-zero value θ_i, and the DFF determines whether the total delay difference is greater or less than θ_i. The leftmost DFF_1 is placed closest to the left selector chain and farthest from the right one, and therefore, $\delta_{L_1} - \delta_{R_1}$ will be the smallest negative value θ_1. To the contrary, the rightmost DFF will give the largest positive value θ_n. Arranging multiple DFFs from left to right, we can obtain delay differences such that $\theta_n > \cdots > \theta_2 > \theta_1$.

Consequently, using multiple DFFs with different delay biases θ_i, we can achieve multi-threshold delay detection, as illustrated in Fig. 6. For example, using three DFFs is equivalent to dividing the delay difference distribution into four segments, while the conventional Arbiter PUF using one DFF divides the distribution into two segments. Using the model in Sect. 2.5, the response of the fDTM PUF r is calculated as

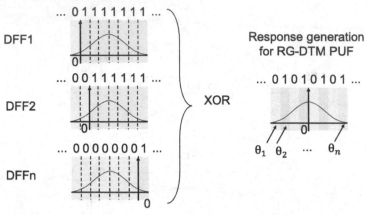

Fig. 6. Multi-threshold response generation in fDTM PUF.

$$r = \begin{cases} 1 & (\Delta \geq \theta_n) \\ 0 & (\theta_n > \Delta \geq \theta_{n-1}) \\ \cdots \\ 1 & (\theta_2 > \Delta \geq \theta_1) \\ 0 & (\Delta < \theta_1) \end{cases} \tag{6}$$

where θ_i represents the threshold of the delay difference, as illustrated in Fig. 6.

The concrete implementation method of the fDTM PUF is explained in Sect. 4.3.

4   Implementation

4.1   Experimental Setup

The experimental setup of the FPGA implementation and response generation of fDTM PUF is shown in Fig. 7. A CW305 FPGA board made by NewAE Technology equipped with Xilinx Artix-7 is used as the evaluation environment. The operating frequency of the board is 10 MHz. The PUF and control circuits are described in Verilog HDL. The design and development tool used is Vivado 2022.1. The challenge is input from the host PC to the PUF, and the response is transferred from the PUF to the host PC via USB.

4.2   Implementation of Arbiter PUF

Since the fDTM PUF performs the arbiter-based response generation, we first explore the optimum structure of Arbiter PUF. The parameters used in the Arbiter PUF implementation and experimentation are listed in Table 1.

Fig. 7. Experimental setup for implementation and evaluation of the PUFs

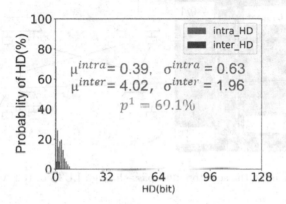

Fig. 8. Intra- and inter-HD of Arbiter PUF without any placement constraints.

As mentioned earlier, achieving the high performance of the Arbiter PUF on FPGAs is difficult because the fine adjustment of wiring is unavailable for FPGAs. Figure 8 shows the intra- and inter-HD of the Arbiter PUF without any placement constraints. The mean and standard deviation of the distributions are far from the ideal values ($\mu^{inter} = 128 \cdot 0.5 = 64, \sigma^{inter} = \sqrt{128}/2 = 5.66$). In this study, we give strict placement constraints for the selector chain and the arbiter circuit to make the two signal paths as equal in length as possible. The best placements of the selector chain and the arbiter circuit are explored through trial-and-error experiments.

The selectors that switch signal paths are arranged with a distance between left and right, as shown in Fig. 9. The first selector stage to which the rising signal is input is placed on the lower side, and the 128th stage connected to the arbiter circuit is placed on the upper side. To enable equal-length wiring between the left and right selectors, pass-through LUTs are added to the four paths input to the selectors, and their locations are specified by the constraint settings.

Table 1. Parameters of the Arbiter PUF.

Description	Value
Number of selector stages	128
Number of evaluated devices	4
Number of iterations to obtain responses	16
Length of the response block for evaluation	128
Number of different challenges	65536

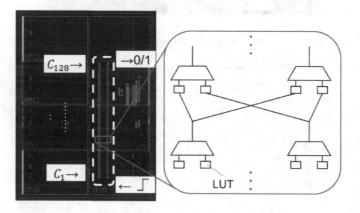

Fig. 9. Placement of the selectors and pass-through LUTs of the Arbiter PUF

The arbiter circuit that judges the positive and negative difference in the delay time of the two paths is implemented using a D flip-flop (DFF). The arbiter circuit is placed just above the 128th stage selector.

Figure 10 illustrates the placement of the left and right selectors with distance 24 and the candidate positions of the arbiter circuit (DFF). The distance between selectors means the difference in the X coordinate of the slice where the left and right selectors are located. When the distance is zero, the left and right selectors are located in the same slice. The candidate positions of the DFF are numbered from (1) through (25). The position of the DFF is one slice above the selector. If the delay of the left and right paths are equivalent, the responses of the Arbiter PUF are expected to be unbiased, i.e., the probability of the response being 1 is 50%.

Figure 11 shows the relationship between the response and the position of the Arbiter DFF. The probability of the response being 1 (p^1) gradually decreases as the DFF is moved from the left selector side to the right side. As the figure depicts, using the DFF (13) produces the most unbiased responses ($p^1 \simeq 50\%$). This indicates that the delay difference between the two paths observed at the DFF is almost zero when the DFF is located near the center; the farther the DFF is located from the center, the larger the delay difference becomes.

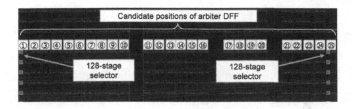

Fig. 10. Selector chains with distance of 24 and candidate positions of arbiter circuit (DFF).

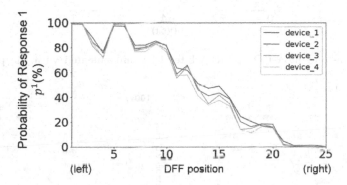

Fig. 11. Relationship between the response bias (p^1) and DFF position.

Using the above experimental results, we can realize a high-performance Arbiter PUF by placing the DFF so that p^1 approaches 50%. To find the best placement of the Arbiter PUF, we change the following three parameters and evaluate the performance in each case:

- Distance between left and right selectors (7 different distances: 0, 1, 2, 6, 12, 18, and 24);
- Position of the arbiter circuit (DFFs between the left and right selectors);
- Region to place the entire Arbiter PUF.

Compared to Fig. 8, the most significant improvement is observed in the layout where the selector distance is 24 and the DFF is implemented on DFF (13) (Fig. 12). The mean and standard deviation of intra- and inter-HD are close to the ideal value ($\mu^{inter} = 64, \sigma^{inter} = 5.66$).

4.3   Implementation of fDTM PUF

In the implementation of fDTM PUF, the distance between the left and right selectors is 24. From the results in Sect. 4.2, we choose (7), (13), and (19) DFFs for a 4-split fDTM PUF and (5), (9), (13), (17), and (21) DFFs for a 6-split fDTM PUF.

Figures 13 and 14 show the intra-HD (steadiness) and inter-HD (uniqueness) of the 4-split and 6-split fDTM PUFs, respectively. Compared to Fig. 12, the

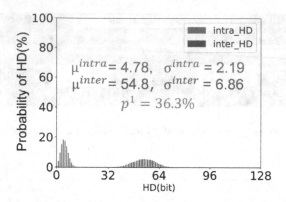

Fig. 12. Intra- and inter-HD of the Arbiter PUF implemented with the placement constraints.

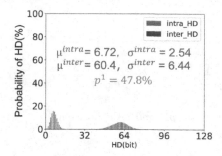

Fig. 13. Evaluation of 4-split fDTM PUF.

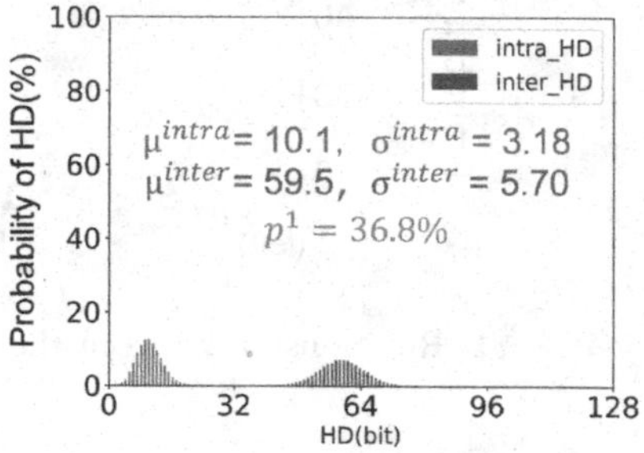

Fig. 14. Evaluation of 6-split fDTM PUF.

fDTM PUFs accomplish steadiness and uniqueness performances as high as the Arbiter PUF. In particular, the standard deviation of the inter-HD (σ^{inter}) of the 6-split fDTM PUF is improved from 6.86 to 5.70, closer to the ideal value of 5.66. Note that if the standard deviation of the inter-IID becomes larger, more PUFs can have small inter-HD and possibly impersonate the genuine PUF.

On the other hand, the standard deviation of the intra-HD (σ^{intra}) of the fDTM PUF becomes slightly worse as the number of arbiter DFFs increases. This would be because, in arbiter-type PUFs, the delay difference near the threshold is subject to noise. Since the fDTM PUF has multiple thresholds, its responses are more noise-prone than those of the Arbiter PUF are. Nevertheless, the distributions of the intra- and inter-HD are clearly separated; therefore, the performance of the fDTM PUF is sufficient for practical use.

5 Security Evaluation

We conduct a modeling attack using deep learning (DL) to evaluate the security of fDTM PUF implemented on FPGA (*cf.* Sect. 4.3). We compare the attack resistance of fDTM PUFs with other arbiter-type PUFs in FPGA implementation and simulation.

Table 2. Structure of the DNN.

	Number of nodes	Activation function	Dropout
Input layer	129	–	–
Hidden layer 1	5,000	ReLU	0.5
Hidden layer 2	1,000	ReLU	0.2
Hidden layer 3	500	ReLU	0.2
Hidden layer 4	200	ReLU	0.2
Output layer	1	Sigmoid	–

5.1 Experimental Setup for Modeling Attack

We evaluate the modeling attack resistance of the Arbiter PUF and the fDTM PUF in the FPGA implementation (*cf.* Sect. 4) and simulation. The structure of the deep neural network (DNN) used in the DL modeling attack is listed in Table 2 with reference to [19]. The hidden layers are all fully connected in this experiment; the optimizer used is Adam; the learning rate is 0.001; the loss function is binary cross entropy; the batch size is 100. The response is 1 if the output of the DNN is greater than 0.5; otherwise, it is 0. As seen from [20], the input to the DNN is the parity $\vec{\Phi}$ converted from the challenge $\vec{C}$. The reason for using $\vec{\Phi}$ for the input to the DNN is that using $\vec{C}$ results in low attack accuracy, as reported in [21].

The responses of the FPGA-implemented PUFs are obtained by 15-bit temporal majority voting to eliminate noise, i.e., the responses are taken 15 times each with the same challenges. In the simulation of Arbiter and fDTM PUFs, $\vec{w}$ is randomly generated from a normal distribution with a mean and standard deviation of 0 ps and 5.7 ps, respectively, which are taken from the measured results in [22]. $\vec{\Phi}$ is calculated from the randomly generated binary challenges. The responses of the Arbiter and fDTM PUFs are calculated according to Eqs. (5) and (6), respectively.

5.2 Results

The results of the DL modeling attacks against the Arbiter and fDTM PUFs are shown in Fig. 15. The attack success rate indicates the probability for the DNN model to correctly predict the response to the given challenge. The attack success rate (= prediction accuracy of the model) is evaluated using 10,000 test CRPs. The number of training CRPs is varied from 1,000 to 16,000. The 2-split is the result of the Arbiter PUF; the 4- and 6-splits are the result of the fDTM PUF. The solid lines are the results of the measured data, and the dashed lines are simulation data. The simulation results of the 2-split Arbiter PUF and 4-split fDTM PUF match the measured results remarkably. The simulation results of the 6-split fDTM PUF eventually comes close to the measured ones, though a further investigation should be needed to explain the difference.

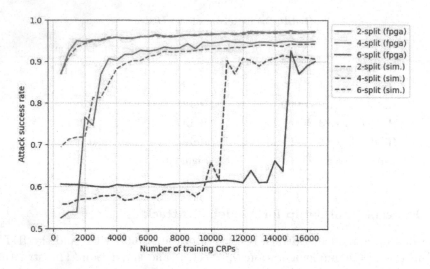

Fig. 15. Success rate of the DL modeling attacks.

Basically, the attack resistance of the fDTM PUF increases with the number of splits, as Fig. 15 illustrates. Even higher attack resistance is expected with more number of splits. The security and performance evaluation of fDTM PUFs with more splits is left as future work.

We also compare the attack resistance of our fDTM PUF with other attack-resistant PUF proposals: n-XOR PUF, lightweight secure PUF (LSPUF), MUX PUF and its variants (MPUF, cMPUF, rMPUF), and interpose PUF (IPUF). The attack resistance of the fDTM PUF is evaluated by the minimal number of CRPs needed to achieve an attack success rate greater than 90%. In this study, the threshold is set to a relatively moderate value (90%) not to overestimate the required number of CRPs. The simulation results of other PUFs are taken from [20], in which the number of CRPs is provided with the attack success rate of 96–99.5%.

Table 3 describes the attack resistance (= required number of CRPs) and area of different PUFs. All PUFs comprise the 128-stage selector chains. The area factor indicates how many times larger the PUF is than the Arbiter PUF. Here, the additional resources such as DFFs, MUXs, and LUTs are not considered, as they are negligible in size compared to the resources used in the Arbiter PUF. Figure 16 plots the relationship between the attack resistance and area utilization of the PUFs.

Usually, it is not easy to compare performance with previous studies because the parameters of the PUFs, the hyper-parameters of the DNN, and the evaluation criteria used in between studies are different. For example, we use a quite large DNN to attack all the developed PUFs (*cf.* Table 2). Our DNN has four hidden layers with 6,700 nodes in total. [20] uses small DNNs with different structures for different PUFs: 1 hidden layer with 3 nodes for the Arbiter PUF, 4 hidden layers with 400 nodes in total for the 5-XOR PUF, and 4 hidden layers

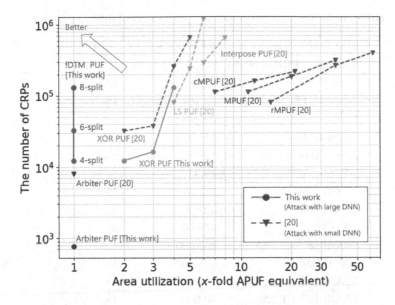

Fig. 16. Plot of attack resistance and area utilization of different PUFs.

with 1,600 nodes in total for the 5-XOR LSPUF. Thus, the figures in Table 3 cannot be strictly comparable or even give pessimistic comparison results for our PUF, but would provide rough estimation of relative attack resistance.

6 Discussion

As seen from Figs. 15 and 16 and Table 3, the number of required CRPs needed to attack the fDTM PUF increases with the number of splits, indicating that the attack resistance improved with the number of delay thresholds. Comparing within this work, the results indicate that the fDTM PUF accomplished 170 times higher attack resistance than the Arbiter PUF, with almost the same area as the Arbiter PUF. It is also deduced from the results that an fDTM PUF with more splits is expected to have a higher attack resistance. However, an fDTM PUF with more delay thresholds can be more noise-prone, resulting in lower steadiness. It is left as future work to investigate the relationship between the number of splits, attack resistance, and the steadiness of the fDTM PUF.

Note that, as mentioned in Section V-B, the DNN used in this work is quite large, while it is very small in [20]. Therefore, our DNN is expected to have quite high attack ability. Additionally, in this work, the thresholds of the attack accuracy with which the attack is considered successful is set to the lower value (90%), resulting in the relatively small number of CRPs in Table 3. Even in the pessimistic estimation, the fDTM PUF achieves an at least 16 times higher attack resistance than the Arbiter PUF in [20].

Other PUFs in Fig. 16 such as LSPUF, MPUF, and IPUF have higher resistance than our fDTM PUF, but their area penalty is also high. These PUFs use

Table 3. Attack resistance and area utilization of different PUFs.

PUF type	#CRPs required	Area factor
Arbiter PUF (this work)	768	baseline
Arbiter PUF [20]	8,000	1×
4-split fDTM (this work)	12,288	1×
6-split fDTM (this work)	32,768	1×
8-split fDTM (this work)	131,072	1×
2-XOR (this work)	12,288	2×
3-XOR (this work)	16,384	3×
4-XOR (this work)	131,072	4×
2-XOR [20]	32,000	2×
3-XOR [20]	37,600	3×
4-XOR [20]	255,000	4×
5-XOR [20]	655,000	5×
6-XOR [20]	1,200,000	6×
3-XOR LSPUF [20]	80,000	4×
4-XOR LSPUF [20]	240,000	5×
5-XOR LSPUF [20]	1,200,000	6×
6-XOR LSPUF [20]	(1,200,000)*	7×
(128,3)-MPUF [20]	112,000	11×
(128,4)-MPUF [20]	184,000	20×
(128,5)-MPUF [20]	312,000	37×
(128,3)-cMPUF [20]	112,000	7×
(128,4)-cMPUF [20]	160,000	12×
(128,5)-cMPUF [20]	215,000	21×
(128,3)-rMPUF [20]	80,000	15×
(128,4)-rMPUF [20]	264,000	31×
(128,5)-rMPUF [20]	400,000	63×
(3,3)-IPUF [20]	288,000	6×
(4,4)-IPUF [20]	647,000	8×
(5,5)-IPUF [20]	(1,200,000)*	10×

*Attack failed.

multiple Arbiter PUFs as components, and therefore, replacing their Arbiter PUFs with the fDTM PUFs will (1) reduce the area penalty without decreasing the attack resistance, or (2) further enhance the attack resistance without increasing the area penalty.

7 Conclusions

This paper introduced the FPGA implementation of a Physically Unclonable Function (PUF) based on a delay-time measurement (DTM) method that achieves high attack resistance against deep learning (DL) attacks. The DTM-based PUF was first implemented using a multi-offset sense amplifier in [18], but this technique was difficult to implement on FPGAs. In this paper, we proposed the DTM method for FPGAs (fDTM) using multiple D flip-flops (DFFs) that were placed in unbalanced locations. The proposed method enabled a multi-threshold delay arbitration that had equivalent functionality to a multi-offset sense amplifier.

We implemented the fDTM PUF on a Xilinx Artix-7 FPGA and applied DL attacks to evaluate the security of the PUF. We also evaluated the security of the fDTM PUF via simulation. The fDTM PUF achieved much higher attack resistance than the Arbiter PUF, with almost the same area utilization. Compared to other attack-resistant PUF proposals, the fDTM PUF achieved equivalent security with areas around several to dozens of times smaller.

The future directions of this study include: (1) implementing fDTM PUFs with more splits and investigating the relationship between the number of splits, attack resistance, and the steadiness of the fDTM PUF;

(2) improving DL attacks against fDTM PUFs; (3) applying the fDTM method to other attack-resistant PUFs, and (4) evaluating the effectiveness and security of the fDTM PUF in real applications such as lightweight device authentication and cryptographic key generation.

ACKNOWLEDGMENT. A part of this work was supported by JSPS KAKENHI Grant Number JP22H03593 and JP21H03413 and by JST, the establishment of university fellowships towards the creation of science technology innovation, Grant Number JPMJFS2146.

References

1. Pappu, R., Recht, B., Taylor, J., Gershenfeld, N.A.: Physical one-way functions. Science **297**, 2026–2030 (2002)
2. ISO/IEC. ISO/IEC 20897-1:2020: Information security, cybersecurity and privacy protection—Physically Unclonable Functions—Part1: Security Requirements (2020)
3. Lee, J., Lim, D., Gassend, B., Suh, G., van Dijk, M., Devadas, S.: A technique to build a secret key in integrated circuits for identification and authentication applications. In: 2004 Symposium on VLSI Circuits. Digest of Technical Papers (IEEE Cat. No.04CH37525), pp. 176–179 (2004)
4. Cherif, Z., Danger, J.-L., Guilley, S., Bossuet, L.: An easy-to-design PUF based on a single oscillator: the loop PUF. In: 2012 15th Euromicro Conference on Digital System Design, pp. 156–162 (2012)
5. Suh, G.E., Devadas, S.: Physical unclonable functions for device authentication and secret key generation. In: Proceedings of the 44th Annual Design Automation Conference, Series DAC 2007, pp. 9–14. Association for Computing Machinery, New York (2007). https://doi.org/10.1145/1278480.1278484

6. Guajardo, J., Kumar, S.S., Schrijen, G.-J., Tuyls, P.: FPGA intrinsic PUFs and their use for IP protection. In: Paillier, P., Verbauwhede, I. (eds.) CHES 2007. LNCS, vol. 4727, pp. 63–80. Springer, Heidelberg (2007). https://doi.org/10.1007/978-3-540-74735-2_5

7. Global field-programmable gate array (FPGA) market 2023 — analysis of the latest industry trends by 2030 (2023). https://www.marketwatch.com/press-release/global-field-programmable-gate-array-fpga-market-2023-analysis-of-the-latest-industry-trends-by-2030-2023-05-09

8. A.B.: Field-programmable gate array (FPGA) market is expected to reach around usd 22.10 billion by 2030, grow at a cagr of 15.12 period 2023 to 2030 — data by contrive datum insights pvt ltd. (2023). https://www.globenewswire.com/en/news-release/2023/02/21/2612772/0/en/Field-Programmable-Gate-Array-FPGA-Market-Is-Expected-To-Reach-around-USD-22-10-Billion-by-2030-Grow-at-a-CAGR-Of-15-12-during-Forecast-Period-2023-To-2030-Data-By-Contrive-Datum-I.html

9. Saha, S.: FPGA market (2023). https://www.futuremarketinsights.com/reports/fpga-market

10. Rührmair, U., Sehnke, F., Sölter, J., Dror, G., Devadas, S., Schmidhuber, J.: Modeling attacks on physical unclonable functions. In: Proceedings of the 17th ACM Conference on Computer and Communications Security, Series CCS 2010, pp. 237–249. Association for Computing Machinery, New York (2010). https://doi.org/10.1145/1866307.1866335

11. Lim, D., Lee, J.W., Gassend, B., Suh, G.E., Van Dijk, M., Devadas, S.: Extracting secret keys from integrated circuits. IEEE Trans. Very Large Scale Integr. (VLSI) Syst. 13(10), 1200–1205 (2005)

12. Majzoobi, M., Koushanfar, F., Potkonjak, M.: Testing techniques for hardware security. In: IEEE International Test Conference 2008, pp. 1–10 (2008)

13. Majzoobi, M., Koushanfar, F., Potkonjak, M.: Lightweight secure PUFs. In: IEEE/ACM International Conference on Computer-Aided Design, pp. 670–673. IEEE (2008)

14. Sahoo, D.P., Mukhopadhyay, D., Chakraborty, R.S., Nguyen, P.H.: A multiplexer-based arbiter PUF composition with enhanced reliability and security. IEEE Trans. Comput. 67(3), 403–417 (2017)

15. Nguyen, P.H., Sahoo, D.P., Jin, C., Mahmood, K., Rührmair, U., Van Dijk, M.: The interpose PUF: secure PUF design against state-of-the-art machine learning attacks. Cryptology ePrint Archive (2018)

16. Machida, T., Yamamoto, D., Iwamoto, M., Sakiyama, K.: A new mode of operation for arbiter PUF to improve uniqueness on FPGA. In: Federated Conference on Computer Science and Information Systems 2014, pp. 871–878 (2014)

17. Gu, C., Liu, W., Cui, Y., Hanley, N., O'Neill, M., Lombardi, F.: A flip-flop based arbiter physical unclonable function (APUF) design with high entropy and uniqueness for FPGA implementation. IEEE Trans. Emerg. Top. Comput. 9(4), 1853–1866 (2021)

18. Fruhashi, K., Shiozaki, M., Fukushima, A., Murayama, T., Fujino, T.: The arbiter-PUF with high uniqueness utilizing novel arbiter circuit with delay-time measurement. In: IEEE International Symposium of Circuits and Systems (ISCAS) 2011, pp. 2325–2328 (2011)

19. Yashiro, R., Hori, Y., Katashita, T., Sakiyama, K.: Deep learning attack against large n-XOR PUFs on 180nm silicon chips. In: Proceedings of 2020 International Workshop on Nonlinear Circuits, Communications and Signal Processing (NCSP) (2020)

20. Santikellur, P., Bhattacharyay, A., Chakraborty, R.S.: Deep learning based model building attacks on arbiter PUF compositions. Cryptology ePrint Archive, Paper 2019/566 (2019). https://eprint.iacr.org/2019/566
21. Ikezaki, Y., Nozaki, Y., Yoshikawa, M.: Deep learning attack for physical unclonable function. In: 2016 IEEE 5th Global Conference on Consumer Electronics, pp. 1–2 (2016)
22. Shiozaki, M., Hori, Y., Oyama, T., Shirahata, M., Fujino, T.: Cause analysis method of entropy loss in physically unclonable functions. In: IEEE International Symposium on Circuits and Systems (ISCAS), pp. 1–5. IEEE (2020)

Incorporating Cluster Analysis of Feature Vectors for Non-profiled Deep-learning-Based Side-Channel Attacks

Yuta Fukuda[✉] [iD], Kota Yoshida[iD], and Takeshi Fujino[iD]

Ritsumeikan University, Kusatsu, Shiga, Japan
ri073pi@ed.ritsumei.ac.jp, y0sh1d4@fc.ritsumei.ac.jp,
fujino@se.ritsumei.ac.jp

Abstract. Differential deep learning analysis (DDLA) was proposed as a side-channel attack (SCA) with deep learning techniques in non-profiled scenarios at TCHES 2019. In the proposed DDLA, the adversary sets the LSB or MSB of the intermediate value in the encryption process assumed for the key candidates as the ground-truth label and trains a deep neural network (DNN) with power traces as an input. The adversary also observes metrics such as loss and accuracy during DNN training and estimates that the key corresponding to the best-fitting DNN is correct. One of the disadvantages of DDLA is the heavy computation time for the DNN models because the number of required models is the as same as the number of key candidates, which is typically 256 in the case of AES. Furthermore, the DNN models have to be trained again if the adversary changes a ground-truth label function from LSB to other labels such as MSB or HW. We propose a new deep-learning-based SCA in a non-profiled scenario to solve these problems. Our core idea is to conduct dimensionality reduction on the leakage waveform using DNN. The adversary conducts cluster analysis using the feature vectors extracted from power traces using DNN. Only one DNN needs to be trained to reveal all key bytes. In addition, once the DNN is trained, multiple label functions can be tested without the additional cost of training DNNs. We provide two case studies of attacking against AES, including AES without SCA countermeasures and the ASCAD database. The results show that the proposed method requires fewer waveforms to reveal all key bytes than DDLA. In addition, the proposed method requires 1/75 less computation time than DDLA.

Keywords: side-channel attacks · deep-learning · cluster analysis

1 Introduction

1.1 Background and Related Works

Side-channel attacks (SCAs) reveal secret information, such as cryptographic keys, by observing leakage waveforms, such as power consumption and electromagnetic radiation. The adversary constructs a statistical model between leakage waveforms and values calculated from the internal state of the encryption process The methods used to calculate intermediate values depend on the assumed leakage models and implementation of the target device. When attacking against software implementation, Hamming weight (HW) of intermediate value is used most often.

SCA involves two types of scenarios: profiled and non-profiled attacks. In a profiled scenario, the adversary uses a profiled device whose cryptographic key is known. The adversary constructs a statistical model using leakage waveforms acquired from the profiled device and reveals the cryptographic key in a targeted device by utilizing the model. Attack assessment and countermeasures studies are considered essential requirements because adversaries have easy access to profiled devices, often purchasing them in response to the recent increase in the number of IoT devices. Conventional attacks in profiled scenarios include template attacks [5]. In a non-profiled scenario, the adversary does not use a profiled device. The adversary assumes a statistical model and directly reveals a cryptographic key in a targeted device without a profiled device. Typical attacks in non-profiled scenarios include differential power analysis focusing on the difference of leakage waveforms [11] and correlation power analysis that assumes a correlation between leakage waveforms and intermediate value [2]. In this paper, we deal with non-profiled scenarios.

Since 2016, deep-learning-based side channel attacks (DL-SCAs) have been discussed as an approach that differs from conventional SCAs [3,10,12,16,18]. In many cases, the attack based on the profiled scenario had been studied. On the other hand, differential deep learning analysis (DDLA) was proposed in the non-profiled scenario by Timon [21]. In DDLA, the adversary must train as many deep neural networks (DNNs) as key candidates. The DNN is trained to predict the intermediate values calculated from plaintext and each key candidate. Then, the adversary guesses that the key corresponding to the DNN model with the best learning metrics (loss, accuracy, etc.) among those models is the correct key. Timon evaluated its attack performance with ASCAD, which is a public dataset [19], and software-implemented AES without SCA countermeasures in Atmel XMEGA128, software-implemented AES with misalignment, and software-implemented AES with second-order masking. Kuroda et al. studied practical DDLA aspects against software-implemented AES with two kinds of masking countermeasure, including rotating s-boxes masking, and the full key bytes (16 bytes) were successfully revealed [13,14]. Alipour et al. provided hiding countermeasures to interfere with model learning in DDLA [1]. Kwon et al. applied an early stopping method to prevent over-fitting in DDLA [15]. They also improved the speed by training DNNs in parallel. Hoang et al. introduced DDLA based on multi-output classification [9]. This enables faster attacks than parallel networks. Do et al. also introduced DDLA using multi-output classification and multi-output regression [7]. It performs faster and achieves higher attack performance than single-output approaches. Do et al. investigated DNN models for DDLA and the effect of hiding countermeasures due to noise generation [6]. Meanwhile, Wu et al. took a different approach which used plaintext labeling to conduct non-profiled DL-SCA [22].

1.2 Our Contribution

In this study, we propose a non-profiled DL-SCA based on an approach different from DDLA. This attack uses DNN to reduce the dimensionality of the waveform and reveals the key via cluster analysis of reduced feature vectors. We provide a method using two kinds of DNNs, autoencoder (AE) and convolutional neural network (CNN). In our attacks against software implementations, we provide an efficient method for training DNNs by taking advantage of the fact that encryption is a sequential process. We provide two case studies. These include two attacks against software implementations, which are AES without SCA countermeasures and the ASCAD database. These attacks can be analyzed in much less time than DDLA.

The contributions of this study are summarized as follows.

- We propose a new non-profiled DL-SCA which is a different approach from DDLA. We provide two types of attacks: AE-based attacks and CNN-based attacks.
- We provide two case studies on software implementation (Case study S-1 and S-2). Case study S-1 involves AES without SCA countermeasures. Case study S-2 involves the ASCAD database. These case studies explain how to take advantage of the fact that the AES function is sequential byte-by-byte to improve the training efficiency of the DNN model.

1.3 Paper Organization

The remainder of this paper is organized as follows. Section 2 provides preliminary information on DDLA. Section 3 describes a new non-profiled attack using cluster analysis as the proposed method. Section 4 provides two case studies describing attacks against software implementations. Section 5 summarizes our work.

2 Differential Deep-Learning Analysis

In TCHES 2019, Timon proposed differential deep-learning analysis (DDLA) as deep-learning-based side-channel analysis in non-profiled scenarios [21]. The adversary prepares the DNN of the number of candidate keys, trained with intermediate values as ground-truth labels calculated from plaintext and each candidate key. Cryptographic keys are estimated by comparing the evaluation metrics (loss and accuracy) when each model is trained. When focusing on loss, the candidate key corresponding to the model with the lowest loss score is estimated as the correct key. When focusing on accuracy, the candidate key corresponding to the model with the highest accuracy score is estimated as the correct key. The algorithm of DDLA, when focusing on loss metrics, is shown in Algorithm 1, where $I(\cdot)$ denotes the label computation function, which is used to compute intermediate values during the encryption process using the plaintext $\mathbb{P}$ and key candidate k. In the case of attacks against software-implemented AES, $I(\cdot)$ is given as follows.

$$I(k, \mathbb{P}) = \text{LSB}(\text{S-Box}(k \oplus \mathbb{P})), \tag{1}$$

where S-Box$(\cdot)$ denote the S-Box function of the AES and LSB$(\cdot)$ is a function used to get the least significant bit (LSB) when the argument is converted to binary. Adversary can change LSB$(\cdot)$ to MSB$(\cdot)$ that means the most significant bit (MSB). Meanwhile, $L(\mathcal{M}_{\theta_k}(\mathbb{T}), I(k, \mathbb{P}))$ denotes the loss with the ground-truth label $I(k, \mathbb{P})$ when the leakage waveforms $\mathbb{T}$ are input to the DNN model $\mathcal{M}_{\theta_k}$ with model parameter θ_k.

Advantage of DDLA. In this attack, the DNN builds the relationship between leakage waveforms and intermediate values from scratch during the key-dependent encryption process. Unlike CPA, this relationship is not limited to correlation. For example, it is possible to construct a DNN that combines the features of the two points where the mask and masked values are processed during masking countermeasures. The relationship exists when the key candidate is correct and the training loss is reduced. In contrast, when the key candidate is incorrect, the relationship does not exist, and the training loss is not reduced. Therefore, the adversary can estimate the key by comparing the training loss.

Disadvantage of DDLA. DDLA requires 256×16 models to reveal all key bytes (128bit) in AES. Thus, a very long computation time is required. Furthermore, the re-training of the model is necessary when the adversary attempts to change the label function applied to the intermediate values.

3   Proposed Method

3.1   Core Idea

We propose a non-profiled SCA method via cluster analysis of feature vectors which are extracted by dimensionality reduction of leakage waveforms using deep-learning techniques. This method offers the following advantages.

- The number of deep learning models trained for dimensionality reduction is greatly reduced compared to DDLA, which requires many deep learning models. This is highly effective for the reduction of computing resources for model training.
- The adversary can try many kinds of cluster analysis by changing different leakage models such as HW and HD (details will be described in Sect. 3.3) once the feature vectors have been extracted from DNN models.

Algorithm 1. Differential deep-learning analysis (using loss metrics)

Input: Leakage Traces $\mathbb{T}$, Plain-text $\mathbb{P}$, Key space $\mathcal{K}$,
    Number of epoch N_{ep}, DNN model parameters $\theta_k (k \in \mathcal{K})$,
    Base DNN model parameters θ_{base}
Output: Estimated key k^*
1: **for** k in $\mathcal{K}$ **do**
2:    $\theta_k = \theta_{base}$
3:    **for** epoch $= 1$ to N_{ep} **do**
4:       Training $\mathcal{M}_{\theta_k}$ with $(\mathbb{T}, \mathrm{I}(k, \mathbb{P}))$
5:       $\mathrm{l}_{loss}[N_{ep}] = L(\mathcal{M}_{\theta_k}(\mathbb{T}), \mathrm{I}(k, \mathbb{P}))$
6:    **end for**
7:    $\mathrm{L}_{loss}[k] = \min \mathrm{l}_{loss}$
8: **end for**
9: $k^* = \arg \min_i \mathrm{L}_{loss}[i]$
10: **return** k^*

– SCA countermeasures such as masking can be successfully analyzed by introducing supervised training on models for dimensionality reduction.

Hereafter, we refer to this method as cluster-analysis-based side-channel attacks (CA-SCAs).

The basics of CA-SCAs are explained below. An overview of CA-SCAs is shown in Fig. 1. First, the adversary trains a DNN model for dimensionality reduction of the leakage waveform. Next, the adversary extracts feature vectors from the leakage waveforms by using the trained DNN. It is noted that each feature vector is corresponding to the intermediate values which is determined by plaintext and key candidate. Finally, the adversary conducts cluster analysis on the feature vectors by using the label (i.e., LSB, MSB, HW, HD) of the intermediate values. Figure 1 shows the schematic diagram of cluster analysis using LSB. If the labeling is performed with the correct key, the dots with the same label are clustered together, and the dots with different labels are plotted apart from each other as shown $\hat{k} = $ correct_key in the figure. On the other hand, the dots are randomly scattered in case of incorrect key as shown as $\hat{k} = $ 0x00 in the figure. The adversary estimates the candidate key corresponding to the most appropriately clustered plot to be the correct key.

The quantitative score used in the cluster analysis is the Calinski-Harabasz index, which is described in Sect. 3.2. In this study, auto-encoder (AE) and convolutional neural network (CNN) are used as DNN models, and their respective attack procedures are described in Sects. 3.4 and 3.5, respectively.

3.2 Calinski-Harabasz Index

We used the Calinski-Harabasz index (CH index) for cluster analysis. The CH index is the variance ratio criterion, and a higher score indicates a better-defined cluster [4]. When inputting data x and labels c indicating the class, the CH index is formulated as follows.

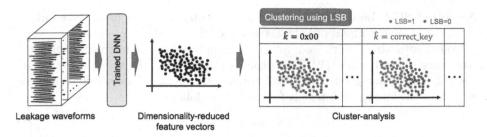

Fig. 1. Overview of cluster-analysis-based side-channel attacks (CA-SCAs)

$$\text{CHscore}(x, c) = \frac{B_k}{W_k} \times \frac{N - k}{k - 1}, \qquad (2)$$

where k, N, B_k, and W_k denote the number of classes, the size of all data, between-class variance, and within-class variance, respectively. In addition, B_k and W_k are formulated as follows.

$$B_k = \sum_{i=1}^{k} n_i ||m_i - m||_2^2, \qquad (3)$$

$$W_k = \sum_{i=1}^{k} \sum_{x \in C_i} ||x - m_i||_2^2, \qquad (4)$$

where C_i, m_i, m, and n_i denote the cluster of class i, the center of gravity of class i, the overall center of gravity, and the number of samples in class i, respectively. Meanwhile, $||x - m_i||_2$ and $||m_i - m||_2$ denote the L2 norm of the two vectors.

The score has no upper limit. A higher score indicates that the cluster is well formed. In contrast, a score closer to 0 indicates an inappropriate cluster, i.e., a mixture of classes.

3.3 Selected Function for Calculation of CH Index

Once a DNN model is trained for dimensionality reduction, CA-SCA can try multiple attacks using various leakage models. The calculation of the CH index requires labels indicating which cluster the input vector belongs to, and the function that calculates the labels can be changed. Here, we provide a list of possible functions that an adversary can choose from. The functions described below are the samples when the target is AES-128.

Known Plaintext. The target round the adversary focuses on depends on whether they know the plaintext $\mathbb{P}$ or the ciphertext $\mathbb{C}$. The adversary focuses on the first round of AES when they know the plaintext $\mathbb{P}$.

Assumed SCA Leakage Model. The adversary generally assumes a leakage model in SCA. Examples of SCA leakage models include HW.

When attacking a software-implemented application on a microcontroller, the adversary typically uses HW. This exploits the fact that the value of the microcontroller's precharge bus affects the power consumption. The selected function in case of the known plaintext is formulated as follows:

$$v = \text{S-Box}(k_t \oplus \mathbb{P}_t), \tag{5}$$

where S-Box$(\cdot)$, k_t, and $\mathbb{P}_t$ denote the S-Box function, the t-th byte cryptographic key, and the t-th byte plaintext, respectively.

Other Options. When the selected function is a bijection, CA-SCAs do not work. This is because the grouping based on the labels calculated for each candidate key is the same. It is necessary to disable the bijection using the following function.

- **Hamming weight of HW (Eq. 5):** The adversary conducts cluster analysis on the label of HW, as same as attack with CPA. In this case, the number of label is nine from HW=0 to HW=8. In this paper, the function is defined as follows.

$$f_{\text{hw}}(v) = \text{HW}(v), \tag{6}$$

where HW$(\cdot)$ is a function that calculates the Hamming weight of its arguments.
- **Mono-bit including LSB/MSB:** The adversary conducts cluster analysis in mono-bit labeling, including LSB/MSB, as it does when attacking with DDLA. For example, in the case of LSB labeling, there are two classes which are LSB=0 group and LSB=1 group. In this paper, the function is defined as follows.

$$f_{\text{mono}}(v, b) = v \oplus 2^b, \tag{7}$$

where b is the bit position to be selected. For example, when LSB labeling is selected, b is 0.
- **Multi-bit:** This is an extension of mono-bit labeling. For this option, the cluster analysis of the two classes focusing on mono-bit labeling is conducted eight times, changing the bit positions. As a result, the CH index for each of the 8-bit positions is calculated, and the sum of these values is calculated as follows.

$$f_{\text{multi}}(x, v) = \sum_{b=0}^{7} \text{CHscore}(x, f_{\text{mono}}(v, b)), \tag{8}$$

where x, v, and b denote the dimension-reduced waveform, the value calculated using Eq. (5), and the bit position, respectively. The adversary calculated and compared these sum values for each candidate key.

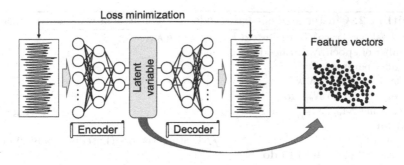

Fig. 2. Feature vectors extraction using auto-encoder in CA-SCA

3.4 Procedure of CA-SCA with Autoencoder

Auto-encoder (AE) is a type of DNN for achieving dimensionality reduction via unsupervised training [8]. AE learns to make the input and output the same, then the difference between them are often used for anomaly detection. In this study, we train AE by the leakage waveforms to obtain feature vectors which will be used for clustering on the CA-SCAs.

AE consists of an encoder and decoder, as shown in Fig. 2. The input data are compressed into latent variables (feature vectors) using the encoder and then reconstructed to its original dimensions using the decoder. AE is unsupervised learning in which the loss between the output and input data is minimized.

The attack procedure of CA-SCA with AE is shown in Algorithm 2. First, an AE consisting of an encoder $\mathcal{M}_{\theta_e}$ with parameters θ_e and a decoder $\mathcal{M}_{\theta_d}$ with parameters θ_d is trained unsupervised using waveforms set $\mathbb{T}$ (lines 1–3 in algorithm 2). Next, the waveforms in the S-Box process corresponding to the target byte are input to the trained encoder $\mathcal{M}_{\theta_e}$, and their latent variables $\mathbb{Z}$ are calculated (line 4 in algorithm 2). Finally, the adversary performs a cluster analysis of $\mathbb{Z}$ using the label computed from the candidate keys and plaintext according to the assumed leakage model (e.g., LSB of S-Box out in the first round). This cluster analysis is performed for each candidate key, and the candidate key with the highest CH index is estimated to be the correct key.

3.5 Procedure of CA-SCA with Convolutional Neural Network

CA-SCA, described in the previous section, can be extended to a method using supervised learning. One method of supervised learning is convolutional neural networks (CNNs). The procedure of CA-SCA with CNNs is described below.

It is necessary to consider how to label the leakage waveforms since CNN is supervised learning that requires ground-truth label. CA-SCA with CNN uses plaintext/ciphertext as labels. Here, we explain why plaintext labeling is effective in CA-SCA against software-implemented AES. SCAs against software-implemented AES generally focus on the S-Box output v at the first round shown below.

Algorithm 2. Cluster-analysis-based side-channel attacks with auto-encoder

---

Input: Leakage Traces $\mathbb{T}$, Plain-text $\mathbb{P}$, Key space $\mathcal{K}$,
    Number of epoch N_{ep}, Encoder parameter θ_e,
    Decoder parameter θ_d
Output: Estimated key k^*
1: **for** epoch $= 1$ to N_{ep} **do**
2:    Training $\mathcal{M}_{\theta_e}, \mathcal{M}_{\theta_d}$ with $\mathbb{T}$ // Training of AE
3: **end for**
4: $\mathbb{Z} = \mathcal{M}_{\theta_e}(\mathbb{T})$ // Feature vectors (Latent Variables) on AE
5: **for** target_byte $= 0$ to 15 **do**
6:    **for** k in $\mathcal{K}$ **do**
7:        $L_{cal}[k] = \text{CHscore}(\mathbb{Z}, I(k, \mathbb{P}))$ // Calculation of clustering score
8:    **end for**
9:    $k^*[\text{target\_byte}] = \arg\max_i L_{cal}[i]$
10: **end for**
11: **return** k^*

$$v = \text{S-Box}(k^* \oplus \mathbb{P}), \tag{9}$$

where k^*, $\mathbb{P}$ and S-Box($\cdot$) denote correct key, plaintext, and S-Box function. In case of the DDLA training, the intermediate value v is used as the supervised output label. In our CA-SCAs, the plaintext $\mathbb{P}$ is used as the supervised output label, but the same effect can be achieved because of the following reason. The key k implemented on the target device is fixed, then the plaintext $\mathbb{P}$ and the intermediate value v are bijective according to the Eq. (9).

The procedure of CA-SCAs using CNN is explained using Algorithm 3. At first, a CNN consisting of a feature extraction layer $\mathcal{M}_{\theta_f}$ and a classification layer $\mathcal{M}_{\theta_c}$ as shown Fig. 3 is trained using a waveform set $\mathbb{T}$ and plaintext $\mathbb{P}$ (lines 1–3 in Algorithm 3). The trained CNN outputs the probability of plaintext given the waveforms w (it is illustrated as $p(\text{Plaintext} = 0x00|w_0)$ in Fig. 3). Next, feature maps are calculated using the trained feature extraction layer $\mathcal{M}_{\theta_f}$ (line 4 in Algorithm 3). The feature map corresponds to dimensionality-reduced feature vectors and can be treated the same as the latent variables in the previous section. Finally, the target byte and key candidates are set, and the CH index is calculated for each. The adversary assumes that the key candidate with the highest CH index is the correct key.

Algorithm 3. Cluster-analysis-based side-channel attacks with convolutional neural network

---

Input: Leakage Traces $\mathbb{T}$, Plaintext $\mathbb{P}$, Key space $\mathcal{K}$,
   Number of epoch N_{ep}, feature extractor layers parameter θ_f,
   classification layers parameter θ_c

Output: Estimated key k^*

1: **for** epoch = 1 to N_{ep} **do**
2:    Training $\mathcal{M}_{\theta_f}, \mathcal{M}_{\theta_e}$ with $(\mathbb{T}, \mathbb{P})$ // Training of CNN
3: **end for**
4: $\mathbb{Z} = \mathcal{M}_{\theta_f}(\mathbb{T})$
                    // $\mathbb{Z}$ is the feature vectors which is used for cluster-analysis.
5: **for** target_byte = 0 to 15 **do**
6:    **for** k in $\mathcal{K}$ **do**
7:       $L_{cal}[k] = \text{CHscore}(\mathbb{Z}, \text{I}(k, \mathbb{P}))$ Calculation of clustering score
8:    **end for**
9:    $k^*[\text{target\_byte}] = \arg\max_i L_{cal}[i]$

10: **end for**
11: **return** k^*

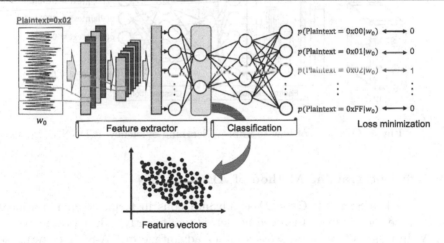

Fig. 3. Feature vectors extraction using convolutional neural network in CA-SCA

4   Evaluation with Software-Implemented AES

4.1   Overview

This section describes the attack evaluation of CA-SCAs against software-implemented AES. Section 4.2 describes how to improve learning efficiency for DNN models when attacking against software-implemented AES with CA-SCA using AE, as explained in Sect. 3.4, and CA-SCA using CNN, as described in Sect. 3.5. Section 4.3 evaluates attacks against AES without SCA countermeasures. Section 4.4 evaluates attacks against the ASCAD database. Section 4.5 discusses these evaluations.

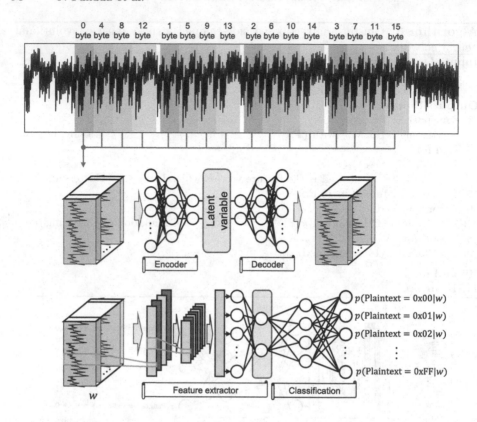

Fig. 4. Overview of how to improve learning efficiency at DNN.

4.2 Efficient Training Method of AE and CNN

As discussed in Sect. 3.1, CA-SCA is advantageous in terms of computational cost because the number of trained models is significantly reduced compared to DDLA. In this section, we discuss another advantage of CA-SCA in terms of learning efficiency, i.e., the ability to train models with fewer waveforms.

Each byte is processed sequentially when encryption is processed on a microcontroller with a single core. In other words, the attacked SubByte is processed byte by byte. Therefore, SCA leakage corresponding to the 16 key bytes appears in 16 separate locations in the leakage waveform. The SubBytes processing details at these locations are generally the same. In the proposed method, the leakage waveforms of 16 bytes are concatenated, and AE and CNN are trained with these waveforms dataset as shown in Fig. 4. It is possible to obtain 16 waveforms from a single encryption as training data.

In CA-SCA with AE, the reconstruction error is minimized. On the other hand, in CA-SCA with CNN, the CNN is trained using waveforms focused on a byte as input and plaintexts of the byte as output. A concatenated dataset of 16 bytes is used for training. The trained AE or CNN is input with the waveforms focused on the target byte, and feature vectors are extracted. Cluster analysis is then applied to reveal cryptographic keys.

4.3   Case Study S-1: Software-Implemented AES Without SCA Countermeasures

This section provides the results of attack evaluations of software-implemented AES without SCA countermeasures. We evaluated four attack methods: CA-SCA with AE, CA-SCA with CNN, DDLA, and CPA. The the setup for the evaluation is described in detail below.

Details of Waveforms. ChipWhisperer-Lite (CW1173), developed by new AE Technology, was used as the environment for waveform acquisition. CW303-XMEGA target, also developed by New AE Technology, was used as the target microcontroller board. This board is equipped with an 8-bit microcontroller, ATXmega128D4-AU. Power consumption during encryption operations was acquired using the A/D converter on CW1173, which has a sampling rate of 29 MS/s.

Setup for Analysis. The number of waveforms used in the analysis was set from 50 to 1,000 at 50 intervals, and multiple runs were performed. An autoencoder consists of an Encoder with one Conv 1D layer and two fully connected layers and a decoder with two fully connected layers and two transposed Conv1D layers. A CNN consists of one Conv 1D layer and three fully connected layers.

Experimental Results. Attacks were conducted when the selected function for the calculation of the CH index was varied. The functions to be evaluated were as follows.

- **HW labeling:** The CH index is calculated using CHscore($w, f_{hw}(v_{hw})$), where w denotes leakage waveforms, and v_{hw} and $f_{hw}(\cdot)$ are defined in Eq. (5) and (6).
- **LSB labeling:** The CH index is calculated using CHscore($w, f_{mono}(v_{hw}, 0)$), where $f_{mono}(\cdot)$ is defined in Eq. (7).
- **Multi-bit:** The CH index is calculated using $f_{multi}(w, v_{hw})$, where $f_{multi}(\cdot)$ is defined in Eq. (8).

The results of CA-SCA with AE and CA-SCA with CNN are shown in Fig. 5a and 5b, respectively. The horizontal axis shows the number of waveforms used in the analysis, and the vertical axis shows the number of revealed key bytes. In CA-SCA with AE, all key bytes were revealed in 450 waveforms for clustering with HW labeling and 500 waveforms for clustering with multi-bit. On the other hand, only 11 key bytes were revealed by clustering with LSBs, even with 1,000 waveforms. In CA-SCA with CNN, all key bytes were revealed in 350 waveforms for clustering with HW labeling and 400 waveforms for clustering with multi-bit.

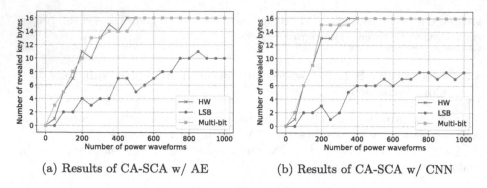

(a) Results of CA-SCA w/ AE   (b) Results of CA-SCA w/ CNN

Fig. 5. Comparison results of the selected functions on the CA-SCAs

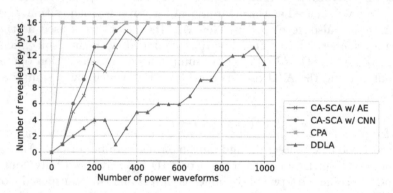

Fig. 6. Comparison with other non-profiled attacks when attacking against software-implemented AES without SCA countermeasures

On the other hand, only eight key bytes were revealed by clustering with LSBs, even with 1,000 waveforms. These results indicate that the selected function for CA-SCA with AE and CNN is important. However, as mentioned above, once the model has been trained, the selected function can be changed, and the attack can be conducted in many kinds. The computational cost for clustering is very small compared to that of DNN training.

We compared the results with other non-profiled attacks (CPA and DDLA). In CA-SCA, HW labeling was adopted as the selected function. The results of the evaluation are shown in Fig. 6, where the horizontal axis shows the number of waveforms used in the analysis, and the vertical axis shows the number of revealed key bytes. In CA-SCA using AE and CNN, all key bytes were revealed in 450 and 350 waveforms, respectively, as described above. In CPA, all key bytes were revealed in 30 waveforms. In DDLA, only 13 key bytes were revealed, even if 1,000 waveforms were used. CPA is most advantageous for software implementation without SCA countermeasures, where there is a correlation between the HW of intermediate value and the waveforms. On the other hand, we showed that CA-SCA is superior to DDLA in attacks using deep learning techniques.

4.4   Case Study S-2: ASCAD Database

In this section, we provide the results of attack evaluations of the ASCAD database. We evaluated the following attack methods: CA-SCA with AE, CA-SCA with CNN, DDLA, and CPA. The setup for the evaluation is described below.

Details of Waveforms. The ASCAD database is a public dataset that provides the electromagnetic (EM) emission waveforms during the operation of AES with a table re-computation masking countermeasure on AVR ATMega8515, which is an 8-bit microcontroller[1]. These waveforms were acquired using an oscilloscope with a sampling rate of 2 GS/s. The waveforms corresponding to the first round of AES processing are available in this dataset. In general, the evaluation is often limited to the SubBytes processing of the 2nd byte of the first round, but waveforms corresponding to SubBytes processing for all bytes are used in this study. This dataset has table re-computation masking countermeasure, but the mask value is fixed to 0 for the 0th and 1st byte. Note that masking is disabled for these two bytes.

Setup for Analysis. The number of waveforms used in the analysis was set from 1,000 to 20,000 at 1,000 intervals, and multiple runs were performed. The waveforms corresponding to SubBytes other than the 2 bytes for which masking was disabled were used to train for training the DNN. An autoencoder consists of an Encoder with three Conv 1D layers and three fully connected layers and a decoder with four fully connected layers and four transposed Conv1D layers. A CNN consists of three Conv 1D layers and four fully connected layers.

Experimental Results. We compared the results with other non-profiled attacks (CPA and DDLA). In CA-SCA, multi-bit was adopted as the selected function. The results of the evaluation are shown in Fig. 7, where the horizontal axis shows the number of waveforms used in the analysis, and the vertical axis shows the number of revealed key bytes. In CA-SCA using CNN, all key bytes were revealed in 12,000 waveforms. In CA-SCA using AE, only 2 bytes that are unmasking bytes were revealed. In CPA, only 3 bytes that include unmasking bytes were revealed. In DDLA, only 5 key bytes were revealed, even if 20,000 waveforms were used. The above results show that CA-SCA using CNN has the highest attack efficiency of the four methods.

4.5   Discussion

It is expected that the computation time to attack is greatly smaller than DDLA since CA-SCA trains only one DNN model. Thus, we measured and compared the computation time. We used a workstation equipped with a CPU: Intel Xeon

---

[1] The ASCAD database is available at https://github.com/ANSSI-FR/ASCAD.

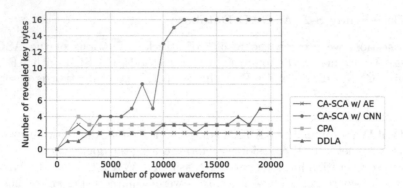

Fig. 7. Comparison with other non-profiled attacks when attacking against ASCAD database

Table 1. Comparison of computation time in case study S-1

Method	CPA	DDLA	CA-SCA with AE	CA-SCA with CNN
Time	2 s	50 m 8 s	41 s	37 s

Cold6226R (2.98GHz), DDR4 memory: 192GB, and a GPU: RTX-A5000 24GB to measure the computation time. The scope of time measurement focused on parts of the DNN training, calculations of a correlation coefficient, and the CH index. Note that data loading and label calculation are not included in the scope.

Table 1 summarizes the computation time required for the four attacks in case study S-1. CPA assumes a correlation between intermediate values and waveforms and is very fast, taking only 2 s, because it only calculates the correlation coefficient. On the other hand, DDLA, which is SCA using deep learning techniques, is very slow, taking 50 min and 8 s. This is because 16×256 DNN models are trained to estimate 16 key bytes. CA-SCAs using AE and CNN had computation times of 41 and 37 s, respectively. The computation time of CA-SCAs with AE and CNN was approximately 1/75 of the computation of DDLA.

The CA-SCA with AE in case study S-2 did not reveal the key. This is because AE is an unsupervised learning method that does not provide ground-truth labels for training. There is a correlation between the product of the two points, where the mask value and the masked value are processed, in the waveforms and the HW of the true intermediate value [17]. The model cannot learn this relationship because unsupervised learning does not provide a ground-truth label that depends on the true intermediate value. Therefore, CA-SCA with AE did not work for the ASCAD database.

Table 2. Summary of the number of waveforms required to reveal all key bytes in attacking against software implementation

Method	CPA	DDLA	CA-SCA with AE	CA-SCA with CNN
Case study S-1 AES w/o SCA countermeasures	30	1,000 (13 key bytes)	450	350
Case study S-2 ASCAD database	20,000 (3 key bytes)	20,000 (5 key bytes)	20,000 (2 key bytes)	12,000

5 Conclusion

We examined new non-profiled side-channel attacks (SCAs) using deep learning techniques. We proposed cluster-analysis-based side-channel attacks (CA-SCAs) where correct key is revealed by the score of cluster analysis on feature vectors extracted from waveforms by using deep neural networks (DNNs). We used auto-encoder (AE) and convolutional neural networks (CNNs) as DNNs. Our method requires only one trained DNN model to reveal all key bytes, whereas DDLA requires 256×16 trained DNN models. Therefore, the computation time for model training is very short. Another advantage of our method is that once the DNN model is trained, it is not necessary to re-train the DNN model when trying attacks with different labels. We provided 2 case studies to demonstrate the effectiveness of the proposed method.

We evaluated attacks against the AES without SCA countermeasures and the ASCAD database in case studies S-1 and S-2. We used a method that effectively trains DNNs by utilizing byte-by-byte sequential processing. In both case studies, we showed that all key bytes are revealed using fewer waveforms than DDLA. We also showed that the computation time for our attack is reduced compared to DDLA. Table 2 summarizes the number of waveforms required for the attack.

We confirmed the effectiveness of the proposed method through the above four case studies. In our future work, we plan to study leakage assessment, e.g., test vector leakage assessment [20], using CA-SCAs.

Acknowledgments. This work was supported by JSPS KAKENHI Grant Number JP22H03593 and JST, the establishment of university fellowships towards the creation of science technology innovation, Grant Number JPMJFS2146.

References

1. Alipour, A., Papadimitriou, A., Beroulle, V., Aerabi, E., Hély, D.: On the performance of non-profiled differential deep learning attacks against an AES encryption algorithm protected using a correlated noise generation based hiding countermeasure. In: 2020 Design, Automation & Test in Europe Conference & Exhibition, DATE 2020, Grenoble, France, 9–13 March 2020, pp. 614–617. IEEE (2020). https://doi.org/10.23919/DATE48585.2020.9116387

2. Brier, E., Clavier, C., Olivier, F.: Correlation power analysis with a leakage model. In: Joye, M., Quisquater, J.-J. (eds.) CHES 2004. LNCS, vol. 3156, pp. 16–29. Springer, Heidelberg (2004). https://doi.org/10.1007/978-3-540-28632-5_2

3. Cagli, E., Dumas, C., Prouff, E.: Convolutional neural networks with data augmentation against jitter-based countermeasures. In: Fischer, W., Homma, N. (eds.) CHES 2017. LNCS, vol. 10529, pp. 45–68. Springer, Cham (2017). https://doi.org/10.1007/978-3-319-66787-4_3

4. Caliński, T., Harabasz, J.: A dendrite method for cluster analysis. Commun. Stat.-Theory Methods 3(1), 1–27 (1974)

5. Chari, S., Rao, J.R., Rohatgi, P.: Template attacks. In: Kaliski, B.S., Koç, K., Paar, C. (eds.) CHES 2002. LNCS, vol. 2523, pp. 13–28. Springer, Heidelberg (2003). https://doi.org/10.1007/3-540-36400-5_3

6. Do, N.T., Hoang, V.P., Doan, V.S., Pham, C.K.: On the performance of non-profiled side channel attacks based on deep learning techniques. IET Inf. Secur. 17(3), 377–393 (2023). https://doi.org/10.1049/ise2.12102. https://ietresearch.onlinelibrary.wiley.com/doi/abs/10.1049/ise2.12102

7. Do, N.T., Le, P.C., Hoang, V.P., Doan, V.S., Nguyen, H.G., Pham, C.K.: MODLSCA: deep learning based non-profiled side channel analysis using multi-output neural networks. In: 2022 International Conference on Advanced Technologies for Communications (ATC), pp. 245–250 (2022). https://doi.org/10.1109/ATC55345.2022.9943024

8. Hinton, G.E., Salakhutdinov, R.R.: Reducing the dimensionality of data with neural networks. Science 313(5786), 504–507 (2006). https://doi.org/10.1126/science.1127647. https://www.science.org/doi/abs/10.1126/science.1127647

9. Hoang, V.P., Do, N.T., Doan, V.S.: Efficient non-profiled side channel attack using multi-output classification neural network. IEEE Embed. Syst. Lett. 1 (2022). https://doi.org/10.1109/LES.2022.3213443

10. Ito, A., Ueno, R., Homma, N.: Perceived information revisited new metrics to evaluate success rate of side-channel attacks. IACR Trans. Cryptogr. Hardw. Embed. Syst. 2022(4), 228–254 (2022). https://doi.org/10.46586/tches.v2022.i4.228-254

11. Kocher, P., Jaffe, J., Jun, B.: Differential power analysis. In: Wiener, M. (ed.) CRYPTO 1999. LNCS, vol. 1666, pp. 388–397. Springer, Heidelberg (1999). https://doi.org/10.1007/3-540-48405-1_25

12. Kubota, T., Yoshida, K., Shiozaki, M., Fujino, T.: Deep learning side-channel attack against hardware implementations of AES. In: 2019 22nd Euromicro Conference on Digital System Design (DSD), pp. 261–268 (2019). https://doi.org/10.1109/DSD.2019.00046

13. Kuroda, K., Fukuda, Y., Yoshida, K., Fujino, T.: Practical aspects on non-profiled deep-learning side-channel attacks against AES software implementation with two types of masking countermeasures including RSM. In: Proceedings of the 5th Workshop on Attacks and Solutions in Hardware Security, ASHES 2021, pp. 29-40. Association for Computing Machinery, New York (2021). https://doi.org/10.1145/3474376.3487285

14. Kuroda, K., Fukuda, Y., Yoshida, K., Fujino, T.: Practical aspects on non-profiled deep-learning side-channel attacks against AES software implementation with two types of masking countermeasures including RSM. J. Cryptogr. Eng. 1–16 (2023)

15. Kwon, D., Hong, S., Kim, H.: Optimizing implementations of non-profiled deep learning-based side-channel attacks. IEEE Access 10, 5957–5967 (2022). https://doi.org/10.1109/ACCESS.2022.3140446

16. Maghrebi, H., Portigliatti, T., Prouff, E.: Breaking cryptographic implementations using deep learning techniques. In: Carlet, C., Hasan, M.A., Saraswat, V. (eds.) SPACE 2016. LNCS, vol. 10076, pp. 3–26. Springer, Cham (2016). https://doi. org/10.1007/978-3-319-49445-6_1

17. Messerges, T.S.: Using second-order power analysis to attack DPA resistant software. In: Koç, Ç.K., Paar, C. (eds.) CHES 2000. LNCS, vol. 1965, pp. 238–251. Springer, Heidelberg (2000). https://doi.org/10.1007/3-540-44499-8_19

18. Picek, S., Heuser, A., Jovic, A., Bhasin, S., Regazzoni, F.: The curse of class imbalance and conflicting metrics with machine learning for side-channel evaluations. IACR Trans. Cryptogr. Hardw. Embed. Syst. **2019**(1), 209–237 (2019). https:// doi.org/10.13154/tches.v2019.i1.209-237

19. Prouff, E., Strullu, R., Benadjila, R., Cagli, E., Dumas, C.: Study of deep learning techniques for side-channel analysis and introduction to ASCAD database. IACR Cryptology ePrint Archive, p. 53 (2018). http://eprint.iacr.org/2018/053

20. Schneider, T., Moradi, A.: Leakage assessment methodology. In: Güneysu, T., Handschuh, H. (eds.) CHES 2015. LNCS, vol. 9293, pp. 495–513. Springer, Heidelberg (2015). https://doi.org/10.1007/978-3-662-48324-4_25

21. Timon, B.: Non-profiled deep learning-based side-channel attacks with sensitivity analysis. IACR Trans. Cryptogr. Hardw. Embed. Syst. **2019**(2), 107–131 (2019). https://doi.org/10.13154/tches.v2019.i2.107-131

22. Wu, L., Perin, G., Picek, S.: Hiding in plain sight: non-profiling deep learning-based side-channel analysis with plaintext/ciphertext. Cryptology ePrint Archive, Paper 2023/209 (2023). https://eprint.iacr.org/2023/209

Creating from Noise: Trace Generations Using Diffusion Model for Side-Channel Attack

Trevor Yap[1,2] and Dirmanto Jap[2]

[1] School of Physical and Mathematical Sciences, Nanyang Technological University, Singapore, Singapore
trevor.yap@ntu.edu.sg

[2] Temasek Laboratories, Nanyang Technological University, Singapore, Singapore
djap@ntu.edu.sg

Abstract. In side-channel analysis (SCA), the success of an attack is largely dependent on the dataset sizes and the number of instances in each class. The generation of synthetic traces can help to improve attacks like profiling attacks. However, manually creating synthetic traces from actual traces is arduous. Therefore, automating this process of creating artificial traces is much needed. Recently, diffusion models have gained much recognition after beating another generative model known as Generative Adversarial Networks (GANs) in creating realistic images. We explore the usage of diffusion models in the domain of SCA. We proposed frameworks for a known mask setting and unknown mask setting in which the diffusion models could be applied. Under a known mask setting, we show that the traces generated under the proposed framework preserved the original leakage. Next, we demonstrated that the artificially created profiling data in the unknown mask setting can reduce the required attack traces for a profiling attack. This suggests that the artificially created profiling data from the trained diffusion model contains useful leakages to be exploited.

Keywords: Side-channel · Neural Network · Deep Learning · Profiling attack · Generative Models · Diffusion Model

1 Introduction

Side-channel Attacks (SCA) are one of those crucial threats that are required to be evaluated. Information on the secret data could be leaked in physical properties such as power consumption [13], and electromagnetic emanation [1]. Many of such physical properties come in a form known as traces. SCA analyzes these traces to recover the secret data in various ways. Profiling attacks and non-profiling attacks are common forms of SCA. Very often, the success of these attacks relies heavily on the number of traces. However, in a practical setting, there might be a limitation on the number of traces that can be collected by

© The Author(s), under exclusive license to Springer Nature Switzerland AG 2024
M. Andreoni (Ed.): ACNS 2024 Workshops, LNCS 14586, pp. 102–120, 2024.
https://doi.org/10.1007/978-3-031-61486-6_7

the adversary, presumably due to some factors; for example, the device itself is protected, which only allows limited access to the device. Due to this limitation, the performance of the SCA could be affected, for example, making it hard to generalize the leakages. As such, there is a need for more data or traces to analyze. However, manually creating artificial traces can be quite complicated and tedious as it needs to capture the leakage information and its characteristics properly.

In recent years, there has been a rise in using machine learning techniques to tackle the automation of creating such artificial traces. One common approach is to use Generative Adversarial Networks (GAN) [7], a popular technique commonly used in the image processing domain for generating synthetic images. Recently, a few of the previous works [23] and [16] have investigated creating artificial traces using GAN. However, in the image domain community, another generative model known as the Denoising Diffusion Probabilistic Model (DDPM) has risen in popularity recently due to its performance in producing more realistic images exceeding that of GAN. As such, in this work, we aim to explore and investigate how to adopt DDPM into the SCA domain.

Our Contributions. In this work, our contributions are stated as follows:

1. We investigate the applicability of the DDPM approach for traces generation in the context of SCA. We proposed two different frameworks in which a diffusion model can be used: Known mask setting and unknown mask setting.
2. In the known mask setting, we highlight that the generated traces can exhibit the original leakages as observed in the original traces by evaluating the traces with Correlation Power Analysis (CPA).
3. On the other hand, we show the effectiveness of the diffusion model in generating artificial data in the unknown mask setting. By increasing the downsampled profiling traces with the newly generated data from the diffusion model, we show that the number of attack traces needed for a profiling attack decreases.

In this work, we target synchronized and desynchronized traces. We validate our approach on traces up to the first-order masking for real traces. We leave higher-order masking of real traces to future works. The results can be publicly accessed on the following weblinks[1].

Paper Organization. The paper is organized as follows. In Sect. 2, we give an overview of related works over the recent years. Section 3 will provide the necessary background on side-channel analysis and DDPM. In Sect. 4, we present the datasets and the building blocks of the neural network being used. Section 5 provides a visualization of the leakages that an diffusion model could provide Subsequently, we present the results of profiling attack when using artificial data created by the trained diffusion model for profiling in Sect. 6. Lastly, in Sect. 7, we conclude the paper and outline some future works.

---

[1] https://github.com/yap231995/Diffusion-SCA.

2   Related Works

One of the common approaches adopted in the machine learning domain is the data augmentation approach. A form of data augmentation is the Synthetic Minority Over-sampling Technique (SMOTE), which was explored in [19]. They applied data augmentation to deal with data imbalance due to the Hamming Weight (HW) leakage model. As such, after balancing the training data, it could improve the attack performance. Another work on different data augmentation was reported in [14], where the authors investigate data augmentation techniques against masked AES with hiding countermeasures. It reported that the data augmentation could help in decreasing the effectiveness of hiding countermeasures, albeit requiring specific configuration when dealing with different Deep Neural Network (DNN) architectures. Another work by Cagli *et al.* [4] proposed using data augmentation for Deep-Learning (DL)-based SCA. They proposed a data augmentation method by manually adding jitters into the original traces to increase the number of traces for profiling.

Recently, more works have performed more in-depth investigations on the applicability of data augmentation through the automatic generation of synthetic traces through the use of DNN. [23] introduced a new approach to generating new traces through the usage of Conditional Generative Adversarial Network (CGAN). They show that CGAN can generate new traces that learn the leakage from both unprotected and protected implementations. However, the leakage model considered in their work is the Hamming Weight (HW) leakage model, resulting in fewer classes. Furthermore, the correlation of the traces evaluated did not consider any comparison with other keys. In [16], the authors proposed another approach when generating traces automatically based on CGAN and Siamese networks. They used the proposed approach to generate datasets for both symmetric and public-key cryptographic implementations. Compared to previous work, they also investigate and analyze the effect of the GAN network on data generation. However, they only considered the dataset with fixed key profiling and attack traces called ASCADf and an ECC dataset. In [11], the authors proposed another CGAN-based approach. In their approach, the generator receives real traces as input and is not conditioned with label class, which allows it to extract the features from the unlabeled set. Therefore, their approach did not create new artificial data but as a form of feature extraction and dimensionality reduction.

In all recent works, the idea is to use data augmentation to generate artificial data, which can also capture the characteristics of the leakage as well as the countermeasures, such as hiding or masking leakage. Most of the works have been utilizing GAN as the main approach for data generation and work under the unknown mask setting. In this work, we investigate an alternative approach using diffusion model for data generation for both known mask and unknown mask settings and investigate how the approach could learn the leakage characteristics.

3 Background

In this section, we provide basic backgrounds on the topics that we will use throughout the whole paper.

3.1 Correlation Power Analysis (CPA)

One of the most commonly used attacks is the CPA [3]. The general approach is to use Pearson correlation to establish the relation between different intermediate values from different secret hypotheses and the actual leakage values. The attacker will use the intermediate values computed as function f of known inputs p and (hypothetical) secret $k \in K$. In this case, the attacker will compute $H = f(p, k)$. These intermediate values will then be compared with the actual leakage traces T obtained while processing actual secret k^*. The secret k with the highest (absolute) correlation can then be estimated as the secret value.

The Pearson correlation between x and y can be computed as follow:

$$r(x, y) = \frac{\sum_{i=1}^{N}((x_i - \bar{x})(y_i - \bar{y}))}{\sqrt{\sum_{i=1}^{N}(x_i - \bar{x})^2}\sqrt{\sum_{i=1}^{N}(y_i - \bar{y})^2}}. \tag{1}$$

For the intermediate values, they have to be mapped to the leakage. In general, a leakage model is used to approximate the behavior of the measured traces. For the software implementation, the leakage is usually assumed to follow the HW model. In contrast, for hardware implementation, it is the Hamming distance (HD) model. In addition to the mentioned leakage values, an identity mapping (ID) can also be used as an alternative leakage model. In this work, we will mainly focus on the ID leakage model.

3.2 Profiling Attacks

Profiling attacks assume a worst-case scenario where the adversary has access to a clone device and a target device. These two devices are similar to each other. In this setting, the adversary can manipulate or know the device's key of the clone device while the key for the target device is unknown to him. Furthermore, the adversary has the ability to collect multiple traces from a known set of random plaintexts (or ciphertexts) from both devices. The adversary will obtain the profiling traces from the clone device while acquiring the attack traces from the target device. The goal of the adversary is to recover the unknown key from the target device.

Profiling attacks can be divided into the profiling phase and the attack phase. In the profiling phase, a distinguisher $\mathcal{F}$ is built from the set of profiling traces. This distinguisher will return a conditional probability mass function $\Pr(T|Z = z)$. During the attack phase, the distinguisher returns a probability score for each hypothetical sensitive value. In other words, we obtain $\boldsymbol{y}_i = \mathcal{F}(\boldsymbol{t}_i)$ where t_i represents an attack trace. We compute the log-likelihood score for every key $k \in \mathcal{K}$ as follows:

$$s_{N_a}(k) = \sum_{i=1}^{N_a} \log(\boldsymbol{y}_i[z_{i,k}]),$$

where N_a as the number of attack traces used and $z_{i,k} = C(p_i, k)$ are the hypothetical sensitive values based on the key k with p_i being the corresponding public variable to the trace $\boldsymbol{t}_i$ and C is the cryptographic primitive. Next, we rank the key of the log-likelihood score in decreasing order and classify them into a guess vector $\boldsymbol{G} = [G_0, G_1, \ldots, G_{|\mathcal{K}|-1}]$ with the score G_0 corresponds to the score of the most likely key candidate, and the score $G_{|\mathcal{K}|-1}$ to be the score for is the least likely key candidate. The rank of the key shall be denoted as the index of guess vector $\boldsymbol{G}$. The guessing entropy GE is defined as the average rank of the correct key k^* over multiple experiments [22]. If $GE = 0$, when using N_a attack traces, the attack is considered successful. We denote $NTGE$ to be the least number of traces required to attain $GE = 0$.

The most known profiling attack is Template Attacks (TA). The distinguisher is built using the Bayes' Theorem with the assumption that the conditional probability $Pr(\boldsymbol{T}|Z = z)$ follows the multivariate Gaussian distribution [5]. Overall, it outputs the following as the posterior probability,

$$\Pr(Z = z_k | \boldsymbol{T} = \boldsymbol{t}) = -\frac{D}{2}\log(2\pi) - \frac{1}{2}\log(det(\Sigma_k)) - \frac{1}{2}(\boldsymbol{t} - \overline{\boldsymbol{t}_k})^T \Sigma_k (\boldsymbol{t} - \overline{\boldsymbol{t}_k}),$$

where $\overline{\boldsymbol{t}_k}$ is the sample mean of class z_k and Σ_k is the covariance matrix of class z_k with determinant $det(\Sigma_k)$.

3.3 Denoising Diffusion Probabilistic Models (DDPM)

DDPM was first created by [9] in 2020 to generate images and was extensively improved [17]. In fact, recently [6] shows that with enough tuning, DDPM could attain better performance compared to GAN. DDPM is a type of Markovian Hierarchical Variational Autoencoder (H-VAE), which can be viewed as stacking multiple Variational Autoencoder together (VAE). Figure 1 illustrates how DDPM works visually. Given a data distribution $x_0 \sim q(x_0)$, we define the forward noising process q which iteratively adding Gaussian noise at each time t with a variance $\beta_t \in (0, 1)$ to x_0 to obtain x_1 to x_T as

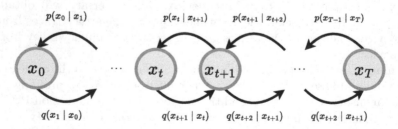

Fig. 1. Visualization representation of DDPM. x_0 represents the original data while x_T denote the pure Gaussian noise. The intermediate x_t portrays the noisy version of x_0 at time step t.

$$q(x_1, \ldots, x_T | x_0) = \prod_{t=1}^{T} q(x_t | x_{t-1}),$$

$$q(x_t | x_{t-1}) = \mathcal{N}(x_t; \sqrt{1 - \beta_t} x_{t-1}, \beta_t I).$$

Suppose T is sufficiently large and the β_t follows a schedule, for example linear or cosine schedule, then the latent x_T is almost isotropic Gaussian distribution (i.e., $x_T \sim \mathcal{N}(0, I)$). This means that we can sample $x_T \sim \mathcal{N}(0, I)$ and reverse the process to obtain data from $q(x_0)$. Throughout this work, we set β_t to follow the cosine schedule as proposed in [17].

We estimate the reverse process by using a neural network by defining the reverse process as

$$p(x_{t-1} | x_t) = \mathcal{N}(x_{t-1}; \mu_\theta(x_t, t), \Sigma_\theta(x_t, t)).$$

As noted in [9], because noising process q is modeled from a Gaussian distribution, one can show that it is allowed to sample x_t for any t directly from the input data x_0,

$$x_t = \sqrt{\bar{\alpha}_t} x_0 + \sqrt{1 - \bar{\alpha}_t} \epsilon$$

$$q(x_t | x_0) = \mathcal{N}(x_t; \sqrt{\bar{\alpha}_t} x_0, 1 - \bar{\alpha}_t I)$$

where $\alpha_t = 1 - \beta_t$, $\bar{\alpha}_t = \prod_{s=0}^{t} \alpha_s$ and $\epsilon \sim \mathcal{N}(0, I)$.

By Bayes' Theorem, we can reformulate $q(x_{t-1} | x_t, x_0)$ in terms of $\bar{\beta}_t$ and $\mu_q(x_t, x_0)$:

$$q(x_{t-1} | x_t, x_0) = \mathcal{N}(x_t; \mu_q(x_t, x_0), \bar{\beta}_t I)$$

where

$$\bar{\beta}_t = \frac{1 - \bar{\alpha}_{t-1}}{1 - \bar{\alpha}_t} \beta_t, \text{ and } \mu_q(x_t, x_0) = \frac{\sqrt{\bar{\alpha}_{t-1}} \beta}{1 - \bar{\alpha}_t} x_0 + \frac{\sqrt{\bar{\alpha}_t}(1 - \bar{\alpha}_{t-1})}{1 - \bar{\alpha}_t} x_t.$$

There are various way to approximate $\mu_\theta(x_t, t)$ to $\mu_q(x_t, x_0)$. One can rewrite $\mu_\theta(x_t, t)$ as $\mu_\theta(x_t, t) = \frac{1}{\sqrt{\alpha_t}}(x_t - \frac{\beta_t}{\sqrt{1-\bar{\alpha}_t}} \epsilon_\theta(x_t, t))$. We simply train a neural network ϵ_θ to minimize $\|\epsilon - \epsilon_\theta(x_t, t)\|^2$. We call this neural network to be the diffusion model.

Conditional Free Guidance. Very often, one would want to produce data based on their label. In other words, we are also interested in modeling $p(x | y)$ where y is the label. Especially in SCA, we would like to create a diffusion model that could obtain traces based on their leakage model. [10] first introduces the concept of Conditional Free Guidance (CFG) by ditching the idea of using a separate classifier to predict newly generated data and train two diffusion models. CFG trains both the unconditional diffusion model and conditional diffusion simultaneously (in practice, this is just one model). The idea is to let the unconditional diffusion model guide the conditional model for more exploration, which allows for more diversity. An equivalent goal when training a diffusion model is known as the score-based formulation, where the objective is to maximize the score $\nabla_{x_t} \log p(x_t | y)$. One can formulate this score as

$$\nabla_{x_t} \log p(x_t \mid y) = \gamma \nabla_{x_t} \log p(x_t \mid y) + (1 - \gamma) \nabla_{x_t} \log p(x_t)$$

where the term $\nabla_{x_t} \log p(x_t \mid y)$ corresponds to the score of the conditional diffusion model while $\nabla_{x_t} \log p(x_t)$ is the score of the unconditional diffusion model, with γ being the hyperparameter that controls how much the conditional diffusion model cares about the label. Throughout this paper, we consider γ to be 0.7. We refer readers to [15] for a more holistic understanding of the diffusion model and CFG.

4   Datasets and Neural Network Used for Experiment

In this section, we present the datasets that will be used for any of the experiments and the neural network used as the diffusion model.

4.1   Datasets

Simulated Traces. We generate simulated traces of 24 sample points. These traces are leaking with the value of the Advance Encryption Standard (AES) substitution box. Suppose each trace is defined as an array, $trace[0, \ldots, 23]$, and $d \in \{0, 1, 2, 3\}$ to be the masking order of the simulated dataset. The sample points that consist of the values of the masks are presented in Table 1. Here, we denote $Z = Sbox(pt \oplus k^*)$ where pt is the plaintext byte and k^* is the correct key. Here, we fix $k^* = 0x03$. Furthermore, m_i are randomly generated bytes for secret sharing. We randomly generate random byte values for the remaining points. Then, we add a small noise sampled from the normal distribution to every sample point with zero mean and variance of 0.01. We generated 14,000 traces for training the diffusion models.

Table 1. Leakage points of the traces generated in simulated data based on the masking order.

Masking Order d	Leakage Point
0	$trace[5, \ldots, 10] = Z$
1	$trace[10, \ldots, 15] = Z \oplus m_1$
	$trace[0, \ldots, 5] = m_1$
2	$trace[0, \ldots, 4] = Z \oplus m_1 \oplus m_2$
	$trace[9, \ldots, 14] = m_1, trace[18, \ldots, 22] = m_2$
3	$trace[0, \ldots, 3] = Z \oplus m_1 \oplus m_2 \oplus m_3$
	$trace[7, \ldots, 9] = m_1, trace[13, \ldots, 17] = m_2, trace[18, \ldots, 22] = m_3$

ChipWhisperer (CW). The CW dataset provides a standard comparison base for the evaluation of different algorithms [18]. The dataset we consider runs the unprotected AES-128 implementation on the CW308 Target. We will refer to this dataset as CW throughout this paper. This dataset targets the first byte in the first round of the AES Sbox, $Sbox(pt \oplus k^*)$, with a fixed key k^*. The dataset consists of 10,000 traces.

ASCADf and ASCADr. The ASCAD dataset consists of a first-order masked AES implementation on an 8-bit AVR microcontroller (ATMega8515) [2]. We target the third byte of the first round AES Sbox. This is a first-order masked key byte. Two versions known as ASCADf and ASCADr are part of the ASCAD dataset. ASCADf contains traces corresponding to the same fixed key for both profiling and attack. ASCADr contains profiling traces generated from a random key setting, while the attack traces are obtained from the fixed key target device. The dataset consists of 50,000 profiling traces and 10,000 attack traces for both datasets. The traces in ASCADf are composed of 700 sample points, while the traces in ASCADr consist of 1400 sample points.

4.2   Neural Network Used: UNet

We train UNet [21] as the diffusion model. A simple illustration of an UNet is shown in Fig. 2. We consider the UNet to consist of 1-dimensional convolutional layers, where each convolution layer is followed by a group normalization [24] and the activation, SiLU [8]. In the UNet, we applied multiple skipped connections (see Fig. 2). Furthermore, the UNet also contains attention mechanisms to improve its performance. We refer to the weblink for the full architecture used. We train the UNet together with an Exponential Moving Averages (EMA) [12] to help to enhance the stability of the training. In order for the neural network to understand which timestamp t the noise is from, it is first applied as a word embedding and followed by a shallow perceptron with GeLU as the activation function. Similarly, in order for the UNet to learn the information of the label y, we feed y into another shallow perceptron with GeLU [8] as the activation function. The output of these two embeddings are concatenated and fed to every convolutional layer of the UNet.

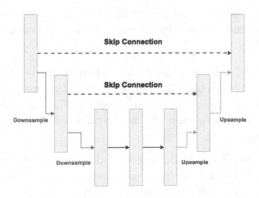

Fig. 2. UNet architecture.

5   Known Mask Setting: Evaluation of the Generated Traces Using CPA

In this section, we consider the scenario where we train a diffusion model under the known mask setting. Here, we can consider this trained diffusion model (together with the autoencoder) as a "portable oscilloscope" of the target device. If an adversary obtains this trained "portable oscilloscope" without access to any traces, they could essentially recover the secret key with the artificially generated data from this trained diffusion model.

In this part, we evaluate the quality of the generated traces from such diffusion model. To perform an evaluation of the quality, we conducted CPA on both original traces and generated traces. The idea is to observe if the generated traces can preserve the crucial leakages from the original traces. As such, while we are performing CPA in key recovery mode, we assume that for higher-order masking, the mask is known, and we assess if the mask leakage is also captured in the generated traces.

5.1   Evaluation Framework

Side-channel traces could go up to thousands of sample points. The time required to sample/generate new traces increases with the number of dimensionality. We propose to use the framework to be applied with CPA. We note that this framework can be used also in any non-profiling setting. This framework was first proposed in [20] to help speed up the sampling process in generating high-resolution images. The framework is as follows:

1. **(Autoencoder phase)** Train an autoencoder to encode and decode the traces into a latent space with reduced dimension.
2. **(Training phase)** We first encode every attack trace into the latent space by applying the encoder and train the diffusion model based on these attack traces.
3. **(Generative phase)** Next, for a given label class, we used the trained diffusion model to generate new latent embeddings by denoising randomly initialized embedding.

This framework introduces an autoencoder to help decrease the dimension of the traces into a latent space. This will help reduce the time required to sample new traces as the diffusion model generates a new latent embedding with smaller dimensional. We can then obtain the new traces by decoding the new latent embeddings (Fig. 3).

Autoencoder Phase. To train the autoencoder, we have to first find the architecture of the model. To find the hyperparameters, we perform a random search (see Appendix A.1). In order to identify the best performing parameters, we use the trace correlation metric. In short, we compute the average correlation between the actual and reconstructed traces from the autoencoder and keep the

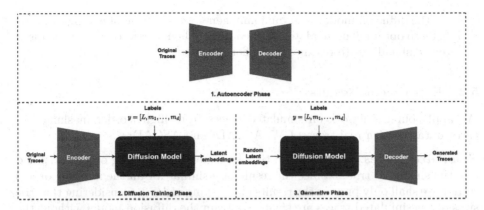

Fig. 3. Framework for using diffusion model in CPA. We define Z to be the corresponding mask data (e.g., $L = Z \oplus m_1 \oplus \cdots \oplus m_d$).

parameter that resulted in the highest correlation. Given traces T and reconstructed T', we compute $r(T, T')$ as described in Eq. 1.

After the autoencoder has been trained with the best performing parameters, we proceed with the trace generation using the diffusion model. We trained the diffusion model with the latent embedding instead of the actual traces. Once the model is trained with their proper labels, we can generate the new latent embedding with their corresponding labels. In the case of higher-order masking, for each trace, we generated corresponding mask share(s), and using this information, with knowledge of the secret, one can compute back the corresponding plaintext (or in the profiling setting, we can directly use the corresponding label for training). After the latent embeddings are generated, we use the autoencoder to decode these embeddings back to get the generated traces. If necessary, one can also normalize the generated traces as post-processing.

Training Phase. We train the diffusion model conditionally with a generalized CFG. In our setting, we consider a known mask setting where one would have the mask value and the mask data value. We set the label given to the diffusion to be both the mask and the mask data, namely $y = (Z \oplus m_1 \oplus \cdots \oplus m_{d-1}, m_1, \ldots, m_d)$ where d is the masking order of the dataset and Z is the hypothetical sensitive values. We train the diffusion model according to Sect. 3.3. Note that $y, m_1, \ldots, m_d$ are in real values when used to train the diffusion model.

Generative Phase. In this phase, one can choose the number of artificial data/latent embeddings one would want to generate.

1. Firstly, we generate n_g latent embeddings for each value of L.
2. Then, we randomly generate values of each mask values $m_1, \ldots, m_d$ and obtain the label $y = (L, m_1, \ldots, m_d)$.

3. Feed the diffusion model with randomly generated latent embeddings and the label y to obtain denoised latent embeddings. Then, we decode these denoised latent embeddings to obtain the artificial traces.

5.2 Experiment Results

We apply our framework on simulated traces from higher-order masking and three datasets with real traces: CW, ASCADf and ASCADr.

Simulated Traces. We performed the assessment for masking order $0, 1, 2$ and 3 of the simulated traces. Since the results are similar for all the masking orders tested, we shall only present the results on masking order 3. Considering that the sizes of the simulated traces are small. We train the diffusion model without the use of an autoencoder. We train the diffusion model using a batch size of 512, a learning rate of 0.0005, and 50 epochs. We sample $n_g = 10$ artificial data for each value of $L = Sbox(pt \oplus k^*) \oplus m_1 \oplus m_2 \oplus m_3$ with randomly generated m_1, m_2 and m_3. We get a total of $256 * 10 = 2560$ artificial latent embeddings and apply the decoder to obtain the newly generated traces. We apply the CPA on these newly generated traces. The result of the CPA for each mask is shown in Fig. 4. The correlation of the original traces is illustrated in Fig. 4a while the correlation of the generated traces is depicted in Fig. 4b. We see that the generated traces from the diffusion model obtain similar correlations on every share in comparison with the corresponding correlations within the original traces. In fact, we see that the correlation of mask m_1 is amplified within around the sample point 11. This shows that the diffusion model could potentially generate traces that amplify the leakages.

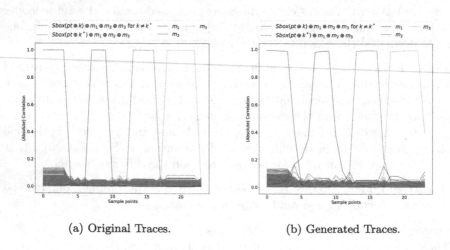

| (a) Original Traces. | (b) Generated Traces. |

Fig. 4. CPA on original and generated simulated data of order 3 (with known shares).

CW. We then test the approach on real datasets. Our first target is the CW dataset. Using random search, we found an autoencoder that mapped the traces into a latent embedding of size 992. Afterward, we generate new traces using the diffusion model. Here, we are using the ID leakage model, resulting in 256 classes. We then generate 2,000 traces in total using the diffusion model. We perform CPA on the original traces as well as on the generated traces, both using 2,000 traces in total. In Fig. 5a, we show the CPA on original CW traces, and in Fig. 5b, we show the CPA on generated CW traces. Overall, we could see that the generated leakage could preserve the important leakages from different sample points. Similarly, we also see the correlation with respect to $Sbox(pt \oplus k^*)$ is amplified in areas that are not correlated previously, showing that diffusion models could possibly increase the intensity of the leakages in areas that are previously not correlated.

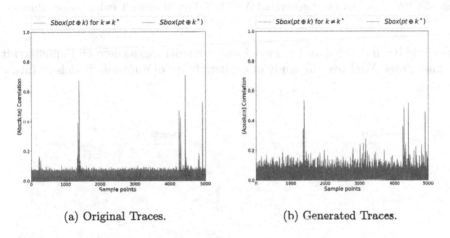

(a) Original Traces.   (b) Generated Traces.

Fig. 5. CPA on original and generated CW data.

ASCADf. Next, we test the approach on the ASCADf dataset. Similar to the previous experiment, we employ random search on the hyperparameters to find an autoencoder. We then constructed an autoencoder that mapped the traces into a latent embedding of size 192. Afterward, we generate new traces using the diffusion model. Again, we are using the ID leakage model with 256 classes. We then generate for each class 10 traces, so we have 2,560 traces in total. We perform CPA on the original traces as well as on the generated traces, both using 2,560 traces in total. In Fig. 6a, we showed the CPA on original ASCADf traces, and in Fig. 6b, we showed the CPA on generated ASCADf traces. Here, we can observe that the leakage of the intermediate value, as well as the mask, can be preserved in the generated leakage. In observe that there is increase in correlation with respect to $Sbox(pt \oplus k^*) \oplus r$. Especially between sample points 0 to 200,

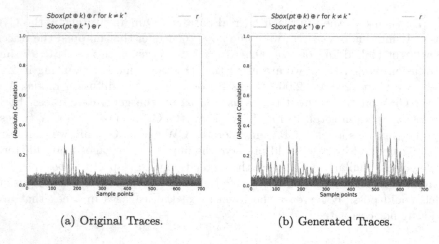

(a) Original Traces.   (b) Generated Traces.

Fig. 6. CPA on original and generated ASCADf data of order 1 (with known shares).

this could be that the diffusion model learns the leakages there and amplified it in those areas. We leave the study of explainability of diffusion models to future works.

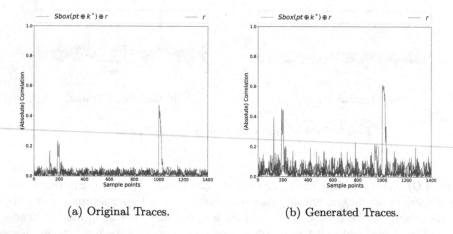

(a) Original Traces.   (b) Generated Traces.

Fig. 7. CPA on original and generated ASCADr data of order 1 (with known shares).

ASCADr. Lastly, we test the approach on ASCADr dataset. Since the key is not fixed, we cannot perform key recovery, instead, we plot the correlation on the intermediate value and the mask for the original (Fig. 7a) and the generated traces (Fig. 7b). Here, we can observe that similar to the ASCADf case, the generated traces can preserve the leakages from the original traces.

In general, from the experiments conducted on these three datasets, we can clearly observe that the diffusion model can generate new traces that can preserve and even amplified the important leakages from the original dataset in the known mask setting.

6 Unknown Mask Setting: Profiling Attack

We will first provide the framework when using DDPM in a profiling attack, followed by the experimental results. As mentioned earlier, we will be using the ID leakage model throughout this section.

6.1 Framework for Profiling Setting

In this section, we explore the effectiveness of using a diffusion model in the profiling attack setting. Figure 8 depicts the overall framework of using a diffusion model in a typical profiling setting. The framework for profiling can be described as follows:

1. Use a dimensionality reduction on the profiling traces to obtain its corresponding latent embeddings.
2. Train the diffusion models with the profiling latent embeddings.
3. Generate new latent embeddings with the trained diffusion model. If necessary, we can also normalize the generated traces as post-processing.
4. Use these new latent embeddings with the original latent embeddings as the new profiling set for the profiling attack.

We choose Principle Component Analysis (PCA) as the dimensionality reduction technique. For each of the datasets, we pick the dimension that managed to recover the key with the least $NTGE$ required. Therefore, for each dimension ranging from 8 to 48 with an interval of 8, we apply PCA and subsequently perform TA.

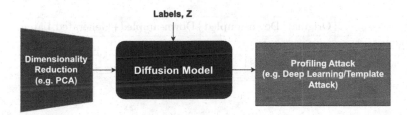

Fig. 8. Framework for using diffusion model in Profiling attack. Z is defined to be the hypothesis sensitive variable (e.g., $Z = Sbox(pt \oplus k^*)$)

We note here that the labels used to guide the diffusion model are the same as the ones used in the profiling attack. This means that this framework is in an unknown mask setting, unlike the previous framework in Sect. 5.1. The label y is the hypothetical sensitive variable Z.

In order to test the efficacy of the diffusion model for profiling attacks, we apply TAs in various settings. We use TA over the deep learning-based attack, as the deep learning-based attack has too many factors that could affect the $NTGE$ attained. For example, even when using the same architecture, the weights are randomly initialized, which could result in different performances in two different training. Therefore, TA is a much better baseline for exploring diffusion models' effectiveness than using deep learning-based profiling attacks.

Various Setting Tested. We apply TA in three different settings. Firstly, we perform TA on the original dataset. We denote this as Original. Next, we decrease the dataset to balance every class to the minimum number of traces within a class. For example, in ASCADf, the class 213 obtains the least number of traces with 139 traces. Therefore, we downsample every class to 139 and obtain traces of size $139 \times 256 = 35584$ for profiling. This is to simulate when there is a lack of profiling traces. Then, we run TA on this downsampled dataset. We call this setting Downsampled. As the next step, we want to determine if using the diffusion model to generate new latent embedding would help in TA. We simply double the traces of each class within the downsampled dataset. We denote this scenario as Downsampled+Generated Latent. Subsequently, we train all our diffusion models with a batch size of 200, a learning rate of 0.001, and 2000 epochs for each dataset experimented.

6.2 Experiment Results for Profiling Attacks

ASCADf. We consider the use of PCA to compress the dimension of the traces to 24 as it successfully breaks the dataset and obtains the least number of $NTGE$ with TA. We presented the results in Table 2. Here, we observed that Downsampled+Generated Latent slight improvement over the Downsampled scenario. This shows that when the adversary has the diffusion model and with limited traces, it could improve the attack.

Table 2. $NTGE$ for ASCADf when applying TA in the various setting.

	Original	Downsampled	Downsampled+Generated Latent
$NTGE$	1,194	1,552	1,531
Dataset Size	45,000	35,584	71,168

ASCADr. For ASCADr, we compress the dimension to 16. We show the performance in Table 3. Similarly to the above, we see an improvement in $NTGE$ when adding newly generated latent from the diffusion model into the down-sampled dataset. Since there is a reduction of approximately 200 traces in the $NTGE$. This shows that the generated latent/traces with the diffusion model could help to slightly improve the performance when the number of traces is limited to build the template.

Table 3. $NTGE$ for ASCADr when applying TA in the various setting.

	Original	Downsampled	Downsampled+Generated Latent
$NTGE$	3,953	4,742	4,598
Dataset Size	45,000	34,816	69,632

ASCADf_desync50: Here, we consider desynchronization within the ASCADf dataset, denoted as ASCADf_desync50. The dataset is created by considering random desynchronization up to 50 sample points in each trace within the raw traces before extracting the 700 sample points. For ASCADf_desync50, we reduce the dimension of the traces to a size of 48. Table 4 shows the performance results of the TA for ASCADf_desync50. Surprisingly, we observe that Downsampled+Generated Latent obtained a significant decrease in $NTGE$. The $NTGE$ decreases by around 4000 traces, which is almost half of the $NTGE$ attained when training with the original dataset. When adding the new latent created by the diffusion model into the downsampled dataset, it even attained the best $NTGE$ out of all the three settings. This shows that the diffusion model is effective even in desynchronized datasets.

Table 4. $NTGE$ for ASCADf_desync50 when applying TA in the various setting.

	Original	Downsampled	Downsampled + Generated Latent
$NTGE$	9,606	9,017	5,730
Dataset Size	45,000	35,584	71,168

7   Conclusion and Future Works

In this work, we have investigated and explored the applicability of using the DDPM approach for artificial trace generation in the context of SCA. We have conducted the study on two different frameworks, namely the known and unknown mask settings. We then performed the experiments on several datasets to create a new set of traces using the diffusion model. Our experimental results have shown that the generated traces can preserve the original leakages in the known mask setting. We have also demonstrated that in the unknown mask setting, the diffusion model can create artificial data that can help to improve the profiling attack, suggesting that leakages are learned within the generated data. In the future, we will investigate more on improving the performance of the proposed DDPM approach; for example, one direction is to optimize or speed up the sampling process. We would like to investigate if this can also be adapted for portability scenarios on custom traces from different setups.

Acknowledgment. This research is supported by the National Research Foundation, Singapore, and Cyber Security Agency of Singapore under its National Cybersecurity Research & Development Programme (Cyber-Hardware Forensic & Assurance Evaluation R&D Programme ¡NRF2018NCRNCR009-0001). Any opinions, findings and conclusions or recommendations expressed in this material are those of the author(s) and do not reflect the view of National Research Foundation, Singapore and Cyber Security Agency of Singapore.

A   Appendix

A.1   Random Search Hyperparameters for Autoencoder

We conducted random search to find hyperparameters for the autoencoder. In the following table, we listed down the range of values used for each parameters (Table 5).

Table 5. Range for hyperparameter random search

Parameters	Start	Max	Step
Number of Layers	2	6	1
Number of Batch Size	64	2048	32
Embedding Size	128	Trace length	32
Epoch Size	40	100	1
Learning Rate (10^x)	−5	−2	1
Node Size per Layer	32	2048	32

A.2   Hyperparameters Used on Autoencoder

In the following tables, we reported the hyperparameters found through random search (Table 6).

Table 6. Hyperparameters used for each dataset, found through random search

Parameters	CW	ASCADf	ASCADr
Number of Layers	3	3	3
Number of Batch Size	896	800	1536
Embedding Size	992	192	256
Epoch Size	86	97	97
Learning Rate (10^x)	−4	−3	−3
Size of Nodes	[928, 448, 992]	[704, 992, 192]	[704, 992, 256]
Correlation	0.87	0.97	0.85

References

1. Agrawal, D., Archambeault, B., Rao, J.R., Rohatgi, P.: The EM side—channel(s). In: Kaliski, B.S., Koç, K., Paar, C. (eds.) CHES 2002. LNCS, vol. 2523, pp. 29–45. Springer, Heidelberg (2003). https://doi.org/10.1007/3-540-36400-5_4
2. Benadjila, R., Prouff, E., Strullu, R., Cagli, E., Dumas, C.: Deep learning for side-channel analysis and introduction to ASCAD database. J. Cryptogr. Eng. **10**(2), 163–188 (2020). https://doi.org/10.1007/s13389-019-00220-8
3. Brier, E., Clavier, C., Olivier, F.: Correlation power analysis with a leakage model. In: Joye, M., Quisquater, J.-J. (eds.) CHES 2004. LNCS, vol. 3156, pp. 16–29. Springer, Heidelberg (2004). https://doi.org/10.1007/978-3-540-28632-5_2
4. Cagli, E., Dumas, C., Prouff, E.: Convolutional neural networks with data augmentation against jitter-based countermeasures. In: Fischer, W., Homma, N. (eds.) CHES 2017. LNCS, vol. 10529, pp. 45–68. Springer, Cham (2017). https://doi.org/10.1007/978-3-319-66787-4_3
5. Choudary, O., Kuhn, M.G.: Efficient template attacks. In: Francillon, A., Rohatgi, P. (eds.) CARDIS 2013. LNCS, vol. 8419, pp. 253–270. Springer, Cham (2014). https://doi.org/10.1007/978-3-319-08302-5_17
6. Dhariwal, P., Nichol, A.: Diffusion models beat GANs on image synthesis (2021)
7. Goodfellow, I.J., et al.: Generative Adversarial Networks (2014)
8. Hendrycks, D., Gimpel, K.: Gaussian error linear units (GELUs) (2023)
9. Ho, J., Jain, A., Abbeel, P.: Denoising diffusion probabilistic models (2020)
10. Ho, J., Salimans, T.: Classifier-free diffusion guidance (2022)
11. Karayalcin, S., Krouk, M., Wu, L., Picek, S., Perin, G.: It's a kind of magic: a novel conditional GAN framework for efficient profiling side-channel analysis. Cryptology ePrint Archive (2023)
12. Klinker, F.: Exponential moving average versus moving exponential average. Math. Semesterber. **58**(1), 97–107 (2010). https://doi.org/10.1007/s00591-010-0080-8
13. Kocher, P., Jaffe, J., Jun, B.: Differential power analysis. In: Wiener, M. (ed.) CRYPTO 1999. LNCS, vol. 1666, pp. 388–397. Springer, Heidelberg (1999). https://doi.org/10.1007/3-540-48405-1_25
14. Li, H., Perin, G.: A systematic study of data augmentation for protected AES implementations. Cryptology ePrint Archive (2023)
15. Luo, C.: Understanding diffusion models: a unified perspective (2022)
16. Mukhtar, N., Batina, L., Picek, S., Kong, Y.: Fake it till you make it: data augmentation using generative adversarial networks for all the crypto you need on small devices. In: Galbraith, S.D. (ed.) CT-RSA 2022. LNCS, vol. 13161, pp. 297–321. Springer, Cham (2022). https://doi.org/10.1007/978-3-030-95312-6_13
17. Nichol, A., Dhariwal, P.: Improved denoising diffusion probabilistic models (2021)
18. O'Flynn, C., Chen, Z.D.: ChipWhisperer: an open-source platform for hardware embedded security research. In: Prouff, E. (ed.) COSADE 2014. LNCS, vol. 8622, pp. 243–260. Springer, Cham (2014). https://doi.org/10.1007/978-3-319-10175-0_17
19. Picek, S., Heuser, A., Jovic, A., Bhasin, S., Regazzoni, F.: The curse of class imbalance and conflicting metrics with machine learning for side-channel evaluations. IACR Trans. Cryptogr. Hardware Embed. Syst. 209–237 (2019)
20. Rombach, R., Blattmann, A., Lorenz, D., Esser, P., Ommer, B.: High-resolution image synthesis with latent diffusion models (2022)
21. Ronneberger, O., Fischer, P., Brox, T.: U-net: convolutional networks for biomedical image segmentation (2015)

22. Standaert, F.-X., Malkin, T.G., Yung, M.: A unified framework for the analysis of side-channel key recovery attacks. In: Joux, A. (ed.) EUROCRYPT 2009. LNCS, vol. 5479, pp. 443–461. Springer, Heidelberg (2009). https://doi.org/10.1007/978-3-642-01001-9_26
23. Wang, P., et al.: Enhancing the Performance of Practical Profiling Side-Channel Attacks Using Conditional Generative Adversarial Networks (2020)
24. Wu, Y., He, K.: Group normalization (2018)

Diversity Algorithms for Laser Fault Injection

Marina Krček[1][(✉)] and Thomas Ordas[2]

[1] Delft University of Technology, Delft, The Netherlands
m.krcek@tudelft.nl
[2] STMicroelectronics, Grenoble, France

Abstract. Before third-party evaluation and certification, manufacturers often conduct internal security evaluations on secure hardware devices, including fault injection (FI). Within this process, FI aims to identify parameter combinations that reveal device vulnerabilities. The impracticality of conducting an exhaustive search over FI parameters has prompted the development of advanced and guided algorithms. However, these proposed methods often focus on a specific, critical region, which is beneficial for attack scenarios requiring a single optimal FI parameter combination.

In this work, we introduce two novel metrics that align better with the goal of identifying multiple optima. These metrics consider the number of unique vulnerable locations and clusters (regions). Furthermore, we present two methods promoting diversity in tested parameter combinations - Grid Memetic Algorithm (GridMA) and Evolution Strategy (ES). Our findings reveal that these diversity methods, though identifying fewer vulnerabilities overall than the Memetic Algorithm (MA), still outperform Random Search (RS), identifying at least ≈8× more vulnerabilities. Using our novel metrics, we observe that the number of distinct vulnerable locations is similar across all three evolutionary algorithms, with ≈30% increase over RS. Importantly, ES and GridMA prove superior in discovering multiple vulnerable regions, with ES identifying ≈55% more clusters than the worst-performing MA.

Keywords: Laser Fault Injection · Parameter Search · Evolutionary Algorithms · Diversity Algorithms · Multiple Optima

1 Introduction

Small embedded devices frequently employ cryptographic algorithms to provide security. According to Kerckhoff's principle, it is expected that security is intact when the secret key is unknown, even if all the other information about the cryptographic system is public. Consequently, these algorithms are often mathematically secure, rendering brute-force attacks impractical. Regardless, implementation attacks, such as side-channel attacks (SCA) and fault injection (FI) attacks, can potentially lead to a successful security breach of such cryptographic systems. Side-channel attacks are passive, with the attacker measuring

© The Author(s), under exclusive license to Springer Nature Switzerland AG 2024
M. Andreoni (Ed.): ACNS 2024 Workshops, LNCS 14586, pp. 121–138, 2024.
https://doi.org/10.1007/978-3-031-61486-6_8

the time [12], power consumption [11], or other side-channel data emanating from the target device. Given a correlation between the processed data and measured side-channel information, the attacker can obtain secret information. On the other hand, fault injection attacks are active, where the attacker purposely interacts with the device, inducing errors during the execution of the underlying algorithm. Specifically, the attack can use external sources, such as electromagnetic radiation [18], lasers [26], temperature [9], and voltage glitching [10], to manipulate data in memory, skip instructions, or alter instructions themselves. These implementation attacks are commonly used in security evaluations and are consequently extensively investigated [1,23]. The objective is to establish an enhanced and automated evaluation process that surpasses the current standard in terms of efficiency. The new algorithms should excel in uncovering more potential vulnerabilities while making more efficient use of available resources or possibly even reducing the required resources.

We focus on laser fault injections (LFI), as introduced by Skorobogatov et al. [26]. The issue with laser injection (and other types of fault injections) comes from the injection parameters determined by equipment. With the laser, we have to define the location of the laser shot on the targeted hardware device (x and y coordinates), the distance from the microscope lens, which is commonly used with lasers, and, lastly, we also have the laser settings, such as laser *intensity*, *delay*, and *pulse width*. Additionally, lasers can have pulses that demand several more parameters to define. Another critical component of successful injections is the trigger on when to perform the injection. In security evaluation, the worst scenario is often considered, where it is assumed that we have open access to the targeted device, and the trigger can be placed at any point in the execution. Obviously, there are *many parameters* we should consider. Additionally, the *possible values and combinations* of those parameters increase to the extent that exhaustive search is not feasible for security evaluation or attack.

In the attack, the adversary aims to find the parameters that lead to exploitable fault injection effects. These desired effects also depend on the method for the attack, where some of the popular attacks are differential fault analysis (DFA) [3], statistical fault attack (SFA) [7], and statistical ineffective fault attacks (SIFA) [6]. Each attack can require different characteristics of the FI effects. Still, some commonly desired and possibly exploitable faults include causing the device to skip instructions or change values in memory [1]. This work does not address identifying exploitable faults but focuses on a scenario within the internal security evaluation. During the security evaluation, a target characterization is performed, striving to uncover all vulnerabilities that can later be categorized based on their level of critical exploitability. While executing an exhaustive search would ensure that all possible vulnerabilities are observed, this process is not feasible as there are many products to be evaluated, and the search is impractical even for a single target. The aim is then adjusted to find as many vulnerabilities as possible within reasonable time and resources. Therefore, the FI parameter search is a process that should observe many vulnerabilities and provide high confidence that little to no vulnerabilities are overlooked. Instead of an exhaustive search, the location on the target is often searched in a grid-like manner using the same laser settings. Defined laser settings could come from previous experience, which might be misleading if the target or the bench is entirely new [28]. If more options for laser settings are tested over the whole target area, this process becomes time-consuming, so alternatively, a random search is applied. However, both methods could omit parameter sets that lead to faults. In grid search, while the location is relatively thoroughly inspected, fixing the laser settings can contribute to overlooking many vulnerabilities. By including different laser settings, the search converges to an exhaustive search where the security analysts aim to reduce the search space based on previous knowledge, but the execution time for these algorithms could still be measured in weeks. On the other hand, random search is unreliable as different runs can lead to very different observations, which causes misrepresentation of the target's security level. Therefore, there is an incentive to improve the process of exploring the FI parameter search space more efficiently in an automated way.

Evolutionary algorithms (EAs) were explored for laser fault injection [14], voltage glitching [4,21,22], and electromagnetic fault injection [16,24] since laser fault injections are not the only type of injections suffering from the previously described issues. From the machine learning domain, hyperparameter optimization techniques [27], reinforcement learning [17] and Generative Adversarial Networks (GANs) [25] were also investigated. Additionally, the prediction ability of machine learning methods was explored for portability issues in the FI parameter search [13] and estimating the full target characterization [28].

The issue with aforementioned search algorithms, like evolutionary algorithms and tuning techniques, lies in their tendency to converge on a single vulnerable area as they are designed to obtain a single optimal solution. Previous works show a significant increase in the observed faults clustered in one sensitive region [16,21]. While that can be highly effective for attackers, we focus on security evaluation, where identifying multiple vulnerable regions is deemed a more favorable outcome. To better assess algorithm success in parameter search concerning the security evaluation goals, we propose to use the number of unique locations (x-y) and clusters with faults as additional metrics. We investigate the performance of several algorithms: random search, memetic algorithm, and two novel algorithms not explored before in the FI context - Grid Memetic Algorithm (GridMA) and Evolution Strategy (ES). The new algorithms are introduced as they promote the diversity of the parameter combinations. This diversity aims to achieve a more diverse search, uncovering distant vulnerabilities and identifying multiple optima instead of a single sensitive region. Experiments are performed with laser fault injections but should be suitable for other fault injection types.

Our main contributions are:

- We propose two methods that promote diversity among the tested FI parameter combinations. Promoted diversity ensures fewer vulnerabilities are overlooked, and multiple optima are uncovered during the search.
- We investigate other aspects of the algorithm performance for the FI parameter search, such as unique locations and clusters.

- The results show that the evolutionary algorithms find ≈30% more unique vulnerable locations than random search.
- The GridMA and ES algorithms found around 41% and 55% more vulnerable clusters than the worst-performing MA in this aspect, respectively. Thus, the diversity algorithms help determine more vulnerable regions.

2   Preliminaries

2.1   Random Search (RS)

Random Search (RS) is a widely used optimization method when exhaustive search is impractical. In the context of FI parameter search, it explores a pre-defined search space by randomly selecting parameter values and assessing their performance, with each value having an equal probability of selection. We ensure that only unique parameter combinations are considered, eliminating duplicates.

2.2   Memetic Algorithm (MA)

The memetic algorithm (MA) enhances the genetic algorithm (GA) by incor-porating local search [19]. We apply the local search at the end of each GA iteration, constituting the first generation of memetic algorithms. This specific method has been successfully utilized in previous research [14,16]. The flow of the MA is depicted in Fig. 1. MA is a population-based optimization technique, operating on a set of individuals, each representing a potential solution to a specific optimization problem. The algorithm begins by generating an initial population using an *initialization method*, where a random sampling approach is often used. The algorithm then uses a problem-specific *fitness function* to evaluate each solution's performance. After evaluation, the genetic operators, including selection, crossover, and mutation, that drive the learning process are performed. The *selector operator* identifies solutions from the current popula-tion for reproduction. Usually, the best-performing solutions are favored as they are more likely to yield improved solutions. The selected solutions, called parent solutions, undergo the *crossover operator*, which combines their traits to cre-ate one or more offspring solutions. The new solutions (offspring) undergo the *mutation operator*, which introduces random variations into the new solutions. The mutation probability is commonly kept low, preventing the algorithm from acting like random sampling. The process generates a new population that con-tinues into another algorithm iteration. To ensure the best-performing solutions are not lost, *elitism* is employed. Elitism explicitly preserves one or more of the best solutions from the current population for the next generation. Lastly, some solutions are selected for further improvement using the *local search*. In this work, we use the memetic algorithm introduced in [14], where the algorithm incorporates the Hooke-Jeeves as local search [8]. The algorithm runs until a predefined *termination condition* is satisfied. These termination conditions com-monly consider the number of iterations or evaluations for ending the execution.

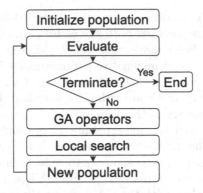

Fig. 1. Flow of the Memetic Algorithm.

2.3   Clustering Method

In the analysis, we use a clustering method called Mean Shift [5], an unsupervised clustering algorithm designed to identify clusters in a continuous distribution of data points. It is a centroid-based algorithm that updates candidates for centroids by computing the mean of points within a specific region (referred to as the *bandwidth*). Subsequently, these candidates are filtered in a post-processing stage to eliminate nearly identical centroids, forming the final set of centroids. We opted for the Mean Shift clustering algorithm because, unlike some other popular methods such as K-Means [15], it does not require users to predefine the number of clusters. While several different algorithms share this characteristic, we chose Mean Shift due to its simplicity as a centroid-based algorithm with only one hyperparameter. We believe it will provide satisfactory results for our analysis. However, we do not claim Mean Shift as the superior clustering algorithm. Note that the considered algorithms were those provided by a Python package called *scikit-learn* [20] to enable quick implementation and usage, as clustering is not the main topic of this work.

3   Related Work

Carpi et al. [4] investigated various search strategies for voltage glitch parameters, specifically the glitch shape and timing, for a successful FI attack. They explored glitch voltage and length with Monte Carlo (random), FastBoxing, Adaptive Zoom&Bound, and a Genetic Algorithm (GA). The genetic algorithm, without fine-tuning, required more measurements than the superior Adaptive Zoom& Bound algorithm. Picek et al. [22] extended the GA for the same voltage glitch parameters by employing a specialized crossover operator and selection mechanism, finding more faults than random search. Later, Picek et al. [21] introduced a memetic algorithm considering three voltage glitching parameters, namely glitch length, voltage, and offset. The authors mentioned the impracticality of specific algorithms used in previous work [4] due to increased dimensionality, excluding them from comparison. Their objective was to efficiently identify favorable parameters within minimal time, seeking both successful parameter combinations and regions with consistent behavioral outcomes. Maldini et al. [16] increased the parameter search space by optimizing five parameters for Electromagnetic Fault Injection (EMFI) using a memetic algorithm. Krček et al. [14] demonstrated the effectiveness of a similar memetic algorithm for laser fault injection (LFI). These studies showcased the efficacy of the memetic algorithm across various FI types. Werner et al. [27] employed two hyperparameter optimization techniques from machine learning to enhance the parameter search for voltage glitching. They proposed a two-stage optimization strategy to reduce the dimensionality of the parameter space, similar to Carpi et al. [4]. Rais-Ali et al. [24] compared three different methods for EMFI, with the GA consistently outperforming the others in identifying areas of interest. The authors emphasize that, from an attacker's perspective, the goal is to identify a single exploitable fault using a specific FI parameter set. However, in the evaluation context, the objective is to ensure device security without excessive time investment, requiring a high-dimensional search to avoid overlooking potential parameter combinations. In [16,21,24], the authors evaluated performance based on the number of observed vulnerabilities, considering the notion of distinct regions and faults. We introduce diversity methods within the evolutionary approach to improve the algorithms' ability to discover more distinct regions with vulnerabilities. Related work on voltage glitching parameter search typically involved optimization of two or three parameters, while EMFI and LFI examined five. We optimize the same five parameters for LFI, performing a high-dimensional parameter search.

Wu et al. [28] focused on laser settings' impact on a specific building block. The authors noted that the complete characterization took over a week to execute. This underscores the need for faster and more efficient algorithms in the field. However, their work differs from ours, as our research investigates fault injection considering five distinct parameters, intending to uncover vulnerabilities across various building blocks within an integrated circuit (IC). Krček et al. [13] explored the transferability of results to different samples of the same target using decision tree models, falling outside the scope of this work for comparison as this work focuses on improving the parameter search without prior knowledge. Lastly, Moradi et al. [17] and Sedaghatbaf et al. [25] applied reinforcement learning and Generative Adversarial Networks (GANs), respectively, for efficiently exploring the fault injection space in simulations for adaptive cruise control systems in autonomous vehicles domain. These techniques could potentially extend to fault injection on hardware devices, aligning with our work.

Comparing all methods from the mentioned related work is time-consuming and complex. Hence, we leave this task to future work, recognizing the importance of unifying and evaluating these advanced methods to determine the state-of-the-art approach for parameter search in the scope of security evaluation, target characterization, and FI attacks. In this study, we compare new algorithms with random search and memetic algorithm, previously employed for high-dimensional parameter search on EMFI and LFI.

4   Diversity Algorithms

This section explains the newly proposed diversity algorithms that should help identify multiple vulnerable regions within the FI parameter search.

4.1   Grid Memetic Algorithm (GridMA)

We propose a novel approach, named the Grid Memetic Algorithm, that involves partitioning the target area for exploration into a grid and running the previously explained memetic algorithm within each grid region. The primary objective of the GridMA approach is to ensure attention (time and evaluations) of the algorithm to all target regions, mitigating the risk of overlooking vulnerabilities in specific $(x\text{-}y)$ locations. For instance, if the target area is divided into a 3×3 grid, resulting in nine distinct regions, GridMA executes the MA independently in each region during a single run. As the search space size within each grid region decreased, we reduced the MA hyperparameters, specifically the population and elite sizes. GridMA represents a minor adaptation to the established MA. Nevertheless, it is a valuable initial step in evaluating diversity algorithms, precisely when we aim to obtain multiple vulnerable target regions.

4.2   Evolution Strategy (ES)

Evolution Strategy, like genetic algorithms, belongs to the class of evolutionary algorithms inspired by the principles of natural evolution [2]. The initial version of ES consisted of a single-parent solution from which one offspring was produced through a mutation-like procedure. The superior solution between the parent and offspring is preserved, and it resumes the same iterative process until it fulfills specific termination criteria. These termination conditions align with those described for MA in Sect. 2.2, consisting of attributes such as the number of iterations, evaluations, or acquiring a specified fitness level. Over time, ES has evolved, and in its more general form, it adopts the notation of $(\mu \overset{+}{,} \lambda)$-ES. For instance, the original version can be denoted as $(1 + 1)$-ES, suggesting the presence of only one parent and one offspring in the process. Thus, μ represents the number of parents, and λ indicates the number of offspring. Additionally, a μ/ρ notation can be used for parents, where μ denotes existing parents, and ρ indicates the number of parents selected for producing offspring. Typically, ρ is less than or equal to μ, meaning that a subset of the best individuals is chosen for reproduction. In the notation, we use symbols + or , to indicate whether the solutions selected for the following generation are derived from both parents and offspring $(\mu + \lambda)$ or the parents (μ) are discarded, and only the offspring (λ), regardless of their fitness, continue to the next generation.

In the context of the described notation, we employ the $(\mu + \lambda)$-ES. The original, $(1 + 1)$-ES, using one single parent and an offspring, still converges to one optimal solution. Thus, to achieve diversity and reduce the risk of focusing on a single optimal solution, we set $\mu > 1$, effectively creating a population of size μ as employed in MA. The initial set of solutions is distributed across different locations, and in each iteration, new offspring are generated from each of these parent solutions as we set $\lambda > 1$. Consequently, ES maintains a population of diverse solutions that evolve through iterations. This iterative process may lead to finding distinct solution clusters representing local optima. Thus, by employing ES, we expect to decrease the chances of overlooking vulnerabilities within the target area and observe more distinct solutions with optimal fitness.

5   Experimental Setup

5.1   Target

In collaboration with STMicroelectronics, we utilize their products for our experiments. Due to confidentiality reasons, we cannot disclose the details of the targets and the utilized laser bench. The target for our experiments is an IC constructed with 40nm technology. Since we use lasers for fault injection, mechanical thinning, a standard procedure, was part of the preparation for the experiments. During security evaluation, test programs can be deployed on the targeted products. The program running on our target device is a test program where data words are loaded into a register from the non-volatile memory (NVM). This test program can commonly be a part of the functionalities occurring within different algorithms on these devices. The target has no security countermeasures as the purpose here is not an attack breaking the device's security and countermeasures. Additionally, this provides the worst-case scenario. The implementation is done in the C programming language, and the pseudocode is displayed in Pseudocode 1.1. The pseudocode shows calls to three functions, where the first function is the `trigger_event`. The trigger event is a monitored event used to trigger the laser shot to inject faults at the desired time. In this case, the injection is aimed during the execution of the following function. That function loads the data from the NVM into a register. Lastly, we read the register and compare the value with the expected data. There is a fault if the register value has changed (fault class *fail*). On the other hand, if the injection was unsuccessful and the data is unmodified, equal to the expected value, then we give this response a fault class *pass*. Lastly, if there is no response from the device due to a time-out error or reset, we categorize this as a fault class *mute*. Note that the IC was reset to the initial state after each injection to provide a clean condition for each injection.

Pseudocode 1.1. Pseudocode of the program running on the target device.

```
...
trigger_event ()
load_register () // injection here
read_register ()
...
```

The FI parameter search is done on the following five parameters - *x, y, delay, laser pulse width,* and *intensity*. These parameters are commonly used in literature and practice during a security evaluation [13, 16]. We use a subset of the available values for each of the five parameters, defined according to the known layout and target cartography. Step sizes are defined based on the minimum possible step according to the utilized bench equipment, and the target area size includes different building blocks of the IC. The intervals are kept the same for all experiments. While we cannot share the parameter intervals as they are specific to the product and laser bench, we note that there are 370 772 710 possible combinations of the parameter values. The exhaustive search with the defined subset of possible values will take around 643 days if we consider that one laser shot takes ≈0.15 s.

While we focus on a single target in this study, the parameter search algorithms we introduce are versatile and applicable across various targets, bench configurations, and FI types. On average, the relative performance of these algorithms is expected to remain similar across mentioned scenarios. The obtained target responses guide these algorithms. Therefore, regardless of the selected target and setup, they strive to identify optimal solutions within the current setup and measured responses. The extent of improvements is limited by the finite number of detectable vulnerabilities associated with a specific target and bench setup.

5.2   Algorithm Details

In all our experiments, we specified a maximum limit of 6 000 evaluations of unique FI parameter combinations as a termination condition. Since we perform injection five times with the same parameter combination, we allow 30 000 laser shots. The number of evaluations is a practical upper bound on the algorithm's execution time. Previous work [13] indicates that a similar evaluation count leads to successful convergence, thus further justifying its selection.

In our approach, as we perform five measurements with the same parameter combination, we can acquire distinct fault class responses given the same parameters. Thus, there is a slight variation in our fault classification compared to related work. In our results, we present classes so that if there is even a single *fail* response within the measurements, we consider it a critical outcome and label it under *fail comb.* notation, signifying a *fail combination*. This approach aggregates all *fail* occurrences, disregarding the specific combinations that led to them. A more fine-grained categorization might be beneficial if we consider a specific attack, as parameter combinations with consistent outcomes might be more suitable for attacks. However, since we are in a security evaluation scenario, any occurrence of a *fail* response is considered critical. Other classes we include are those with *mute* response, a combination of *mute* and *pass* referred to as *mute_pass*, and lastly, there is a *pass* class where only *pass* class occurred in five measurements. The fitness function for all algorithms is calculated as

$$fitness = \frac{f_P \cdot N_P + f_M \cdot N_M + f_F \cdot N_F}{N_P + N_M + N_F},$$

where f_P, f_M, and f_F correspond to the fitness values assigned to the fault classes *pass*, *mute*, and *fail*, respectively. Similarly, N_P, N_M, and N_F represent the frequency of these classes occurrences within the number of measurements for a specific parameter combination. The sum of N_P, N_M, and N_F constitutes the total number of measurements per parameter combination. This fitness function definition follows the previous works [13,14]. In our case, the fitness values for f_P, f_M, and f_F are 1, 2, 10, respectively. These values differ slightly from prior works, as we choose to create a more pronounced distinction in fitness value between each fault class. This design decision emphasizes the significance of any *fail* combination by assigning it a significantly higher fitness value. Before evaluating the entire population, we conduct a sorting operation using a greedy approach that considers the Manhattan distance between different locations of the FI parameter combinations within the population as described in [14].

MA Hyperparameters. We employ a population of size 100, with an *elite_size* of 10. The initialization method employs a random sampling strategy while preventing duplicates. For selection, we implement the roulette wheel method. We use uniform crossover and a uniform mutation with a mutation probability of 0.05. Lastly, the Hooke-Jeeves algorithm is applied for local search. Note that the hyperparameters in our experiments remain the same and have been taken based on information from previous work [14].

GridMA Hyperparameters. We dedicated additional experiments to exploring the hyperparameters of the GridMA algorithm, as it is a newly proposed method. We performed a minor hyperparameter search focused on the grid size, the population size, and the elite size of the MA. This section outlines the hyperparameters for the final version of the GridMA, whose results are shown in Sect. 6. The MA instances running in each grid have the same hyperparameters as described in Sect. 5.2, except for the mentioned hyperparameters that we were able to decrease due to the reduced scope of exploration within each grid region. Accordingly, the population size is set at 30 individuals, with an *elite_size* of 5. We divide the area in 4×4 grid, effectively conducting a total of 16 MA algorithms during a single run of GridMA. Since we maintain the total number of evaluations at 6000 parameter combinations, each grid region is limited to evaluating only 375 FI parameter combinations.

ES Hyperparameters. Evolution Strategy is a new approach, so we explored several hyperparameters. Specifically, we assessed the algorithm's performance concerning the number of parents and offspring and the mutation probability. While we quickly obtained reported results, further fine-tuning may improve performance. The reported results are derived from ES employing 40 parent solutions and 5 offspring with the initial generation of parents established through random sampling. This algorithm uses the mutation operator as the sole source of introducing solution modifications, so a higher mutation probability will be necessary. We observed that the mutation probability of 0.4, much higher than used with MA, produces the best results without converging to a purely random search approach. The mutation probability applies to each specific dimension within the parameter combinations. For example, with 40% probability, mutation will occur from uniformly distributed values of the given parameter. Uniform mutation encourages more substantial modification, allowing more 'jumps', particularly beneficial in the context of FI parameter search, as there are more non-vulnerable areas than vulnerable ones. In Sect. 6.4, we explore several modifications to the ES algorithm, including the Gaussian mutation approach, which is more commonly utilized to ensure a higher probability of local changes.

6   Experimental Results

This section presents results from applying the described algorithms to the same IC and laser bench. We aim to identify more locations with a *fail* outcome and uncover multiple vulnerable regions. To achieve this, we avoid restricting our search to a $2D$ location exploration, as it could overlook numerous parameter combinations due to the need for fixed laser settings. To effectively assess and identify algorithms that perform well for our objective, we compare them not only based on the observed $5D$ parameter combinations with a *fail* outcome but also on the number of unique locations ($2D$) and clusters. We executed each algorithm five times and reported the average results to ensure statistically relevant observations.

6.1   Number of Unique Parameter Combinations ($5D$)

We initially assess the number of unique parameter combinations with *fail* outcomes, where we use percentages from total tested combinations as in previous work for a more straightforward comparison. The results, shown in Table 1, reveal a comparable increase in *fail* responses between random search (RS) and memetic algorithm (MA) to the reported results in [13,14,16]. The MA identified ≈55.6× more FI parameter combinations leading to *fail* response than RS. In contrast, the two new methods, which provide greater diversity in the population of the FI parameters, obtained a lower percentage of *fail* responses compared to the MA. Compared to RS, we still find ≈12.4× more *fails* with GridMA, and ≈7.8× more with the ES. This decrease in the percentage arises from GridMA's exploration of areas where vulnerabilities might not exist. The ES, which relies solely on mutation, introduces more randomness than the MA, leading to a decrease in the number of identified vulnerabilities. Moreover, each parent evolved independently, resulting in more dispersed parameters and less exploitation of sensitive locations. These features should enhance our current objective but are shown to impact this metric negatively. Considering only the number of unique $5D$ parameter combinations tested, MA outperforms the other tested algorithms. However, the evolutionary approaches with diversity still offer advantages and should be preferred over random search.

Table 1. The average percentage of observed fault classes from all tested parameter combinations (6 000) using four different algorithms on the same IC. The average is calculated over five runs.

	RS	MA	GridMA	ES
fail comb.	0.61%	33.84%	7.54%	4.77%
mute	1.23%	3.23%	4.44%	4.53%
mute_pass	0.79%	1.21%	2.24%	2.83%
pass	97.36%	61.72%	85.79%	87.88%

6.2   Number of Unique Locations (2*D*)

In this work, we explore other metrics that could be used to evaluate the performance of different parameter search algorithms employed for fault injection. As we explain, MA converges commonly to one region sensitive to the utilized FI type and exploits it, leading to many observed FI parameter combinations with *fail* outcome. These parameter combinations come from a cluster of close x-y locations that can be detected visually (see Fig. 1b in [16] and Fig. 2 in [21]). In security evaluation, there should be a certain confidence that not many vulnerabilities are missed during the assessment of the IC. Also, we aim to find multiple regions with vulnerabilities, so we explore algorithms that promote diversity as it should help produce vulnerabilities distant in the utilized 5*D* space. More importantly, we want distant solutions when looking at the observed vulnerabilities' location (x-y). Thus, in Table 2, we report the number of unique parameter combinations with different fault classes and the number of unique locations per fault class from those parameter combinations. The table has two columns per algorithm, with the first showing the numbers from all the tested parameter combinations and the second showing the number of unique x-y locations. We also calculate what we refer to as location coverage, dividing the number of unique locations (2*D*) by the number of total tested unique 5*D* parameter combinations. This number shows the ratio of covered area within the tested parameter combinations. The numbers are rather small if we look at the absolute possible locations instead of relative to the tested parameters. To put it into perspective, from all possible combinations ($\approx$370 million), we only test 0.00162% with 6 000 combinations. Unique tested locations from all possible locations (2*D*) per algorithm are 4.27%, 1.67%, 2.02%, and 3.07% for RS, MA, GridMA, and ES, respectively. We see an increase in the absolute location coverage between different evolutionary approaches, but RS has the best result. In the table, we report the relative location coverage as it provides an easier comparison. The relation between the algorithms is the same when we compare the absolute and relative location coverage. The results show that RS has the best coverage with 97.95% as the algorithm has no guidance. The worst location coverage is with MA (38.24%), supporting the motivation for this work. GridMA and ES improve coverage with 46.36% for GridMA and 70.29% for ES. Location coverage can serve as a measure of the algorithm's confidence in not overlooking vulnerable areas. Comparing the unique locations with *fail* response between MA, GridMA, and ES, we see that the algorithms find a similar number of unique locations with *fail* - around 48, which is around 30% more than with RS (36.4). While similar in the number of unique locations with *fail* outcome, GridMA found the most unique locations on average with higher location coverage than MA. This improvement over MA is not as significant as the difference in performance between the evolutionary approaches and RS. Still, it shows the potential of diversity algorithms for security evaluation as they provide better coverage and thus confidence in identified vulnerabilities while delivering a similar improvement over RS in the number of unique, vulnerable locations.

Table 2. The average number of unique parameter combinations and x-y locations per fault class, and in total for all four algorithms. The average is calculated over five runs.

	RS		MA		GridMA		ES	
Nb. comb. | Nb. loc.	6000	5877.2	6000	2294.6	6000	2781.4	6000	4217.4
Location coverage	0.9795		0.3824		0.4636		0.7029	
fail comb.	37	36.4	2030.2	48.4	452	**49.2**	285.6	47
mute	74	73	194	60.4	266.2	70.4	271.6	93.2
mute_pass	47.4	47	72.8	45.8	134 6	61.4	169.8	67 6
pass	5841.6	5723.4	3703	2218.8	5147.2	2704.8	5273	4088.6

6.3   Number of Location Clusters

Finding distant, vulnerable locations is considered more valuable as the smaller regions could further be explored with an exhaustive search on a significantly reduced search space [24]. Thus, we compare the algorithms based on the number of observed location clusters with a specific fault class. We calculate the number of clusters using the Mean Shift clustering algorithm. The bandwidth hyperparameter for the Mean Shift algorithm defines the window/region from which the mean is calculated. We executed the clustering with different bandwidth values, precisely $0.1, 0.2, 0.3, 0.4$. With a bandwidth of 0.3, the region was large enough to categorize all the x-y points as one cluster for all fault classes. Table 3 shows the number of clusters averaged over five runs with bandwidth set to 0.1. Using the same bandwidth ensures the number of clusters is comparable as the same window size is considered. Note that if the number of clusters is more significant, the vulnerabilities are observed in more distant and distinct locations on the target, which is the desired objective. The results show that GridMA finds the most clusters with *fail* outcome, implying that the observed locations are more distant than other algorithms. GridMA and ES obtain a similar number of clusters on average, closely followed by RS. MA, on the other hand, clearly shows a smaller number of clusters observed. These results further emphasize the benefits of diversity methods for security evaluation and finding multiple regions

Table 3. The number of clusters based on Mean Shift clustering algorithm over the unique x-y locations per fault class. The bandwidth size is 0.1. The number of clusters is averaged over five runs.

	RS	MA	GridMA	ES
fail comb.	7.8	5.8	**8.2**	8
mute	11.4	8.6	9.6	10.6
mute_pass	9.6	8.4	10.8	10.2
pass	41.8	37	34.2	33.8

sensitive to the utilized FI type. We checked the clustering model's predictions visually for several cases to ensure that classified clusters are meaningful. While some more distinct locations were still clustered together using this bandwidth, the predicted clusters seemed reasonable. Moreover, we use the same bandwidth to ensure comparable results, as relative correlation is essential.

6.4 Further Exploring the Evolution Strategy Algorithm

The results show that evolutionary algorithms perform better than random search when considering the number of unique FI parameter combinations and unique locations with *fail* response. Considering the number of clusters, RS was better than MA, but the diversity algorithms were better overall. Thus, while the performance was not significantly improved using the diversity algorithms considering these metrics, the observed minor improvements show promising results. Therefore, we deem it necessary to explore these algorithms more within the scope of future work. In this section, we explore several ES versions to obtain enhanced performance.

We test the ES algorithm with a more common Gaussian mutation, which uses the Gaussian distribution to set the probabilities of each of the parameter values getting selected. The mutation probability will then be used as a standard deviation σ parameter, while the parameter's current value will be the mean μ. This mutation makes local changes more likely, while the more distant significant changes have a low probability of occurring, but not zero. We refer to this version of ES as *ES gauss*. Another modification we test is the initialization method, where we use a grid approach to set the parents of ES in distinct regions over the target area, considering only the location parameters. This way, the location parameters within the initial population are well-distributed, and the evolution should have a better chance of observing more distant and distinct regions with *fail* response. This version of ES is named *ES grid*. We then combine both modifications into a third version of ES referred to as *ES grid gauss*. Lastly, we execute a GridES, similar to GridMA, where we run ES within each grid cell over the target area. The grid is split in the same manner as for GridMA. We ran the GridES with the *ES grid* version as it was the best considering the number of clusters, and it performed similarly to the best ES versions

Table 4. The average percentage of observed fault classes from all tested parameter combinations (6 000) using five different versions of ES algorithm on the same IC. The average is calculated over three runs.

	ES gauss	ES grid	ES grid gauss	GridES grid
fail comb.	0.61%	4.19%	0.82%	0.82%
mute	1.83%	6.31%	2.02%	1.68%
mute_pass	1.17%	2.85%	1.08%	0.94%
pass	96.39%	86.66%	96.08%	96.57%

considering the other two metrics. Note that the reported results from the new ES versions are mean values from three runs, while the previous experiments ran five times. From the results in Table 4, considering **the number of unique FI parameter combinations** with *fail* response, the initial ES version performs the best on average, followed by the *ES grid* version. The versions with Gaussian mutation perform more closely to the results observed with random search. However, applying grid initialization for the version with Gaussian mutation did help increase the number of observed vulnerabilities. Still, using uniform mutation proved better within these experiments. Similar to *ES gauss* and *ES grid gauss*, GridES obtained a similar number of faults as RS. Considering the **number of unique locations** with *fail* response, versions *ES grid* and *ES grid gauss* were better than the initial ES version, as seen in Table 5. On average, the number of unique locations is now closer to the best GridMA algorithm, and it remains in the scope of previously observed improvements over RS using any of the evolutionary approaches. Considering this metric, *ES gauss* and GridES perform similarly to RS. Gaussian mutation increases the location coverage to the same level as RS, as evident from the results with the *ES gauss* and *ES grid gauss*. Finally, we consider **the number of clusters** with *fail* response in Table 6, and the *ES grid* version found 9 clusters on average, while the GridMA, had 8.2 clusters which was the previous best result. We also note that all the ES versions observed more clusters than the initial version, and GridES had the same number on average. Thus, we improved the initial ES, with the crucial modification being the grid initialization. Gaussian mutation provided more randomness in the location parameters, which led to enhanced location coverage but less vulnerable parameter combinations and locations. However, interestingly, all ES versions provided more clusters than RS and MA, demonstrating the potential of diversity methods.

Table 5. The number of unique parameter combinations and x-y locations per fault class, and in total for all four algorithms. The average is calculated over three runs.

	ES gauss		ES grid		ES grid gauss		GridES grid	
Nb. comb. | Nb. loc.	6000	5869	6000	4235.5	6000	5857.3	6000	4322
Location coverage	0.9782		0.7059		0.9762		0.7203	
fail comb.	36.3	36	251	48	49	**48.7**	48.7	35.7
mute	110	107.3	378.5	124.5	121.3	121	101	78
mute_pass	70	69.7	171	86.5	64.7	64.7	56.3	47
pass	5783.7	5666	5199.5	4075	5765	5632	5794	4216.3

Table 6. The number of clusters based on the Mean Shift clustering algorithm over the unique x-y locations per fault class. The bandwidth size is 0.1. The number of clusters is averaged over three runs.

	ES gauss	ES grid	ES grid gauss	GridES grid
fail comb.	8.3	**9**	8.3	8
mute	11.3	10	9.6	10.3
mute_pass	9	12	10	9.3
pass	32.3	31.5	27.6	40

7   Conclusions and Future Work

Previous works show the benefits of algorithms such as memetic algorithm in finding more FI parameter combinations with vulnerabilities compared to commonly used random search. However, the observed results commonly come from a single sensitive region, and during security evaluation, we do not want to neglect possibly exploitable vulnerabilities. Thus, we propose diversity algorithms that promote diversity in the population of evolutionary algorithms and test the GridMA and Evolution Strategy and its variations. While we evaluate algorithms considering the number of unique FI parameter combinations as in related work, we additionally assess algorithm success based on the number of unique locations (x-y) and clusters with faults as two additional metrics that better align with the objective of finding multiple vulnerable regions. MA performs best only when the number of faults is concerned. However, GridMA and ES with grid initialization and Gaussian mutation (*ES grid gauss*) found more unique locations with faults. Nonetheless, all evolutionary algorithms, including MA, found around 30% more unique locations with *fail* responses than RS, performing similarly. Considering the number of clusters, MA performed the worst, while ES with grid initialization (*ES grid*) had the most clusters, followed by the GridMA algorithm and other ES versions. This work shows that the diversity approach helps find more distant locations with the desired outcome. However, the improvements are less significant than the difference between evolutionary algorithms and RS regarding the number of FI parameter combinations. Thus, while this work showcases the potential enhancement using the diversity approaches, future work could consider (μ, λ)-ES and more advanced diversity algorithms to provide more significant improvements.

References

1. Barenghi, A., Breveglieri, L., Koren, I., Naccache, D.: Fault injection attacks on cryptographic devices: theory, practice, and countermeasures. Proc. IEEE **100**(11), 3056–3076 (2012)
2. Beyer, H.G., Schwefel, H.P.: Evolution strategies-a comprehensive introduction. Nat. Comput. **1**, 3–52 (2002)
3. Biham, E., Shamir, A.: Differential fault analysis of secret key cryptosystems (1997)
4. Carpi, R.B., Picek, S., Batina, L., Menarini, F., Jakobovic, D., Golub, M.: Glitch it if you can: parameter search strategies for successful fault injection. In: Francillon, A., Rohatgi, P. (eds.) CARDIS 2013. LNCS, vol. 8419, pp. 236–252. Springer, Cham (2014). https://doi.org/10.1007/978-3-319-08302-5_16
5. Comaniciu, D., Meer, P.: Mean shift: a robust approach toward feature space analysis. IEEE Trans. Pattern Anal. Mach. Intell. **24**(5), 603–619 (2002)
6. Dobraunig, C., Eichlseder, M., Korak, T., Mangard, S., Mendel, F., Primas, R.: SIFA: exploiting ineffective fault inductions on symmetric cryptography. IACR Trans. Cryptogr. Hardw. Embed. Syst. **2018**(3), 547–572 (2018). https://doi.org/10.13154/tches.v2018.i3.547-572. https://tches.iacr.org/index.php/TCHES/article/view/7286
7. Fuhr, T., Jaulmes, E., Lomné, V., Thillard, A.: Fault attacks on AES with faulty ciphertexts only. In: Proceedings of the 2013 Workshop on Fault Diagnosis and Tolerance in Cryptography, FDTC 2013, USA, pp. 108–118. IEEE Computer Society (2013). https://doi.org/10.1109/FDTC.2013.18
8. Hooke, R., Jeeves, T.A.: "Direct search" solution of numerical and statistical problems. J. ACM **8**, 212–229 (1961)
9. Hutter, M., Schmidt, J.-M.: The temperature side channel and heating fault attacks. In: Francillon, A., Rohatgi, P. (eds.) CARDIS 2013. LNCS, vol. 8419, pp. 219–235. Springer, Cham (2014). https://doi.org/10.1007/978-3-319-08302-5_15
10. Kim, C.H., Quisquater, J.-J.: Fault attacks for CRT based RSA: new attacks, new results, and new countermeasures. In: Sauveron, D., Markantonakis, K., Bilas, A., Quisquater, J.-J. (eds.) WISTP 2007. LNCS, vol. 4462, pp. 215–228. Springer, Heidelberg (2007). https://doi.org/10.1007/978-3-540-72354-7_18
11. Kocher, P., Jaffe, J., Jun, B.: Differential power analysis. In: Wiener, M. (ed.) CRYPTO 1999. LNCS, vol. 1666, pp. 388–397. Springer, Heidelberg (1999). https://doi.org/10.1007/3-540-48405-1_25
12. Kocher, P.C.: Timing attacks on implementations of Diffie-Hellman, RSA, DSS, and other systems. In: Koblitz, N. (ed.) CRYPTO 1996. LNCS, vol. 1109, pp. 104–113. Springer, Heidelberg (1996). https://doi.org/10.1007/3-540-68697-5_9
13. Krček, M., Ordas, T., Fronte, D., Picek, S.: The more you know: improving laser fault injection with prior knowledge. In: 2022 Workshop on Fault Detection and Tolerance in Cryptography (FDTC), pp. 18–29. IEEE (2022)
14. Krček, M., Fronte, D., Picek, S.: On the importance of initial solutions selection in fault injection. In: 2021 Workshop on Fault Detection and Tolerance in Cryptography (FDTC), pp. 1–12 (2021). https://doi.org/10.1109/FDTC53659.2021.00011

15. MacQueen, J., et al.: Some methods for classification and analysis of multivariate observations. In: Proceedings of the Fifth Berkeley Symposium on Mathematical Statistics and Probability, Oakland, CA, USA, vol. 1, pp. 281–297 (1967)
16. Maldini, A., Samwel, N., Picek, S., Batina, L.: Genetic algorithm-based electromagnetic fault injection. In: 2018 Workshop on Fault Diagnosis and Tolerance in Cryptography (FDTC), pp. 35–42. IEEE (2018)
17. Moradi, M., Oakes, B.J., Saraoglu, M., Morozov, A., Janschek, K., Denil, J.: Exploring fault parameter space using reinforcement learning-based fault injection. In: 2020 50th Annual IEEE/IFIP International Conference on Dependable Systems and Networks Workshops (DSN-W), pp. 102–109. IEEE (2020)
18. Moro, N., Dehbaoui, A., Heydemann, K., Robisson, B., Encrenaz, E.: Electromagnetic fault injection: towards a fault model on a 32-bit microcontroller. In: 2013 Workshop on Fault Diagnosis and Tolerance in Cryptography, pp. 77–88. IEEE (2013)
19. Moscato, P.: On evolution, search, optimization, genetic algorithms and martial arts - towards memetic algorithms. Caltech Concurrent Computation Program (2000)
20. Pedregosa, F., et al.: Scikit-learn: machine learning in Python. J. Mach. Learn. Res. 12, 2825–2830 (2011)
21. Picek, S., Batina, L., Buzing, P., Jakobovic, D.: Fault injection with a new flavor: memetic algorithms make a difference. In: Mangard, S., Poschmann, A.Y. (eds.) COSADE 2014. LNCS, vol. 9064, pp. 159–173. Springer, Cham (2015). https://doi.org/10.1007/978-3-319-21476-4_11
22. Picek, S., Batina, L., Jakobović, D., Carpi, R.B.: Evolving genetic algorithms for fault injection attacks. In: 2014 37th International Convention on Information and Communication Technology, Electronics and Microelectronics (MIPRO), pp. 1106–1111. IEEE (2014)
23. Picek, S., Perin, G., Mariot, L., Wu, L., Batina, L.: SoK: deep learning-based physical side-channel analysis. ACM Comput. Surv. 55(11), 1–35 (2023)
24. Rais-Ali, I., Bouvet, A., Guilley, S.: Quantifying the speed-up offered by genetic algorithms during fault injection cartographies. In: 2022 Workshop on Fault Detection and Tolerance in Cryptography (FDTC), pp. 61–72. IEEE (2022)
25. Sedaghatbaf, A., Moradi, M., Almasizadeh, J., Sangchoolie, B., Van Acker, B., Denil, J.: DELFASE: a deep learning method for fault space exploration. In: 2022 18th European Dependable Computing Conference (EDCC), pp. 57–64. IEEE (2022)
26. Skorobogatov, S.P., Anderson, R.J.: Optical fault induction attacks. In: Kaliski, B.S., Koç, K., Paar, C. (eds.) CHES 2002. LNCS, vol. 2523, pp. 2–12. Springer, Heidelberg (2003). https://doi.org/10.1007/3-540-36400-5_2
27. Werner, V., Maingault, L., Potet, M.L.: Fast calibration of fault injection equipment with hyperparameter optimization techniques. In: Grosso, V., Pöppelmann, T. (eds.) CARDIS 2021. LNCS, vol. 13173, pp. 121–138. Springer, Cham (2022). https://doi.org/10.1007/978-3-030-97348-3_7
28. Wu, L., Ribera, G., Beringuier-Boher, N., Picek, S.: A fast characterization method for semi-invasive fault injection attacks. In: Jarecki, S. (ed.) CT-RSA 2020. LNCS, vol. 12006, pp. 146–170. Springer, Cham (2020). https://doi.org/10.1007/978-3-030-40186-3_8

One for All, All for Ascon: Ensemble-Based Deep Learning Side-Channel Analysis

Azade Rezaeezade[1(✉)], Abraham Basurto-Becerra[2], Léo Weissbart[2], and Guilherme Perin[3]

[1] Delft University of Technology, Delft, The Netherlands
`a.rezaeezade-1@tudelft.nl`
[2] Radboud University, Nijmegen, The Netherlands
[3] Leiden University, Leiden, The Netherlands

Abstract. In recent years, deep learning-based side-channel analysis (DLSCA) has become an active research topic within the side-channel analysis community. The well-known challenge of hyperparameter tuning in DLSCA encouraged the community to use methods that reduce the effort required to identify an optimal model. One of the successful methods is ensemble learning. While ensemble methods have demonstrated their effectiveness in DLSCA, particularly with AES-based datasets, their efficacy in analyzing symmetric-key cryptographic primitives with different operational mechanics remains unexplored.

Ascon was recently announced as the winner of the NIST lightweight cryptography competition. This will lead to broader use of Ascon and a crucial requirement for thorough side-channel analysis of its implementations. With these two considerations in view, we utilize an ensemble of deep neural networks to attack two implementations of Ascon. Using an ensemble of five multilayer perceptrons or convolutional neural networks, we could find the secret key for the Ascon-protected implementation with less than 3 000 traces. To the best of our knowledge, this is the best currently known result. We can also identify the correct key with less than 100 traces for the unprotected implementation of Ascon, which is on par with the state-of-the-art results.

Keywords: Side-channel Analysis · Deep Learning · Ensemble · Ascon

1 Introduction

Introducing the Ascon family as a new standard for authenticated encryption [NIS23] has raised interest in the available implementations that could be used in embedded devices and their security. Then, evaluating the physical security of cryptographic implementations against side-channel analysis (SCA) is a crucial step in developing secure embedded devices.

SCA is an implementation attack that exploits measurements of unintended physical leakages of sensitive information from a device through side channels

© The Author(s), under exclusive license to Springer Nature Switzerland AG 2024
M. Andreoni (Ed.): ACNS 2024 Workshops, LNCS 14586, pp. 139–157, 2024.
https://doi.org/10.1007/978-3-031-61486-6_9

such as power consumption, electromagnetic emission, or timing. The analysis methods for SCA have evolved since the first works on the subject, introducing simple power analysis (SPA) and differential power analysis (DPA) [KJJ99]. Today, SCA methods are numerous and are classified into two main categories: profiled and non-profiled attacks.

Non-profiled attacks, including Differential Power Analysis (DPA) [KJJ99], Correlation Power Analysis (CPA) [BCO04], and Mutual Information Analysis (MIA) [GBTP08], are techniques where an attacker uses a large set of measurements and statistical tools to exploit the leakage of secret information.

Profiled attacks include techniques like template attack [CRR02], stochastic attacks [SLP05], and machine learning-based attacks [MPP16], where the attacker mounts the attack in two phases. In the first phase, known as profiling/template building, the attacker needs access to a clone device to build profiles. In the second phase, which is known as the attack/template matching phase, the attacker matches the built profiles to recover the secret data.

Deep learning-based side-channel analysis (DLSCA) has become a research hot spot from 2016 [MPP16]. The studies have reported many advantages for this approach, including the robustness to different masking and hiding countermeasures [MBC+20, MPP16, CDP17] and removing the need for pre-processing [CDP17, KPH+19]. Despite all these advantages, it is frequently emphasized that the principal challenge in DLSCA is the selection of a neural network model that is tailored to the specific nuances of the problem at hand [PPM+23].

To overcome that challenge, different works have used various approaches, including hyperparameter tuning [WPP22, RWPP21, AGF21], regularization techniques [RB22], or designing a methodology for model selection [ZBHV20]. An interesting and effective strategy proposed to circumvent (or, at least alleviate) the challenge of finding an optimal model is the utilization of ensemble techniques [PCP20], where multiple sub-optimal neural network models combine to enhance the overall performance of DLSCA. While the results presented in that work demonstrate the utility of the ensemble method in enhancing attack performance, a gap in generalization across various cryptographic primitive implementations is evident. Until recently, the publicly available datasets for symmetric-key cryptography were centered around the AES primitive, as discussed in [PPM+23].

Consequently, the effectiveness of many proposals, including the ensemble, has been validated using only AES-based datasets. This raises a question about the efficiency of diverse proposals in DLSCA for AES when considering other cryptographic primitives. Ascon, the NIST lightweight cryptography competition winner, currently being standardized for broad public use, is an ideal subject for such investigation. The known vulnerability of the Ascon encryption mode of operation to side-channel analysis and the availability of its datasets make it an ideal candidate for this research. This shift toward considering Ascon as a benchmark in DLSCA research not only aligns with its growing use but also provides a broader perspective on the adaptability and efficiency of DLSCA across different cryptographic primitives.

In this research, we attack two software implementations (one unprotected and one protected) of the Ascon primitive using the ensemble method. The key contributions of our work are:

- **Extension beyond AES-based experiments:** Previous research demonstrated the effectiveness of the ensemble method in DLSCA, only focusing on the AES primitive. Our study extends this, showing that the ensemble method is also effective for other cryptographic primitives. We particularly highlight improved attack performance on protected Ascon implementations, where the challenge is more significant, and the attacks have not been very successful so far. The successful results with ensembles give hope that other DLSCA proposals aiming at AES may generalize for other cryptographic primitives.
- **Exploring Ascon in the context of side-channel analysis:** With Ascon being standardized by NIST and its usage expected to increase, there is a pressing need for comprehensive side-channel analysis of its implementations. In this research, we successfully attack both protected and unprotected Ascon implementations using the ensemble method. Our attack using the ensemble method outperforms the state-of-the-art results, emphasizing the necessity of designing and implementing adequate countermeasures for vulnerable operations in Ascon's implementation.

2   Preliminaries

2.1   Ascon Primitive

Ascon is a family of cryptographic algorithms designed to provide secure encryption and authentication in resource-constrained environments. This family of cryptography primitives is based on sponge construction [BDPVA12] and was selected by NIST in February 2023 to be standardized [NIS23] for lightweight applications. Ascon is an authenticated encryption algorithm that includes associated data, meaning it not only encrypts a message to maintain its confidentiality but also attaches a tag to the encrypted message and associated data to ensure integrity. The algorithm can take four inputs: plaintext P, associated data A, nonce M, and a key k. It outputs the authenticated ciphertext C and an authentication tag T. The algorithm includes four operation phases: *initialization, associated data process, plaintext process (ciphertext process in decryption), and finalization.* Figure 1 shows these four phases of Ascon.

In Ascon-128, the input of the initialization phase is a 320-bit initial state ($IV||k||M$ in Fig. 1 consisting of the 64-bit constant IV, the 128-bit key k, and the 128-bit fresh nonce M) in the form of five 64-bit words x_0 to x_4. This five-word state updates through the algorithm phases and is used as the secret state (or the sponge state) for encryption (decryption) and tag generation. The initialization phase includes twelve (same) permutation functions (shown as p^a in Fig. 1) that update the initial state. The permutation function consists of three parts: 1) the addition of the round constants, 2) a non-linear five-bit S-box (substitution layer), and 3) a linear diffusion layer.

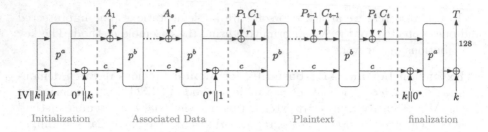

Fig. 1. Ascon's mode of operation and S-box.

During a data exchange, data like headers and metadata must remain in plaintext, but maintaining integrity is crucial for this data. The optional associated data processing phase maintains its integrity. In this phase, when an associated data block (A_i) is received, its first $r = 64$ bits is XORed to the first $r = 64$ bits of the sponge state, then the whole sponge state is permuted $b = 6$ times (p^b in Fig. 1). The associated data processing phase updates the sponge state using the associated data blocks. Then, the updated sponge state attains the plaintext process phase. The plaintext process phase XORs the 64-bit plaintext block P_i with the first $r = 64$ bits of the sponge state to produce ciphertext block C_i. Then, the whole state is transformed by the permutations $p^b, b = 6$ to update the sponge state for the next plaintext block. The finalization phase XORes the key with the sponge state and transforms the results with $p^a, a = 12$, to provide the 128-bit authentication tag T. For more details about different parts of the Ascon primitive, refer to [DEMS16].

2.2   Ensembles

Ensemble techniques combine multiple predictors (machine learning models or deep neural networks) to reduce generalization error [GBC16]. The predictor can be a simple machine learning method like a decision tree or an advanced one like a deep neural network. Ensemble techniques work because different predictors may capture various aspects of the data, and by combining them, one can often achieve better performance than every single model contributing to the ensemble. There are different techniques for ensemble predictors, including voting, bagging, boosting, and stacking. These techniques are different in how they create and combine the models. For example, bagging involves training multiple models independently and averaging their predictions. This method is useful for reducing variance and overfitting. Boosting, on the other hand, trains models sequentially, with each new model focusing on the data points that previous models miss-classified, aiming to improve the predictive performance iteratively. In deep learning, ensemble methods typically involve different architectures or configurations of neural networks, such as varying numbers of layers, nodes, or activation functions [PCP20].

The ensemble method has also been used in the domain of SCA (see Sect. 3). Our ensembling approach is aligned with the one Perin et al. used in [PCP20]. Their technique is specialized bagging (bootstrap aggregating), where the models in the ensemble are selected through a random search, and each model is trained on the entire dataset (the "bag" used for training every single model is equal to the whole training dataset). The models are trained independently. We diverge from common practices like majority voting or averaging to integrate the models' output. That is because, in the context of DLSCA, models often provide uncertain predictions about the class of a trace[1]. The accuracy of models in an attack phase is marginally better (or sometimes even worse) than a random guess [PCP20]. Consequently, techniques like majority voting or averaging are ineffective in enhancing attack performance. As an alternative, we exploit the small bias of the model outputs toward the correct class by utilizing the guessing entropy metric. Section 2.3 provides more information about this side-channel metric.

2.3   Deep Learning-Based Side-Channel Analysis

As mentioned in Sect. 1, profiling SCA has a phase of template building where the attacker gathers many traces from a clone device and builds the templates using those traces and a phase of template matching where the attacker matches the traces from the device under attack with the templates to find out to which template the traces belong. The output of the template matching phase is a matrix of probabilities showing with what probability each trace belongs to each template. Looking into the procedure of profiling SCA, deep learning (machine learning) classification is a natural choice for profiling attacks. Template building is equivalent to learning the classes[2] using many examples during the training phase and template matching is equivalent to classification on not previously seen data in the test phase. Using softmax as the last layer of a deep neural network, we can obtain the probability matrix as before. Using that matrix, we can calculate the common metrics like guessing entropy and the required number of attack traces to measure the performance of profiling SCA.

Guessing Entropy. In the attack phase of a profiled attack, guessing entropy [Mas94,KB07] is the average number of guesses that must be made before finding the correct key. The output of a profiling side-channel attack with Q attack traces is a probability vector of key hypotheses $\mathbf{h} = [h_1, h_2, \ldots, h_{|\mathbb{K}|}]$ in decreasing order (i.e., h_1 has the highest probability and $h_{|\mathbb{K}|}$ the lowest probability of being the correct key), where $|\mathbb{K}|$ is the key space. The information about each key candidate is calculated using $h_i - \Sigma_{j=1}^{Q} \log p(x_j, y)$, where $p(x_j, y)$ is the probability that the trace x_i belongs to class y. Thus, guessing entropy is

---

[1] Trace is the whole or part of the measurement given as input to the neural network.

[2] Usually, classes are all the possible intermediate values specified by the selected leakage model, something we know like the plaintext or public nonce, and the secret key.

the average position of the correct key, k^*, in $\mathbf{h}$. Equation (1) shows the formal definition of guessing entropy:

$$GE = E(rank_{k^*}(\mathbf{h})), \tag{1}$$

where $rank_{k^*}(\mathbf{h})$ denotes the position of the correct key k^* in the probability vector $\mathbf{h}$, and E is the expectation operator. An attack is considered a successful attack if $GE = 1$.

For the ensemble of models, we accumulate all individual models' output probabilities class-wise for each trace, and then the rest of the procedure is the same as above.

Required Number of Attack Traces. The required number of attack traces is the minimum number of traces needed to always place the correct key in the first position of $\mathbf{h}$.

3   Related Work

Two research streams are closely related to the work presented in this paper. The first stream employs ensemble methods to improve SCA. The second stream targets implementations of Ascon. The following section briefly summarizes what has been done so far.

Ensemble methods were used in the SCA domain as soon as the community started to use machine learning. For example, Picek et al. in [PHJ+17] used Random Forest (which is an ensemble of decision trees), Rotation Forest, and MultiBoosting, all methods that use ensembling to improve the accuracy of predictions. In [LMBM13] and [MPP16], researchers again used Random Forest, which is one of the most popular options for machine learning-based SCA (next to Support Vector Machines). In a recent work, which we consider as the first and the most relevant from the DLSCA perspective, Perin et al. used bagging of multiple deep neural networks for attacking different AES implementation [PCP20]. One can find more details about [PCP20] in Sect. 2.2.

Several researchers have analyzed Ascon's side-channel resistance since its submission to the NIST lightweight competition. In [RAD20], a method named SCARL is used to recover the secret key of an Ascon Artix-7 FPGA implementation. SCARL uses LSTM autoencoders for dimensionality reduction of S-box operations power measurements and reinforcement learning for clustering key candidates. In [SS23], transfer learning is used from gate-level power simulation traces for an Ascon software implementation running on a custom-made RISC-V SoC to improve the performance of DLSCA using raw power traces as input (measured from a chip prototype of the same design). In [WP23], multi-task learning is used to evaluate the side-channel resistance of protected and unprotected Ascon datasets.

4   Experimental Setup

4.1   Attack Point and Leakage Model

During the initialization and finalization phases of the Ascon encryption mode of operation as described in Fig. 1, the secret key is directly involved with the nonce, a user input data. Since this phase processes something we know (the nonce) and the secret information we aim to obtain (the key), it can be the target of side-channel analysis. As is the usual case for symmetric cryptography, the best point to attack is the non-linear S-box output of first-round permutation. The S-box operation in Ascon takes 5-bit inputs from the sponge state and gives 5-bit outputs (Fig. 2). The S-box operates column-wise, i.e., the input includes only one bit from each word x_0 to x_4 at a time.

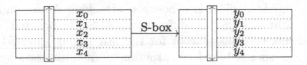

Fig. 2. Ascon column-wise S-box. S-box operation takes 5-bit input that includes only one bit from each word x_i and gives 5-bit output that contains one bit from each word y_i.

The Ascon S-box layer is a column-wise operation on the sponge state, applied to an individual column of the sponge state with 64 columns. One significant benefit of the Ascon S-box operation is its ability to be executed through XOR and AND operations on x_is [DEMS16]. Taking x_is as the inputs of the S-box layer and y_is as the outputs of this layer, the outputs of the non-linear S-box can be calculated as:

$$y_0 = x_0 + x_1 + x_2 + x_3 + x_1 x_2 + x_0 x_1 + x_1 x_4$$
$$y_1 = x_0 + x_1 + x_2 + x_3 + x_4 + x_1 x_2 + x_1 x_3 + x_2 x_3$$
$$y_2 = x_1 + x_2 + x_4 + x_3 x_4 + 1 \tag{2}$$
$$y_3 = x_0 + x_1 + x_2 + x_3 + x_4 + x_0 x_3 + x_0 x_4$$
$$y_4 = x_1 + x_3 + x_4 + x_0 x_1 + x_1 x_4 = x_1(1 + x_0 + x_4) + x_3 + x_4.$$

In our approach to target the first round of permutation, we substitute the x_i values with their original values, which consist of the public constant, the key's high and low parts, and the nonce's high and low parts for x_0 to x_4, respectively. By examining Eq. (2), it is evident that in y_4, all components are public except for x_1 (the key's high part). This characteristic makes y_4 a practical intermediate value for side-channel attacks. Furthermore, it is feasible to deduce

x_1 using a divide-and-conquer[3] strategy and retrieve x_1 with 8-bit chunks. We use the following leakage model to recover the whole x_1 in eight attacks.

$$Y = k_i^{(1)} \& (255 \oplus IV_i \oplus M_i^{(1)}) \oplus M_i^{(1)} \oplus M_i^{(2)} \quad i = 0, ..., 7 \tag{3}$$

To obtain the remaining key bits (x_2), we use y_0 or y_1 (since they have non-linear terms including x_2) as the intermediate value. The other half of the key, x_1, can be taken as a known, and the recovered value can be replaced in the selected intermediate value.

Comparing with Attacking AES: As mentioned in Sect. 1, most of the published research in the DLSCA domain focused on AES-based datasets. Here, we mention some similarities and differences between the side-channel analysis of AES and Ascons to make our attack easier to understand.

The most highlighted difference between attacking Ascon and AES stems from these algorithms' structure differences. AES-128 has ten rounds of S-box, shift rows, mix columns (except for the last round), and add round key, while Ascon has a sponge-based construction with initialization and finalization phases. In the AES, the side-channel attacks target the first or last rounds because only these two rounds operate on a known value (plaintext in the first round and ciphertext in the last round) and the key. The structure of the Ascon algorithm is entirely different from AES, and only the initialization and finalization phases of this algorithm seem to be vulnerable against SCA. While the known values in the case of AES are plaintext or ciphertext, they are nonce and the tag in the case of Ascon. Consequently, there are fundamental differences in the S-box implementation of Ascon and AES. For instance, in the case of AES, S-box input is a combination of key and plaintext, while it is a combination of two bits of the key, two bits of the nonce, and one bit of the initial value in the case of the Ascon. However, in both cases, the S-box output seems the most effective point to attack as this point offers non-linearity. Also, divide-and-conquer is helpful in both cases.

4.2   Datasets

Considering the primary goal of this research is evaluating the effectiveness of the ensemble method for attacking Ascon primitive implementation, we use two publicly available datasets[4] introduced in [WP23]. The first dataset, referred to as Ascon-Unprotected from this point, is provided using the 32-bit optimized implementation of Ascon-128 v1.2. The other dataset, referred to as Ascon-Protected, is provided using a first-order protected implementation of Ascon. This implementation uses bit-interleaved and a specific masking countermeasure designed

---

[3] Divide-and-conquer strategy is a strategy to recover a long key by retrieving its smaller parts separately.

[4] https://zenodo.org/records/10229484.

to be efficient with the Ascon S-box[5]. The C implementations by the Ascon team are available in their GitHub repository [SDG+20]. Traces are collected using a ChipWhisperer Lite board and an 8-bit precision oscilloscope, coupled with the STM32F4 target running at a frequency of 7.37MHz. Both datasets contain traces of Ascon's first-round permutation during the initialization phase. We use 60 000 traces from the datasets; the first 50 000 traces are collected with random keys, used for training, and 10 000 traces are collected using a fixed key, used for the attack phase. Traces from the Ascon-Unprotected dataset have 772 samples, and from the Ascon-Protected dataset have 1 408 samples.

4.3   Neural Network Architectures

Multilayer Perceptron (MLP) is a class of feedforward artificial neural networks (ANNs) that consist of at least three layers of nodes: an input layer, one or more hidden layers, and an output layer. Each layer has one or more neurons connected to the neurons in the following layer through weighted edges. These neurons typically include a non-linear activation function, which allows the network to learn non-linear relationships between input and output data. The MLP learns to map input data to the correct output through an iterative optimization algorithm that adjusts the weights of the connections by minimizing a loss function. To minimize the loss function, ANNs mostly use gradient descent and back-propagation. MLPs are usually used for tasks like classification and regression.

Convolutional Neural Network (CNN) is another class of feedforward neural networks. CNNs have one or more convolutional layers followed by one or more fully connected layers. The convolutional layers apply a set of learnable filters (sometimes known as kernels) to the input. Filters are simply vectors (in the one-dimensional convolution) or matrices (in the two-dimensional convolution) of coefficients that update during a process similar to that of MLPs. An activation function is used after each convolution layer to add non-linearity. Then, there can be a max/average pooling layer that simply reduces the spatial size of the representation expanded by the filters. The network extracts the most important features using a combination of filters and pooling layers. CNNs are commonly used for classification, but their architecture can be adapted for regression by altering the final layer and the loss function.

4.4   Methodology

This section provides a set of experiments to inspect the ensemble method's effectiveness for DLSCA. To evaluate the efficacy of ensembles, we compare

---

[5] The masking technique used in the implementation is called Domain-Oriented Masking (DOM). It is a specialized technique used in cryptographic hardware, but it can also be applied in software implementation. It involves dividing a circuit into separate domains, each handling only one part of the data. This separation ensures that each domain only accesses a specific portion of the data, reducing the risk of data leakage through side-channel attacks. For more reading, one can look into the implementation of Ascon and [GIB18].

Table 1. Random search range for MLP and CNN hyperparameters.

Hyperparameter	Range
MLP's Architecture Hyperparameters	
Number of neurons	[30, 40, 50, 60, 70, 80, 90, 100, 120, 150]
Number of layers	[2, 8], step = 1
CNN's Architecture Hyperparameters	
Number of convolution layers	[2, 4], step = 1
Number of filters	[4, 20], step = 2
First layer's filter size	[4, 24], step = 2
$i^{(}th)$ layer filter size	$((i-1)filter\_size)^2$
Stride	[2, 10], step = 2
Pooling	"Average", "Max"
Pooling size	[4, 10], step = 2
Pooling stride	[4, 10], step = 2
Number of dense layers	[2, 4], step = 1
Number of neurons in dense layers	[50, 100, 150, 200, 300, 400, 500]
Common Learning Hyperparameters in MLP and CNN	
Learning rate	random.uniform(0.0001, 0.001)
Activation function	"relu", "tanh", "selu", "elu"
Optimizer	"Adam"
Weight initialization	"he_uniform"
Batch size	128
Epochs	10

the performance of the ensemble (a group of the neural network models) with the performance of *the best model*. To show that the results can be generalized, the experiments are conducted on two different datasets introduced in Sect. 4.2(Ascon-Unprotected and Ascon-Protected). To assure that the results are valid for various neural network topologies, we employed MLP and CNN models (Sect. 4.3) combined with the leakage model introduced in Sect. 4.1. Using two datasets, two neural network topologies, and a single leakage model gives us four combinations. In each combination, we aim to retrieve x_1, which is eight bytes of the sixteen-byte secret key. We use a divide-and-conquer strategy, i.e., we repeat the following steps eight times for each combination, and each time, we retrieve a sub-key of size one byte.

– **Acquiring best predictor:** In [WPP22], Wu et al. showed that random search can reach neural network models with top performance when one attacks relatively easy datasets. Considering this, we generate fifty different models using random search. The range of hyperparameters for the random search is given in Table 1). Then, we use guessing entropy to compare the performance of these fifty models and take the model with the best performance as *the best model*. It is worth mentioning that the selected model is not the best possible model. Other, more advanced hyperparameter tuning techniques (like reinforcement learning [RWPP21] or Bayesian optimization [WPP22]) or searching with a wider range of hyperparameters with more randomly generated models can lead to models with better performance. Hence, our experiments aim not to find an optimal model, and we only want to investigate whether the ensemble performs better than the single best model. We report the best model's guessing entropy (GE-Best) and its required number of attack traces (NT-Best) as the performance of the best model.

- **Acquiring ensemble:** To benefit from the ensemble method in general, a group of neural networks that individually can learn the problem and give predictions better than random guesses is needed. Since accuracy is not a good metric to judge the performance of a model in the side-channel analysis domain, we use guessing entropy to select models that perform the best among the randomly generated models. We take five[6] models with the smallest guessing entropy from the pool of randomly generated models to be used in the ensemble.

  The selected models do not necessarily need to find the key (reach $GE = 1$); they only need to reduce the GE to small values. In Sect. 2.3, we have seen that guessing entropy can be calculated by accumulating the probability that the neural network gives for each key hypothesis over the attack traces. We sum up the probabilities for each key hypothesis from all individual models in the ensemble and accumulate that over the attack traces. We report the final guessing entropy as the ensemble guessing entropy and refer to it as GE-Ensemble. The required number of attack traces can be calculated using the GE-Ensemble, which we call NT-Ensemble.

- **Comparing the best model and the ensemble performance:** The final step is comparing the performance of the best-acquired models (GE-Best and NT-Best) and the performance of the ensemble model (GE-Ensemble and NT-Ensemble). The selected group of predictors for the ensemble always includes the best predictor, and improved performance means that the ensemble method was effective.

5   Experimental Results

The objective of this section is to demonstrate the effectiveness of using the ensemble method for side-channel analysis of the Ascon primitive implementation. As noted in Sect. 1, the ensemble method has only been utilized to attack AES primitive implementations. Thus, its effectiveness for other primitives is unclear. We demonstrate that the ensemble technique enables successful attacks on both unprotected and protected implementations of the Ascon primitive. Our

---

[6] This number can vary depending on the problem, the complexity of individual models, and the desired balance between performance and complexity. In our experiments, we observed that five models could already offer good performance improvement.

results confirm that the ensemble method is the most efficient technique to attack Ascon's protected implementation so far. Moreover, the success of the ensemble method attacking Ascon's unprotected implementation matches the success of a model selected through Bayesian optimization [WP23], again confirming that the ensemble of weaker learners can match the performance of a single model selected through an advanced hyperparameter tuning process.

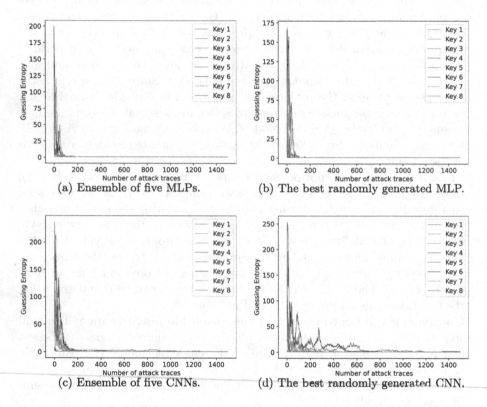

(a) Ensemble of five MLPs.   (b) The best randomly generated MLP.

(c) Ensemble of five CNNs.   (d) The best randomly generated CNN.

Fig. 3. Guessing entropy for Ascon-Unprotected. On top, each color shows the evolution of guessing entropy for ensemble of five MLPs (a) and the best-found MLP (b) selected from a pool with fifty randomly generated MLP for each sub-key. On the bottom, each color shows the evolution of guessing entropy for ensemble of five CNNs (c) and the best-found CNN (d) among fifty randomly generated ones for each sub-key. (Color figure online)

5.1   Ascon-Unprotected

This section presents experimental results when attacking Ascon-Unprotected, an unprotected software implementation of Ascon, using the ensemble method, and compares the results with the performance of the best-found models with random search. Figure 3a shows the evolution of guessing entropy using the ensemble method for eight sub-keys. For each sub-key, the ensemble combines

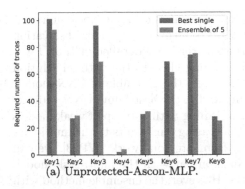 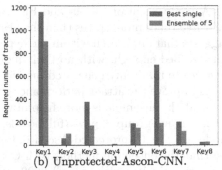

(a) Unprotected-Ascon-MLP.   (b) Unprotected-Ascon-CNN.

Fig. 4. The required number of attack traces with and without ensemble method in the Ascon-Unprotected dataset. On the left side, the required number of attack traces using the best MLP (green) and the ensemble of five MLPs (orange) is compared. On the right side, the required number of attack traces using the best CNN (green) and the ensemble of five CNNs (orange) is compared. (Color figure online)

the five best MLP neural networks selected among fifty randomly generated ones. In contrast, Fig. 3b depicts the guessing entropy evolution for the same sub-keys but employing the best-found MLP model. Observe that the reduction in guessing entropy is generally fast, though slightly slower for certain sub-keys. Figure 4a offers a clearer view of the impact of using the ensemble method. The effectiveness is most evident for key 3, where the required number of attack traces drops from 100 to 70. However, in half of the cases, using the ensemble method slightly increased the required number of attack traces. This observation is not unusual in scenarios where the problem tackled by the deep neural networks is relatively straightforward. For instance, a closer look into the performance of all randomly generated MLPs for sub-key 4 (key 4 in Fig. 3a) shows that more than 80% of the models could reveal the key with fewer than 10 traces, indicating that the attack is relatively easy for all the generated models. Consequently, finding an optimal model for this sub-key does not need much effort, and using the ensemble method does not offer additional performance benefits.

Turning to CNNs, Fig. 3c and Fig. 3d show the guessing entropy evolution for the same eight sub-keys, using an ensemble of the five best CNNs and the best-found CNN among fifty randomly generated ones for each sub-key. The ensemble's overall performance generally surpasses that of the best CNNs. However, when comparing MLP and CNN performances, it is apparent that either the best MLP or the ensemble of MLPs is typically more effective in key recovery. This observation has been mentioned in [RB22] as the "general ability of MLP models to find the key" and the "potential ability of CNN models to find the key". As discussed in [RB22], a limited number of MLP neural networks are more successful in reducing guessing entropy on average than the same number of CNN neural networks. Yet, with a more detailed architecture search, usually the best-found CNN outperforms the best-found MLP in key recovery.

A comparison of Fig. 4a and Fig. 4b reveals that the best CNN requires at least five times more traces than the best MLP to recover a key. This observation suggests that our search within the hyperparameter space detailed in Table 1 was not detailed enough, with no CNN model coming close to the optimal solution among the randomly generated models. However, the ensemble of CNN models could improve the attack performance compared to the best-found CNN, indicating that the ensemble is more helpful when dealing with a group of weak models rather than a group of powerful models. Comparing our results to the multi-task model on the Unprotected-Ascon dataset from previous work [WP23], we can see that the ensemble method with CNNs is on par with the multi-task model, recovering the key with around 1 000 traces. However, the ensemble method with MLPs can recover the key with about 100 traces, which is significantly better than the multi-task model where for some sub-keys more than 1 000 traces were needed.

5.2 Ascon-Protected

Next, we outline experimental results when attacking Ascon-Protected, a first-order protected software implementation of Ascon. The experiments in this section present a more challenging test for the efficacy of the ensemble method, particularly because the considered dataset is not easy to break [WP23]. Figure 5a illustrates the evolution of guessing entropy using an ensemble of five MLP neural networks. Figure 5b shows the same attack using the best-found MLP for each sub-key. Comparing these two figures shows that the reduction in guessing entropy using the ensemble method is much faster than the best-found MLP. The superior performance of the ensemble method is highlighted when analyzing the required number of attack traces. Figure 6a compares the required number of attack traces for both the ensembles and the best MLP. Clearly, the best MLP could only reveal sub-key 3 (key 3 in Fig. 6a) and sub-key 8 (key 8 in Fig. 6a), whereas the ensemble of MLPs successfully recovered all the sub-keys except sub-key 2 (key 2 in Fig. 6a)[7].

Similar observations apply to the CNN models, as shown in Fig. 5c and Fig. 5d. The ensemble method allows for the reduction of all sub-keys guessing entropy to $GE = 1$, except for sub-key 4 (key 4 in Fig. 5c), while none of the best-found CNNs in the pools of randomly generated CNN models could reduce GE to one. The stark contrast is further evident in Fig. 6b.

Considering the results from the ensemble learning on the Ascon-Protected and Ascon-Unprotected datasets, we can conclude that the ensemble method is significantly more effective for challenging datasets, where finding optimal models is more difficult. This conclusion can be supported by the similar performance

---

[7] This observation again emphasizes that extracting some sub-keys is more challenging than others. This difficulty stems from the difference in the amount of leakage for each sub-key. This difference in leakage can come from the architecture of the target (related to the hardware) or the implementation of the algorithm (related to the software). However, this is a common phenomenon in SCA, and to justify it, we need to get deeper into hardware and software implementations.

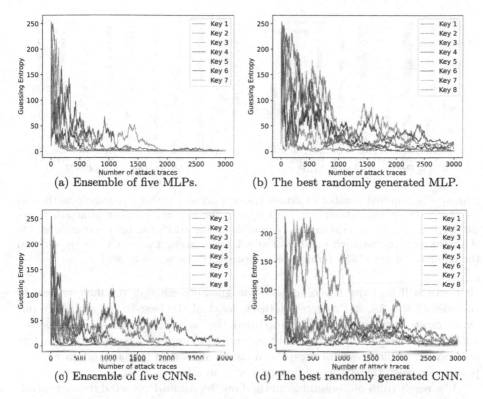

Fig. 5. Guessing entropy for Ascon-Protected. On top, each color shows the evolution of guessing entropy for ensemble of five MLPs (a) and the best-found MLP (b) selected from a pool with fifty randomly generated MLP for each sub-key. On the bottom, each color shows the evolution of guessing entropy for ensemble of five CNNs (c) and the best-found CNN (d) among fifty randomly generated ones for each sub-key.

of both the ensembles and the best-found MLP model in the Ascon-Unprotected dataset and the considerably improved results using the ensemble method in the Ascon-Protected dataset. The difference in the effectiveness of using the ensemble method in these two datasets stems from the difficulty of finding optimal and sub-optimal neural network models. Since it is relatively easy to find powerful models for the Ascon-Unprotected dataset, the ensemble method does not offer much improvement. In contrast, in the case of Ascon-Protected, almost all the best-found models performed poorly. However, combining those weak models through the ensemble method could still significantly improve the attack performance.

It is worth mentioning that using an ensemble of good models is more effective compared to an ensemble of poor models (as expected). While the ensemble method can offer better performance even using poor models, combining good models provides more performance benefits [MK23]. One should consider that with a good model, we do not mean an optimal model but a sub-optimal one

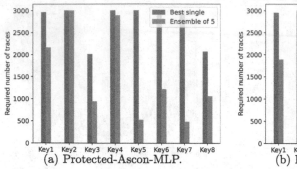
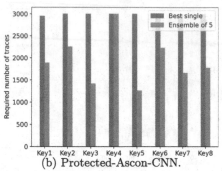

(a) Protected-Ascon-MLP.   (b) Protected-Ascon-CNN.

Fig. 6. The required number of attack traces with and without ensemble method in the Ascon-Protected dataset. On the left side, the required number of attack traces using the best MLP (green) and the ensemble of five MLPs (orange) is compared. On the right side, the required number of attack traces using the best CNN (green) and the ensemble of five CNNs (orange) is compared. (Color figure online)

that can still find the key or reduce the guessing entropy to small values. In the case of the Ascon-Protected dataset, most of the best-found models in our experiments were not good enough to break the target. To find individual models with better performance, we could extend the range of the hyperparameters outlined in Table 1 and increase the number of models in the random models' pool to increase the chance of finding better models.

The result from our ensemble method on the Ascon-Protected dataset significantly improved over the previous work [WP23], where the authors could not recover all the bits of the key with their multi-task model. We can recover the key with less than 3 000 traces using the ensemble method.

6   Conclusions and Future Work

This research investigated the effectiveness of applying an ensemble method to attack both protected and unprotected implementations of the Ascon primitive. While the ensemble method was considered before in DLSCA, its effectiveness for symmetric-key primitives was only validated using AES-based datasets, leading to questions about its applicability to primitives with different operational logic. Our research demonstrated the successful application of ensemble methods to Ascon implementations. Besides, using the ensemble of neural network models, we improved state-of-the-art attacks on Ascon's protected implementation, underscoring that future implementations should consider the current vulnerabilities and that stronger countermeasures are needed to prevent DLSCA. Our experimental results show that with an ensemble of (only) five neural network models, it is possible to extract the secret key with less than 3 000 traces from the protected implementation and, at most, with 100 traces from the unprotected implementation. One possible future work in this direction is using better (and more) models for the ensemble, where we stipulate it can improve the final performance even further.

As the next step, we intend to investigate whether an ensemble of neural networks of different types (ensemble of different topologies like MLP and CNN) trained using different leakage models can improve the attack performance. Our intuition is that a model with a particular topology trained with the same leakage model tends to generate less diverse predictions than models with a different topology trained with different leakage models. Indeed, when we use a dataset and a specific combination of neural network topologies and leakage models, the acquired models are less diverse and mostly focus on similar leakage (points of interest). By integrating diverse neural network types and leakage models into our ensemble, we aim to extract a richer spectrum of information from individual traces, potentially leading to more potent and efficient DLSCA.

References

[AGF21] Acharya, R.Y., Ganji, F., Forte, D.: InfoNEAT: information theory-based neuroevolution of augmenting topologies for side-channel analysis. CoRR, abs/2105.00117 (2021)

[BCO04] Brier, E., Clavier, C., Olivier, F.: Correlation power analysis with a leakage model. In: Joye, M., Quisquater, J.-J. (eds.) CHES 2004. LNCS, vol. 3156, pp. 16–29. Springer, Heidelberg (2004). https://doi.org/10.1007/978-3-540-28632-5_2

[BDPVA12] Bertoni, G., Daemen, J., Peeters, M., Van Assche, G.: Duplexing the sponge: single-pass authenticated encryption and other applications. In: Miri, A., Vaudenay, S. (eds.) SAC 2011. LNCS, vol. 7118, pp. 320–337. Springer, Heidelberg (2012). https://doi.org/10.1007/978-3-642-28496-0_19

[CDP17] Cagli, E., Dumas, C., Prouff, E.: Convolutional neural networks with data augmentation against jitter-based countermeasures. In: Fischer, W., Homma, N. (eds.) CHES 2017. LNCS, vol. 10529, pp. 45–68. Springer, Cham (2017). https://doi.org/10.1007/978-3-319-66787-4_3

[CRR02] Chari, S., Rao, J.R., Rohatgi, P.: Template attacks. In: Kaliski, B.S., Koç, K., Paar, C. (eds.) CHES 2002. LNCS, vol. 2523, pp. 13–28. Springer, Heidelberg (2003). https://doi.org/10.1007/3-540-36400-5_3

[DEMS16] Dobraunig, C., Eichlseder, M., Mendel, F., Schläffer, M.: Ascon v1. 2. Submission to the CAESAR Competition 5(6), 7 (2016)

[GBC16] Goodfellow, I.J., Bengio, Y., Courville, A.C.: Deep Learning. Adaptive Computation and Machine Learning. MIT Press, Cambridge (2016)

[GBTP08] Gierlichs, B., Batina, L., Tuyls, P., Preneel, B.: Mutual information analysis. In: Oswald, E., Rohatgi, P. (eds.) CHES 2008. LNCS, vol. 5154, pp. 426–442. Springer, Heidelberg (2008). https://doi.org/10.1007/978-3-540-85053-3_27

[GIB18] Groß, H., Iusupov, R., Bloem, R.: Generic low-latency masking in hardware. IACR Trans. Cryptogr. Hardw. Embed. Syst. 2018(2), 1–21 (2018)

[KB07] Köpf, B., Basin, D.A.: An information-theoretic model for adaptive side-channel attacks. In: Ning, P., De Capitani di Vimercati, S., Syverson, P.F. (eds.) Proceedings of the 2007 ACM Conference on Computer and Communications Security, CCS 2007, Alexandria, Virginia, USA, 28–31 October 2007, pp. 286–296. ACM (2007)

[KJJ99]   Kocher, P., Jaffe, J., Jun, B.: Differential power analysis. In: Wiener, M. (ed.) CRYPTO 1999. LNCS, vol. 1666, pp. 388–397. Springer, Heidelberg (1999). https://doi.org/10.1007/3-540-48405-1_25

[KPH+19] Kim, J., Picek, S., Heuser, A., Bhasin, S., Hanjalic, A.: Make some noise. Unleashing the power of convolutional neural networks for profiled side-channel analysis. IACR Trans. Cryptogr. Hardw. Embed. Syst. **2019**(3), 148–179 (2019)

[LMBM13] Lerman, L., Medeiros, S.F., Bontempi, G., Markowitch, O.: A machine learning approach against a masked AES. In: Francillon, A., Rohatgi, P. (eds.) CARDIS 2013. LNCS, vol. 8419, pp. 61–75. Springer, Cham (2014). https://doi.org/10.1007/978-3-319-08302-5_5

[Mas94]   Massey, J.L.: Guessing and entropy. In: Proceedings of 1994 IEEE International Symposium on Information Theory, p. 204 (1994)

[MBC+20] Masure, L., et al.: Deep learning side-channel analysis on large-scale traces. In: Chen, L., Li, N., Liang, K., Schneider, S. (eds.) ESORICS 2020. LNCS, vol. 12308, pp. 440–460. Springer, Cham (2020). https://doi.org/10.1007/978-3-030-58951-6_22

[MK23]   Mohammed, A., Kora, R.: A comprehensive review on ensemble deep learning: opportunities and challenges. J. King Saud. Univ. Comput. Inf. Sci. **35**(2), 757–774 (2023)

[MPP16]   Maghrebi, H., Portigliatti, T., Prouff, E.: Breaking cryptographic implementations using deep learning techniques. In: Carlet, C., Hasan, M.A., Saraswat, V. (eds.) SPACE 2016. LNCS, vol. 10076, pp. 3–26. Springer, Cham (2016). https://doi.org/10.1007/978-3-319-49445-6_1

[NIS23]   NIST Information Technology Laboratory. NIST lightweight cryptography standardization process. The National Institute of Standards and Technology (2023). https://csrc.nist.gov/News/2023/lightweight-cryptography-nist-selects-ascon

[PCP20]   Perin, G., Chmielewski, L., Picek, S.: Strength in numbers: improving generalization with ensembles in machine learning-based profiled side-channel analysis. IACR Trans. Cryptogr. Hardw. Embed. Syst. **2020**(4), 337–364 (2020)

[PHJ+17] Picek, S., et al.: Side-channel analysis and machine learning: a practical perspective. In: 2017 International Joint Conference on Neural Networks, IJCNN 2017, Anchorage, AK, USA, 14–19 May 2017, pp. 4095–4102. IEEE (2017)

[PPM+23] Picek, S., Perin, G., Mariot, L., Wu, L., Batina, L.: SoK: deep learning-based physical side-channel analysis. ACM Comput. Surv. **55**(11), 227:1–227:35 (2023)

[RAD20]   Ramezanpour, K., Ampadu, P., Diehl, W.: SCARL: side-channel analysis with reinforcement learning on the Ascon authenticated cipher. arXiv preprint arXiv:2006.03995 (2020)

[RB22]   Rezaeezade, A., Batina, L.: Regularizers to the rescue: fighting overfitting in deep learning-based side-channel analysis. IACR Cryptology ePrint Archive, p. 1737 (2022)

[RWPP21] Rijsdijk, J., Lichao, W., Perin, G., Picek, S.: Reinforcement learning for hyperparameter tuning in deep learning-based side-channel analysis. IACR Trans. Cryptogr. Hardw. Embed. Syst. **2021**(3), 677–707 (2021)

[SDG+20] Schläffer, M., Dobraunig, C., Großschädl, J., dos Santos, L.C., Bachmann, F., Eichlseder, M.: ASCON-C Implementation. Github repository (2020). https://github.com/ascon/ascon-c

[SLP05] Schindler, W., Lemke, K., Paar, C.: A stochastic model for differential side channel cryptanalysis. In: Rao, J.R., Sunar, B. (eds.) CHES 2005. LNCS, vol. 3659, pp. 30–46. Springer, Heidelberg (2005). https://doi.org/10.1007/11545262_3

[SS23] Shanmugam, D., Schaumont, P.: Improving side-channel leakage assessment using pre-silicon leakage models. In: Kavun, E.B., Pehl, M. (eds.) COSADE 2023. LNCS, vol. 13979, pp. 105–124. Springer, Cham (2023). https://doi.org/10.1007/978-3-031-29497-6_6

[WP23] Weissbart, L., Picek, S.: Lightweight but not easy: side-channel analysis of the Ascon authenticated cipher on a 32-bit microcontroller. IACR Cryptology ePrint Archive, p. 1598 (2023)

[WPP22] Wu, L., Perin, G., Picek, S.: I choose you: automated hyperparameter tuning for deep learning-based side-channel analysis. IEEE Trans. Emerg. Top. Comput. 1–12 (2022)

[ZBHV20] Zaid, G., Bossuet, L., Habrard, A., Venelli, A.: Methodology for efficient CNN architectures in profiling attacks. IACR Trans. Cryptogr. Hardw. Embed. Syst. 2020(1), 1–36 (2020)

CNN Architecture Extraction on Edge GPU

Péter Horváth[1]([✉]), Lukasz Chmielewski[2], Leo Weissbart[1], Lejla Batina[1], and Yuval Yarom[3]

[1] Radboud University, Nijmegen, The Netherlands
peter.horvath@ru.nl
[2] Masaryk University, Brno, Czech Republic
[3] Ruhr University, Bochum, Germany

Abstract. Neural networks have become popular due to their versatility and state-of-the-art results in many applications, such as image classification, natural language processing, speech recognition, forecasting, etc. These applications are also used in resource-constrained environments such as embedded devices. In this work, the susceptibility of neural network implementations to reverse engineering is explored on the NVIDIA Jetson Nano microcomputer via side-channel analysis. To this end, an architecture extraction attack is presented. In the attack, 15 popular convolutional neural network architectures (EfficientNets, MobileNets, NasNet, etc.) are implemented on the GPU of Jetson Nano and the electromagnetic radiation of the GPU is analyzed during the inference operation of the neural networks. The results of the analysis show that neural network architectures are easily distinguishable using deep learning-based side-channel analysis.

Keywords: Deep Learning · Side Channel Attack · NVIDIA GPU

1 Introduction

The field of machine learning has seen an enormous amount of interest and use in recent years. One specific area of machine learning, namely deep learning, has proven to be versatile and provides state-of-the-art performance for many real-world applications. Deep learning refers to multi-layer Artificial Neural Networks (ANNs) that learn to solve a task by extracting the important features from data and generalizing well to that task. These tasks, such as games, object detection, image classification, or natural language processing, can be vastly different.

AlphaGo [32] is one of the deep learning-based breakthroughs where a neural network learned to play Go and was able to beat one of the best human Go players at the time. Similarly, AlphaZero [33] was developed to play chess and outperformed human players. Lastly, AlphaStar [39] achieved superior levels, compared to human players, in the StarCraft 2 real-time strategy computer game, beating multiple of the best players in the world.

M. Andreoni (Ed.): ACNS 2024 Workshops, LNCS 14586, pp. 158–175, 2024.
https://doi.org/10.1007/978-3-031-61486-6_10

Additionally, image classification is a fundamental problem of computer vision where deep learning models have achieved state-of-the-art results and continue to provide improvements [6,8,17,20,34]. A more general problem in computer vision concerns the field of object detection, which has also seen enormous improvements in accuracy due to neural networks [21].

Similarly, deep learning provided multiple breakthroughs in Natural Language Processing (NLP) in recent years [26]. NLP is a broad field that aims to solve practical issues concerning human languages, such as information retrieval, summarisation, or machine translation. Google Translate [2] and ChatGPT [25] are popular NLP applications based on the Transformer [38] neural network architecture.

Neural networks are changing many areas of our lives and are becoming indispensable in our everyday lives. However, the design and training of neural networks can be expensive in many ways, as follows:

1. Collecting the training dataset can be time-consuming and expensive;
2. Designing and training neural networks requires people with expertise;
3. The time it takes to train and validate a model can range from hours to weeks;
4. The cost of training and tuning can be high due to requiring specialized, high-performance hardware, e.g., graphics processing units (GPUs).

Additionally, sometimes sensitive data is used to train a neural network, and this data can also be vulnerable to reverse engineering. Therefore, keeping the architecture and parameters of the trained models secret becomes an important issue.

Beyond their great successes, neural networks also face a wide variety of adversarial attacks. These attacks can have different goals, such as causing misclassification, input recovery, or reverse engineering architecture.

One kind of technique that attackers can employ is Side-Channel Analysis (SCA). SCA exploits the physical leakages of electronic devices to extract secret information. Despite existing countermeasures against SCA-based attacks, it is not always possible to utilize these countermeasures, especially in resource-constrained environments, because countermeasures usually come at a price of speed and cost.

Therefore, this work will focus on the following research question: **Are neural network implementations of large-scale convolutional neural networks on the GPU of NVIDIA Jetson Nano vulnerable to reverse engineering using deep learning-based side-channel analysis?**

The GPU platform is targeted because neural network implementations, especially convolutional neural networks, in practice, often run on GPUs because the core operations of neural networks are matrix operations (e.g., multiplications). These operations are highly parallelizable, which makes GPUs more suitable than CPUs for neural network-based applications.

1.1   Comparison with Related Work

In this work, we analyze electromagnetic and timing side channel information similarly to the CSI-NN paper, which analyzed NNs running on microcontrollers [3]. However, we focus on well-known and widely used, large-scale convolutional neural network architectures in computer vision with a different and more popular platform for neural networks as the target, i.e. the GPU. In practice, since GPUs provide efficiency through parallelism, they are commonly used to run neural networks, especially large-scale ones. This GPU parallelism also poses a big challenge in analyzing side-channel signals, as the number of concurrently executing threads is much larger than that of microcontroller applications. Moreover, the attacks presented in this paper do not require the decapsulation of the target chip, contrary to [3].

The work of Chmielewski and Weissbart [5] targets the same platform as we do in this work, with the goals and methods similar to those of [3]. Basically, the number of neurons, number of layers, and activation function types are recovered based on using electromagnetic side-channel and timing information. However, our work goes further in extending the approach to large-scale architectures and showing that recovering neural net architectures used in real-world application is viable.

In addition, some other works target desktop GPUs to extract hyperparameters [19,23] but not an embedded system like the Jetson Nano that might be deployed in an environment where an adversary is more likely to have physical access.

A side-channel-based attack on neural networks is also presented in [40], where the architecture extraction of neural networks, implemented on the CPU of Raspberry Pi, is demonstrated using power-side channel analysis and machine learning. The extracted architectures are similar to those in this work, but the classification method, the target platform, and the used side channel are different as they classify power traces with a Support Vector Machine (SVM) classifier.

1.2   Contributions and Outline

The target device in this work is the NVIDIA Jetson Nano, which is a microcomputer tailored to run AI applications in a resource-constrained environment. As already stated above, we demonstrate an architecture extraction attack by distinguishing among a number of well-know neural net architectures on this platform.

To summarize, the main contributions of this work are:

1. We demonstrate how complex convolutional neural network architectures can be extracted by visually inspecting electromagnetic side-channel measurements. To that end, 15 well-known neural network architectures from computer vision are classified based on the electromagnetic radiation of the device's GPU.
2. We also show how the process of distinguishing the architectures can be automated using a deep learning classifier.

This papers is organized as follows. Prior to discussing the experiments and results, Sect. 2 gives an introduction to related topics. First, the investigated neural network architectures are discussed in detail. Next, the relevant concepts from side-channel analysis are introduced. Section 3 discusses the experimental setup as well as the results of reverse engineering. Section 4 provides a discussion about the results and possible countermeasures. Section 5 concludes the paper.

2 Background

2.1 CNN Architectures

This section introduces the convolutional neural network architectures that are analyzed in this work. Most of these architectures are suitable for resource-limited devices, such as the Jetson Nano, but there are other well-known architectures besides the ones analyzed in this work, such as ResNets [8], ShuffleNets [42] and Xception [6].

MobileNet. MobileNets [11] are convolutional neural networks suitable for real-time applications in constrained environments. The architecture relies on depthwise separable convolutional blocks to speed up computations. These blocks consist of a depthwise convolutional layer and a pointwise convolutional layer. First, the depthwise convolutional layer applies 3×3 kernels on only one input channel of the input. Second, the produced feature map of the depthwise convolutional layer is the input to the pointwise convolutional layer with 1×1 kernels, which are applied to all input channels. In standard convolutions, the 3×3 kernels would be applied to all input channels. Empirically, it has been shown that depthwise separable convolutions provide less latency with a negligible decrease in accuracy compared to standard convolutional layers. This is very important for embedded systems as the resources such as area and power consumption are typically limited.

MobileNetV2. MobileNetV2 [31] is an optimized version of MobileNets. In this architecture, the depthwise separable convolutional blocks are expanded with linear bottleneck layers and residual connections [8,41] to form *inverted residual blocks*.

EfficientNets. EfficientNet [36] proposes a compound scaling method that uniformly scales model depth, width, and resolution with scaling coefficients. This compound scaling method is based on the intuition that all dimensions of a network have to be balanced to achieve better accuracy and efficiency. The baseline network, EfficientNetB0, is similar to that of MobileNetV2 as it is based on the same inverted residual blocks with bottleneck layers. In addition, squeeze-and-excitation [12] is added to the blocks. The upscaled versions of the baseline architecture, such as EfficientNetB1, -B2, -B3, -B4, -B5, and -B6, are scaled up using the compound scaling method mentioned earlier.

DenseNets. DenseNets [13] do not use depthwise separable convolutions, they are based on the idea of feature reusing. In terms of the architecture, this means that feature maps produced by a layer are inputs to all subsequent layers. The architecture of DenseNets employs dense blocks and transition layers. Dense blocks use the principle of feature reusing, while transition layers are responsible for downsampling.

NasNetMobile. The NasNet [43] architecture is quite distinct when compared to the previous architectures. The main building blocks of the NasNet architecture are the *normal* and *reduction* cells. These cells have multiple branches that apply different operations on the inputs in parallel, and the results of the branches are concatenated to form the output of the cell. The operations in the branches consist of standard convolution, separable convolutions, pooling or identity.

MobileNetV3. MobileNetV3 [10] is the further optimized version of MobileNetV2 with various new additions. Similarly to MobileNetV2, MobileNetV3's main building blocks are the inverted residual blocks with bottleneck layers, but with the addition of squeeze-and-excitation [12] in some blocks in the new architecture. Additionally, the ReLU nonlinearity is substituted with the swish activation [30] in some blocks. The paper specifies the MobileNetV3small architecture for environments where resources are limited and the MobileNetV3large architecture for high-resource use cases. These architectures are very similar, with MobileNetV3large having more bottleneck blocks.

2.2   Side-Channel Analysis

Side-channel analysis (SCA) exploits the physical leakages of electronic devices to extract secret information [15,16]. Such leakages could be power consumption, electromagnetic (EM) emanations, timing, optical, or sound, while secret information could be anything that has to remain confidential. The attacks based on side-channel information were first introduced in the 90's, targeting constrained firmly cryptographic devices such as smartcards [15,16] and they pose ever since a constant threat to the security of various embedded systems. In this work, we exploit the timing and EM side channels.

Timing Analysis. Timing vulnerabilities in implementations arise from different sources, such as branching, cache hits/misses, and instructions. These vulnerabilities also pose a threat to cryptographic algorithms [4,16,27]. Timing attacks are typically based on the vulnerability of implementations where an operation takes a varying amount of time to complete, where this variation is due to the private key or other data being manipulated or even different instructions executed.

Power Analysis. Kocher et al. (1999) [15] introduced power consumption-based attacks called Simple Power Analysis (SPA) and Differential Power Analysis (DPA) by measuring the power consumption of microcontrollers during the execution of cryptographic algorithms. These attacks exploit the dependence between the power consumption of a device and the executed operations and processed data by the device. SPA is a method to visually analyze and interpret the collected power consumption measurements, also called *traces*. It often requires a few or just a single trace to extract information about the operations and data used in the targeted algorithm. DPA exploits the dependency of power consumption on the processed data. The small variations in power due to different data being processed can allow an adversary to extract secret information (e.g., secret key) about the targeted algorithm using power measurements.

Electromagnetic Emanations. Electromagnetic (EM) emanations have been exploited since the Second World War [35] and pose a massive security issue for sensitive systems. Wim van Eck [37] was the first to publish a paper about the risk of information leakage due to electromagnetic radiation using equipment that anyone can acquire. His work demonstrated the danger of EM radiation by reconstructing the frames of the video from display units using EM radiation.

Since then, EM radiation has also been used to break cryptographic implementations [18,29] or eavesdrop on display units [7,9,22]. Similar to power analysis, Simple EM Analysis (SEMA) and Differential EM Analysis (DEMA) are methods that work exactly the same way as their counterparts in power analysis, with the exception of the traces consisting of EM measurements. In this work, we use electromagnetic emanations in combination with timing information to distinguish the architectures.

3   Architecture Extraction

3.1   Threat Model

In our threat model, the adversary has the following knowledge and capabilities.

A1: Physical access to the target device.
A2: Access to an identical device for profiling.
A3: Capability to collect electromagnetic side-channel measurements.
A4: Knowledge that one of the 15 architectures listed in Table 1 is executed on the target device.

The capabilities **A1–A3** are standard assumptions in profiled side-channel attacks [28]. The assumption of **A1** can be relaxed as the adversary requires limited amount of physical access to the target device because the attack requires only a single trace to identify the correct architecture. In addition, the assumption of **A4** is motivated by the investigated architectures' efficiency in resource-constrained environments like embedded devices. Furthermore, developers may choose to pick an off-the-shelf architecture that is proven to work instead of developing custom architectures, which can be an expensive and time-consuming process. In our experiments, we use the same device for profiling and attacking.

Table 1. Analyzed convolutional neural network architectures

Name	# parameters
EfficientNetB0	5.3 M
EfficientNetB1	7.9 M
EfficientNetB2	9.2 M
EfficientNetB3	12.3 M
EfficientNetB4	19.5 M
EfficientNetB5	30.6 M
EfficientNetB6	43.3 M
MobileNet	4.3 M
MobileNetv2	3.5 M
MobileNetv3small	2.5 M
MobileNetv3large	5.4 M
Densenet121	8.1 M
Densenet169	14.3 M
Densenet201	20.2 M
NASNetMobile	5.3 M

3.2   NVIDIA Neural Network Implementations

In our attack, we are considering the implementations from NVIDIA's TensorRT deep learning inference framework. TensorRT is a library written by NVIDIA to support deep learning inference by running neural networks efficiently and quickly on NVIDIA hardware.

TensorRT works as follows:

1. the user defines the neural network model
2. the user defines the desired optimizations for the model
3. TensorRT builds an engine based on the defined model and desired optimizations

Optimizations include layer fusions and calibration of the precision of calculations. Given the precision constraints, TensorRT times different implementations and chooses the fastest ones for the model. The built engine includes layer implementations and model weights, which can be subsequently used for inference. In our experiments, we restricted the models to use implementations with half-precision calculations to decrease the memory footprint of the architectures as some of them require more than the available DRAM in the device if single-precision calculations are used.

Fig. 1. Heatmap of 78 MHz clock frequency after scanning the chip of the Jetson Nano device. The heatmap was generated by applying the Fourier-transform on traces collected at each point on the chip. Purple indicates no activity of the 78 MHz clock frequency while yellow indicates the highest activity of this frequency at a certain point. Multiple yellow points can be used to mount a successful architecture extraction attack. (Color figure online)

Fig. 2. Location of the Riscure EM probe. The probe tip is located above the chip.

3.3 Measurement Collection

We use the PicoScope 3207B oscilloscope with a Riscure EM probe [1] and Riscure EM probe station [1] to collect electromagnetic side-channel measurements in the architecture extraction attack. In order to capture the inference of the neural networks from the device, a GPIO pin on the Jetson Nano's board is used as a trigger for the oscilloscope to signal when the inference operation is about to start. In the architecture extraction experiment, we set the GPU cores of the device to operate at 76 MHz clock frequency, so we set the sampling rate of the oscilloscope at 1GS/s. In order to detect where the chip of the Jetson Nano leaks the most information, the whole chip was scanned. The results of the

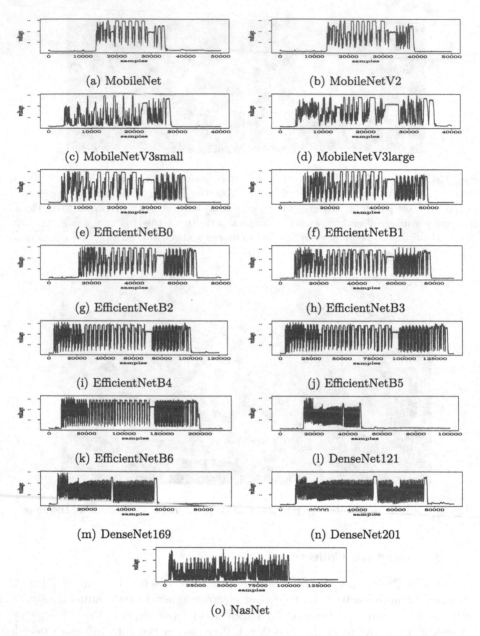

Fig. 3. Example traces of the investigated architectures.

scan are shown in Fig. 1. Based on the figure and experiments, there are multiple locations where the architectural information of neural networks leaks. The final location of the probe is shown in Fig. 2.

3.4   Architecture Extraction Using SEMA and Timing Analysis

Here we discuss Simple EM Analysis and timing analysis on the collected traces using. The traces shown in this section are not the raw traces but the preprocessed versions of those. For preprocessing, we applied windowed averaging of size 1 000 on the absolute value of the measurements. Alignment of the traces is not required for this attack.

Figure 3 shows example traces of the architectures that are investigated in this paper. For the MobileNet and MobileNetv2 architectures, there are clear timing differences between them, showing the MobileNetV2 takes more time to execute. According to the benchmarks in the original paper [31], MobileNetV2 is faster than MobileNetV1. However, the experiments in the original paper were carried out on the CPU of the Google Pixel 1 smartphone, using TensorFlow Lite, so this might explain the difference. The displayed patterns are similar for the architectures, which is expected as MobileNetV2's building block is based on MobileNet's building block. Regarding the MobileNetV3small and MobileNetV3large architectures, the execution time for the MobilNetV3large architecture is substantially larger than that of MobileNetV3small, as expected. However, the execution time for the MobileNetV3small architecture is very similar to that of the MobileNetV2. The DenseNet 121, DenseNet169, and DenseNet201 architectures display very different EM patterns than the rest of the architectures. In addition, the displayed patterns are very similar when compared to each other. However, the timing differences clearly identify the correct architecture DenseNet architecture. Regarding the EfficientNet architectures, the EM patterns are similar to that of the MobileNet architectures, as expected, but the timing differences give away the correct architecture. Lastly, the EM patterns shown by the NasNet architecture are quite distinct compared to the previous architectures. In terms of execution times, NasNet is very similar to EfficientNetB4, but NasNet's EM amplitude frequently drops near zero.

3.5   Architecture Extraction Using Deep Learning

In this section, we present how the architecture extraction attack can be automated using deep learning by framing the problem as a classification problem. The models for each architecture for training were created using TensorFlow. For some architectures, the TensorFlow implementation involves preprocessing layers that actually do not belong to the architecture. These preprocessing layers make it possible for the network to receive inputs that are not preprocessed. These layers were removed before creating the models so that every architecture uniformly does not have preprocessing layers. Besides this, the default parameter values of the TensorFlow implementations were used.

To train and validate the deep learning classifier, $n = 5$ models $M_{a,i}$ were created for every architecture ($g = 15$). For testing, $t = 3$ models were created per architecture. These only differ in their weights $W_{a,i}$ as all the weights are sampled randomly from a normal distribution (with mean 0 and variance 1) for every model.

Table 2. Classifier architecture and hyperparameters

Layer type	Hyperparameters	Activation
Conv1D	filters: 32, kernel-size: 500, strides: 50	ReLU
Conv1D	filters: 32, kernel-size: 300, strides: 10	ReLU
Max-pool	pool-size: 10, strides: 5	–
Flatten	–	–
Dense	neurons: 32	ReLU
Dropout	dropout rate: 0.2	–
Dense	neurons: 15	softmax

Formally,

$$M_{a,i} = f_a(x; W_{a,i})(i = 1, \ldots, n+t; a = 1, \ldots, g)$$

which means that i'th model for the a-th architecture is defined as a function of its weights and its inputs (x). Additionally,

$$W_{a,i} \neq W_{a,j}$$

where $j \in \{1, 2, .., n+t\} \setminus \{i\}$. The function f_a depends on the architecture of the model. Overall, $g \times (n+t) = 120$ models were created. The input and batch size of the models during the experiments were set to $32 \times 32 \times 3$ and 1, respectively.

We define a simple convolutional neural network as our classifier, shown in Table 2, as they have proven to be effective in the SCA context [14,28]. We collect 200 measurements for each model in the training and validation sets and 20 measurements per model in the test set, which amounts to 15 900 traces altogether. Out of the 15 900 traces, the test set contains 900 measurements, and the remaining 15 000 traces are divided into training and validation sets in a 70:30 ratio, i.e., the model is trained using 10 500 traces and validated using 4 500 traces. In addition, early stopping is used to avoid overfitting. After the model is trained, it is evaluated on the test set and the accuracy of the model was 99%. Note from the previous section that distinguishing the architectures is not difficult; hence, the almost perfect accuracy is not surprising.

4   Discussion

4.1   Limitations

The attacks described are specific to this device's GPU and the CUDA kernel implementations provided by the specific TensorRT version used. In addition, we work with the assumption that well-known architectures are used by the victim. If a target device runs a different architecture, that is not in the dataset used for profiling, then the attack does not work unless profiling is extended to more architectures. However, with extensive profiling, we believe it is possible to cover a wide array of architectures with different types of layers.

4.2   Mitigation

Traditional ways to contain electromagnetic radiation, such as proper shielding or introducing noise to decrease the Signal-to-Noise ratio, could alleviate the problem [24].

Additionally, the architectures investigated in this work are popular because of their efficiency and accuracy. However, ignoring these architectures and designing custom networks could make an adversary's job significantly harder. A custom-designed neural network basically means an infinite number of possible combinations of layers, layer sizes, etc. On the other hand, there are common design principles for neural networks which narrow down the search space. For instance, if a neural network performs classification, then it is safe to assume that the last layer has a softmax activation.

Profiling also applies to custom-made neural networks, and a persistent adversary could make a comprehensive profile that could also identify the types of layers and layer sizes, as these are the main factors that influence EM measurements.

4.3   Alternative Method

In this work, analyzing traces of whole architectures is enough to show that reverse engineering the architecture is possible. However, one could reverse engineer a whole architecture by running just parts of the architecture on the unprotected device. In other words, starting with only the first layer of the architecture, then with the first two, then the first three, and so on. With this perhaps a bit of a time-consuming (due to the large number of layers in the investigated architectures) method, the individual layers can be identified in the traces, not just the whole architecture. Since the number of parameters for these architectures is constant, except perhaps for the first and last layers, this method remains viable. The traces for the first and last layers can potentially be different because input and output sizes are specific to each problem.

4.4   Example of Breaking down Network

In order to identify individual layers, one has to consider the layer type as well as the activation (if any) of the layer. As we have seen in the classification results, different weights barely impact the overall EM trace. Thus, we can concentrate on building templates for one-layer MLPs with and without activation, 2-layer MLPs with and without activation, and so on. To that end, a 3-layer MLP will be reverse-engineered using this method. In the experiment, the input batch size is 1, the input size is 100, and every fully connected layer has 32 neurons.

Figure 4 shows how the EM trace changes if a ReLU activation is removed. The top figure is a trace of a 3-layer MLP where the fully connected layers are followed by ReLU activation. The bottom figure is a trace of the same MLP, except that a ReLU layer does not follow the last fully connected layer.

3-layer MLP with three and two relu activations

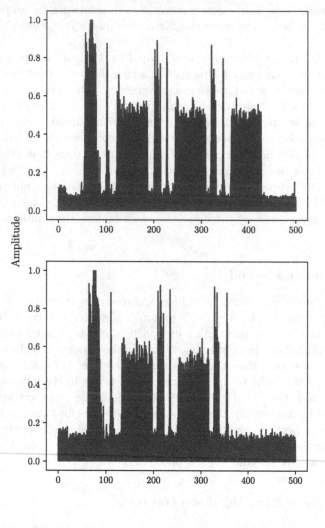

Fig. 4. 3-layer MLP with 3 ReLU activations (top) and 2 ReLU activations (bottom)

Continuing the removal of layers and activations one by one, the top figure in Fig. 5 shows how the EM trace changes if a fully connected layer is removed. The MLP in the bottom figure in Fig. 4 has a third fully connected layer, and the top figure in Fig. 5 is the same MLP except that the last fully connected layer is missing. Next, the removal of the ReLU activation that follows the second fully connected layer leads to a trace as that of the bottom figure in Fig. 5.

2-layer MLP with two and one relu activations

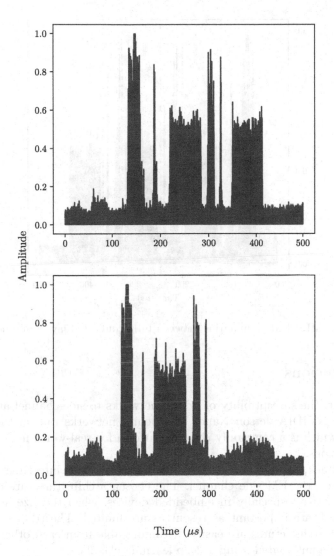

Fig. 5. 2-layer MLP with 2 ReLU activations (top) and 1 ReLU activation (bottom)

Removing layers one by one helps identify layer boundaries. Figure 6 shows the trace for the 3-layer MLP with boundaries drawn with red dashed lines after every fully connected layer and every activation. Overall, profiling can also be executed on a more granular level, e.g. layer level, but this requires more profiling to cover all the possible layer types with varying sizes.

3-layer MLP with three relu activations

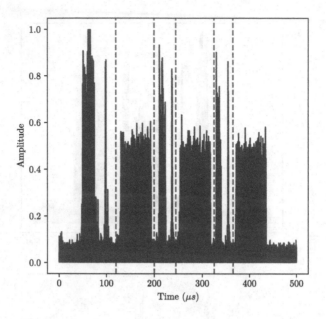

Fig. 6. 3-layer MLP with boundaries between fully connected layers and activations.

5   Conclusions

In this paper, the susceptibility of neural networks to side-channel attacks was analyzed on NVIDIA Jetson Nano. The neural networks ran on the GPU of the device, which is a commonly chosen platform for real-world neural network implementations.

In our attack, popular convolutional neural network architectures were classified based on the EM side channel. The chosen architectures are a common choice in practice, especially in embedded devices, when the size and latency of the network are important as resources are limited. The results show that the analyzed architectures are easily distinguishable from each other, and this process can be automated using a deep learning classifier.

Overall, the neural network implementations of NVIDIA's TensorRT framework are vulnerable to architecture extraction using side-channel attacks despite the networks running in a highly parallel and noisy environment.

References

1. https://web.archive.org/web/20220119062522/.   https://www.riscure.com/uploa ds/2017/07/inspector_brochure.pdf. Accessed 25 Jan 2022
2. Google translate research. https://ai.googleblog.com/2020/06/recent-advances-in-google-translate.html

3. Batina, L., Bhasin, S., Jap, D., Picek, S.: CSI–NN: reverse engineering of neural network architectures through electromagnetic side channel. In: 28th USENIX Security Symposium USENIX Security 2019, pp. 515–532 (2019)

4. Bernstein, D.J.: Cache-timing attacks on AES (2005)

5. Chmielewski, Ł, Weissbart, L.: On reverse engineering neural network implementation on GPU. In: Zhou, J., et al. (eds.) ACNS 2021. LNCS, vol. 12809, pp. 96–113. Springer, Cham (2021). https://doi.org/10.1007/978-3-030-81645-2_7

6. Chollet, F.: Xception: deep learning with depthwise separable convolutions. In: Proceedings of the IEEE Conference on Computer Vision and Pattern Recognition, pp. 1251–1258 (2017)

7. Elibol, F., Sarac, U., Erer, I.: Realistic eavesdropping attacks on computer displays with low-cost and mobile receiver system. In: 2012 Proceedings of the 20th European Signal Processing Conference (EUSIPCO), pp. 1767–1771. IEEE (2012)

8. He, K., Zhang, X., Ren, S., Sun, J.: Deep residual learning for image recognition. In: Proceedings of the IEEE Conference on Computer Vision and Pattern Recognition, pp. 770–778 (2016)

9. Hongxin, Z., Yuewang, H., Jianxin, W., Yinghua, L., Jinling, Z.: Recognition of electro-magnetic leakage information from computer radiation with SVM. Comput. Secur. 28(1–2), 72–76 (2009)

10. Howard, A., et al.: Searching for MobileNetV3. In: Proceedings of the IEEE/CVF International Conference on Computer Vision, pp. 1314–1324 (2019)

11. Howard, A.G., et al.: MobileNets: efficient convolutional neural networks for mobile vision applications. arXiv preprint arXiv:1704.04861 (2017)

12. Hu, J., Shen, L., Sun, G.: Squeeze-and-excitation networks. In: Proceedings of the IEEE Conference on Computer Vision and Pattern Recognition, pp. 7132 7141 (2018)

13. Huang, G., Liu, Z., Van Der Maaten, L., Weinberger, K.Q.: Densely connected convolutional networks. In: Proceedings of the IEEE Conference on Computer Vision and Pattern Recognition, pp. 4700–4708 (2017)

14. Kim, J., Picek, S., Heuser, A., Bhasin, S., Hanjalic, A.: Make some noise. Unleashing the power of convolutional neural networks for profiled side-channel analysis. IACR Trans. Cryptogr. Hardware Embed. Syst. 148–179 (2019)

15. Kocher, P., Jaffe, J., Jun, B.: Differential power analysis. In: Wiener, M. (ed.) CRYPTO 1999. LNCS, vol. 1666, pp. 388–397. Springer, Heidelberg (1999). https://doi.org/10.1007/3-540-48405-1_25

16. Kocher, P.C.: Timing attacks on implementations of Diffie-Hellman, RSA, DSS, and other systems. In: Koblitz, N. (ed.) CRYPTO 1996. LNCS, vol. 1109, pp. 104–113. Springer, Heidelberg (1996). https://doi.org/10.1007/3-540-68697-5_9

17. Krizhevsky, A., Sutskever, I., Hinton, G.E.: ImageNet classification with deep convolutional neural networks. In: Advances in Neural Information Processing Systems, vol. 25, pp. 1097–1105 (2012)

18. Kuhn, M.G., Anderson, R.J.: Soft tempest: hidden data transmission using electromagnetic emanations. In: Aucsmith, D. (ed.) IH 1998. LNCS, vol. 1525, pp. 124–142. Springer, Heidelberg (1998). https://doi.org/10.1007/3-540-49380-8_10

19. Liang, S., Zhan, Z., Yao, F., Cheng, L., Zhang, Z.: Clairvoyance: exploiting far-field EM emanations of GPU to "see" your DNN models through obstacles at a distance. In: 2022 IEEE Security and Privacy Workshops (SPW), pp. 312–322 (2022). https://doi.org/10.1109/SPW54247.2022.9833894

20. Lin, M., Chen, Q., Yan, S.: Network in network. arXiv preprint arXiv:1312.4400 (2013)

21. Liu, L., et al.: Deep learning for generic object detection: a survey. Int. J. Comput. Vis. **128**(2), 261–318 (2020)
22. Liu, Z., et al.: Screen gleaning: a screen reading TEMPEST attack on mobile devices exploiting an electromagnetic side channel. In: 28th Annual Network and Distributed System Security Symposium, NDSS 2021, Virtually, 21–25, February 2021. The Internet Society (2021). https://www.ndss-symposium.org/ndss-paper/screen-gleaning-a-screen-reading-tempest-attack-on-mobile-devices-exploiting-an-electromagnetic-side-channel/
23. Maia, H.T., Xiao, C., Li, D., Grinspun, E., Zheng, C.: Can one hear the shape of a neural network?: snooping the GPU via magnetic side channel. In: Butler, K.R.B., Thomas, K. (eds.) 31st USENIX Security Symposium, USENIX Security 2022, Boston, MA, USA, 10–12 August 2022, pp. 4383–4400. USENIX Association (2022). https://www.usenix.org/conference/usenixsecurity22/presentation/maia
24. Mangard, S., Oswald, E., Popp, T.: Power Analysis Attacks: Revealing the Secrets of Smart Cards, vol. 31. Springer, Cham (2008)
25. OpenAI: GPT-4 technical report (2023). https://doi.org/10.48550/arXiv.2303.08774
26. Otter, D.W., Medina, J.R., Kalita, J.K.: A survey of the usages of deep learning for natural language processing. IEEE Trans. Neural Netw. Learn. Syst. **32**(2), 604–624 (2020)
27. Page, D.: Theoretical use of cache memory as a cryptanalytic side-channel. Cryptology ePrint Archive (2002)
28. Picek, S., Perin, G., Mariot, L., Wu, L., Batina, L.: SoK: deep learning-based physical side-channel analysis. ACM Comput. Surv. (2022)
29. Quisquater, J.-J., Samyde, D.: ElectroMagnetic analysis (EMA): measures and counter-measures for smart cards. In: Attali, I., Jensen, T. (eds.) E-smart 2001. LNCS, vol. 2140, pp. 200–210. Springer, Heidelberg (2001). https://doi.org/10.1007/3-540-45418-7_17
30. Ramachandran, P., Zoph, B., Le, Q.V.: Searching for activation functions. arXiv preprint arXiv:1710.05941 (2017)
31. Sandler, M., Howard, A., Zhu, M., Zhmoginov, A., Chen, L.C.: MobileNetV2: inverted residuals and linear bottlenecks. In: Proceedings of the IEEE Conference on Computer Vision and Pattern Recognition, pp. 4510–4520 (2018)
32. Silver, D., et al.: Mastering the game of go with deep neural networks and tree search. Nature **529**(7587), 484–489 (2016)
33. Silver, D., et al.: Mastering chess and shogi by self-play with a general reinforcement learning algorithm. arXiv preprint arXiv:1712.01815 (2017)
34. Simonyan, K., Zisserman, A.: Very deep convolutional networks for large-scale image recognition. arXiv preprint arXiv:1409.1556 (2014)
35. Singh, S.: The Code Book, vol. 7. Doubleday New York (1999)
36. Tan, M., Le, Q.: EfficientNet: rethinking model scaling for convolutional neural networks. In: International Conference on Machine Learning, pp. 6105–6114. PMLR (2019)
37. Van Eck, W.: Electromagnetic radiation from video display units: an eavesdropping risk? Comput. Secur. **4**(4), 269–286 (1985)
38. Vaswani, A., et al.: Attention is all you need. In: Advances in Neural Information Processing Systems, vol. 30 (2017)
39. Vinyals, O., et al.: Grandmaster level in StarCraft II using multi-agent reinforcement learning. Nature **575**(7782), 350–354 (2019)

40. Xiang, Y., et al.: Open DNN box by power side-channel attack. IEEE Trans. Circuits Syst. II Express Briefs **67**(11), 2717–2721 (2020). https://doi.org/10.1109/TCSII.2020.2973007
41. Xie, S., Girshick, R., Dollár, P., Tu, Z., He, K.: Aggregated residual transformations for deep neural networks. In: Proceedings of the IEEE Conference on Computer Vision and Pattern Recognition, pp. 1492–1500 (2017)
42. Zhang, X., Zhou, X., Lin, M., Sun, J.: ShuffleNet: an extremely efficient convolutional neural network for mobile devices. In: Proceedings of the IEEE Conference on Computer Vision and Pattern Recognition, pp. 6848–6856 (2018)
43. Zoph, B., Vasudevan, V., Shlens, J., Le, Q.V.: Learning transferable architectures for scalable image recognition. In: Proceedings of the IEEE Conference on Computer Vision and Pattern Recognition, pp. 8697–8710 (2018)

Harnessing the Power of General-Purpose LLMs in Hardware Trojan Design

Georgios Kokolakis[✉], Athanasios Moschos, and Angelos D. Keromytis

Georgia Institute of Technology, Atlanta, USA
{gkokolakis6,amoschos,angelos}@gatech.edu

Abstract. Large language models (LLMs) are becoming a powerful transformative force of automation in the areas of software engineering and cybersecurity. In software-centric security research, the LLMs have undertaken a prime role in the identification and repair of security vulnerabilities and bugs. However, in hardware related fields such as logic design and hardware security, use of LLMs has only recently started to get traction. In this work we aim to explore the potential of LLMs in the offensive hardware security domain. More specifically, we explore the level of assistance that LLMs can provide to attackers for the insertion of vulnerabilities, known as hardware trojans (HTs), in complex hardware designs (*e.g.,* CPUs). Having in mind high-level attack outlines, we test the ability of a general-purpose LLM to act as a "filter" that correlates system level concepts of security interest with specific module abstractions of hardware designs. By doing so, we tackle the challenges posed by the context length limit of LLMs, that become prevalent during LLM-based analyses of large code bases. Next, we initiate an LLM analysis of the reduced code base, that includes only the register transfer level code of the identified modules and test the LLM's ability to locate the parts that implement the queried security related features. In this way, we reduce the complexity of the overall analysis performed by the LLM. Lastly, we instruct the LLM to insert suitable trojan functionalities by modifying the identified code parts accordingly. To showcase the potential of our automated LLM-based hardware trojan insertion flow, we craft a realistic HT for a modern RISC-V micro-architecture. We test the functionality of the LLM-generated HT on an FPGA board, by attacking the integrity and the availability of the RISC-V CPU. Hence, we demonstrate how general-purpose LLMs can navigate attackers through complex hardware designs and assist them in the implementation of realistic HT attacks.

Keywords: Hardware Trojans · Large Language Models · ChatGPT · RISC-V

G. Kokolakis and A. Moschos—All student authors contributed equally to this paper.

1   Introduction

Large language models are artificial intelligence algorithms that utilize deep learning techniques to perform various natural language processing tasks. By implementing deep learning techniques (*e.g.,* transformer architectures [58]) language models are able to process vast amounts of text data and generate coherent human language responses. This is due to their remarkable ability of assimilating the context and relationships between human words. By dint of their diverse dataset, LLMs have shown great potential in performing a series of complex tasks both in the software and the hardware engineering domain.

In software engineering, LLMs are mainly employed as tools that assist in the generation of code [1,18,26,31,35–37,39,41,42,50,53,61,65], the identification of vulnerabilities and bugs [19,20,29,32,60] and recently bug correction [25,47,62]. In parallel, domain-specific LLMs have been developed to address more specialized tasks, like in the all-important fields of medical diagnosis and healthcare assistance [24].

On the hardware engineering domain, encompassing of language models seems to be more challenging due to the limited hardware description language (HDL) code bases available in the wild. Furthermore, generation of bug-free HDL code is usually more challenging and demands particular attention and expertise. Another issue attributed to the restricted availability of HDL, is the frequent inability of LLMs to produce syntactically correct and synthesizable HDL code.

A recent academic attempt tried to tackle this problem by fine-tuning pre-trained LLMs on Verilog datasets [56]. Another work [57], focused on the generation of an automated framework called Autochip, that aims to correct bugs in LLM-generated HDL code. Chang et al. [5] discuss the ways LLMs can aid hardware engineers in producing more efficient logic designs through natural language interaction. The authors developed an LLM-based design environment, named ChipGPT, that can generate optimal logic designs through the use of natural language specifications.

The hardware security community has only recently started to explore ways in which LLMs can be utilized in system on chip (SoC) security. So far, LLMs have showed promising results in formal verification tasks [33,45,54], as well as generation of secure hardware [38,40,46,54]. The works explore different aspects of the SoC security, pertaining to the correct generation of assertions (e.g., SystemVerilog Assertions), the extraction of security properties dedicated to hardware design, the generation of code for hardware security assertion and lastly the detection of hardware vulnerabilities.

A universal characteristic of LLMs, is their ability to receive inputs written in natural languages. The inputs are then further processed, taking the form of tokens. Depending on the underlying algorithm, the representation of a token can be a word [4], a sub-word [51,52,59] or a character [28]. Tokenization is important, as it contributes to the reduction of computational and memory costs and can assist in the assimilation of complex words and concepts by the model [3]. However, LLMs do not posses the ability to receive unlimited amount of tokens with each input. This can have a negative impact in cases where the input length is considerably large (*i.e.,* software programs consist usually of numerous lengthy code files). Consequently, it is important to identify *effective filtering strategies* that can address the challenge of context length limit when there is need of analyzing complex code databases with LLMs. Commonly used filtering strategies so far include either manual inspection or employment of external tools to help locate only the necessary files or code segments for the analysis.

In this work, we aim to leverage the use of a general-purpose LLM, to tackle the challenge of efficiently filtering through complex hardware design databases, for the purpose of hardware trojan insertion. Hardware trojans are malicious modifications made in the logic of hardware designs, that can alleviate the implementation of attacks on the systems that host them. To that extent, we explore the potential of LLMs in the implementation of efficient hardware trojan attacks. Our contributions are the following:

- We discuss how the challenge of context length limit has been addressed in relevant literature.
- We present an automated flow that encompasses a general-purpose LLM, to identify suitable candidate modules in large HDL databases for the insertion of trojans.
- Using our methodology, we perform among others, an end-to-end HT attack on a complex RISC-V micro-architecture.

We observe that our methodology can help in the exploration of potential attack routes available for the implementation of HT functionalities in hardware designs. Thus, our methodology reduces the overall complexity associated with the design of a hardware trojan attack.

Paper Organization: Section 2 presents relevant works around the use of large language models in the detection, repair and insertion of hardware vulnerabilities. Section 3 outlines the threat model considered for the use of our attack methodology. Section 4 introduces our LLM-based automated design flow and explores the implementation of trojan attacks in a diverse design dataset. In Sect. 5 we showcase the power of our insertion flow, in a proof of concept hardware trojan attack against a modern RISC-V CPU. In Sect. 6 we discuss possible limitations of our flow and provide future research directions in the intersection of LLMs with hardware trojan design. We conclude in Sect. 7.

2   Background and Related Work

The use of artificial intelligence (AI) programs has recently started to take shape in the system on chip security domain through the use of LLMs and LLM-based frameworks. Ahmad et al. [2] investigated the use of natural language guidance for the remediation of security-related hardware vulnerabilities. To that end, the authors generated a bug-fixing framework based upon the use of two general-purpose LLMs, namely OpenAI's Codex [43] and CodeGen [42]. For the quantitative evaluation of the framework, the authors collated a database of hardware

Table 1. Use of automation in context length filtering for hardware vulnerability related works.

Publication	Vulnerability-Related Operation	Context Length Filtering Automation	LLM Type Utilized	Design Database
[2]	Repair	✗	General-Purpose	CPU, Security Modules
[27]	Detection, Repair	✓	Domain-Specific	CPU
[49]	Detection, Repair, Insertion	✗	General-Purpose	CPU, Security Modules, FSMs
Our Work	Insertion	✓	General-Purpose	CPU, Security Modules

designs that featured security related bugs, taken either from MITRE's common weaknesses enumeration (CWE) list or relevant hardware security competitions (*e.g.*, Hack@DAC). The database was then used in the construction of appropriate prompts that were used as input to the framework, in order to generate efficacy metrics about the LLM-proposed solutions in the remediation of the vulnerabilities. To formulate the prompts, only the parts of the buggy RTL code were provided as part of the prompts. The code selection process included either feedback taken by bug detector tools or the assumption of *a priori knowledge* of the code at fault. The necessity of assistance for the bug location identification (*e.g.*, code selection) is further acknowledged and discussed as one of the framework's limiting factors.

In [27], the authors showcase a unique approach in the training of domain specific LLMs for the purposes of identification and subsequent correction of hardware defects. Their approach utilized the version control data available in open-source hardware designs, in order to assemble a dataset of hardware design defects accompanied with their remediation steps. This special dataset was subsequently used for the generation of a framework that enabled the domain-specific training of medium sized language models. The authors proceeded to assess the efficacy of the hardware debugging framework by comparing the domain-specific LLMs against state of the art general-purpose LLMs (*e.g.*, Chat-GPT and Bard) in the generation of hardware remedies. The "hardware-patches" proposed by the fine-tuned models, were indeed more efficient than the solutions proposed by their general-purpose counterparts. An important part of the training methodology, is that of data sanitization. This is considered to be essential due to the LLMs' adherence to specific context length constraints. Therefore, the prompt generation process needs to be cost-aware. To that end, while files with insufficient information were excluded from partaking in the dataset generation process, the larger ones were segmented in appropriate lengths through a tokenization process, in order to be further considered in the generation of the dataset.

Saha et al. [49] published an in-depth analysis on the use of generative pre-trained transformers (GPTs) in state of the art works related to SoC software and hardware security. In their work, a thorough investigation is attempted over the possibilities stemming from the integration of a variety of LLM architectures in domains related to vulnerability detection, repair and insertion in

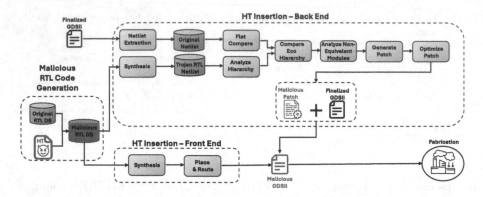

Fig. 1. Abstract view of the insertion options for an LLM-generated hardware trojan.

SoCs. Among others, their work tests the ability of ChatGPT-3.5 to efficiently integrate CWE-based vulnerabilities in hardware designs and more specifically inside finite state machines. The primary method pursued for the introduction of the vulnerabilities is that of one/few-shot learning. To that end, ChatGPT was presented with the part of the RTL code that needs to be maliciously modified, as well as an informative description of the hardware modifications that need to be implemented in the provided piece of code. The part of the code that was adjusted, was considered again to be known a priori. A deciding factor for choosing ChatGPT in the implementation of the experiments was the model's ability to handle extended context lengths in the provided prompts. However, the context length limits in LLM chatbots is discussed by the authors to be a significant challenge, especially when it comes to handling larger design tasks. Therefore, they consider this to potentially adversely affect the models' efficiency in performing security related tasks.

All of the works in Table 1 attempt to operate on databases of complex hardware designs (*e.g.,* CPUs). Irrespective of the LLM-framework basis (domain-specific or general-purpose), *the constrained context length limit* remains a reality for all of the suggested LLMs. In the SoC domain, this problem particularly manifests when dealing with complex RTL databases (*i.e.,* micro-architecture implementations) which consist of dozens of HDL files and tens of thousands of code lines, as seen in Table 4. Therefore, *an automated strategy* is necessary in the identification of code parts of interest, so that *context length is reduced.*

The works in [2,49] consider the HDL code of interest that is included in prompts, to be either already known or made known through the use of external code vulnerability detectors [2]. We consider these approaches to be non-automated as seen in Table 1. For the work in [27], the files are scrutinized for inefficiencies and then tokenized before their use in prompts. We therefore consider this work to include sufficient automation in the code of interest selection process. From these works, only [49] includes a detailed discussion about use of LLMs for hardware trojan insertion. However, as mentioned, the respective RTL is manually selected and then provided to the GPT model for the vulnerability insertion. Our work aims to address this gap in the use of LLMs in the offensive hardware security domain. *We provide a methodology that automates the filtering of large design databases for context length purposes*, to alleviate the insertion of vulnerabilities known as hardware trojans, in complex RTL designs. We now proceed to explain the threat model under which our LLM-automated methodology can be used by an attacker for the insertion of a hardware trojan.

3   Threat Model

We consider the use of general-purpose LLMs to be an attractive option for a rogue entity inside a design house tasked with the insertion of a hardware trojan. The scenario of a design stage attacker has been featured before in several works [21,22,30,34]. The presence of a design stage attacker means that the rogue entity is familiar with IC design practices, like logic design, simulation, physical implementation and verification. For the successful introduction of a HT the malicious actor would need to either have knowledge of the design under attack or perform code review to get an understanding of the underlying design. However, especially for large designs (*e.g.*, SoCs) such an analysis, proves impractical as it requires significant time and effort. Consequently, the introduction of an LLM in this process can help alleviate the cumbersome task of pinpointing the parts of code to be altered. We show the practicality of this approach in Sect. 5. Another interesting outcome from the use of an LLM at this stage, is that it allows for a more relaxed assumption in terms of the attacker's familiarity with the specifics of the design to be modified. For example, the malicious actor can be a company engineer with access to the design servers but not directly working on the design under attack. The above rationale leads to the following scenarios in terms of an LLM-guided trojan insertion:

i) The HT is added at the front-end phase. The malicious actor, using the LLM as a guide, adjusts the RTL database of the design to include the malicious functionality. If the change goes unnoticed, the malicious RTL database will proceed to the synthesis and the physical implementation stages for the generation of the malicious finalized layout as seen in Fig. 1. The malicious finalized layout, represented in a GDSII file form, is then sent for fabrication.

ii) The HT is added at the back-end phase via engineering change orders (ECO) on the finalized layout. Functional ECOs are logic modifications made directly to the gate level netlist of the finalized layout and correspond to RTL code changes. In this scenario, the finalized layout has been generated and is ready to be shipped for fabrication. Therefore, a change at this point is considered to be more stealthy, as the attacker tampers directly the ready to tape out layout. The steps for this scenario are depicted in Fig. 1. Similar to the front-end scenario, the attacker uses the LLM as a guide, to make the necessary adjustments in the RTL code of the design for the inclusion of the trojan. The attacker then passes the malicious RTL database through

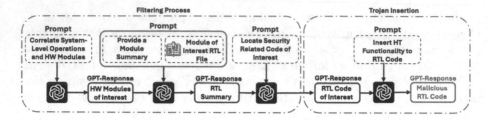

Fig. 2. Our LLM-based Hardware Trojan Design Flow

a synthesis round and generates a malicious synthesized netlist. As a next step, the malicious netlist is compared to the extracted netlist from the original layout, using logic equivalence check tools. The outcome of this check is the difference in logic between the two netlists, that is translated to a *digital patch*, ready to be applied on the existing finalized layout. This digital patch basically contains only the extra malicious logic that describes the trojan functionality. As a last step, the attacker uses physical implementation tools to apply the patch through the use of ECOs on the original layout and generates the new malicious finalized layout. Since the ECOs can keep the existing layout intact and avoid the deterioration of the layout's timings, the inclusion of the HT can fly under the radar and not raise any suspicion about possible changes in the finalized layout.

Next, we proceed to describe our LLM-based automated filtering method, that reduces the context length of the prompts used for the hardware trojan insertion. We also show our experimental results by applying this method and attacking different hardware designs (*e.g.,* a RISC-V microarchitecture, cryptographic algorithms) using the GPT-3.5/4 models.

4   An LLM-Based Hardware Trojan Design Flow

Typical system on chip designs comprise of numerous modules described usually in Verilog or VHDL hardware description languages. As mentioned in Sect. 2, these complex databases consist of tens of thousands of code lines. The naive approach of providing to the LLM under use the complete HDL database for analysis, is not feasible. This is because the input LLM prompts need to abide to a maximum context length limit that sets an upper bound to the number of words that a prompt can have. Therefore, to automate the vulnerability insertion through the use of LLMs, an attacker needs to create a filtering process that would provide to the LLM only the part of the HDL code that is necessary for the introduction of the hardware trojan. This naturally brings up the need for a *filtering process*, that will allow the attacker to navigate through the complexity of the respective design under attack and filter out any modules not fit for the attack implementation. *We observe that this filtering process can be implemented through the use of general-purpose GPT models.*

Table 2. Correlating system level concepts with hardware modules of a CPU architecture.

System-Level Concept	User-GPT Dialogue	# of Prompts	# of Repetitions
Hardware modules involved in read operations	[8]	1	0
Hardware modules handling illegal memory accesses exceptions	[6]	1	0
Hardware modules involved in high cache miss rate operations	[11]	1	0
Hardware modules handling privilege level separation	[7]	1	0
Hardware modules involved in time-expensive operations	[9]	1	0

More specifically, we show that through LLM prompting an attacker can correlate system-level concepts with different hardware modules and deduce information about the modules of attack interest. Next, the attacker can provide as input to the language model only the HDL code of the identified module(s). This approach can successfully reduce the amount of code submitted for inspection to the LLM, therefore minimizing the overall analysis complexity performed by the LLM and making it easier to abide by the LLM's context length limit. Figure 2 illustrates our proposed flow for automating the identification of candidate HT host modules in complex designs and the subsequent implanting of hardware trojans. Our flow is based on task decomposition [49] in order to streamline the attack into simple, actionable steps, that can be performed even by an attacker with incomplete knowledge about the specifics of the design under attack. We proceed now to explain our trojan design flow in more detail and provide experimental results.

4.1   Context Length Reduction

The objective of the first step in our automated trojan design flow, is to utilize the LLM as a filter that will provide to the attacker the names of the HW modules that are of attack interest. To that end, an attacker can query the general-purpose LLM about the names of modules that take part in the implementation of different system level tasks performed by the design under attack. To showcase the aforementioned ability of LLMs to correlate system level concepts with hardware modules of interest, we questioned OpenAI's GPT-3.5 and GPT-4 models about different system level operations that happen inside a CPU and asked for the CPU modules that implement them. Table 2 showcases the system concept that the GPT was queried for, the number of prompts used to receive back a useful response, as well as references to the dialogues between the user and the GPT model. For all the queries, the LLM was able to provide a detailed description of each module and its involvement in the specific system-level operation. The questions were formulated under the rationale that such system level functionalities and modules can be utilized by a malicious entity for the purposes of a hardware trojan design. For instance, information about the CPU module that generates exceptions related to unauthorized memory accesses can be exploited by an attacker, in order to create a HT that facilitates such unauthorized accesses, as we see later in Sect. 5.

4.2   Identifying RTL Code of Interest

Once the name of the module of attack interest is identified, the second step is to provide as input to the general-purpose LLM the HDL code that describes it. As seen in Fig. 2, the module's HDL code is included in a prompt that is provided to the LLM, so that a synopsis of the module's functionalities is received back as a response. This synopsis can provide a valuable insight to the attacker about the characteristics of the module's design.

Having in mind the high level attack scenario, the malicious actor then proceeds to ask for more information about the way specific security related functionalities are implemented in the design. Moreover, the attacker requests from the LLM to pinpoint to the code locations associated with the realization of these functionalities. Once the respective locations are identified, the attacker can provide more specialized requests for the appropriate modification of the HDL code, in order to introduce the trojan functionality. Care must be taken, so that the changes performed by the LLM do not break any of the original code functionality. To that end, the attacker we consider in our threat model is in a position to verify that the original functionality is kept intact by functionally testing the modules.

To test the ability of ChatGPT to successfully pinpoint the security-related code parts, we perform five different attacks on a set of cryptographic hardware designs and the design of an open-source RISC-V micro-architecture. The scenarios we consider can be seen in Table 3, along with the number of prompts and repetitions used to receive back a useful response, as well as references to the dialogues between the user and the GPT model. We include bellow a succinct summary of the attack scenarios that the GPT model was asked to perform. The scenarios range from traditional leakage information attacks (*e.g.*, leaking the AES key) to more sophisticated CPU memory attacks (*e.g.*, tampering privileged memory areas without privilege escalation). For the attacks on the hardware security modules we use an open-source implementation of a DES algorithm [48] and an open-source implementation of an AES algorithm [55]. For the implementation of the more sophisticated attacks, we target the implementation of a modern, Linux-capable, 64-bit RISC-V microprocessor, named CVA6 [63,64].

Reduction in DES Encryption Rounds. This scenario involves an attack against a hardware implementation of a DES encryption algorithm. The attack aims to reduce the number of rounds in its encryption scheme [23], thus making it less secure. Our goal is to evaluate if ChatGPT can locate the Verilog code segment responsible for performing the encryption rounds. We asked the LLM to provide the name of the module that needs to be adjusted in order to perform the encryption round reduction attack. The LLM successfully located the Verilog file and the encryption round loop code, giving us instructions on how to modify it to reduce the encryption rounds.

Leakage of an AES Secret Key. In this scenario we examine if ChatGPT can guide us in the implementation of an HT that would leak an AES secret

Table 3. High level description and prompt metrics for different hardware trojan attack scenarios.

Module	High-Level Description of the Attack Scenario	User-GPT Dialogue	# of Prompts	# of Repetitions
DES	Reduction in DES encryption rounds	[13]	3	0
AES	Leakage of the AES secret key	[10]	4	1
CVA6	Speculative execution of wrong-path instructions	[14]	4	5
CVA6	Performance reduction via thermal attacks	[11, 12]	4, 5	2, 0
CVA6	Violation of OS-enforced memory policies	[15–17]	3, 3, 6	6, 0, 5

key. Our goal is to evaluate if ChatGPT can locate Verilog code segments that upon modification can lead to a key leakage. The LLM located the module that is responsible for handling the AES key, including its generation and storage. Subsequently, it provided suggestions with respect to modifications that can lead to a key leakage.

Speculative Execution of Wrong-Path Instructions. In this scenario we explore the possibility of a privilege escalation attack. The rationale is to interfere with the branch prediction logic of the CVA6 CPU, in order to execute non-privileged Instructions while the CPU is in privilege mode. We asked the LLM to identify the modules associated with the branch prediction in the CVA6 micro-architecture. We then provided as input the HDL description of the identified module and queried the model for code changes that an attacker can explore to perform the above mentioned attack. As seen in [14], the model responded with suggestions that involved modifications in code parts that describe the prediction logic and the logic that updates the branch target address.

Thermal Attacks on CPU Performance. In this scenario we explore the possibility of CPU performance degradation through the introduction of inefficiencies in the CPU's pipeline. We examined two possible attacks, namely introduction of dummy loops and generation of frequent cache misses.

- Dummy Loop Introduction: in this attack we aim to introduce inefficiencies or loops in the instruction scheduler or the execution stage that will cause the CPU to perform intensive operations continuously, thus increasing heat generation. To achieve that ChatGPT pointed us to the ALU module of the CPU and suggested code changes that would add dummy logic, to increase the switching activity and inevitably the CPU's temperature.
- Cache Evictions: in this attack the cache controller was targeted by the GPT model, to cause frequent cache misses. Suggested modifications included altering the code of the FSM responsible for the cache eviction policies.

Violation of OS Memory Policies. This attack scenario attempts to perform an attack against the integrity and availability of the CPU. Specifically modifi-

Table 4. Complexity of hardware designs measured by number of HDL files and lines of code.

Design Name	GitHub Repository	# of HDL Files	# of Code Lines
DES	[48]	15	1007
AES	[55]	7	2714
CVA6	[63]	96	28559

cations in the micro-architecture are required, so that under certain conditions, a user space process will be able to access the restricted kernel space memory. For that, the LLM targeted the modules that handle the privilege level checks inside the memory management unit (MMU). The LLM successfully located the code that generates an exception when the user process attempts to access memory areas assigned to the kernel. Then it suggested changes that included the modification of specific bits of page table entries (PTE), in order to circumvent the generation of an exception and allow the illegal access. In the next section, we further explore this attack scenario and use our automated methodology in conjunction with GPT-3.5 and GPT-4 models, to implement a fully functional hardware trojan inside the CVA6 micro-architecture.

5   Evaluation of an LLM-Generated HT

In this section, we present the implementation of a fully functional hardware trojan inside the CVA6 CPU design. Having in mind the high level attack we want to implement, we provide prompts to the GPT model, that help in the identification of host modules in the CVA6 micro-architecture suitable for implementation of the hardware trojan payload.

Identifying Suitable HT Host Modules. As can be seen in Table 4, the CVA6 design is considerably complex, as it is comprised of 96 HDL files and a total of 28.5K lines of System Verilog code. We utilize the GPT model to filter through the micro-architecture's design modules and find suitable host candidates for the integration of the trojan's malicious functionality. The attack we want to implement aims to violate the separation of the memory address space, enforced by the operating system, between privileged and non-privileged areas. More specifically, we want to enable a user space process controlled by a malicious actor, to access and modify arbitrary addresses in the kernel space memory without the need for privilege escalation. To circumvent any ethical objections posed by the LLM model, we express our prompts in the context of exploring new micro-architectural features. To that end, we craft the prompts seen in Figs. 3 and 4. The GPT model identifies the memory management unit (MMU) to be responsible for supporting the virtual memory management and the enforcement of memory protections. Consequently, this process filters down the candidate host modules that need to be adjusted for the implementation

User Prompt:

CVA6 is a Linux-capable 64-bit RISC-V microarchitecture. What modules in CVA6 enable the support of a Linux OS?

GPT Response:

...

However, for a RISC-V micro-architecture to support a Linux-based operating system, it needs to have several key components and features in place:

...

2. Memory Management Unit: A Linux-capable micro-architecture should have an MMU to support virtual memory management, address translation, and memory protection.

...

Fig. 3. Identify micro-architecture modules that support an operating system.

User Prompt:

Assume the CPU architect of CVA6 wants to allow a user process, under specific conditions, to overwrite parts of the kernel address space. The architecture of which CVA6 module should be altered for this change to take effect?

GPT Response:

...altering a RISC-V micro-architecture like CVA6 to allow such behavior (again, not recommended), you would likely need to modify the Memory Management Unit (MMU) module. The MMU ...enforces memory protection and access control by distinguishing between user and kernel address spaces ...

Fig. 4. Identify micro-architecture modules responsible for the separation of the memory address space.

of the payload, to only one, that of the MMU. For more information on the identification of the MMU as a sutibale host module, we direct the reader to [15]. Next, the attacker needs to provide for code analysis to the LLM the HDL files that implement the MMU, in order to integrate the payload functionality. We now proceed to describe the implementation of the payload and the trigger circuit of the hardware trojan.

Designing the Payload Circuit. The CVA6 micro-architecture is written in System Verilog and the description of the MMU consists of a single HDL file out of a total of 96. At first, the GPT model reads the HDL file and provides as feedback a high-level description of the module's functionalities. Since we are interested in discovering the code responsible for the memory address space separation, we ask the GPT model to trace the code responsible for the generation of an exception in the event of an illegal memory access. The illegal access of interest happens upon accessing kernel space addresses while the CPU is in user mode privilege level. In a traditional scenario, a kernel memory access is valid only when the CPU has elevated privilege rights (supervisor or machine mode). In any other case, the access is obstructed with the generation of an exception. As seen in Fig. 5, the LLM model returns the part of the code that implements the exception mechanism of the memory management unit. The exception mechanism is responsible for the generation of page fault errors related to faulty load and store instructions.

The next step is to ask ChatGPT to modify the exception mechanism, so that our malicious functionality is added to the micro-architecture. In our attack scenario, upon triggering, the payload disables the generation of exceptions that happen during the execution of faulty store instructions. A faulty store instruction is considered to be one that attempts to alter the value of an address for which the privilege state of the processor does not concur with the privilege rights required to access it. Consequently, once activated, the trojan will enable a malicious user space process to access and modify addresses in the kernel space memory without the need for privilege escalation. We show in Fig. 6 that the LLM is able to add the requested trojan functionality by properly adjusting the identified Verilog code. For more information on how the GPT adjusted the memory management unit, we direct the reader to [16].

Designing the Trigger Circuit. The stealthiness of a hardware trojan is directly related to the specific conditions that enable the trigger signal and how easily these conditions can be met outside of an attack scenario. Ideally, the triggering conditions should be instigated only by the attacker. To generate the trigger signal, we target the register file (RF) module of CVA6. The RF is comprised by 32 integer and 32 floating-point registers, with each one being 64-bits long. The register file of CVA6 is flip-flop based and the architectural registers correspond one-for-one to the RF's physical entries. We ask the GPT model to attach the triggering circuit on two of the integer general purpose registers (GPRs). For the attack to be feasible, any set of architectural registers that can be reliably controlled (*i.e.*, load values) by the attacker, is suitable to insert the trigger. The triggering circuit passively monitors the values loaded in these two registers. When two specific 64-bit values are placed simultaneously in the chosen set of general-purpose registers, the HT is enabled and allows the tampering of arbitrary kernel space memory addresses by a user process. For more information on how the GPT adjusted the register file, we direct the reader to [17].

5.1 Hardware Trojan Attack Implementation

We implement the GPT-generated hardware trojan using Xilinx's Vivado and create a new HT-CVA6 bitstream. Table 5 shows the utilization of the overall CVA6 design inside the FPGA, along with the minimal footprint of the HT implementation with respect to the CVA6's size. We include these metrics, as they are typical in papers evaluating the HT's stealthiness.

To test the HT functionality we download the bitstream on a Genesys 2 FPGA board and boot inside a Linux OS. The effectiveness of the HT is tested

---

User Prompt:

Find the Verilog check that generates an error signal when kernel address space is accessed while in user mode. The check should be about data and not instructions. Show me the code.

GPT Response:

The Verilog code you provided includes a section where data access errors are checked for while considering the privilege level (user mode or supervisor mode) ...Specifically, it checks whether kernel address space is accessed while in user mode. The relevant code for this check is as follows: ...

Fig. 5. Identify the code part responsible for the generation of an exception in an illegal memory access.

User Prompt:

Now I want a new functionality to be added, without breaking the existing. Add next to signal "X" a new signal of type wire that will allow writing from the user address space to the kernel address space upon the signal's activation. The new signal is activated from a trigger condition I will provide later.

GPT Response:

...

In the above code:

- We declare a new wire signal called "Y" to control the ability to write from the user address space to the kernel address space.
- In the exception signal calculation, we modify the second condition ...to include "Y" as well. This means that if "Y" is not active (high), it will prevent writes from the user space to the kernel space, even if the user is in user mode ...

Fig. 6. Modify the conditions for illegal memory access exception generation to add the trojan functionality.

in two different attack scenarios: *(i)* against the integrity and *(ii)* against the availability of the CVA6 system. For both of the attacks, a malicious user process enables the trojan and proceeds to alter the values of arbitrary addresses in the kernel address space. The integrity attack is performed in a controlled setting and the affected addresses belong to custom-made Linux kernel modules (LKMs). At the end of the attack, the LKMs hold attack-influenced values, thus violating the integrity of the kernel. In the availability attack, the user process modifies addresses belonging to the *init_task* structure of the *init* process, leading to a kernel panic.

Table 5. CVA6 and HT utilization of resources inside the Genesys 2 FPGA board.

Module Name	LUTs	FFs
CVA6	72606	47178
Trigger Circuit	26	1
Payload Circuit	4	3

6 Discussion

Our experiments showcased that LLMs can provide an effective assistance to attackers looking to insert HTs in complex hardware designs. Nevertheless, we acknowledge that our study is limited to the use of a single general-purpose LLM on a small design dataset. Future research in the automation of hardware trojan attacks through large language models, should encompass an examination of a wider range of LLMs (both general-purpose and domain-specific) and a larger sample of hardware designs. Moreover, it is worth examining how fine-tuning of LLM parameters (*i.e.,* the temperature parameter in charge of the response creativity) can affect the quality of the LLM outputs and therefore the effectiveness of the generated HT designs. On top of that, it is important to focus research efforts on the implementation of frameworks that can verify the effectiveness of LLM-generated HTs.

As discussed in Sect. 4.1, our methodology provides a way to address the problem of context length limit in LLM prompts. However, we recognize that our solution can prove to be inefficient, if the size of the submitted for analysis HDL file surpasses the context length limit of the LLM's prompts. In such a scenario, an attacker will have to develop a more sophisticated strategy, similar to the tokenization approach of the LLM4SecHW framework [27], to segment the HDL code submitted for analysis. In our study, we did not encounter any such issue. We consider the 4096 tokens limit [44] for ChatGPT to be adequate enough to process typically-sized HDL files.

A future interesting direction in the intersection of language models with hardware trojans research would be to investigate how introduction of relevant HT publications in the feedback loop of LLMs, can lead to more efficient (*e.g.,* stealthy, smaller) hardware trojan designs. We consider such a technique to be attractive for attackers that want to encompass the latest advancements in hardware trojan design, to reshape or enhance the characteristics of their trojan implementations.

7 Conclusions

In this paper we presented an automated methodology that utilizes general-purpose LLMs for the analysis of complex hardware designs and the subsequent insertion of hardware trojans in them. Our methodology is primarily segmented in two phases, the filtering process and the trojan insertion. During the first phase, an attacker can utilize the LLM as a fine-grained filter, to navigate through the design's large HDL database and discover information about the modules of attack interest. To do that, the attacker is considered to have an abstract idea of the desired attack and then proceeds to craft appropriate prompts that will drive the LLM responses to pinpoint to specific candidate modules. This way, an attacker manages to reduce the context length of the subsequent LLM prompts, as only the RTL code of the identified module(s) needs to be submitted for analysis to the LLM. After the initial analysis, the attacker requests from the LLM to locate parts in the RTL code that correlate with the attack target. During the second phase, the attacker using natural language instructions, prompts the LLM with the modifications necessary for the inclusion of the trojan functionality in the identified code. Using the above method, we examined several attack scenarios on different hardware security modules, as well as a complex RISC-V micro-architecture. To highlight the efficiency of our automated methodology, we showcased a complete proof of concept trojan implementation inside the utilized RISC-V CPU. For this attack scenario, our method overcame the context length limitations by reducing the overall attack space analysis from almost a hundred HDL files to only a single. Thus, our work highlights the power LLMs can provide when integrated in the design cycle of hardware trojan attacks.

References

1. GitHub Copilot: Your AI pair programmer (2021). https://copilot.github.com/
2. Ahmad, B., Thakur, S., Tan, B., Karri, R., Pearce, H.: Fixing hardware security bugs with large language models. arXiv preprint arXiv:2302.01215 (2023)
3. Ali, M., et al.: Tokenizer choice for LLM training: negligible or crucial? arXiv preprint arXiv:2310.08754 (2023)
4. Bengio, Y., Ducharme, R., Vincent, P.: A neural probabilistic language model. In: Advances in Neural Information Processing Systems, vol. 13 (2000)
5. Chang, K., et al.: ChipGPT: how far are we from natural language hardware design. arXiv preprint arXiv:2305.14019 (2023)
6. ChatGPT: Hardware modules handling illegal memory accesses exceptions. OpenAI ChatGPT (2023). https://chat.openai.com/share/b4acf148-f31b-438f-a60b-9570ed1ad4b4
7. ChatGPT: Hardware modules handling privilege level separation. OpenAI ChatGPT (2023). https://chat.openai.com/share/9436a01d-3d3e-4fed-a8be-780638dc2b7e
8. ChatGPT: Hardware modules involved in read operations. OpenAI ChatGPT (2023). https://chat.openai.com/share/b4acf148-f31b-438f-a60b-9570ed1ad4b4
9. ChatGPT: Hardware modules involved in time-expensive operations. OpenAI ChatGPT (2023). https://chat.openai.com/share/9436a01d-3d3e-4fed-a8be-780638dc2b7e
10. ChatGPT: Leakage of the AES secret key. OpenAI ChatGPT (2023). https://chat.openai.com/share/01888ff9-ace8-4eb3-b496-802c9b704a4d
11. ChatGPT: Performance reduction via thermal attacks (cache). OpenAI ChatGPT (2023). https://chat.openai.com/share/c9cfdae6-71ea-4f7f-8696-cc7b7a92d770

12. ChatGPT: Performance reduction via thermal attacks (loop). OpenAI ChatGPT (2023). https://chat.openai.com/share/3ec61ff4-5cd1-4474-9a68-e4e813999435
13. ChatGPT: Reduction in des encryption rounds. OpenAI ChatGPT (2023). https://chat.openai.com/share/1319eccf-9d6b-4d90-9487-a7a7150bf9d4
14. ChatGPT: Speculative execution of wrong-path instructions. OpenAI ChatGPT (2023). https://chat.openai.com/share/27438636-70c4-4786-8eac-24b445c772f1
15. ChatGPT: Violation of OS-enforced memory policies. OpenAI ChatGPT (2023). https://chat.openai.com/share/31d55383-37dd-4f09-bf78-9599f50eb704
16. ChatGPT: Violation of OS-enforced memory policies (payload circuit). OpenAI ChatGPT (2023). https://chat.openai.com/share/777c995d-108c-48ab-8ce0-83a46aec5cd0
17. ChatGPT: Violation of OS-enforced memory policies (trigger circuit). OpenAI ChatGPT (2023). https://chat.openai.com/share/2974bd05-573b-406b-95b9-ec7bba16053c
18. Chen, M., et al.: Evaluating large language models trained on code. arXiv preprint arXiv:2107.03374 (2021)
19. Chen, T., et al.: VulLibGen: identifying vulnerable third-party libraries via generative pre-trained model. arXiv preprint arXiv:2308.04662 (2023)
20. Chen, Y., Ding, Z., Alowain, L., Chen, X., Wagner, D.: DiverseVul: a new vulnerable source code dataset for deep learning based vulnerability detection. In: Proceedings of the 26th International Symposium on Research in Attacks, Intrusions and Defenses, pp. 654–668 (2023)
21. De, A., Khan, M.N.I., Nagarajan, K., Ghosh, S.: Hartbleed: using hardware trojans for data leakage exploits. IEEE Trans. Very Large Scale Integr. (VLSI) Syst. **28**, 968–979 (2020)
22. Dharsee, K., Criswell, J.: Jinn: hijacking safe programs with trojans. In: 32nd USENIX Security Symposium (USENIX Security 2023), Anaheim, CA, pp. 6965–6982. USENIX Association (2023)
23. Dunkelman, O., Sekar, G., Preneel, B.: Improved meet-in-the-middle attacks on reduced-round DES. In: Srinathan, K., Rangan, C.P., Yung, M. (eds.) INDOCRYPT 2007. LNCS, vol. 4859, pp. 86–100. Springer, Heidelberg (2007). https://doi.org/10.1007/978-3-540-77026-8_8
24. Esteva, A., et al.: A guide to deep learning in healthcare. Nat. Med. **25**(1), 24–29 (2019)
25. Fakhoury, S., Chakraborty, S., Musuvathi, M., Lahiri, S.K.: Towards generating functionally correct code edits from natural language issue descriptions. arXiv preprint arXiv:2304.03816 (2023)
26. Feng, Z., et al.: CodeBERT: a pre-trained model for programming and natural languages. arXiv preprint arXiv:2002.08155 (2020)
27. Fu, W., Yang, K., Dutta, R.G., Guo, X., Qu, G.: LLM4SecHW: leveraging domain-specific large language model for hardware debugging. In: Asian Hardware Oriented Security and Trust (AsianHOST) (2023)
28. Gao, Y., Nikolov, N.I., Hu, Y., Hahnloser, R.H.: Character-level translation with self-attention. arXiv preprint arXiv:2004.14788 (2020)
29. Hajipour, H., Holz, T., Schönherr, L., Fritz, M.: Systematically finding security vulnerabilities in black-box code generation models. arXiv preprint arXiv:2302.04012 (2023)
30. Hepp, A., Sigl, G.: Tapeout of a RISC-V crypto chip with hardware trojans: a case-study on trojan design and pre-silicon detectability. In: Palesi, M., Tumeo, A., Goumas, G.I., Almudéver, C.G. (eds.) CF 2021: Computing Frontiers Conference, Virtual Event, Italy, 11–13 May 2021, pp. 213–220. ACM (2021)

31. Huang, D., Bu, Q., Zhang, J., Xie, X., Chen, J., Cui, H.: Bias assessment and mitigation in LLM-based code generation (2023)
32. Jin, M., et al.: Inferfix: end-to-end program repair with LLMs. arXiv preprint arXiv:2303.07263 (2023)
33. Kande, R., et al.: LLM-assisted generation of hardware assertions. arXiv preprint arXiv:2306.14027 (2023)
34. King, S.T., Tucek, J., Cozzie, A., Grier, C., Jiang, W., Zhou, Y.: Designing and implementing malicious hardware. In: Monrose, F. (ed.) First USENIX Workshop on Large-Scale Exploits and Emergent Threats, LEET 2008, San Francisco, CA, USA, 15 April 2008, Proceedings. USENIX Association (2008)
35. Li, R., et al.: Starcoder: may the source be with you! arXiv preprint arXiv:2305.06161 (2023)
36. Li, Y., et al.: Competition-level code generation with alphacode. Science **378**(6624), 1092–1097 (2022)
37. Luo, Z., et al.: WizardCoder: empowering code large language models with evol-instruct. arXiv preprint arXiv:2306.08568 (2023)
38. Meng, X., et al.: Unlocking hardware security assurance: the potential of LLMs (2023)
39. Murr, L., Grainger, M., Gao, D.: Testing LLMs on code generation with varying levels of prompt specificity (2023)
40. Nair, M., Sadhukhan, R., Mukhopadhyay, D.: Generating secure hardware using chatGPt resistant to CWEs. Cryptology ePrint Archive (2023)
41. Nijkamp, E., Hayashi, H., Xiong, C., Savarese, S., Zhou, Y.: CodeGen2: lessons for training LLMs on programming and natural languages. arXiv preprint arXiv:2305.02309 (2023)
42. Nijkamp, E., et al.: CodeGen: an open large language model for code with multi-turn program synthesis. arXiv preprint arXiv:2203.13474 (2022)
43. OpenAI: Openai codex (2021). https://openai.com/blog/openai-codex/. Accessed 24 Jan 2024
44. OpenAI: Chat completions API guide (2024). https://platform.openai.com/docs/guides/text-generation/chat-completions-api. Accessed 26 Jan 2024
45. Orenes-Vera, M., Martonosi, M., Wentzlaff, D.: Using LLMs to facilitate formal verification of RTL (2023)
46. Paria, S., Dasgupta, A., Bhunia, S.: Divas: an LLM-based end-to-end framework for SoC security analysis and policy-based protection. arXiv preprint arXiv:2308.06932 (2023)
47. Pearce, H., Tan, B., Ahmad, B., Karri, R., Dolan-Gavitt, B.: Examining zero-shot vulnerability repair with large language models. In: 2023 IEEE Symposium on Security and Privacy (SP), pp. 2339–2356. IEEE (2023)
48. Pszczołowski, J.: Data encryption standard (DES) (2020). https://github.com/jpszczolowski/des-verilog
49. Saha, D., et al.: LLM for SoC security: a paradigm shift (2023)
50. Sandoval, G., Pearce, H., Nys, T., Karri, R., Dolan-Gavitt, B., Garg, S.: Security implications of large language model code assistants: a user study. arXiv preprint arXiv:2208.09727 (2022)
51. Schuster, M., Nakajima, K.: Japanese and Korean voice search. In: 2012 IEEE International Conference on Acoustics, Speech and Signal Processing (ICASSP), pp. 5149–5152. IEEE (2012)
52. Sennrich, R., Haddow, B., Birch, A.: Neural machine translation of rare words with subword units. arXiv preprint arXiv:1508.07909 (2015)

53. Shen, B., et al.: PanGu-coder2: boosting large language models for code with ranking feedback. arXiv preprint arXiv:2307.14936 (2023)
54. Srikumar, P.: Fast and wrong: the case for formally specifying hardware with LLMs. In: Proceedings of the International Conference on Architectural Support for Programming Languages and Operating Systems (ASPLOS). ACM. ACM Press (2023)
55. Strömbergson, J.: Advanced encryption standard (AES) (2023). https://github.com/secworks/aes
56. Thakur, S., et al.: Benchmarking large language models for automated verilog RTL code generation (2022)
57. Thakur, S., Blocklove, J., Pearce, H., Tan, B., Garg, S., Karri, R.: Autochip: automating HDL generation using LLM feedback (2023)
58. Vaswani, A., et al.: Attention is all you need. In: Advances in Neural Information Processing Systems, vol. 30 (2017)
59. Wang, C., Cho, K., Gu, J.: Neural machine translation with byte-level subwords. In: Proceedings of the AAAI Conference on Artificial Intelligence, vol. 34, pp. 9154–9160 (2020)
60. Wang, J., Huang, Y., Chen, C., Liu, Z., Wang, S., Wang, Q.: Software testing with large language model: survey, landscape, and vision. arXiv preprint arXiv:2307.07221 (2023)
61. Wong, M.F., Guo, S., Hang, C.N., Ho, S.W., Tan, C.W.: Natural language generation and understanding of big code for AI-assisted programming: a review. Entropy 25(6) (2023). https://doi.org/10.3390/e25060888. https://www.mdpi.com/1099-4300/25/6/888. ISSN 1099-4300
62. Wu, Y., et al.: How effective are neural networks for fixing security vulnerabilities. arXiv preprint arXiv:2305.18607 (2023)
63. Zaruba, F.: CVA6 (2019). https://github.com/openhwgroup/cva6
64. Zaruba, F., Benini, L.: The cost of application-class processing: energy and performance analysis of a Linux-ready 1.7-GHz 64-bit RISC-V core in 22-nm FDSOI technology. IEEE Trans. Very Large Scale Integr. (VLSI) Syst. 27(11), 2629–2640 (2019). https://doi.org/10.1109/TVLSI.2019.2926114. ISSN 1557-9999
65. Zheng, Q., et al.: CodeGeex: a pre-trained model for code generation with multilingual evaluations on HumanEval-X. arXiv preprint arXiv:2303.17568 (2023)

Everything All at Once: Deep Learning Side-Channel Analysis Optimization Framework

Gabriele Serafini[✉], Léo Weissbart, and Lejla Batina

Radboud University, Nijmegen, The Netherlands
{gabriele.serafini,leo.weissbart,lejla.batina}@ru.nl

Abstract. Deep learning is becoming an increasingly proficient tool for side-channel analysis. While deep learning has been evolving around the tasks of image and speech recognition for decades, it is still lacking maturity for side-channel analysis. One of the challenges to train a good model is the fine-tuning of its hyperparameters. Many methods have been developed for Hyperparameter Optimization, but a few have been applied for deep learning side-channel analysis.

We study the use of sampling algorithm and early-stopping mechanism in the hyperparameter optimization search for deep learning side-channel analysis models. We also offer a scalable deep learning framework to extend results obtained for other problems and datasets.

Our results show that hyperparameter optimization methods can save time and resources while leading to models that can lead to the best possible output and at the same time are providing more confidence whether to look for a better model.

Keywords: Deep Learning · Side-Channel Analysis · Hyperparameter Optimization · Pruning

1 Introduction

From personal smart gadgets to sophisticated industrial machinery, devices embedded with sensors, software, and other technologies are becoming an integral part of our daily lives. These devices, collectively referred to as the Internet of Things (IoT), communicate over a common network, and the security of this network depends on the reliability of the least secure device. However, as the integration of IoT devices expands, the need for secure cryptographic implementations grows bigger. One of the most critical concerns is the potential vulnerability of these devices to cyberattacks, which can lead to unauthorized access, data theft, or even taking control over the device's functions, thus posing significant risks to users' privacy and security.

While strong cryptographic designs can give guaranties on the security of an application, there remains numerous possibles threats. Side-Channel Analysis (SCA) is a set of techniques aimed to explore the possible vulnerabilities of

© The Author(s), under exclusive license to Springer Nature Switzerland AG 2024
M. Andreoni (Ed.): ACNS 2024 Workshops, LNCS 14586, pp. 195–212, 2024.
https://doi.org/10.1007/978-3-031-61486-6_12

implementations of secure designs on physical devices. These techniques entail the analysis of information contained in unintentional leakages from electronic devices during operations involving sensitive secrets. This analysis can provide insights into the device's internal workings, exposing vulnerabilities to security breaches.

The assessment of side-channel leakages is a part of standard evaluations for electronics in commercial use, and typically involves the use of classic techniques e.g., Differential Power Analysis [10] or Template attack [6]. While research on SCA becomes more mature, new analysis methods are developed that add up to the standard techniques for side-channel evaluators, such as Deep-Learning SCA.

Among the various deep learning techniques, Convolutional Neural Networks (CNNs) turned out to be particularly suited for in profiling SCA. CNNs are designed to automatically and adaptively learn spatial hierarchies of features, which make them effective at recognizing subtle and complex patterns in side-channel data. When trained on a side-channel dataset, a CNN model can learn to associate the secret key to certain power leakage of a cryptographic operation by extracting the important features it contains.

A fundamental challenge when using CNN, as a profiling SCA tool, is the tuning of its hyperparameters. Hyperparameters define the configuration of a model, and have a significant impact on a model performance. The sheer size of the hyperparameter space to explore to find a fitting model and the cost of evaluating each configuration make the hyperparameter optimization (HO) task computationally expensive and time-consuming. Moreover, there exists no guaranty for a CNN model that, if after the training phase the underlying attack is not successful, no better configuration that would make the attack succeed could be found. Thus, to ensure that an implementation is secure against CNN-based SCA, an exhaustive HO search, exploring all possible configurations of hyperparameters remains the best method.

The use of optimization techniques to tune hyperparameters can help to ease the HO search to some extends. One such method is the use of sampling based on optimization algorithms e.g., Bayesian optimization [25] or Genetic algorithms [12], for exploring the search space of hyperparameter configurations in an educated manner, and increase the chances that the best configurations are explored the earliest possible during the search. Another method used to enhance deep learning is Early Stopping. Based on the results of previous models during the training phase, this method allows for the early termination of an unpromising model training based on an intermediate results [2]. This method can save computational resources and allows the HO process to allocate more time to explore other, potentially better hyperparameter configurations.

In this paper, we aim to provide a first guideline towards a framework that integrates efficiently HO for CNN-based side-channel analysis. We demonstrate how the conjunction of early-stopping and optimization method, namely median Early Stopping and tree-structured Parzen Estimator (TPE), can computationally ease the HO search. The following points provide a more detailed overview of the study's focal areas:

1. We give an introductory analysis to enhance the efficiency of hyperparameter optimization in CNN-based SCA. We show it is possible to speed up the HO process while minimizing the compromise on the quality of results. The integration of sampling method and early-stopping offers more flexibility in dealing with the exploration-exploitation trade-off during hyperparameter tuning.
2. We introduce the use of Guessing Entropy (GE) inside sampling and early-stopping to reach faster convergence to good fitting models.
3. We demonstrate how the use of patience early stopping together with median early stopping can save resources by preventing long training of models that appeared to have already converged and won't learn further, and models that appear to have little likelihood of improving previously run models.
4. We share the code used for model training and HO. The utilization of several machine learning packages simplifies the hyperparameter optimization process and is specifically crafted for SCA, thus paving the way for further exploration with other optimization algorithms or machine learning frameworks in the SCA setting.

The rest of the paper is organized as follows. In Sect. 2, we provide a brief overview of existing research in the area of CNN-based side-channel analysis and hyperparameter optimizations for this type of attacks. In Sect. 3, we provide necessary information on both SCA and deep learning attack. In Sect. 4, we present the methodology we applied to create experiments, and especially the datasets and framework we use. In Sect. 5, we show the results obtained from our experiments with efficiency of the best obtained model, and saving computational resource compared to other results from the literature. Finally, in Sect. 6, we sum up our results and identify some future research directions.

2   Related Works

The studies of deep learning for side-channel analysis have gained great interest in recent years [21]. CNN-based deep learning have been shown many times to be particularly efficient for attacks against masking countermeasure in cryptography [11,15,17,22,28,30]. Wouters et al. in [28] managed to reduce the complexity of the CNNs proposed by Zaid et al. [30] by an average of 52% while maintaining similar performance. The authors argue that increasing the filter size can actually improve the performance of the network. The review also emphasizes the importance of pre-processing side channel traces, and shows that with proper pre-processing the first convolutional block proposed in [30] to extract features can be omitted, which contributes to reducing the complexity of the models. Their work highlights the need for proper evaluation of the hyperparameter search space to conclude on the security of a given dataset.

In an effort to build a universal framework for deep-learning SCA to guaranty better result reproducibility, Perin et al. [20] and Brisfors et al. [5] introduce two publicly available frameworks designed to streamline deep learning based side channel analysis. In these frameworks, the objective is to provide a basis for SCA evaluations with deep learning, and provide useful functionalities published in the literature.

Early-stopping and hyperparameter tuning for deep-learning SCA in discussed in [18,24]. The authors of [24] introduces the six sigma methodology for choosing the best possible hyperparameters. The method is a derivative from a well known methodology for various engineering problems often used to reduce the variability of industrial processes.

In [18], Paguada et al. introduces an early-stopping method designed for SCA model training. The early-stopping of the training is evaluated based on the guessing entropy of the resulting attack, using the newly defined patience and persistence of the guessing entropy. Our approach also uses optimized computation of the guessing entropy and combines an automated search for the best hyperparameters with a tree-structured Parzen optimization. Wu et al. in [29], also suggest an automated method for modifying the hyperparameters, but using Bayesian optimization. This paper also compares the tracking evolution of the guessing entropy, accuracy, and leakage difference distribution of the resulting attack to choose the best fitting hyperparameters, but do not implement early-stopping methods.

3   Background

3.1   Profiling SCA

Profiling SCA is a type of SCA that is opposed to non-profiled SCA (i.e., Single Power Analysis and Differential Power Analysis). Contrary to non-profiled SCA in which an attacker is assumed to have physical access to the device under attack, profiling SCA makes the assumption that an attacker also has access to and full control of an identical copy of the device under attack, and can learn about leakage to profile before accessing the device under attack. This technique is commonly divided in two phases:

1. A profiling phase: during this phase, the attacker collects side channel traces from a copy of the target device while running cryptographic operations with known secret. This data is then used to build a predictive model (i.e. a profile) of the device's behavior.
2. An attack phase: after the profiling phase, the attacker applies the developed model to the target device while it is executing the same cryptographic operations with unknown key. If the model developed during the profiling phase is accurate, the attacker can infer the secret key.

3.2   CNN and Profiling SCA

Convolutional Neural Networks (CNNs) are a specific type of feed-forward neural network that have become standard for tasks involving image and signal processing. A CNN is generally composed of multiple convolutional layers followed by fully connected layers. The input of a convolution layer is multiplied by several filters (also known as kernels) which are shifted along the input data, performing a dot product operation at each position, and creating a so-called feature map. During this convolution operation, the kernels act as feature extractor, each learning to identify a different pattern in the input data. The patterns can range from simple edges to complex shapes or textures, and they emerge automatically during the training process. Once the features are extracted, the output of the convolution layers goes to a fully-connected network that acts as a classifier.

A CNN, as well as other deep learning algorithms, is divided in two stages: a training and an evaluation phase. During training, the neural network is challenged with raw input data and is followed by backpropagation correcting the differential between the predicted and known labels. In the evaluation phase, the network is challenged with a never previously used input data, and outputs a probability distribution to classify the input based on the trained task.

Because of the similar two-stage structure of profiling SCA and deep learning classification, the later can be applied as a profiling method in SCA. In such a framework, the aim is to classify observed side-channel leakages into corresponding secret information. Given this formulation, machine learning techniques emerge as a natural choice for enhancing the efficiency and efficacy of profiled side channel attacks.

SCA often involves extracting useful information from noisy, high-dimensional data, a process that CNNs are exceptionally well-equipped to handle. The properties of CNN align with the requirements of side channel analysis for extracting features in a high dimensional power trace and overcome invariance of a leakage position. The learned features are more representative and discriminative, enabling them to effectively identify and classify patterns in side channel data.

The property of translation invariance of CNNs is useful in the context of side channel analysis. This property ensures that once a feature from a leakage, such as a specific pattern, has been learned, the CNN model can recognize the same pattern regardless of its position in any new side channel trace, making CNNs effective tools to work effectively with raw, unprocessed data. This is particularly beneficial in side channel analysis, where preprocessing steps such as trace alignment can be challenging and time-consuming.

3.3 SCA Metrics

Precision, recall and accuracy, often fall short in deep-learning SCA due to the binary nature of their result. These metrics focus on whether a single prediction is correct, overlooking an attacker's strategy of narrowing down potential keys across many traces. A more informative metric in SCA is Guessing Entropy (GE), which measures the average number of keys as attacker would need to guesses before finding the correct one.

Guessing entropy can be modeled as follows:

$$GE = E\left[rank_{k^*}(\mathbf{g})\right] \tag{1}$$

In this context, $rank_{k^*}$ denotes the position of the correct key k^* in an ordered vector of candidate keys. The vector **g** represents the output array of keys, sorted in an order determined by the likelihood of each candidate key being the correct one according to the classifier. The expectation is computed by averaging the rank value over multiple experiments.

3.4 Leakage Model

A leakage model is a critical component that links the observed side-channel information to the intermediate values of the cryptographic operation being performed. The leakage model thus forms a fundamental bridge between the physical world observations and the mathematical properties of the cryptographic algorithm, allowing for an attacker to make informed deductions about secret data.

The basic premise behind leakage models is that the side-channel emissions of a device are not random, but depend on the device's internal state and operations. In the case of a cryptographic device, these operations are influenced by the data being processed and the secret key. The leakage model aims to describe this relationship, essentially serving as a predictor of side-channel emissions based on the known intermediate values of the cryptographic algorithm.

In this paper, only the Identity Leakage Model (ID) is considered.

This model assumes a direct relationship between the observed side-channel leakage and the secret intermediate values during cryptographic operations.

Under the ID model, the observed leakage is assumed to be the identity of the intermediate value. This suggests that the leakage directly reveals the intermediate value, without any noise or distortion.

Mathematically, this can be expressed as:

$$L = V \tag{2}$$

where, L denotes the observed leakage and V represents the secret intermediate value.

In the context of the Advanced Encryption Standard (AES), for instance, the intermediate value could be the result of the application of the S-box in the first round, which can be expressed as $V = Sbox(key + input)$.

This would result in 256 possible classes (corresponding to the 256 possible values of an 8-bit output), each representing a distinct intermediate value.

3.5 Hyperparameter Optimization

Hyperparameter optimization (HO) is a critical step in the development of ML algorithms. It entails determining an optimal set of hyperparameters, that minimizes or maximizes an established fit function, and so improves the model's performance. The hyperparameters are chosen before training a model and cannot be changed later. Moreover, it is not possible to predict that a configuration of hyperparameters will lead to a good model.

Learning rate, number of layers in a neural network, number of hidden units in each layer, type of activation functions, and many more parameters are examples of hyperparameters. When we initially apply a model, the ideal values for these hyperparameters are often not obvious, and they might be highly problem-dependent.

To find a suitable set of hyperparameters, one needs to explore different configurations of a given model. Common methods for exploring hyperparameters are:

- Grid Search: This is the simplest strategy, in which we establish a subset of the hyperparameter space and methodically attempt all combinations within the defined grid.
- Random Search: Unlike grid search, random search draws hyperparameter values at random from a given space. When the number of hyperparameters is considerable, this method may be more efficient than grid search.
- Bayesian Optimization: This method creates a posterior distribution of functions that best describes the function to be optimized, and then uses it to select the most promising hyperparameters to evaluate in the true function.

3.6   Tree-Structured Parzen Estimator

The process of selecting the hyperparameters that optimize a model's performance can be time-consuming and computationally expensive. It is, nonetheless, critical for developing strong and accurate ML models. In this study, we use the Tree-structured Parzen Estimator (TPE) [4], a Sequential Model-Based Optimization (SMBO) approach.

TPE constructs a model of the objective function with the goal of suggesting more promising hyperparameters for evaluation.

TPE models two probability distributions: $P(x|y)$ and $P(y)$, where x represents the hyperparameters, and y is the corresponding objective function. Through this modelling, TPE assigns greater weight to regions of the hyperparameter space it deems promising.

The operational procedure of TPE consists of the following steps:

1. TPE starts its process by randomly selecting n hyperparameters configurations from the search space and evaluating the objective function for them.
2. These hyperparameters are then fitted into two distinct distributions: one for those that yielded better outcomes of the objective function (termed "good" values), and another for the remainder of the hyperparameters (termed "bad" values).
3. In subsequent iterations, TPE samples more from regions having a high ratio of good to bad hyperparameter values. This ratio is determined by a parameter, γ, which is a quantile threshold separating the good and bad hyperparameters based on their objective function outcomes.

Through this process, TPE continuously adapts its focus towards the promising areas of the hyperparameter space, while diminishing attention on areas known to yield inferior results.

3.7   Early Stopping Strategies in Hyperparameter Optimization

Early stopping strategies in HO to the process of halting training of non-promising hyperparameter configuration as early as possible during the tuning process, saving computational resources. These techniques are particularly useful for tuning complex machine learning architectures, where the computational cost can be quite high [27]. Among early stopping strategies, the most notable are: median early-stopping, asynchronous successive halving algorithm [13], and hyperband algorithm [9,14]. These strategies monitor a model training performance and use it to decide whether to stop the training prematurely. All these strategies are adaptive early-stopping mechanisms that adapt the rules to trigger the training stop based on the tracked monitored value. Early stopping strategies were initially viewed as HO strategies when applied to grid search or random search, but it has been demonstrated how these strategies can actually enhance Optimization algorithms such as Bayesian Optimization [26,27].

In particular, we explore median early-stopping in this paper. Median-early stopping will stop the training of a model when the objective value by the current epoch is worse than the median value of the running averages of all completed previous trials objective values. Another early-stopping rule that can be applied is the Patience-Early stopper. This method can be used to wrap an early-stopping rule with a patience parameter that will trigger the wrapped rule after a fixed number of epochs where no improvement can be observed.

Despite their computational benefits, these strategies bear the risk of prematurely discarding configurations that may start slow but eventually outperforms others. This issue can augment with the double descent phenomena [16], potentially leading to suboptimal final configurations.

3.8   Warm-Up Values in Early Stopping Strategies

Warm-up values refer to the initial set of iterations or epochs during which the performance of the hyperparameter configurations is not evaluated for pruning. This grace period allows the configurations to stabilize and exhibit their potential before any pruning decisions are made. In our experiments, we utilize these warm-up values in conjunction with the Median-Early-Stopper. The Median-Early-Stopper operates by comparing the performance of each configuration against the median performance of all configurations at similar epochs. If a configuration's performance falls below the median, it is stopped, allowing resources to be focused on more promising configurations. To understand the impact of warm-up values on this process, we experiment with warm-up periods of 30, 50, 75, and 100 epochs. By varying these values, we aim to analyze how different lengths of the warm-up period affect the overall hyperparameter optimization process, particularly in terms of the timing and effectiveness of early stopping decisions.

4   Methodologies

4.1   Study Settings

The experiments utilize both the ASCADf and the ASCADr datasets [3]. Those datasets have been introduced in an initiative to provide a ground base for side-channel analysis of smartcard masked AES implementation. ASCADf dataset was the first published, and contains traces collected from encryption operations with a fixed key. The ASCADr dataset contains traces collected from encryptions with random keys and was meant to be more challenging than ASCADf. For both, we use the label obtained by using the Identity Leakage Model.

For the computational aspect, all the deep learning models were trained on an NVIDIA GeForce GTX 1080 TI Graphics Processing Unit (GPU).

The implementation of the experiment was conducted using Python. The TensorFlow [1] and Keras [7] libraries served as the foundation for constructing and training the deep learning models, while Optuna [2] was employed for the optimization of hyperparameters. For the purpose of visualizing results and monitoring the progress of our experiments, we used Matplotlib [8], TensorBoard, and Optuna's built-in visualization features. These tools allowed us to effectively track, analyze, and present the outcomes of our research in a clear and intuitive manner.

4.2   CNN Model Architecture

In this research, we leveraged the benefits of sampling optimization with early-stopping to perform hyperparameter optimization (HO) experiments on two SCA datasets: ASCADr and ASCADf, with the identity leakage model.

The experiments are executed each for 100 models. In these experiments, the HO process is guided using a customized objective function based on GE.

The CNN-based models can be decomposed in a feature extraction part (i.e., one or more convolutional blocks) followed by a multi-layer perceptron that acts as a classifier to recover the guessed intermediate value of an input trace. One convolutional block always is formed with a convolution layer and a pooling layer. An additional normalization layer is inserted every two blocks between the convolution and pooling layers to add regularization of parameters. A representation of the obtained models is showed in Fig. 1. The Table 1 lists the different hyperparameters chosen to explore and their range for this study.

We combined the capabilities of Optuna and Keras to dynamically construct CNN models, the structure, and parameters of which were determined by the Tree-structured Parzen Estimator (TPE) Sampling Algorithm used in the HO process.

To enhance the efficiency of our experiments and explore the potential benefits of early stop strategies, we conducted four tests for each dataset. Each test uses the Median-Early-Stopping and Patience-Early-Stopping techniques with varying degrees of intensity, adjusted by manipulating the warm-up values. For ASCADf, an additional experiment was conducted without employing any early

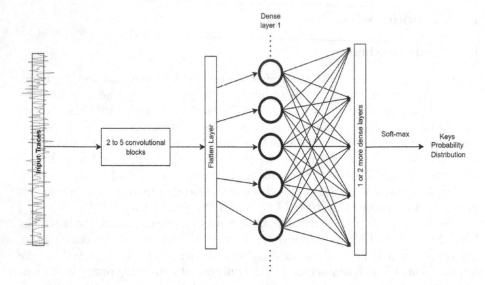

Fig. 1. General overview of how the convolutional neural networks are built

Table 1. Hyperparameter space explored in the optimization process

Hyperparameter	Range	Step
batch_size	$[100, \ldots, 1000]$	100
learning_rate	[1e-5] (Fixed)	None
activation_function	[relu, selu]	None
filters	$[2, \ldots, 64]$	×2
num_conv_layers	$[2, \ldots, 5]$	1
kernel_size	$[2, 3, 5, 7, 11, 17]$ (for each conv layer)	None
num_fc_layers	$[1, 2, 3]$	1
size_fc_layers	$[64, \ldots, 512]$ (for each fc layer)	64
epochs	200 or 300 (fixed)	None
strides	1 (fixed)	None

stopping method, providing a benchmark against which to assess the impact of these resource-saving techniques.

Finally, we assessed the experiments by selecting the best models from each and comparing their performance metrics. We compared the different models using GE.

4.3   Hyperparameter Optimization Process

Optuna was selected as the primary tool for conducting a series of HO experiments. The Tree-structured Parzen Estimator (TPE) sampling algorithm, a

Bayesian optimization algorithm provided by Optuna, was employed for the hyperparameter configuration selection.

An important component of the approach was the use of the averaged GE as the objective function to guide the HO process:

$$GE_{average} = \frac{GE(1) + GE(2) + ...GE(n)}{n} \tag{3}$$

where n is the size of the subset of traces taken from the validation set to estimate the key rank, which correspond to the number of used traces to compute the GE during the training. Utilizing the averaged GE as a metric during the HO process is helpful in comparing the efficiency between different models, since this metric gives an estimation of both the amount of traces needed to reach a low GE, and the amount of attempts needed for guessing the correct value. Optuna ultimately utilized this number as an objective value to guide the Hyperparameter selection of the future models based on TPE Algorithm.

5   Results

This section of our research delves into the results from our analysis of the two distinct datasets: ASCADf and ASCADr. We focus primarily on the hyperparameter optimization experiments conducted at various warm-up values for the Median Early Stopper, methodically studying their impact on resource use, measured in number of epochs, and the performance of the best model. This examination allows us to determine the effects of early stopping on the best models' result for each unique experiment.

5.1   Experiments for ASCADf

Table 2 encapsulates the impact of various warm-up periods on resource utilization during hyperparameter optimization processes. The columns labeled Median-Early-Stopper and Patience-Early-Stopper show the percentages of epochs spared due to the implementation of the respective early stopping strategies. These savings are calculated in comparison to the total number of epochs that would have been required if no early stopping mechanism were employed. This comparison highlights the efficiency gains achieved by employing these early stopping strategies in our hyperparameter optimization process. By saving epochs, we are able to evaluate more configurations using fewer resources, thus enhancing the overall efficiency and scalability of the optimization process.

Specifically, the Median Early Stopper column denotes the percentage of epochs saved because of the application of this strategy, the Patience Early Stopper column represents the percentage of saved epochs attributed to early stopping based on patience. Lastly, the Sum column aggregates these savings, providing an overall view of the resource conservation.

The total savings (represented by the Sum column), which combines the impacts of both the different early stopping strategies, doesn't exhibit a direct

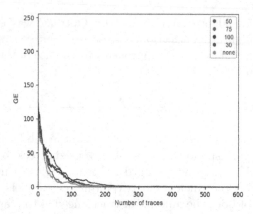

Fig. 2. Guessing entropy for the ASCADf experiments using warm up value of 30, 50, 75 and 100

Table 2. Summary of the effect of different warm-up values on the average number of epochs saved with early stopping during training on ASCADf (in percentage of a complete training)

Warm-up	Median-Early-Stopper	Patience-Early-Stopper	Sum
30	49.085	2.68	51.765
50	36.825	7.34	44.165
75	9.975	24.82	34.795
100	4.79	33.27	38.06

relationship with the warm-up period. This follows from the fact that a lighter early stop based on previous models lead to more space for the early stop mechanism based on the training patience to act.

From the data collected in Table 2 and corresponding performance drawn from Fig. 2, we can analyze the relations between the warm-up steps applied to the training and the performance outcomes of the optimal model in the HO process. All settings perform as well as or better than the run without early-stopping, confirming that early-stopping does not impact on the capacity of HO to find a good fitting model.

The setting with a minimal warm-up phase of 30 steps realizes significant resource savings, with nearly half of the epochs conserved. Notably, the model's performance under this condition doesn't compromise drastically as it recovers the key with approximately 200 traces, like the rest of the configurations. This suggests that even an aggressive early stop schedule can still result in optimal model performance.

Extending the warm-up phase to 50 or 75 steps results in a slight decrease in epoch savings. However, the performance of the model remains similar, requiring around 200 traces for key recovery, which aligns with the performance exhibited by setting the warm up-value to 30.

Increasing the warm-up phase to 100 steps, or even having no early stop at all, maintains a consistent performance level, necessitating around 200 traces for key recovery. This finding reinforces the premise that strategic early stop doesn't compromise finding optimal configurations, but it might instead ensure efficient resource allocation and exploration-exploitation balance.

Table 3. Comparison with other papers of number of traces required to reach a GE of 0 for ASCADf, ID leakage Model

Attempt	Traces to reach GE = 0
[3]	1476
[30]	191
[23]	202
[29]	158
this study	230

5.2   Experiments for ASCADr

Table 4. Summary of the effect of different warm-up values on the average number of epochs saved with early stopping during training on ASCADr (in percentage of a complete training)

Warm-up	Median-Early-Stopper	Patience-Early-Stopper	Sum
30	33.3	14.44	44.74
50	35.63	18.09	53.72
75	24.0	38.12	62.12
100	0.0	39.11	39.11

The Table 4 summarizes the effects of different warm-up values on the 2 early stopping strategies for the ASCADr dataset.

When the warm-up value is set to 30, the Median Early Stopper contributes to 33.30% saving in epochs, while Patience-Early Stopping approximately 14.44%, reaching the total reduction of epochs to approximately 44.74%. Surprisingly, this figure is slightly lower than the reduction seen for higher warm up values (50 and 74), even though a lower warm up value would usually mean more aggressive pruning.

This counterintuitive result can be attributed to the fact that during this particular experiment, effective configurations were relatively quickly identified, and the experiment showed consistent improvements as the models were executed. Considering the Median Early stop mechanism, this scenario naturally led to a decrease and delay of early stopping compared to other scenarios.

Although a lower warm up value generally implies more aggressive early stopping, it is essential to consider the dynamics of the optimization process and the quality of the configurations with the order in which they are found.

At a warm-up value of 50, Median Early Stopper models saved about 35.63% of the total epochs that could have been run, and the early stop saved approximately 18.09% of the epochs. The combined effect led to a reduction of around 53.72% in the number of epochs.

Increasing the warm-up value to 75, the impact of the Median Early Stopper savings decreases to 24.0%, but the effect of early stopping increases to 38.12%, leading to a total reduction of approximately 62.12%.

At a warm-up value of 100, the Median Early Stopper has no effect (0.0% reduction), while the impact of early stopping slightly increases to 39.11%, leading to the overall reduction in epochs to 39.11%.

It's important to explain that the elevated percentage of pruned epochs in the ASCADr experiments, compared to those in the ASCADf experiments, is primarily attributable to the baseline number of epochs set for each dataset. In the ASCADr experiments, the default number of epochs, was set to 300. In contrast, for the ASCADf experiments, this number was lower at 200.

This discrepancy means that, since the warm-up and early stopping values are kept constant across both sets of experiments, the resource-saving techniques, have a larger pool of epochs from which to cut in the ASCADr experiments. As a result, these techniques appear to prune a higher percentage of epochs in the ASCADr experiments compared to the ASCADf ones. This difference, however, is simply a reflection of the different default epoch settings for the two datasets, rather than indicating any inherent differences in the effectiveness of the early stopping strategies.

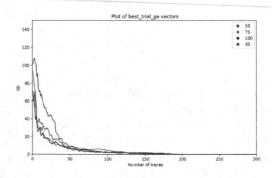

Fig. 3. Guessing entropy for the ASCADr experiments using warm up value of 30, 50, 75 and 100

Analyzing the outcomes of the best models' Guessing Entropy (GE) from various experiments of the ASCADr dataset, depicted in Fig. 3, reveals comparable results across the board for different warm-up values, specifically 30, 50, 75, and 100. Interestingly, the model from the experiment with a warm-up value of 30 exhibited slightly superior performance, reaching a GE of 0 with 170 traces. Meanwhile, the best models from experiments with warm-up values of 50, 75, and 100 also demonstrated commendable performance, requiring slightly more than 200 traces to achieve a GE of 0.

Once more, despite the amounts of computational resources saved across the different warm-up values, all experiments resulted in well performing models. These results suggest that the role of early stopping strategies can be effective in the HO process and can help to focus the process on more promising configurations and lead to better results.

Table 5. Comparison with other papers of number of traces required to reach a GE of 0 for ASCADr, ID leakage Model

Attempt	Traces to reach GE = 0
[19]	105
[23]	490
[20]	1500
this study	170

6   Conclusion and Future Work

In this paper, we investigated the role of HO in CNN-based SCA. We specifically showed how the integration of sampling and early-stopping strategies can help to find a good fitting model and save computing time and resources during the HO process.

Our results showed that the implementation of adaptive early-stopping techniques during the training phase could speed up the HO process without affecting performance. Across all warm-up values used in the experiments, the models consistently required around 200 traces for successful key recovery. This observation suggest that an efficient HO process, facilitated by early-stopping, does not compromise the effectiveness of the CNN models in SCA.

Furthermore, the use of TPE as a sampling algorithm and a GE-based objective value reduce the number of explored configurations during the HO process before finding a first good fitting model. These methods contributed to the effective selection and evaluation of hyperparameter configuration, leading to promising results shown in Tables 3 and 5.

In this work, we focused on the combination of TPE sampling and median early-stopping methods, but there exists many other sampling and early-stopping methods which could alleviate better the HO search. It would be interesting to explore in more depth the different methods available in the machine learning literature and adapt it to the problem of SCA. This work also explored only the case of CNN-based deep learning, and only with a narrowed hyperparameter search space, adapted from the previous research for the given datasets we used for the experiments. When dealing with another dataset, a different search space or even different neural network architecture should be designed. The standardization of a common search space, taking into account width and depth limits of the architecture, could help to increase the confidence of security assessment of deep-learning based SCA.

References

1. Abadi, M., et al.: TensorFlow: large-scale machine learning on heterogeneous systems (2015). https://www.tensorflow.org/. software available from tensorflow.org
2. Akiba, T., Sano, S., Yanase, T., Ohta, T., Koyama, M.: Optuna: a next-generation hyperparameter optimization framework. In: Proceedings of the 25th ACM SIGKDD International Conference on Knowledge Discovery & Data Mining, pp. 2623–2631 (2019)
3. Benadjila, R., Prouff, E., Strullu, R., Cagli, E., Dumas, C.: Deep learning for side-channel analysis and introduction to ASCAD database. J. Cryptogr. Eng. **10**(2), 163–188 (2020)
4. Bergstra, J., Bardenet, R., Bengio, Y., Kégl, B.: Algorithms for hyper-parameter optimization. In: Advances in Neural Information Processing Systems, vol. 24 (2011)
5. Brisfors, M., Forsmark, S.: DLSCA: a tool for deep learning side channel analysis. IACR Cryptol. ePrint Arch. 1071 (2019). https://eprint.iacr.org/2019/1071
6. Chari, S., Rao, J.R., Rohatgi, P.: Template attacks. In: Kaliski, B.S., Koç, C.K., Paar, C. (eds.) Cryptographic Hardware and Embedded Systems - CHES 2002. Lecture Notes in Computer Science, vol. 2523, pp. 13–28. Springer, Berlin (2003). https://doi.org/10.1007/3-540-36400-5_3
7. Chollet, F., et al.: Keras (2015). https://keras.io
8. Hunter, J.D.: Matplotlib: a 2D graphics environment. Comput. Sci. Eng. **9**(3), 90–95 (2007). https://doi.org/10.1109/MCSE.2007.55
9. Jamieson, K., Talwalkar, A.: Non-stochastic best arm identification and hyperparameter optimization. In: Artificial Intelligence and Statistics, pp. 240–248. PMLR (2016)
10. Kocher, P., Jaffe, J., Jun, B.: Differential power analysis. In: Wiener, M. (ed.) Advances in Cryptology — CRYPTO' 99. Lecture Notes in Computer Science, vol. 1666, pp. 388–397. Springer, Berlin (1999). https://doi.org/10.1007/3-540-48405-1_25
11. Kubota, T., Yoshida, K., Shiozaki, M., Fujino, T.: Deep learning side-channel attack against hardware implementations of AES. Microprocess. Microsyst. **87**, 103383 (2021). https://doi.org/10.1016/j.micpro.2020.103383
12. Li, C., et al.: Genetic algorithm based hyper-parameters optimization for transfer convolutional neural network. CoRR **abs/2103.03875** (2021). https://arxiv.org/abs/2103.03875
13. Li, L., et al.: A system for massively parallel hyperparameter tuning. Proc. Mach. Learn. Syst. **2**, 230–246 (2020)

14. Li, L., Jamieson, K., DeSalvo, G., Rostamizadeh, A., Talwalkar, A.: Hyperband: a novel bandit-based approach to hyperparameter optimization. J. Mach. Learn. Res. **18**(1), 6765–6816 (2017)

15. Maghrebi, H., Portigliatti, T., Prouff, E.: Breaking cryptographic implementations using deep learning techniques. In: Carlet, C., Hasan, M., Saraswat, V. (eds.) Security, Privacy, and Applied Cryptography Engineering. Lecture Notes in Computer Science(), vol. 10076, pp. 3–26. Springer, Cham (2016). https://doi.org/10.1007/978-3-319-49445-6_1

16. Nakkiran, P., Kaplun, G., Bansal, Y., Yang, T., Barak, B., Sutskever, I.: Deep double descent: Where bigger models and more data hurt. J. Stat. Mech: Theory Exp. **2021**(12), 124003 (2021)

17. Paguada, S., Armendariz, I.: The Forgotten Hyperparameter: - introducing dilated convolution for boosting CNN-based side-channel attacks. In: Zhou, J., et al. (eds.) ACNS 2020. LNCS, vol. 12418, pp. 217–236. Springer, Cham (2020). https://doi.org/10.1007/978-3-030-61638-0_13

18. Paguada, S., Batina, L., Buhan, I., Armendariz, I.: Being patient and persistent: optimizing an early stopping strategy for deep learning in profiled attacks. IEEE Trans. Inf. Forensics Secur. **17** (2022)

19. Perin, G., Chmielewski, Ł., Picek, S.: Strength in numbers: improving generalization with ensembles in machine learning-based profiled side-channel analysis. IACR Trans. Cryptogr. Hardw. Embedded Syst., 337–364 (2020)

20. Perin, G., Wu, L., Picek, S.: AISY - deep learning-based framework for side-channel analysis. Cryptology ePrint Archive, Report 2021/357 (2021). https://eprint.iacr.org/2021/357

21. Picek, S., Perin, G., Mariot, L., Wu, L., Batina, L.: SoK: deep learning-based physical side-channel analysis. ACM Comput. Surv. **55**(11), 1 35 (2023). https://doi.org/10.1145/3569577

22. Picek, S., Samiotis, I.P., Kim, J., Heuser, A., Bhasin, S., Legay, A.: On the performance of convolutional neural networks for side-channel analysis. In: Chattopadhyay, A., Rebeiro, C., Yarom, Y. (eds.) SPACE 2018. LNCS, vol. 11348, pp. 157–176. Springer, Cham (2018). https://doi.org/10.1007/978-3-030-05072-6_10

23. Rijsdijk, J., Wu, L., Perin, G., Picek, S.: Reinforcement learning for hyperparameter tuning in deep learning-based side-channel analysis. IACR Trans. Cryptogr. Hardw. Embedded Syst., 677–707 (2021)

24. Rioja, U., Paguada, S., Batina, L., Armendariz, I.: The uncertainty of side-channel analysis: a way to leverage from heuristics. ACM J. Emerg. Technol. Comput. Syst. **17**(3), 1–27 (2021). https://doi.org/10.1145/3446997

25. Snoek, J., Larochelle, H., Adams, R.P.: Practical Bayesian optimization of machine learning algorithms. In: Bartlett, P.L., Pereira, F.C.N., Burges, C.J.C., Bottou, L., Weinberger, K.Q. (eds.) Advances in Neural Information Processing Systems 25: 26th Annual Conference on Neural Information Processing Systems 2012. Proceedings of a meeting held 3-6 December 2012, Lake Tahoe, Nevada, United States, pp. 2960–2968 (2012). https://proceedings.neurips.cc/paper/2012/hash/05311655a15b75fab86956663e1819cd-Abstract.html

26. Wang, J., Xu, J., Wang, X.: Combination of hyperband and Bayesian optimization for hyperparameter optimization in deep learning. arXiv preprint: arXiv:1801.01596 (2018)

27. Wistuba, M., Schilling, N., Schmidt-Thieme, L.: Hyperparameter search space pruning – a new component for sequential model-based hyperparameter optimization. In: Appice, A., Rodrigues, P.P., Santos Costa, V., Gama, J., Jorge, A., Soares,

C. (eds.) ECML PKDD 2015. LNCS (LNAI), vol. 9285, pp. 104–119. Springer, Cham (2015). https://doi.org/10.1007/978-3-319-23525-7_7

28. Wouters, L., Arribas, V., Gierlichs, B., Preneel, B.: Revisiting a methodology for efficient CNN architectures in profiling attacks. IACR Trans. Cryptogr. Hardw. Embedded Syst., 147–168 (2020)

29. Wu, L., Perin, G., Picek, S.: I choose you: automated hyperparameter tuning for deep learning-based side-channel analysis. IEEE Trans. Emerg. Top. Comput. (2022)

30. Zaid, G., Bossuet, L., Habrard, A., Venelli, A.: Methodology for efficient CNN architectures in profiling attacks. IACR Trans. Cryptogr. Hardw. Embedded Syst., 1–36 (2020)

AIoTS – Artificial Intelligence
and Industrial IoT Security

Device Fingerprinting in a Smart Grid CPS

Chuadhry Mujeeb Ahmed[1](✉), Nandha Kumar Kandasamy[2],
Darren Ng Wei Hong[3], and Jianying Zhou[3]

[1] Newcastle University, Newcastle upon Tyne, UK
mujeeb.ahmed@newcastle.ac.uk
[2] Liteon Singapore, Singapore, Singapore
Nandha001@e.ntu.edu.sg
[3] Singapore University of Technology and Design, Singapore, Singapore
{darren_ng,jianying_zhou}@sutd.edu.sg

Abstract. Data integrity attacks on the various meter readings found in smart grid systems can be executed to be undetectable by current detection algorithms used in smart grid systems. These unobservable cyber-attacks present a potentially dangerous threat to grid operations. Data integrity attacks that involve the compromise of various meter readings such as voltage and current levels can lead to threats ranging from trivial problems such as energy usage miscalculations to dire consequences resulting from the breakdown of the entire smart grid system through overloading the generators. An efficient detection algorithm to detect these attacks on various sensors embedded in the smart grid system is proposed. Due to manufacturing imperfections, discretizing the sensor readings produces variations in the readings that are unique to each sensor. A fingerprint of this sensor noise (variations in readings) is modeled through the use of machine learning techniques. Under a malicious spoofing attack, the noise pattern deviates from the fingerprinted pattern and hence enabling the proposed detection scheme to identify these attacks. A novel ensemble learning method is used to identify the Intelligent Electronic Device (IED). Experiments are performed on the Electric Power and Intelligent Control (EPIC) testbed. It is shown that a set of IEDs under the different stages of the power generation process can be uniquely identified with an accuracy greater than 90% based on the fingerprint.

Keywords: CPS Security · Device Fingerprinting · Sensor Fingerprinting

1 Introduction

Cyber-Physical Systems (CPS) is an integration of computing and networking elements with physical processes [8]. Embedded Computers and networks, monitor and control the physical processes through the use of Intelligent Electronic

---

C. M. Ahmed—This work was carried out when authors were working at SUTD.

M. Andreoni (Ed.): ACNS 2024 Workshops, LNCS 14586, pp. 215–234, 2024.
https://doi.org/10.1007/978-3-031-61486-6_13

Device (IED) that computes the sensor readings. In particular, we will consider examples of power generation systems in this work, a critical part of smart grid systems. A smart grid system consists of physical components such as electric power generators, power substations, transmission and distribution lines, and cyber components such as smart meters, IEDs, controllers, transmission control centers and Human Machine Interface (HMI) components that are interconnected via a communications network [1]. Advancements in micro-embedded systems and communication networks enabled existing physical systems to become digitized. The digital components also expose the physical processes to malicious entities in the cyber domain [6]. Recent activities of cyber attacks and sabotage on these systems have raised security concerns about the reliability and security of smart grid systems.

Challenges in Smart Grid Systems and CPS are fundamentally different from traditional IT systems [4]. Real-time availability of the service also provides a stricter operational environment than most traditional IT systems and many CPSs are legacy systems, that were designed without security in mind. Because Smart grid systems deal with the generation and supply of electricity, the manipulation through a cyber attack might result in damage to the physical property or the people who depend on these critical infrastructures, as was the case in Ukraine where the power supply was disrupted for the residents due to a cyber attack [7]. Data integrity is therefore an important security requirement for CPS. Sensor readings can be spoofed through the sniffing of packets between the communication of the IEDs and the HMI as classical man-in-the-middle attack [13]. Data integrity attacks on sensor measurements and their impacts and consequences have been studied largely in theory, including data manipulation injection, replay attacks, and stealthy attacks. These previous studies proposed attack detection methods based on statistical fault detectors such as Cumulative Sum (CUSUM) or Chi-square, which can be deceived [11].

In this work, we propose an attack detection framework. The proposed detection scheme is a fingerprinting method to authenticate IEDs in smart grid systems when their readings are received at the HMI. This scheme is unique and provides a novel way of extracting the noise imperfections of the IEDs. The sensor noise is captured during the different stages of the power generation process. Process stages such as the Smart Home, Transmission and Micro-grid readings have been tested and experimented upon. Because of sensor manufacturing imperfections, these IEDs can be differentiated from their noise pattern. These variations are minute in nature and are therefore hard to control or reproduce, making a spoofing of sensor readings of these noise profiles challenging. A fingerprint is based on a set of time domain and frequency domain features that are extracted from the data collection of the IED readings. A multi-class support vector machine (SVM) is used to classify the noise patterns of various line readings found within each IED. Optimization in the decision function used and the use of different kernels, which is a set of mathematical functions used to transform the feature space of the dataset into higher orders for better separation of data have also been experimented on. Bagging algorithms form a class

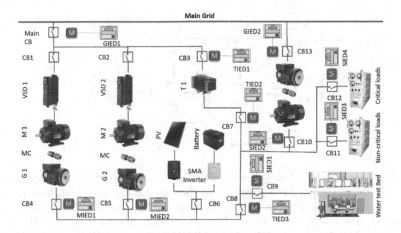

Fig. 1. Electrical layout of the EPIC (actual) test-bed. Electrical power lines are shown in red color lines. MC - Mechanical coupling, CB - Circuit Breaker, IEDs - intelligent electronic devices, the prefix G, M T and S stands for Generation, Micro-grid, Transmission and Smart Home respectively. (Color figure online)

of algorithms that build several instances of a black-box estimator on random subsets of the original training set and then aggregate their predictions to form a final prediction. These methods are used as a way to reduce the variance of a base estimator (e.g., a decision tree), by introducing randomization into its construction procedure and then making an ensemble out of it.

A group of algorithms which includes Random Forest Classifier, Gradient Boosting Classifier, and Ada Boost Classifiers have been experimented on. These algorithms form the overall ensemble algorithm which takes in the output of each of the machine learning algorithms and uses a majority vote to predict the final class labels [12]. Such a classifier can be useful for a set of equally well-performing model to balance out their weaknesses. IED and their respective lines identification accuracy is observed to be as high as 93%, and at least 90% for a range of sensors. The major contribution of this work includes the following: a) A novel fingerprinting framework that is built for the identification of IEDs based on sensor noise. b) A detailed evaluation of the proposed scheme as an IED identification mechanism, for a class of IED spoofing attacks. c) Extensive empirical performance evaluation on the EPIC testbed. A comparison of the performance of the various machine learning algorithms implemented is also presented. This work evaluates the device fingerprinting technique in the context of the smart grid power generation process.

2   Background: EPIC Testbed

This work is carried out on the EPIC (Electric Power and Intelligent Control) testbed which is a smart gird test-bed designed specifically for cyber security

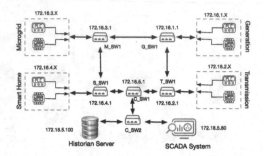

Fig. 2. A simplified network diagram for EPIC test-bed. Each dotted box represents a subnet with the respective IP addresses and corresponds to individual inner rings. An X in the IP address means that a device in that subnet would have a similar subnet mask and then a unique X as its IP. The connection $M_S W1 - - > S_S W1 - - > C_S W1 - - > T_S W1 - - > G_S W1 - - > M_S W1$ is the outer HSR ring

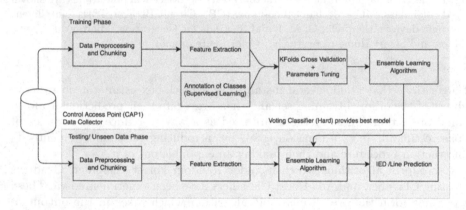

Fig. 3. Overview of the proposed technique.

studies and technology evaluations. The testbed is an industrial-grade system capable of supplying power to a mini water treatment plant and a mini water distribution plant [3,9], thus enabling studies such as the cascading effect of cyber attacks, i.e., how a cyber attack on one critical infrastructure affects the reliability of other. As mentioned above, EPIC has been designed and implemented with industry-grade equipment meeting all the standards and regulations of a smart grid CPS. Further, EPIC provides an emulated environment that cannot be observed in other test-beds, i.e., all four sections of a typical power grid are available. The four sections are not only physically zoned into generation, micro-grid, transmission, and smart home but also via network segregation for IEDs and Programmable logic controllers (PLCs). Advanced metering infrastructure (AMI) meters are integrated along with the IEDs to measure current, voltage, power, and frequency at different electrical nodes. Each section of EPIC is described below,

The electrical layout of EPIC is shown in Fig. 1, and a basic description is given below. For further details on the electrical layout and physical process of EPIC, an interested reader is referred to the EPIC test-bed paper [1].

- **Generation:** Due to the limitation on having fossil fuel-powered prime-movers, the Generation stage is created using two induction motors that are powered by variable speed drives (15kW). The induction motors are mechanically coupled to respective 3-phase synchronous generators (10KVA each) that act as the master (reference grid) for the electrical system.
- **Micro-Grid:** Renewable energy components for the electrical system are provided via solar Photo-voltaic (PV) array (34kW) and energy storage system (18kW) with inverters to harness solar energy and also include the behavior of distributed energy resource dynamics into the system.
- **Transmission:** The transmission stage is sectioned into two groups, 1) a direct connection to downstream loads representing a pure micro-grid and 2) a connection through a transformer (105kVA) to represent the line-impedance and tap-changing functionalities in transmission systems.
- **Smart Home:** The smart home acts as the power distribution system's load, the load is configurable using programmable load banks (45kVA) containing RLC[1] loads and a motor (10kW) load for representing pumps, ventilation systems, etc. Besides, as mentioned before two water test-beds are connected to the EPIC test-bed to form a cluster of critical infrastructure.

Similar to the physical components, the network of epic is also sectioned into four groups each representing the respective control zones, namely, power generation, transmission, micro-grid, and smart home. The IEDs connected to the individual nodes are connected using high-speed seamless redundancy (HSR) rings which ensures $n - 1$ redundancy. The HSR rings connecting the IEDs are referred to as inner rings, and each inner ring has a PLC for controlling the process of the respective section. The IEDs and PLCs are named with suffixes of the corresponding section, for example, an IED in the generator section is named as GIEDx (x is numerical), whereas the IED in the smart home section is named as SIEDx. All the inner rings are connected via another HSR ring referred to as the outer ring, the outer ring enables the communication between the inner rings. $n - 1$ redundancy is ensured for the outer ring as well. The Supervisory Control and Data Acquisition (SCADA) system is connected to the outer ring. Figure 2 shows the communication network architecture in the EPIC testbed. The data flow from IED SIED1 will start at the physical measurement "M" shown in Fig. 1, the measure data is then converted in IEC61850 network data by SIED1 which is then made available to SPLC, and the SCADA system via IEC61850 MMS (Manufacturing Message Specification) variables. IEC61850 GOOSE (Generic Object Oriented Substation Event) variables are used only for the Transmission section and only made available among the IEDs.

---

[1] Resistor-Inductor-Capacitor.

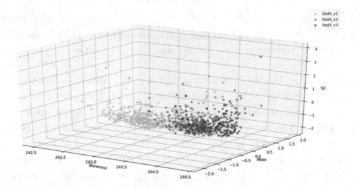

Fig. 4. Scatter plot of TIED v1, v2 and v3 the addition of skewness as the third dimension shows separability in the dataset. The results of these experiments conclude that the noise patterns of these IEDs follow a unique variation.

3   Overview of the Proposed Technique

An overview of the proposed technique is shown in Fig. 3. The data is collected using the log management tool in the testbed. We have studied the system design and functionality of the power generation process of EPIC testbed and identified 3 different key stages and IEDs to focus the experiments on. We collected the data under regular operation (no attack) with the predefined loads. As shown in Fig. 3, we will discuss the process of collecting the dataset from the historian HMI interface. Then, we will present the data preprocessing and chunking process followed by the fingerprinting scheme [2,5] which involves the use of various supervised machine learning algorithms embedded into a single ensemble learning cluster where each of the individual machine learning algorithm learners are trained to solve the same problem and a voting classifier is used [10].

IED Noise: The IEDs send the readings of the sensors through the use of the access point to the control unit. Here, X_k (refers to the set of sensor readings of each of the IEDs at time k. $X_k = \{x_k^1, x_k^2, ..., x_k^z\}$ where z corresponds to the total number of IEDs found in the EPIC testbed system. Due to manufacturing imperfections of the IED components, the IED measurements of the various system variables such as voltage and current contain noise. It has been observed that when the intended value of the system variable is set, the readings are always displaced by a small margin of up to 2 decimal places. For example, when the voltage value is set to 240V, based on more than 5000 different data points observed, the values received by the historian logging system show that the reported value varies around the true value, indicating the presence of noise found in these IEDs. This observation is seen similarly for each of the IEDs and their line readings.

The presence of these noise patterns indicates a possibility that these fluctuations can be individually identified for each of the IEDs. The data collected is preprocessed to remove any possible loss of data during the data collection stage due to unforeseen technical issues and is processed into chunks of size m.

These chunks are then analyzed and statistical features such as mean and standard deviation are extracted. Both frequency domain and time-related features are examined. The noise and its time/frequency domain features exhibit clustering characteristics indicating that the features extracted from the data points belonging to the same IEDs tend to have small distances to data points of the same IEDs thus forming dense areas of clustered points throughout the visualization. Furthermore, these features extracted from the noise are profiled using standard deviation, mean, and skewness to show further possible correlation. In Fig. 4, we can see that there is a distinct separation between TIED4 v1 from TIED4 v2 and v3. Although the separation is distinctively clearer, it is important to note that the noise pattern found in the dataset from v3 is very similar to that of v2 thus, identifying v3 from v2 might not provide desirable results.

Next, a set of machine learning algorithms are used to classify the IEDs from one another. Noise fingerprints can be generated over time as the process of power generation is in progress. During normal operations, the fingerprint will be used to identify if the data reading received by the Control Access Point (CAP) is indeed from the IEDs or if it is injected by the attacker.

Data Preprocessing: Data is collected from the IEDs right at the moment EPIC is started to the end. After the collection of data is done, we would need to do certain data preprocessing to prepare the dataset for both feature extraction and then classification. We first remove all of the intermediate 0 values as we are only concerned with values of the predefined range. For voltage, we have decided that the predefined value would be at 240 V. The dataset is then compiled into their respective IEDs such as TIED4, MIED1, MIED2, and SIED4. In total, there were 3,680 raw data points collected.

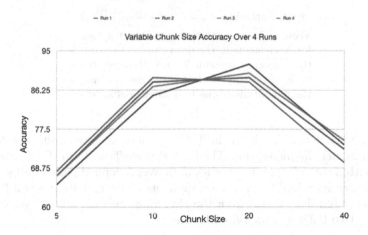

Fig. 5. Accuracy percentage results of varying chunk sizes.

Data Chunking: After the collection of data is done, we would need to create chunks of the dataset. Because the features are statistical, we would need to create chunks of data to extract these features. Chunking allows us to understand the right size of data needed to capture the variance in the set and how much data is needed to train the machine learning algorithm to produce desirable results. A list of varying chunk sizes was tested upon such as (5,10,2,40) and based on the accuracy performance, chunk size 20 produced the best results. Figure 5 shows the accuracy results of the chunk size on the support vector machine algorithm with the only variable difference as the chunk size, m. We could see that chunk size 5 produces a fairly low accuracy performance as 5 data points do not capture a lot of the variance in the data set thus each chunk produced did not tend to follow a similar pattern. On the other spectrum, a chunk size of 40 captures most of the variance in the data set but because the data collected is limited, using a chunk size of 40 meant that the overall number of fingerprint data points to classify is greatly reduced. Hence, the machine learning algorithm is not able to produce a desired accuracy count.

Table 1. List of features used.

Feature	Description
Mean	$\bar{x} = \frac{1}{N}\sum_{i=1}^{N} x_i$
Std-Dev	$\sigma = \sqrt{\frac{1}{N-1}\sum_{i=1}^{N}(x_i - \bar{x}_i)^2}$
Mean Avg. Dev	$D_{\bar{x}} = \frac{1}{N}\sum_{i=1}^{N}|x_i - \bar{x}|$
Skewness	$\gamma = \frac{1}{N}\sum_{i=1}^{N}\left(\frac{x_i - \bar{x}}{\sigma}\right)^3$
Kurtosis	$\beta = \frac{1}{N}\sum_{i=1}^{N}\left(\frac{x_i - \bar{x}}{\sigma}\right)^4 - 3$
Spec. Std-Dev	$\sigma_s = \sqrt{\frac{\sum_{i=1}^{N}(y_f(i)^2)*y_m(i)}{\sum_{i=1}^{N} y_m(i)}}$
Spec. Centroid	$C_s = \frac{\sum_{i=1}^{N}(y_f(i))*y_m(i)}{\sum_{i=1}^{N} y_m(i)}$

Vector x is time domain data from the sensor for N elements in the data chunk. Vector y is the frequency domain feature of sensor data. y_f is the vector of bin frequencies and y_m is the magnitude of the frequency coefficients.

Feature Extraction: As shown in Table 1, there are seven different features used to construct the fingerprint. The Fast Fourier Transform (FTT) algorithm is an algorithm that samples time series data over a defined period and separates it into its corresponding frequency components to extract its spectral features. The fingerprinted data points from the chunking are then labeled according to their respective IEDs for supervised learning.

Cross-Validation: Cross-validation is a type of model validation technique used in the assessment of how the performance results of a given statistical analysis will generalize to an unseen data set. It is a resampling procedure used to evaluate the algorithm model on unseen data, i.e., how the model is expected to perform in general when used to make classifications on data not used during the training phase of the model. It takes in a single parameter k, which is the number of sub-divisions given to the overall dataset. For K different groups, take the first group as the hold-out or test data set and combine the remaining groups as the training data set. The machine learning model is fitted, trained, and evaluated based on the hold-out set. The process is repeated for different hold-out sets and their overall model evaluation score is returned. K-Folds cross-validation is implemented with the use of the scikit-learn python module.

4 Threat Model

In this paper, we will only consider specific cyber-attacks on the data integrity of these IED readings and not physical attacks due to the nature of the smart grid system and the EPIC testbed system, direct contact to these sensors is very dangerous and not easily accessible to both an intruder or even an insider (operator) who has direct access to these physical IEDs. First, we profile the attacker and lay down assumptions of the attacker backed with justification. Following on, we will introduce one such possible cyber-attack on the EPIC testbed system. The attack here is defined as a sequence of one or more malicious actions intended to move a CPS such as EPIC system to an undesirable state while the attacker refers to an individual, or a group, that intends to, or has launched attacks on a CPS. The attacker model is a formal description of the capabilities and knowledge base of an attacker and provides useful information when designing protective and detective measures, and for comparing the chances of successfully launching an attack. The attacker may have its motivation stemming from a set of intentions such as denial of service, falsifying data and the actual usage of the power supply, diverting resources, performance degradation or even damaging a component.

4.1 Attacker Model

Assumptions on the Attacker: It is assumed that the attacker is an Insider, an employee who has information access to the system network and has knowledge of the operational process of the EPIC testbed or smart grid system. On top of that, the attacker knows all of the different IEDs present in each of the 4 stages of the power generation process. The adversary has perfect knowledge of the various sensor readings and can modify them arbitrarily. An example would be the following, the adversary would like to reduce his apparent consumption of electricity and thus would inject falsified readings of current and voltages to make it appear as if he was not using the actual amount of electricity. The goal is to minimize the apparent consumption without being detected.

The attacker is a strong adversary who can launch cyber-attacks both within the premise and outside of the premise of the system. One of the key vulnerabilities of the smart grid system is its communication link between the IEDs and the HMI. As such, an attacker can compromise these communication links simply through the use of a Man-in-The-Middle (MiTM) attack. This could also lead to a data integrity attack against one or more IEDs taking place when legitimate data of the IED is tampered with, replaced, or deleted before its transmission to the data concentrate unit is completed successfully. For example, by interjecting the communication link between the access points to the control unit, the attacker can sniff the packets sent over the communication link and decide to either drop the packet, delay the sending of the packet, or reload it with a different payload. Therefore, we will need to find a robust method to authenticate the IED readings received on the end of the control unit and to the Historian logging system. While a malicious insider can break into the network communication between the IEDs and the control unit, an outsider may also be able to break into the network if an appropriate firewall is not installed. Furthermore, we also assume that the attacker would want to be stealthy and undetected, hence placing this attack under the unobservable attack category.

4.2   Attack Model

Data Injection Attacks: This class of attacks refers to one where the attacker intercepts the communication link, sniffs the packet sent and injects or modifies the actual IED sensor readings with a falsified one that is generated randomly or with a specific intend. The adversary may inject fictitious data into the HMI to either portray increased electricity consumption or to reduce it. It affects the normal operations of the system as power load balances might be redistributed to other areas as a result of this data injection. For example, manipulating the current and voltage readings can lead to a misleading reading of power since $P = IV$. Thus, the system state is disrupted, and power will be redistributed and generated higher than the source needs. This is a direct attack on the integrity of the system. The proposed solution uses a fingerprinting methodology to identify that the readings are indeed coming from the IEDs and not from an attacker. This is made possible due to the intricate nature of the imperfections. Because the current readings and voltage readings have been fingerprinted, changing their values (i.e. if the operating voltage is set to be at 240V but the spoofed reading shows 220 V), the operator might increase the voltage by 20 V and when it has been increased to 260 V, the attacker can send packets showing the desired 240 V but the actual voltage is now at 260 V. Similarly, this scenario works for the Current as well. Because $P = IV$, an increase in either of Current or Voltage will lead to an increase in power supply. Over or under powering over prolonged periods can also be used for fault injection. Under powering can increase signal propagation delay and can lead to setup time violations in hardware platforms. In our experiments, we consider three types of data injection attacks.

Bias Data Injection Attack: The goal of the bias data injection attack is to deceive the controller by sending an increased/decreased value of the actual reading by a constant c, to deceive the controller into thinking that the received values are the true IED sensor readings. For example, in this situation, the voltage measurements are increased while the actual voltage level is invariant.

Hence, the controller will continue to reduce the voltage supplied until it reaches zero. The attack vector is defined as follows:

$$y'(k) = \hat{y}(k) \pm c \tag{1}$$

where c is a constant added at each time instant. A negative constant could be used for attacks such as the one targeting damage by deceiving the controller to increase the current to unacceptable levels.

Geometric Data Injection Attack: Geometric attack is similar to bias data attack but consists of two additional coefficients α and β. The constant is now modified to increase exponentially instead of constantly. The attack vector is defined as follows:

$$y'(k) = \hat{y}(k) \pm \beta\alpha^{n-k} \tag{2}$$

where $\alpha \in (0,1)$ and β is a multiplier to be adjusted for maximum damage. n here represents the last measurement received in the sequence and k is the measurement number starting from 0.

Zero-Alarm Attack: zero-alarm attack is crafted such as to remain undetectable by traditional statistical methods like cumulative sum (CUSUM). The CUSUM detection mechanism is fed with the sequential data of the incoming IED readings. It computes the current cumulative sum and does so by performing a change point detection. Because CUSUM depends largely on two predefined constant values, the threshold, τ, and the bias, b, the adversary can easily remain undetected by choosing the attack vector δ_k that stays within the confines of the threshold value. The impact and limitations of these statistical methods as detection mechanisms have already been widely covered in the literature.

It is important to note that for such zero-alarm attacks if the attacker wants to remain undetected, he cannot damage the system but can always still impact the integrity of the system.

4.3   Attack Execution

Because of the nature of the EPIC testbed system, an actual MiTM attack was not possible to carry out. This is due to the restrictions of the laboratory as attacks can lead to dangerous scenarios. A successful attempt at a data injection attack might bring dire consequences. In reality, however, the adversary would need to intercept the data traffic between the communication lines of the IED's access point to the controller's access point. The attack could be a physical or logical MiTM, in which a physical MiTM is physically intrusive but has no impact on the configuration of the plant and the logical MiTM does not need physical intrusion but has a serious impact on the configurations of the plant as the restoration is likely to consume 4–5 working days. Packets are then inspected and modified (payload changed depending on the type of attack) but modified data readings are injected into the sequence of legitimate data points found in the historian logging system. The above attack is equivalent to malware that modifies the configurations in the SCADA software to assign the IED's IEC61850 server (one under attack) to a local port and feeds the modified data by polling the actual IED and creating a malicious server on the above local port. From there, the CUSUM and the proposed detection mechanism were tested for accuracy and performance.

4.4   Generating Attack Data

As mentioned above, the simulated attack instead focuses on generating the attack data which will be used by the adversary to inject into the controller unit. A script has been written to read an incoming packet payload and modify it according to whether it is a bias, geometric, or zero-alarm attack. For the zero-alarm attack, to remain undetected, the function created to generate the attack falsified data is a random number generator that generates a random floating number based on the current reading received and does so in the ranges of a predefined standard deviation. This allows the random floating numbers to hover around a predefined value, but the changes are within the threshold value set for CUSUM. Thus, allowing the adversary to stay undetected while still being able to manipulate the data readings.

5   Performance Evaluation

In this section, a brief background of the statistical detection scheme, CUSUM will be provided, followed by the performance of the machine learning algorithms in identifying each of the IEDs, the model evaluation methods used as well as the evaluation of the proposed detection mechanism scheme.

5.1   CUSUM

Statistical detectors estimate state values in each turn of the sequence and compare it with the IED measurement reading. The difference between the two values provides a value that stays within the threshold value under normal operation. As such, the threshold value and the bias value are important key variables as they affect the false alarm rate. To begin, we have identified two hypotheses to be tested, $\mathcal{H}_0$ which represents the hypothesis where a given measurement depicts normal process behavior, and $\mathcal{H}_1$, which represents the hypothesis where a given measurement depicts anomalous process behavior (with attack).

CUSUM: $S_{0,i} = 0, \quad i \in \mathcal{I},$

$$\begin{cases} S_{k,i} = \max(0, S_{k-1,i} + z_{k,i} - b_i), & \text{if } S_{k-1,i} \leq \tau_i, \\ S_{k,i} = 0 \text{ and } \tilde{k}_i = k - 1, & \text{if } S_{k-1,i} > \tau_i. \end{cases} \tag{3}$$

Design parameters: bias $b_i > 0$ and threshold $\tau_i > 0$.
Output: alarm time(s) $\tilde{k}_i$.

We have to choose both threshold τ_i and bias b_i such that both are greater than 0.

5.2   Model Evaluation Methods

To prevent cases of over-fitting or under-fitting of the dataset, the technique used to separate the dataset into S_{train} and S_{test} is crucial. Therefore, Cross-validation is used as a means of model evaluation method. Cross-validation belongs to a class of model evaluation methods that has significant performance over the use of residuals. The limitations of residual evaluations include the fact that they do not indicate how well the learner will do when it has to make predictions for unseen data (independent data). A simple solution to eliminate this problem is to prevent the use of the entire data set as a whole when training the classifier. A segment of the data is removed before the training process. After which when the training phase has been completed, the data that was removed earlier can now be used to test the performance of the classification model. This forms the basis for a whole class of model evaluation methods called cross-validation.

Hold Out Method: The simplest form of cross-validation, the data set is first separated into two distinct sets, S_{train} and S_{test}. Next, the model is trained only using the training set that was separated following which the model is then used to predict the classes or labels of the data in the testing set. Hence, the testing set is used to estimate the prediction error rate of the trained classifier algorithm. However, from the experimentation, it is shown that when the dataset is sparse or minute, we may not be able to set aside a portion of the dataset for testing. Therefore, in the initial phase of the project, the Holdout method was removed in favor of the k-fold cross-validation method with three-way data splits so that the parameters of the algorithm could be tuned.

K-Fold Cross-validation: Is an improvement over the standard holdout method. The algorithm works as such, the dataset is divided into k subsets, and the holdout method is repeated k different times with each time, a a sliding window of fixed value (subset) is used as a test set while the rest $k - 1$ subsets are used as training sets. Even though this method takes k times as much computation as compared to the holdout method, the variance of the resulting estimate is reduced as k is increased, thus resulting in better model validation.

Choosing k: The number of k folds can affect the variance of the resulting estimate. With a large k value, the bias of the true rate estimator will be small, hence it will be more accurate. However, the variance of the true error rate will be large, and also the computational time as it has to run k several times. With a small k value, the number of experiments and computation time are reduced, with a small variance of the estimator and the bias of the estimator will be large.

Using the first machine learning algorithm, SVM, K-Folds was running repeatedly with a range of $K \in \{1, 10\}$ and found that the most suitable number of folds based on accuracy against computational time effort is 4. As such, the value of k will be set at 4 when comparing amongst the algorithms.

5.3   Zero-Alarm Attack Design

A zero-alarm attack is designed in such a way that it stays undetected by the CUSUM detectors. As shown in the CUSUM procedure, we can write (3) in terms of the estimation error e_k:

$$S_{k,i} = \max(0, S_{k-1,i} + |C_i e_k + \eta_{k,i} + \delta_{k,i}| - b_i), \tag{4}$$

if $S_{k-1,i} \leq \tau_i$; and $S_{k,i} = 0$, if $S_{k-1,i} > \tau_i$.

Consider the attack:

$$\delta_{k,i} = \begin{cases} \tau_i + b_i - C_i e_k - \eta_{k,i} - S_{k-1,i}, & k = k^*, \\ b_i - C_i e_k - \eta_{k,i}, & k > k^*. \end{cases} \tag{5}$$

For all given $k \geq k*$, zero alarm has been raised. The assumption made here is that the adversary knows exactly $S_{k-1,i}$, the value of the CUSUM sequence one timestamp before inducing the attack. This would allow him to set the falsified data such that it will not trigger the alarm of the CUSUM scheme. The IED readings received by the controller will thus take the following form:

$$\bar{y}_{k,i} = \begin{cases} C_i \hat{x}_{k,i} + \tau_i + b_i + C_i \hat{x}_k - \eta_{k,i} - S_{k-1,i}, & k = k^*, \\ b_i + C_i \hat{x}_{k,i}, & k > k^*. \end{cases} \tag{6}$$

5.4   Performance Metrics

The experiments were carried out for each of the IEDs and their respective line values found within the EPIC testbed system. A binary classification model is used to identify if the measurement received by the controller unit is indeed from the IED access point transmission (normal) or is malicious (attack). Let I be the total number of IEDs. We define TP_i as the true positive for IED i when it correctly classifies the IED based on ground truth while the false positive is defined as FP_i. Similarly, we take the false negative as FN_i and is defined as the wrongly rejected classification while TN_i is the rightly rejected class. Therefore, the overall accuracy for each of the IEDs in I can be defined as the following:

$$acc = \frac{\sum_{i=1}^{c} TP_i + \sum_{i=1}^{c} TN_i}{\sum_{i=1}^{c} TP_i + \sum_{i=1}^{c} TN_i + \sum_{i=1}^{c} FP_i + \sum_{i=1}^{c} FN_i}. \tag{7}$$

Table 2. Multiclass identification between each Line measurement reading for each IED.

IED	Line 1	Line 2	Line 3
TIED4.I	93.12%	89.12%	92.10%
TIED4.V	91.15%	92.15%	78.89%
MIED1.V	93.34%	91.23%	93.14%
MIED1.I	88.12%	83.45%	87.12%
MIED2.V	89.12%	82.45%	93.14%
MIED2.I	86.34%	87.45%	88.34%
SIED4.V	91.23%	93.14%	76.54%
SIED4.I	89.45%	88.34%	85.23%

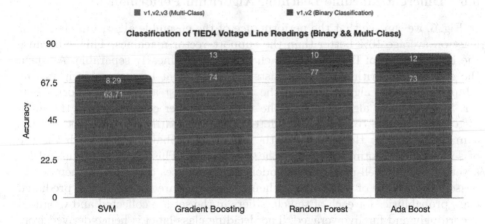

Fig. 6. Machine Learning Classifier comparison when used to identify IED v1, v2, v3 from one another in a multi-class problem.

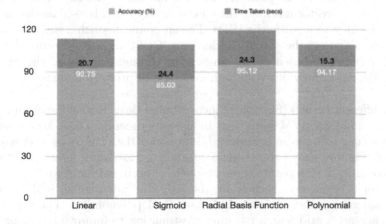

Fig. 7. Graph showing the average performance of each kernel function.

5.5   IED Identification Accuracy

In Table 2, the IED identification accuracies were given for 24 different IEDs. The IEDs belong to 3 different processes found within the power generation process. We can see that the lowest identification accuracy was 76.54% and this is because SIED4.V3 has a very similar noise pattern to both V1 and V2 thus the identification accuracy is a lot lower. This is, however, not a worrying factor as the noise pattern of the IEDs is very difficult for the adversary to mimic. On average, the IED identification hovers around a high 90% range for all 24 IEDs. The results shown in Table 2 is the average of 100 different runs from the ensemble algorithm. In the case of identifying the sensors from one another, a multi-class classification model is used.

5.6   Different Machine Learning Algorithm Performance

In Fig. 6, we can see that the performance of the ensemble algorithm class is at least on average 10% better than the support vector machines. This is because the identification of IEDs among each other is not linearly separable. As such, the ensemble algorithm which consists of the gradient boosting algorithm, the adaptive boosting algorithm, and the Random Forest algorithm performs better. The ensemble algorithm uses the voting classifier concept where the main idea is to combine conceptually different machine learning algorithms and use a majority vote or the average of the predicted probabilities through the use of soft-weighted voting to predict the class labels. This is especially useful for a set of equally well-performing models as it balances out each of their weaknesses. In the case of soft voting, when the weights are provided, the predicted class probabilities for each of the classifiers in the set are collected and weighted accordingly and finally averaged. The deciding class label is hence derived from the class with the highest probability count. The grid search optimizer is also used for the voting classifier to tune the hyper-parameters of the individual estimators. Because of the performance and validity of the ensemble algorithm over the support vector machine, the ensemble algorithm is used as the machine learning classifier to identify the IEDs. The ensemble algorithm was also used as a comparison against the statistical detector, CUSUM. These results show and prove that the noise-based device fingerprint through the use of the ensemble learning algorithm provides very high accuracy in prediction against malicious data.

Four different kernels (Sigmoid, Linear, Radial Basis Kernel Function (RBF), and Polynomial) for SVM were used in the experiments. These were tested on 5 separate runs using k-folds cross-validation and the results are averaged and compared. Figure 7 shows the average accuracy performance for each of the different kernels in the 5 separate runs. From the experimentation, we can conclude that the top 2 performing kernels are the RBF and polynomial. RBF, however, took considerably more computation time than polynomials. These 2 kernels are used against a grid-search parameter estimation to improve the algorithm's performance. The polynomial kernel yields an accuracy rate similar to that of

RBF but computes 21% faster, the kernel polynomial with grid-search parameter estimation will be used for the final comparison against the other algorithms.

5.7   Attack Detection Performance

The experiments were carried out for each of the IEDs and their respective line values found within the EPIC testbed system. A binary classification model is used to identify if the measurement received by the controller unit is indeed from the IED access point transmission or if it is modified data coming from the adversary.

Threshold and Bias Selection: As mentioned in the CUSUM section the threshold and bias should be selected such that the false alarm rate is not too high but also not too low such that it is not able to detect any form of attack. The values of the threshold and bias have been tested, and the final selected values are 3.5 and 2. This in-turn leads to a very low false alarm rate while still being functional to detect if there are any anomalies present. Figure 8 shows the IED measurements of TIED4 current L1 over time. It can be seen that over 2500 s, there are only three false alarms. Further analysis shows that these false alarms correspond to when the process is completed, and the current is reduced to 0. If the threshold and bias are tweaked to remove these false alarms, CUSUM will not be efficient in detecting max-min attacks, where the adversary would set the measurement readings to either 0 (min) or extremely high (max) in an attempt to disrupt the system.

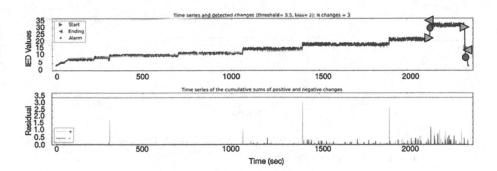

Fig. 8. CUSUM threshold and bias setting with 3 false alarms over 2500 s.

Constant Bias Attack: Figure 9 shows that during the transmission state, the malicious data was injected when $k = 21$ s (21 s since the start of the transmission process in EPIC testbed). The bias attack used was $\delta_1 = 2$. CUSUM was able to detect the attack immediately. The proposed mechanism was able to detect the attack as well but because it uses a chunk size of 20, it has to wait for 20 s before it can detect it.

Geometric Attack: Similar to the constant bias attack, both CUSUM and the proposed mechanism were able to detect the attack. The attack was also launched at $k = 21$ s (21 s since the start of the transmission process in the EPIC testbed).

Zero-Alarm Attack: Figure 10 shows the zero-alarm attack when it was launched at $k = 21$ s (21 s since the start of the transmission process in EPIC testbed). Because the attack was designed such that no alarms were raised, CUSUM was not able to detect when the attack was launched. Since the adversary has complete knowledge of the system including the CUSUM detector, he can deliberately set and launch the attack such that the CUSUM detector would not be able to detect it. Figure 10 shows the measurement readings received during the experiment. It can be seen from the graph plots that the adversary spoofed the measurements in a way that it stays within the confines of the threshold and bias value, thus remaining undetected while reducing the values of the measurement to near zero. On the other hand, because the spoofed values do not follow the intrinsic noise pattern fingerprinted for each IED, the spoofed data does not match the pattern fingerprinted using the proposed mechanism. Our proposed technique here removes the limitation of CUSUM detectors as it was able to detect the attack as the noise pattern coming from the crafted attack does not match the one fingerprinted for the IEDs during the training phase.

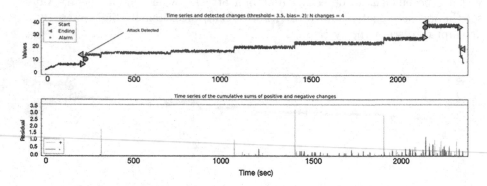

Fig. 9. Constant Bias Attack with CUSUM detector. Attack Detection was made with the The alarm is marked in the diagram.

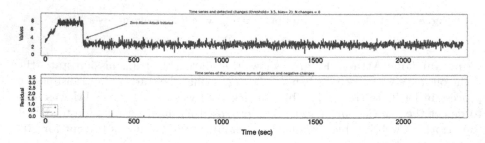

Fig. 10. Zero-Alarm Attack with CUSUM detector. Attack Detection was not made, CUSUM was not able to detect the attack.

6   Conclusions

A novel method to fingerprint the noise patterns present in the IEDs of the smart grid system is presented. From the experiments, it is shown that the noise pattern of each IED can be fingerprinted uniquely and thus can be identified individually with high confidence. With the extraction of both time and frequency domains, these key feature attributes were passed into machine learning classifiers for training purposes. Four different machine learning classifiers were tested and experimented on. The best method as the ensemble learning algorithm comprising adaptive boosting, gradient boosting, and random forest with grid search optimization combined through the use of a voting classifier mechanism where the class label is decided based on the highest probabilities. A binary classification is used to detect malicious data from actual data that is received from the IEDs as opposed to one from the adversary. Our results have shown that the proposed mechanism eliminates the limitations of statistical detectors such as CUSUM and can detect zero-alarm attacks.

References

1. Ahmed, C.M., Kandasamy, N.K.: A comprehensive dataset from a smart grid testbed for machine learning based CPS security research. In: Abie, H., et al. (eds.) CPS4CIP 2020. LNCS, vol. 12618, pp. 123–135. Springer, Cham (2021). https://doi.org/10.1007/978-3-030-69781-5_9
2. Ahmed, C.M., Mathur, A.P., Ochoa, M.: NoiSense print: detecting data integrity attacks on sensor measurements using hardware-based fingerprints. ACM Trans. Priv. Secur. **24**(1), 1–35 (2020). https://doi.org/10.1145/3410447
3. Ahmed, C.M., Palleti, V.R., Mathur, A.P.: WADI: a water distribution testbed for research in the design of secure cyber physical systems. In: Proceedings of the 3rd International Workshop on Cyber-Physical Systems for Smart Water Networks, CySWATER '17, pp. 25–28. ACM, New York (2017).https://doi.org/10.1145/3055366.3055375
4. Ahmed, C.M., Zhou, J.: Challenges and opportunities in cyberphysical systems security: a physics-based perspective. IEEE Secur. Priv. **18**(6), 14–22 (2020). https://doi.org/10.1109/MSEC.2020.3002851
5. Ahmed, C.M., Zhou, J., Mathur, A.P.: Noise matters: Using sensor and process noise fingerprint to detect stealthy cyber attacks and authenticate sensors in CPS. In: Proceedings of the 34th Annual Computer Security Applications Conference, ACSAC '18, pp. 566–581. ACM, New York (2018).https://doi.org/10.1145/3274694.3274748
6. Cardenas, A., Amin, S., Sinopoli, B., Giani, A., Perrig, A., Sastry, S.: Challenges for securing cyber physical systems. In: Workshop on Future Directions in Cyber-Physical Systems Security, p. 5 (2009)
7. Case, D.U.: Analysis of the cyber attack on the Urainian power grid (2016)
8. Lee, E.A.: Cyber physical systems: design challenges. In: 2008 11th IEEE International Symposium on Object and Component-Oriented Real-Time Distributed Computing (ISORC), pp. 363–369 (2008).https://doi.org/10.1109/ISORC.2008.25

9. Mathur, A.P., Tippenhauer, N.O.: SWaT: a water treatment testbed for research and training on ICS security. In: 2016 International Workshop on Cyber-physical Systems for Smart Water Networks (CySWater), pp. 31–36 (2016). https://doi. org/10.1109/CySWater.2016.7469060
10. MR, G.R., Ahmed, C.M., Mathur, A.: Machine learning for intrusion detection in industrial control systems: challenges and lessons from experimental evaluation. Cybersecurity 4(1), 1–12 (2021)
11. Murguia, C., Ruths, J.: Characterization of a CUSUM model-based sensor attack detector. In: 2016 IEEE 55th Conference on Decision and Control (CDC), pp. 1303–1309 (2016). https://doi.org/10.1109/CDC.2016.7798446
12. Umer, M.A., Ahmed, C.M., Jilani, M.T., Mathur, A.P.: Attack rules: An adversarial approach to generate attacks for industrial control systems using machine learning. In: Proceedings of the 2nd Workshop on CPS and IoT Security and Privacy, CPSIoTSec '21, pp. 35–40. Association for Computing Machinery, New York (2021). https://doi.org/10.1145/3462633.3483976
13. Urbina, D.I., et al.: Limiting the impact of stealthy attacks on industrial control systems. In: Proceedings of the 2016 ACM SIGSAC Conference on Computer and Communications Security, pp. 1092–1105. ACM (2016)

Power Quality Forecasting of Microgrids Using Adaptive Privacy-Preserving Machine Learning

Mazhar Ali⬤, Ajit Kumar⬤, and Bong Jun Choi$^{(\boxtimes)}$⬤

School of Computer Science and Engineering, Soongsil University,
Seoul 06978, Republic of Korea
{mazhar,davidchoi}@soongsil.ac.kr, kumar@ssu.ac.kr

Abstract. Microgrids face challenges in monitoring and controlling the power quality (PQ) of integrated electrical systems to make timely decisions. Inverter-based technologies handle small-scale smart grids' power quality parameters (PQPs) and play an important role in condition monitoring. Accurate forecasting of such parameters is difficult due to the stochastic nature of demand, distributed generation, and weather conditions. Moreover, energy clients have concerns over growing privacy and security breaches for collaboration involving data exchanges. This study aims to predict PQPs indices of home microgrids using ANN, LSTM, and CNN-LSTM models. To preserve users' privacy, federated learning has been applied with some adaptive differential privacy on the global model and clients' data. Comparative analysis of the ML model and DP parameters shows that the LSTM model gives better results with adequate privacy parameters to predict the PQPs of five distributed microgrids. LSTM model gives the least MAE of 0.2323 for FL without privacy and 0.3256 test loss for appropriate DP level.

Keywords: Machine Learning · Microgrid · Federated Learning · Power Quality

1 Introduction

Integration of small renewable energy (RE) sources at the user end eases environmental degradation and climate change. Intermittent RE makes power grid stability less reliable, leading to cascading failure due to prolonged disturbances. The growing integration of distributed energy resources (DER), enormous electronic devices such as controllers, power management units (PMUs), relays, and household appliances deteriorate the power quality of modern intelligent grids [8]. Intelligent control and monitoring systems are vital for appropriate, timely decisions to protect sensitive equipment in PQ management activities. Electric appliance operations will be affected due to severe voltage deviation, frequency changes, power factor variations, transients, and current imbalances. Accurate prediction of the PQPs is an emerging problem in intelligent grid

M. Andreoni (Ed.): ACNS 2024 Workshops, LNCS 14586, pp. 235–245, 2024.
https://doi.org/10.1007/978-3-031-61486-6_14

dynamics and stable system operations. It can be helpful for better and quicker responses in case of PQ standards violations.

Microgrids (MG) require intelligent control systems for steady-state operation and monitoring in case of minor disturbances such as PQ parameter fluctuations. The general parameters involve voltage (U), frequency (f), total harmonic distortion of voltage (THD_u), and total harmonic distortion of current (THD_i) [5]. These parameters rapidly fluctuate with the power demand and supply imbalance. Such variance is a significant problem in modern microgrids with highly variable distributed solar and wind energy. Microgrids with long-lasting transient states can lead to the collapse of the whole distribution network. Thus, these parameters are directly or indirectly affected by renewable generations and load patterns, which are influenced by weather conditions. This study forecasts PQ parameters according to the weather patterns such as wind speed, solar irradiance, temperature, humidity, etc.

Previous studies focus on statistical and linear ML models to forecast the PQ parameters in centralized and local setups. In centralized learning, clients share the data with the server; thus, information leakage concerns from the clients. Similarly, in local learning, users face data scarcity issues that need to be improved for ML training. This study uses a time series regression model to predict the PQ parameters in a federated setting to preserve the privacy and data islands.

Moreover, a differential privacy (DP) approach is also adapted to address the issue of poisoning and model inference attacks. The literature needs to include the application of FL and adaptive federated DP in forecasting the PQ parameters of MG. This study opens the research toward distributed secure learning on the regression tasks of PQ forecasting and the tradeoff between model degradation and privacy. The contribution of this research study is summarized as follows:

- Comparatively analyze three data-driven models (ANN, LSTM, CNN-LSTM) as a PQP forecaster in a federated setup to address MG clients' privacy and data scarcity.
- Evaluate the federated ML models based on test loss and use the most appropriate forecasting approach to analyze the DP mechanism in the distributed setting of MG.
- Apply the adaptive differential privacy approach in a federated setup to secure the server and client models against poisoning and inference attacks. Also, compute the threshold of security that does not severely degrade the models during the training.

The paper continues with Sect. 2 as a literature review, which provides insights into the past related studies. Section 3 discusses the proposed method of the study. Section 4 analyzes the simulation setup, data processing, and results of the research work. Lastly, Sect. 5 concludes the study by highlighting key findings and gaps in the current study.

2   Literature Review

Power Quality remains a significant problem in microgrids, and it deteriorates further with multiple intelligent devices and highly variable local renewable generation. PQ parameter prediction is critical for early warning and preparedness in transient disturbances. I.S Jahan et al. [5] predicted five PQ indices, i.e., frequency, voltage, flicker, total harmonics distortion of current and voltage with decision tree and neural network approaches. DT was found to be a suitable model for the off-grid system experiment based on the test loss for six days. Jakub Kosmal and Stranislav Misak [7] analyzed PQ management of a decentralized microgrid predominantly with PV generation and active demand side management (ADSM). The three PQ parameters included ficker severity, frequency, and THD_u. The ADSM controls the consumption plan based on the predicted PQ parameters, which would lead to equipment damage outside limits. Similarly, Ibrahim Jahan et al. [6] carried out clustering approaches for the same data based upon several features like appliance (AC. heating, light, fridge, TV) states with weather variables (temperature, pressure, GHI, U.V., wind speed) to predict five PQ indices (U, PF, PL, THD_u, THD_i). Four forecasting models (DT, KNN, BGDT, BODT) were used for each cluster node and evaluated based on RMSE. All the models better forecast the power factor (PL) and load, while BODT gives the least RMSE for all the parameters except higher error of 6.736 for THD_i

Federated learning is a new paradigm of machine learning where multiple clients collaborate to learn a global model without sharing their data with the central server. The computation is done at edge devices where client data resides. Thus, FL provides a better solution in cases of data scarcity, privacy, and security concerns. FL applications have been seen in intelligent grids for anomaly detection, energy trading, EV scheduling, NILM, and RE forecasting. Several FL studies have been conducted to accurately predict the demand and generation of different building setups and energy resources, such as solar and wind [1,3].V. Venkatesh et al. [9] analyzed the distributed energy forecasting using the BuildFL framework on IoT-based pecan street datasets. FL prediction gives similar load patterns when compared with GridLAB-D generated consumption profile. Similarly, Zhang and Wang [10] performed distributed aggregation of sub-parameters of the probabilistic wind forecasting model. The ADMM algorithm decomposes the problem into sub-parts and evaluates the probabilistic regression models of 10 wind farms based on the quantile score. ADMM and mirror-descent algorithms have been studied in distributed setup for measuring the PQ variables, and the literature still needs to include FL [4].

The probabilistic ADMM approach, in a distributed setup, concatenates the cost function into sub-problems in which clients share their information. Such a technique has limitations over non-convex models and lacks privacy guarantees in collaborative learning. Literature has thorough FL studies on energy demand prediction and renewable generation forecasting. Data-driven ML approaches have provided reasonable solutions in smart grids, and implementing FL is more straightforward than traditional probabilistic methods. However, research on minute time series PQP prediction needs for federated and centralized ML. Thus, current research aims to analyze the application of FL and DP in power quality forecasting in distributed microgrid networks. The study compares non-linear ML models in privacy-preserving distributed learning to address the privacy and security issue in microgrid PQ parameter predictions, which is lacking in the literature.

3 Methodology

Modern power systems aim to be more resilient towards energy security, climate change, cyber-physical attacks, power disturbances, and cascading outages. DERs at the consumer end increase smart grid resiliency, energy, and cyber security by providing energy in case of catastrophic power outages and disturbances. Moreover, flexible energy markets encourage prosumers in cost-effective demand response (DR) tasks through home energy monitoring and control systems. Such intelligent home energy systems make incremental usage of power electronics and IoT devices for energy conversion, storage, monitoring, and control of power quality variables at the user end. The smart home system collects sensitive data from these devices and electrical appliances. We applied distributed ML and differential privacy in a federated setup to preserve the privacy and security of home microgrids. The methodology of the study is provided in detail below (Fig. 1).

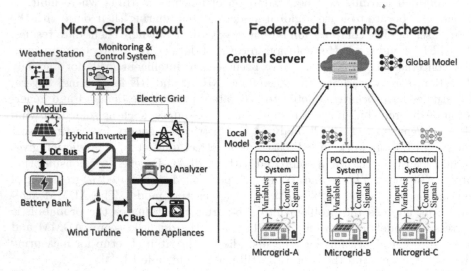

Fig. 1. (Left) Home MG system with DERs, Storage, Inverters, Appliances, and Control System. (Right) Privacy-preserving federated setup for Home MG clients for collaborative ML training without sharing data.

3.1   Microgrid System

The Microgrid concept has been practiced for decades at the distribution, community, and user levels. Prosumers with integrated RE, PEV, and battery storage made themselves small-scale microgrids that involved different tasks, like energy trading, demand response, load management, and protection schemes via monitoring and control systems [2]. Our study considers five home microgrids with PV, a small wind turbine, and a battery bank. The system model has been used in a home hybrid system test platform by Smart Grid Lab of VSB Technical University, Czech Republic [6]. Two buses are connected to two 2 kW PV modules and four 115 Ah lead-acid batteries with respective inverters. The voltage across the DC bus varies from 40.5–64 V (V) due to variable charging and discharging. A 240 V and 50 Hz frequency AC bus is connected with a load, grid, wind turbine, and hybrid inverter responsible for converting DC supply to AC for end usage. The load consists of several electrical appliances used for daily household activities, producing high noise in the AC system due to the appliances' inductive, capacitive, and resistive nature. An energy management system has been used to monitor and control the microgrid operation, which has several input signals from the weather station, electric grid PQ analyzer, etc.

3.2   Data-Driven Model

Prediction has been carried out by analyzing linear and non-linear ML approaches. Comparative analysis on ANN, LSTM, and CNN-LSTM hybrid models has been conducted to predict the PQ variables. ANN models are relatively simple to implement as they better approximate any continuous function but can be problematic for data scarcity and temporal dependencies. LSTM better captures the temporal features but has a complex model and lacks spatial feature extraction. CNN-LSTM is a hybrid model in which the CNN layer extracts spatial features, and LSTM layers handle the time-series patterns. Comparing these three models gives a better understanding of the relationship between single and hybrid ML models for recurrent tasks.

3.3   Privacy Preserving Method

Clients have concerns about data leakage, which can lead to misuse of personal information, malfunction of devices, and potential attacks on microgrids to disturb the whole power system. Federated learning, which can better preserve users' privacy, has been used in the study. In FL, the data reside on clients, and models are trained on edge devices; thus, no information has been shared with a central server. As the goal of FL is to learn a general global model, there is a threat of poison and model inversion attacks. Differential privacy adds noise in the client model weights to protect the user information from a poison attack. Similarly, noise is added to the server model weights to protect the global model from inversion attacks by malicious clients. However, if the noise or security is high, the accuracy declines, and the prediction task will be affected. So, we evaluated different privacy parameters using an adaptive approach.

Algorithm 1. Pseudo Code of Proposed Method

Initialize: Model (M^0), Clients (K), NoiseValue (N), Batch$(d \in D)$
for $t = 1$ to T client$(i \in K)$ **do:**
  Client Updates: $\Delta_i'^t, b_i^t \leftarrow$ **FedAVG**(i, M^t, S^t)
  Server Updates:
    $\bar{\Delta}^t = Agg.(D - i^t) + Noise(N)$
    $M^{t+1} = M^t + n_s \bar{\Delta}^t$
    $S^{t+1} = \text{Adaptive}(S^t)$
end for
LocalUpdate: **FedAVG**(i, M^t, S^t)
  $M \leftarrow M_0, \quad M \leftarrow SGD(M, n_l, d)$
  $\Delta \leftarrow M - M^0, \quad b \leftarrow ClippingNorm(\|\Delta\| \leq S)$
  $\Delta' \leftarrow \Delta \cdot \min(1, S/b)$
return (Δ', b)

Federated Differential Privacy. In federated learning, the model poses a threat from malicious actors to manipulate the raw local information. Encryption schemes present viable protective measures but pose a possibility of cryptographic breach and incur high computational costs. A nascent and promising alternative comes from DP, which offers privacy guarantees during training. FL process starts with the server initializing the forecasting model (M) to the clients (K). Each client $(i \in K)$ locally updates the global model (M) on their private data (D_i) and sends it back to the server with noise bit b_i. The server aggregates the client update at each round with the additional noise under the FedAVG and DP mechanism, as shown in Algorithm 1. Any randomized learning algorithm satisfies (ϵ, δ)−DP for any adjacent input data d and d', by adding noise function as given.

$$M(d) = f(d) + Noise(S_f)$$

where, S_f is the maximum l_2-distance norm $\|f(d) - f(d')\|_2$ and ϵ is the privacy loss parameter with the failure probability $\delta \in [0, 1]$. In the above equation, the $M(d)$ can achieve (ϵ, δ)−DP privacy by adding Gaussian noise $N(0, S_f^2 \sigma^2)$ with $\epsilon \leq 1$ and $\delta \geq 0.8 \cdot exp(-(\sigma\epsilon)^2/2)$ in the function $f(d)$. Here, σ is the noise multiplier that controls the trade-off between privacy and model degradation during the federated training process.

Adaptive Clipping. To ensure better privacy, the FedAVG algorithm made two levels of DP mechanism in a federated setup. In the client updates, local model parameters must be clipped before sending to the server, while the server adds enough noise to the aggregated weights. These measures provide enough security for poisoning and inference attacks from the malicious adversary. It has been seen in past studies that a clipping norm with too small a value will slow the model converge process, while a larger value adds too much noise, which degrades the model performance. Thus adaptive clipping approach

$S \leftarrow S \cdot exp(-n_c S(\bar{b} - \gamma)$, which start will low value S^0 and gradually increase with the learning rate $n_c(=0.2)$ to the target quantile $\gamma(=0.5)$.

4   Simulation and Results

4.1   Dataset

The dataset used for our work is obtained from experimental results of a simulated test bed environment by Smart Grid Lab in the Czech Republic. It consists of several temporal and spatial features, as shown in Table 1. The dataset consists of every 5-min reading of the respective variables for the June and July months of 2019. The power quality parameters have been collected using a PQ analyzer at the AC bus connected to the household load under EN 50160 and EN 61000-2-20 European standards. Minute-wise power load consists of different household appliances such as TV, boiler, kettle, fridge, microwave, lights, etc. These are inductive, capacitive, and resistive loads, thus fluctuating the minute variation. Similar time series weather datasets have been collected from the periphery of the study site in Ostrava, Czech Republic.

Power quality and meteorological datasets used in the study have been collected via a test-bed of a home hybrid system by Smart Grid Lab of VSB Technical University, Czech Republic [5]. The PQ analyzer collected the power load, voltage, frequency, power factor, THD_u, and THD_i parameters from the AC bus. The dataset contains 5-min intervals of input (GHI, WS, Pressure, Temperature, and PL) and output parameters (frequency, voltage, THD_u and THD_i) for two months.

Table 1. Input and Output Parameters used in Power Quality Analysis

Symbol	Description	Range
Weather Parameters		
GHI	Global Horizon Irradiance (W/m^2)	0–1033
W_s	Wind Speed (m/s)	0–5.7
P	Atmospheric Pressure (hPa)	976.4–995.3
T	Atmospheric Temperature (°C)	9.2–32.2
Power Quality Parameters		
PL	Power Load (kW)	0.6–2.61
f	Frequency (Hz)	49.9–50.08
U	Voltage (V)	223.96–245.64
THD_u	THD of Voltage (%)	0.51–5.75
THD_i	THD of Current (%)	4.48–61.68

4.2   Data Preprocessing

The multivariate time series study has several features that are used to predict the desired output variable. In our research, we aim to forecast four parameters that have directly or indirectly influenced the input features and the output variable. The principal component analysis (PCA) approach is used to analyze the correlation among all the input and output parameters. Based on the feature correlation matrix, the respective parameters have been dropped before the training process. Similarly, as time series forecasting depends upon its past trends, a lookback is also given as an input feature. Data normalization is crucial in training the machine learning model to access the optimized weights and connections between neurons. Thus, we normalized the data during preprocessing for flexible training, a robust model, and better prediction results.

4.3   Experiment

Tensorflow federated (TFF) framework is used to perform simulations in a federated setup. The dataset has been used for centralized machine learning, and to address the federated setup, we divide the data among five client modules. It is assumed to be a cross-silo setup, which means the amount of data is the same for each client, but the tabular data are highly different in temporal nature. LSTM and CNN-LSTM models have one dense layer with respective LSTM and CNN/LSTM layers, while only two layers are used for the ANN model. The number of neurons for these layers has been kept the same, i.e., $n = 50$. SGD optimizer has been used for the federated experiment. The MAE metric has been used throughout the simulations to evaluate the model. The model has been trained for global round $R = 500$ and evaluated on the test datasets. Table 2 gives the details about the hyperparameters of ML models used in the experiment of federated learning. Similarly, in the differential privacy, several noise values have been added in global model weights and client model weights to secure the model from malicious attacks and privacy leakage.

Table 2. Details of hyperparameters used in the implementation of ML models.

Hyperparameters	Search Space	Value
No. of Neurons	10, 20, 30, 50	50
Activation Function	ReLU, Tanh	Relu
Server Learning Rate	1.0, 0.10, 0.01	0.1
Batch Size	40, 60, 80, 100	60
Client Learning Rate	0.2, 0.02, 0.002	0.02
Client Epochs	5, 10, 20, 30	10
No. of Global Rounds	200, 300, 500, 750	500

4.4   Results and Discussion

The privacy-preserving FL approach has been analyzed to evaluate the three ML models based on the MAE loss, as shown in Table 3. We only considered the distributed setup of microgrids. We did not analyze the local learning as our main aim is to evaluate the better model in FL due to privacy constraints. The three trained models have been assessed on individual test datasets of microgrids after selecting appropriate hyperparameters during the training stage. After extensive experiments, it has been shown that MG_4 gives a better result for all the ML models used in the experiment. Still, the LSTM model has the lowest average MAE value, i.e., 0.3467. MAE value for MG_3 is 0.2323, depicting that the LSTM model is better learned on client 3. As the LSTM model gives better results than ANN and hybrid models, it is used to analyze the impact of the differential privacy approach in the federated setup. Similarly, the differential privacy insights on clients lead to better secure training results.

Table 3. MAE loss of the ANN, CNN-LSTM and LSTM models on test datasets.

Clients	ANN	CNN-LSTM	LSTM
MG_1	0.4293	0.3296	0.2378
MG_2	0.4148	0.3709	0.3018
MG_3	0.2562	0.2017	**0.2323**
MG_4	**0.2335**	**0.2461**	0.2383
MG_5	0.8538	0.9798	0.6333
Average	0.4355	0.4376	**0.3467**

Different DP parameters have been given for the federated training to learn in a secure environment. During the training, a noise ratio is added to clients and server models to secure them from poison and model inference attacks. Different noise multiplier values [0.0, 0.25, 0.5, 0.65, 0.75, 1.0] have been given to find the tolerance range of the LSTM model from degradation. Extensive simulations have been carried out to determine the optimum noise parameter through the search space approach. Figure 2 shows these noise parameters' results for a training round of 500 rounds. It depicts that the LSTM model can tolerate a noise value of up to 0.5 without degrading model quality. A noise value of 0.65 slightly deviates the model from the optimum, while a higher value of 0.75 and 1.0 significantly degrades the model. That's why we stopped the training for noise $= 1.0$ after rounds $= 200$. Though the noise secures the user's privacy during the training process, there is a trade-off of accurate prediction, which is crucial in power quality parameter forecasting.

The noise values that mimic the global model without DP have been evaluated on the test datasets, as shown in Table 3. It shows the tradeoff between privacy and model precision, as the LSTM model with lesser noise values has

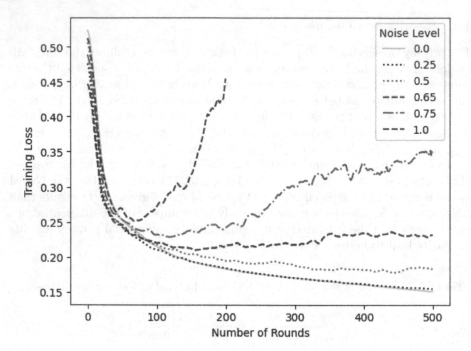

Fig. 2. MAE of LSTM model during the FL training with different level of DP Noise.

the least MAE loss of 0.3809 average. The study addresses the privacy issue in distributed learning through an adaptive DP mechanism. It can be the baseline for future studies that tackle secure aggregation techniques in intelligent grid PQ forecasting applications. However, to address the data heterogeneity and accurate model adaptation, personalized federated learning will give better analysis in the future. Future studies must incline towards a statistical approach or tolerance factor to mitigate the impact of the clipping approach and change the time series forecasting to an anomaly or error detection problem (Table 4).

Table 4. MAE loss of the LSTM model on different noise levels on clients test data.

	MG_1	MG_2	MG_3	MG_4	MG_5	Avg
Noise = 0.25	0.2595	0.4201	0.2941	0.2539	0.6767	0.3809
Noise = 0.5	0.3256	0.4614	0.3701	0.3202	0.7291	0.4332
Noise = 0.65	0.5128	0.5417	0.4989	0.4156	0.9528	0.5844

5   Conclusion

Distributed energy generation made microgrids more intelligent with the proliferation of power electronic devices and monitoring systems. Intelligent ML operation of green microgrids faces privacy and security issues due to sharing power quality parameters. Federated learning is a suitable approach to learning the patterns of predictive ML models to preserve privacy via edge training. Comparative analysis on ANN, LSTM, and CNN-LSTM models evaluate better prediction models in distributed settings. The LSTM model has the least MAE test loss of 0.2323, making it most appropriate for federated predictive learning. FL faces the challenge of potential model inversion and poison attacks at the server and client end. Thus, the study provides an adaptive differential privacy technique to secure the microgrid in such an FL setup. The results showed that a privacy parameter of 0.5 value gave a better solution to secure the server and home microgrid clients. In future studies, we aim to analyze the personalized FL approach with DP under IEEE standards for hybrid energy systems.

Acknowledgment. This research was supported by the MSIT Korea under the NRF Korea (NRF-2022R1A2C4001270) and the Information Technology Research Center (ITRC) support program (IITP-2022-2020-0-01602) supervised by the IITP.

References

1. Ali, M., Singh, A.K., Kumar, A., Ali, S.S., Choi, B.J.: Comparative analysis of data-driven algorithms for building energy planning via federated learning. Energies **16**(18), 6517 (2023)
2. Ali, M., et al.: Techno-economic assessment and sustainability impact of hybrid energy systems in Gilgit-Baltistan, Pakistan. Energy Rep. **7**, 2546–2562 (2021)
3. Cheng, X., Li, C., Liu, X.: A review of federated learning in energy systems. In: 2022 IEEE/IAS Industrial and Commercial Power System Asia (I&CPS Asia), pp. 2089–2095 (2022)
4. Gholizadeh, N., Musilek, P.: Distributed learning applications in power systems: a review of methods, gaps, and challenges. Energies **14**(12), 3654 (2021)
5. Jahan, I., Misak, S., Snasel, V.: Power quality parameters analysis in off-grid platform. In: Kovalev, S., Tarassov, V., Snasel, V., Sukhanov, A. (eds.) IITI 2021. LNNS, vol. 330, pp. 431–439. Springer, Cham (2022). https://doi.org/10.1007/978-3-030-87178-9_43
6. Jahan, I.S., Blazek, V., Misak, S., Snasel, V., Prokop, L.: Forecasting of power quality parameters based on meteorological data in small-scale household off-grid systems. Energies **15**(14), 5251 (2022)
7. Kosmák, J., Mišák, S.: Power quality management in an off-gtrid system. In: 2018 IEEE International Conference on Environment and Electrical Engineering and 2018 IEEE Industrial and Commercial Power Systems Europe (EEEIC/I&CPS Europe), pp. 1–5. IEEE (2018)
8. Luo, A., Xu, Q., Ma, F., Chen, Y.: Overview of power quality analysis and control technology for the smart grid. J. Mod. Power Syst. Clean Energy **4**(1), 1–9 (2016)
9. Venkataramanan, V., Kaza, S., Annaswamy, A.M.: Der forecast using privacy-preserving federated learning. IEEE Internet Things J. **10**(3), 2046–2055 (2022)
10. Zhang, Y., Wang, J.: A distributed approach for wind power probabilistic forecasting considering spatio-temporal correlation without direct access to off-site information. IEEE Trans. Power Syst. **33**(5), 5714–5726 (2018)

Evaluation of Lightweight Machine Learning-Based NIDS Techniques for Industrial IoT

Alex Baron[1,2], Laurens Le Jeune[2,3], Wouter Hellemans[2(✉)],
Md Masoom Rabbani[2], and Nele Mentens[2,4]

[1] Department of Mathematics, University of Padova, Padua, Italy
[2] ES&S-COSIC, KU Leuven, Leuven, Belgium
{alex.baron,laurens.jeune,wouter.hellemans,
md.masoom.rabbani,nele.mentens}@kuleuven.be
[3] EAVISE-PSI, KU Leuven, Leuven, Belgium
[4] LIACS, Leiden University, Leiden, The Netherlands

Abstract. Internet of Things (IoT) devices have revolutionized communication, transportation, healthcare, and many other fields. In particular, the adoption of these devices has propelled the growth of Industry 4.0 to an exponential pace. However, while this vast pool of interconnected devices broadens the opportunities for better business and better lives, it also attracts the attention of cybercriminals. Nevertheless, it has been shown that the resource-constrained nature of these devices inhibits the deployment of traditional security measures.

To this end, we investigate how various lightweight Machine Learning-based intrusion detection systems (IDSs) can be implemented on resource-constrained IoT devices. Specifically, we train various decision tree and neural network-based models and implement them on Raspberry Pi and Field-Programmable Gate Array (FPGA) platforms. Furthermore, we evaluate our implementations on the IoT-23 and TON_IoT datasets and compare the results in terms of classification performance, throughput and resource consumption. We show that tree-based models surpass the neural network-based models in classification performance and throughput but that hardware acceleration on FPGA can aid in closing the gap in terms of throughput. As such, this work opens the path for the deployment of a real-time distributed IDS on low-cost devices.

Keywords: Intrusion Detection System · IIoT · Machine Learning · Embedded platforms · FPGA

This work is partially supported by the COllective Research NETworking (CORNET) project "TrustedIOT: Trusted Computing Architectures for IoT Devices". The Belgian partners are funded by VLAIO under grant number HBC.2021.0895. This work is also partially supported by Cybersecurity Initiative Flanders (VR20192203). Additionally, W.H. is a SB PhD fellow at FWO (Research Foundation Flanders) under grant agreement 1SH3824N. This paper is based on the work of [4].

1   Introduction

The relentless advancement of modern informatization has led Internet of Things (IoT) to play a remarkable role in several aspects of our daily lives. The possibility of being able to manipulate a wide range of devices, all under the control of a single centralized device, such as a smartphone, is making this market grow exponentially over the last few years. IoT has a total potential economic impact of 3.9 trillion to 11.1 trillion dollars a year by 2025 [20]. According to Cisco, there will be 500 billion devices connected to the internet by the year 2030 [29]. These devices may range from home appliances such as thermostats and smart light bulbs to sensors in healthcare or industry.

While very innovative, IoT is also very sensitive to safety problems, as attacks on IoT networks can have devastating consequences. For example, after infecting hundreds of thousands of IoT devices, the Mirai botnet targeted the infrastructure of Dyn, which controlled a significant portion of the internet's Domain Name System (DNS) infrastructure, and brought down sites such as Twitter, Netflix and Reddit [33].

Although traditional defense techniques relying on authentication, encryption and access control may in specific situations be useful, IoT networks need another layer of protection [5]. Intrusion Detection System (IDS) can provide this protection by analyzing system events in an effort to uncover malicious activity, such as unauthorized file or resource access [1]. Recently Machine Learning (ML) techniques have seen increasing application to improve IDS detection performance [8, 21].

With the advancement of technology and the growth of IoT networks, there is a continuous search for highly effective solutions in the field of information security [5]. The purpose of this paper is to present a new perspective in the field of *Edge Machine Learning* regarding the protection of IoT networks, which consists in the use of small board microcontrollers, also called *edge-devices*. Edge ML can be defined as a field of ML which aims to bring ML applications on devices that are cheap, as well as resource and power-constrained. The ultimate goal is to develop and test different lightweight ML models that can fit into resource-constrained devices to be integrated and deployed alongside the components of an IoT network with the aim of guaranteeing network-based protection.

The pipeline of this work starts with the data collection of IoT network traffic. The analyzed traffic is preprocessed after feature extraction which aims to find the best performing features. Both common IoT network traffic and different IoT networks attacks are taken into consideration in the dataset. These attacks mainly include Denial-of-Service (DoS) and Distributed Denial-of-Service (DDoS). ML models are trained to classify the network traffic as benign or malicious and they will alert the system if any malicious packet is encountered. Different kinds of classifiers are compared in this work, including *Neural Networks (NNs), Decision Trees (DTs) and Random Forests (RFs)*. ML models are installed on Raspberry Pis and Field-Programmable Gate Arrays (FPGAs), to build a network-based device-independent IDS that can guarantee a remarkable protection to the whole IoT environment.

The main contributions of this work are:

- We develop and carry out a performance assessment on a set of lightweight ML classifiers for IDS applications in IoT environments;
- We investigate the applicability of the TabNet architecture on resource-constrained devices;
- We provide a proof-of-concept implementation of all classifiers based on Raspberry Pi and/or FPGA platforms;
- We evaluate our models on state-of-the-art datasets and report relevant metrics.

This paper is organized as follows. We present different recent and performing IDSs applied to the IoT field in Sect. 2. In Sect. 3 we give an overview about IoT security and IDSs. Furthermore, we describe ML models that are used in this work. In Sect. 4, we present problems and the methodology assumed. Subsequently, the results of the performed experiments are presented with relative discussions in Sect. 5. Sect. 6 concludes the paper and proposes future works.

2 Related Work

In this section, we introduce various ML-based IDSs for IoT security.

There are many publications showcasing various techniques related to anomaly detection in IoT networks. Common techniques include various NNs [6, 10,13], Conditional Variational Autoencoder (CVAE) [19], Recurrent Neural Network (RNN) [2], RF [15], and Extreme Learning Machine (ELM) [17]. Additionally, some authors introduce more specific approaches. Lee *et al.* [18] analyze the power consumption of sensor nodes in IPv6 to flag malicious activity. Hosseinpour *et al.* [14] base their IDS on an Artificial Immune System (AIS). Nobakht *et al.* [23] analyze device activity in a Software Define Network (SDN). Sarhan *et al.* [28] use a Hierarchical Blockchain-based Federated Learning (HBFL) framework to detect intrusions in a collaborative fashion. We provide an overview of these techniques in Table 1, additionally highlighting whenever implementations are distributed or centralized.

Related anomaly-based work shows considerable promise. However, most systems have been tested on older datasets, even though different attacks on smart and industrial networks are continuously advancing. Most recent IDS systems are centralized or cloud-based, leaving the internal network vulnerable if attackers bypass the single centralized IDS or if the connection between devices and cloud computing fails. Therefore, in this work, we explore distributed solutions.

3 Background

In this section, we briefly review the main tools and components involved in our work. We start by describing the environment security of IoT networks and the features of IDSs. Next, we describe the used ML model architectures. Finally, we introduce FINN, which is used to deploy quantized neural networks on hardware.

Table 1. Overview of relevant anomaly-based IDSs for IoT settings

References	Method	Placement
Lee et al. [18]	IDS over 6LowPAN	Distributed
Hosseinpour et al. [14]	Lightweight IDS based on AIS	Distributed
Hodo et al. [13]	ANN	Centralized
Nobakht et al. [23]	Host-based IDS in SDN	-
Lopez-Martin et al. [19]	CVAE	-
Kozik et al. [17]	IDS based on ELM	Centralized
Doshi et al. [6]	NN	Centralized
Ge et al. [10]	NN	-
Hasan et al. [11]	LR, SVM, DT, RF, ANN	Distributed
Almiani et al. [2]	Full-automated IDS based on RNN	-
Hussein et al. [15]	RF	-
Sarhan et al. [28]	HBFL	-

3.1 Problem Setting

The IoT is growing fast and is widening its fields of application. IoT systems are well characterized for the heterogeneity and diversity of the devices involved. As well as the mixture of devices deployed, several protocols are involved to make IoT networks functional and reliable. Despite the widespread use of IoT networks, they are quite different from a conventional computer network. In particular, IoT systems are constrained in terms of computational capability and complexity. Moreover, due to their heavily distributed and heterogeneous nature, a centralized traditional solution may not be always suitable [5].

It is easy to infer that due to these limitations, most IoT devices are not equipped with efficient defense mechanisms (e.g. memory isolation, address space randomization, encryption and authentication algorithms [34]). Furthermore, another serious threat, due in part to IoT networks' fast and wide proliferation, are botnets that produce DoS and DDoS attacks as explained in Sect. 1.

IDSs aim to identify malware, malicious access or any kind of attack to defend internal networks. They represent one major research problem in cybersecurity and as there are several risks concerning networks there are different systems built to secure an environment from external attacks [31].

Motivated by an increasing number of vulnerabilities, attacks, and information leaks, IoT device manufacturers as well as cloud providers and researchers are working to design security systems and protocols, to explore new vulnerabilities and to seek effective ways to protect data privacy.

3.2 Machine Learning

In this paper, we investigate the deployment of lightweight ML models on tiny and low-power devices. Specifically, we compare different kinds of NNs, Convolutional Neural Networks (CNNs), Decision Trees (DTs) as well as ensembling techniques such as RF, AdaBoost, and Extremely Randomized Trees (ET). In addition, we explore Attentive Interpretable Tabular Learning (TabNet) and consider hardware acceleration of the CNNs using the FINN framework. For the sake of completeness, we provide background information on TabNet and FINN.

TabNet. Attentive Interpretable Tabular Learning [3], or TabNet, is a novel high-performance and interpretable canonical deep tabular data learning architecture that uses sequential attention to choose features for reasoning at each decision step, resulting in more efficient learning. TabNet outperforms various tabular learning models on various datasets for classification and regression tasks.

TabNet's architecture is divided in an *encoder* composed of different feature transformers, attentive transformers and feature masking as well as a *decoder* which is composed of feature transformers. TabNet is appropriate for an intrusion detection task with tabular network datasets, as it inputs raw data without any preprocessing. Moreover, its training via gradient descent enables large flexibility. Although the complexity introduced by the attention transformer and the feature transformer in Tabnet's architecture results in challenging deployment for very small micro-controllers, TabNet performs extremely well for medium-sized controllers.

3.3 FINN

FINN is an experimental tool designed by Xilinx Research Lab in order to implement Deep Learning model on FPGA. In particular, FINN builds a streaming architecture where each layer has its own engine and each layer can be executed as soon as the previous layer has generated the data. FINN targets Quantized Neural Networkss (QNNs) trained in PyTorch with the help of Brevitas [24] which is a Python library to create quantized models. Brevitas also comes with a set of tools to manage the quantization properties and the functionality to export the QNNs to FINN. The workflow of FINN starts once a suitable QNN has been trained, tested and exported to an Open Neural Network Exchange (ONNX) representation. FINN will transform the initial QNN into synthesizable High-Level Synthesis (HLS) layers using different transformations. In particular, FINN's pipeline starts by preparing the model to facilitate the tuning of the layers which is based on setting up the graph model correctly and removing floating point operators. The layers are then turned into HLS and grouped in a *Dataflow Partition* which contains HLS layers suitable for acceleration. Once the sythesizable model is completely ready, FINN uses Xilinx's software called Vivado and/or Vitis to generate the final HLS code, bitstream and driver used to deploy the starting model on hardware.

4   Method

In this section we present the architecture, concept, design principles and the pipeline of the conducted experiments of our work. After stating our objective,

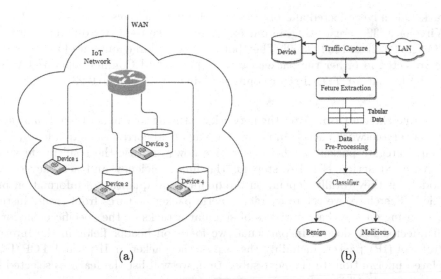

Fig. 1. Proposed network-based IDS applied architecture (a). Workflow of the proposed framework during deployment, starting from the data collection to the classification (b).

we describe the datasets, features and metrics that we use. We describe our metrics in the appendix.

We then show how we train the ML models introduced in Sect. 3 and deploy them on Raspberry Pi and FPGA.

4.1 Research Objective

The main objective of the proposed work is to build different lightweight IDSs, capable of distinguishing between benign and malicious network traffic. We integrate them in individual IoT devices in the Local Area Network (LAN), as shown in Fig. 1a. We assume that any device on the network can exchange data with all the other connected devices and the victim of an attack may be any device which belongs to the LAN. By introducing a high level of flexibility and autonomy in the IDS, we seek to introduce IDSs that can be deployed on various devices. Moreover, the IDSs should not only be accurate, but additionally, they should not influence the overall performance of the IoT devices.

4.2 Proposed Framework

We now give an overview to the computation pipeline performed by the proposed IDS that goes from the traffic capture to the binary classification between benign and malicious traffic as shown in Fig. 1b. We now describe the individual steps.

Traffic Capture. The first step of the workflow consists of real-time and continuous traffic capturing. Raw network data which includes in-going and out-going

packets can be collected and processed with different tools such as Zeek [27] and
Wireshark [32]. For testing, in our experiments, we used two different datasets,
TON_IoT [22] and IoT-23 [9]. They both provide a large amount of network traf-
fic collected in either the packet capture (pcap) and Comma-Separated Values
(CSV) format for TON_IoT or conn.log[1] labelled files for IoT-23.

Feature Extraction. After the network capturing we extract the relevant fields
from every network packet. In particular, each field corresponds to a feature. We
then aggregate packets in their respective flows and use the resulting features.
Feature extraction is a key step for the final efficiency and accuracy of ML
models, as they totally depend on the quality and quantity of information provided. Therefore, we try to extract generic packet features from traffic instead
of focusing on the characteristics of singular attacks or the specific behavior of
an infected IoT device. In particular we focus on header fields in the Internet
Protocol (IP) packet, including the size of the packet or IPv4 and TCP/UDP
related information. In the next subsection, we will list the features selected for
each dataset and the consequent reasons.

Feature Processing. Pre-processing consists of different procedures to make
acceptable and optimize the input data to a ML algorithm. Typically, the
datasets are composed of different types of data (e.g. integers, floats, doubles,
binary, strings, etc.). Non-numeric inputs need to be mapped to numbers or to
be converted into one-hot-encoded values, after which all numeric data needs to
be normalized to improve data quality and ML performance [30].

Training and Classification. Preprocessed data is then used to fit our models
on the training set. Finally, after training our ML models using the preprocessed
data, they can be deployed for new traffic. In our work, we have selected different
ML models to test in different compositions, i.e. in different architectures. During
inference, the classifier takes as input the processed data and outputs whether
this network flow belongs to traffic considered malicious or not.

4.3   Datasets and Feature Importance

In this work we used two different datasets, specifically the TON_IoT (Network) Dataset [22] and the IoT-23 Dataset [9]. These are the most recent data
collections with malicious and benign IoT network traffic, bringing significant
information at the level of malware families that even modern security solutions
are unfamiliar with.

TON_IoT comprises a collection of Industry4.0, IoT and Industrial IoT new
generation data. At UNSW Canberra, the dataset were collected in a large and
realistic network environment. The testbed was designed based on interacting
network, IoT devices and systems. The environment is composed of three layers

---

[1] Obtained by running the Zeek network analyser.

to mimick the implementation of recent realistic IoT networks. Specifically, the *edge layer* involves physical devices, while the *fog layer* and the *cloud layer* determine the computation location. TON_IoT presents malicious scenarios with nine different attack categories launched against vulnerable IoT applications, Operating Systems (OSs) and network systems, as listed in Table 2. Several heterogeneous sources of data are included into the dataset, in particular sensors, OSs and network traffic. In our work we focus on the network traffic records (i.e. traffic flow), which are extracted with Zeek [27]. The TON_IoT dataset comes with the extracted traffic flow in CSV format. The authors also provide a Training and Test collection comprising a smaller portion of the dataset, which we use for our work. Table 2 gives the composition of the network traffic data.

Table 2. Statistics of Network Records of TON_IoT dataset [22]

Labels	All Network Data	Training and Testing
Backdoor	508,116	20,000
DDoS	6,165,008	20,000
DoS	3,375,328	20,000
Injection	452,659	20,000
MIMT	1,052	1,043
Password	1,718,568	20,000
Ransomware	72,805	20,000
Scanning	7,140,161	20,000
XSS	2,108,944	20,000
Normal	796,380	300,000
Total	22,339,021	461,043

The IoT-23 dataset [9] is a recent collection of network traffic from different IoT devices. Data were captured in the Stratosphere Laboratory, AIC group, FEL, CTU University in Czech Republic. The dataset comprises 23 different network captures, also called *sessions*, with 20 malware and 3 benign network traffic captures. During data collection, different malicious scenarios were executed related to a specific malware which performed different actions in a Raspberry Pi. The benign traffic however was collected using three real physical devices. In particular, a Philips HUE smart LED lamp, an Amazon Echo home personal assistant and a Somfy smart door lock. As the devices were not simulated, the collection is characterized by the real network behaviour. We use different scenarios of IoT-23 as shown in Table 3. For each capture, IoT-23 contains a series of *pcap* files and *conn.log.labeled* files, which are the Zeek *conn.log* files obtained by running Zeek network analyser using the original pcap file. We derive a CSV file containing the chosen features with the related data starting from the *conn.log.labeled* files using the *zeek-cut* tool provided by Zeek.

Table 3. IoT-23 Dataset scenarios used in our work. FD stands for FileDownload, PortScan is the short for PartOfHorizontalPortScan and C&C is short for Command and Conquer. Specifically, the *FileDownload* label indicates that a file is being downloaded to the infected device. The *Attack* label refers to some kinds of attack which try to exploit flaws such as telnet login, brute force, command injection etc.

Labels	1-1	8-1	34-1	35-1	44-1
Benign	469,275	2,181	1,923	8,262,389	211
DDos	-	-	14,394	2,185,302	1
C&C	8	8,222	6,706	81	14
C&C-FD	-	-	-	12	11
PortScan	539,465	-	122	-	-
Attack	-	-	-	3	-
Total	1,008,748	10,403	23,145	10,447,787	237

The IoT-23 scenarios contain different kinds of attacks and consequently a considerable amount of information. From the *IoT23-35-1* scenario we extracted a subset where the number of entries has been reduced to avoid data imbalance, composed of $1,048,484$ benign samples and $895,929$ malicious samples. Furthermore, we tested the *IoT23-44-1* scenario with the aim of observing how the selected ML models can perform with extremely reduced amount of data.

From TON_IoT and IoT-23 we extract a subset of features that we use to train the ML models. In particular, we concentrate on features concerning the *connection activity* and the *statistical activity* related to the network and transport layer. Although there are multiple characteristics which can be derived from individual network packets, we have focused on the most consistent information. Specifically, during the traffic analysis it is possible that some protocols are not present in the layers, or the tool used to capture the traffic fails to gather certain non-essential characteristics. We have excluded information regarding DNS, Secure Socket Layer (SSL) as well as Hypertext Transfer Protocol (HTTP) activity, focusing more on addresses, ports, amount of bytes transmitted, amount of packets transmitted, duration of transmission and protocol used. From both TON_IoT and IoT-23 we extract the same 14 features, as shown in Table 4. We additionally use scikit-learn [26] to depict the importance of each feature in an RF in Fig. 2.

4.4 Experimental Setup

We train and validate the chosen ML models on a machine operated with 64-bit Windows 11 Home, and an Intel Core i5-10210U four core CPU having 1.60 GHz base frequency and 4.20 GHz as max turbo frequency. Afterwards, the saved trained models are transferred to Raspberry Pi and FPGA for inference on new input data.

Table 4. Dataset features used in our experiments. Note that some identical features may have different names in the datasets.

No	TON_IoT Name	Type	IoT-23 Name	Type	Specifics
1	ts	Time	ts	Time	Timestamp of connection
2	src_port	Number	id.orig_p	Number	TCP/UDP source port
3	dst_port	Number	id.resp_p	Number	TCP/UDP destination port
4	proto	String	proto	String	Protocol
5	service	String	service	String	DNS, HTTP, SSL, DHCP, etc.
6	duration	Number	duration	Number	Flow duration
7	src_bytes	Number	orig_bytes	Number	Source bytes
8	dst_bytes	Number	resp_bytes	Number	Destination bytes
9	conn_state	String	conn_state	String	Connection state
10	missed_bytes	Number	missed_bytes	Number	Number of missing bytes
11	src_pkts	Number	orig_pkts	Number	Number of source packets
12	src_ip_bytes	Number	orig_ip_bytes	Number	Number of source IP header bytes
13	dst_pkts	Number	resp_pkts	Number	Number of destination packets
14	dst_ip_bytes	Number	resp_ip_bytes	Number	Number of IP destination header bytes

Classifiers are implemented in Python 3.8 via several popular ML libraries, especially PyTorch [25] as well as Scikit-learn [26], which is also used to derive the performance and statistical results. Section A lists our model architectures and their corresponding hyperparameters, and additionally comments on the grid search, optimization and regularization used in our experiments.

In order to run the experiments, the trained and saved models are transferred to the Raspberry Pi running Pi OS Lite ready to perform inference. In particular, the board is a Raspberry Pi Model 3B [7] which is equipped with 1.2 GHz BCM2837 Soc ARM Cortex-A53 CPU with 4 cores, 1024 MB of RAM and a power requirement of 5 V at 2.5 A.

We also implement some models on FPGA using the FINN pipeline described in Sect. 3. At the moment, FINN is open-source and publicly available[2]. We tested the QNN Quant-NN on the PYNQ-Z2 FPGA board. The PYNQ-Z2 features 512MB DDR3 of RAM and it is equipped with a 650MHz dual-core Cortex-A9 processor.

5   Results

In this section, we carry out a detailed performance analysis and we discuss the results of the classifiers described in the previous section.

We start by evaluating the results for TON_IoT and IoT-23 by comparing tree-based and NN-based models in two separate groups. Table 5 and Table 6

---

[2] https://github.com/Xilinx/finn.

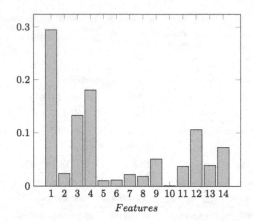

Fig. 2. This histogram depicts the Feature Importance for a Random Forest. In particular, the Feature Importance is provided by the fitted attribute related to the Random Forest, obtained with scikit-learn. In this RF model it is possible to see that the timestamp feature is very important for the correct classification of data. The horizontal axis represents the features numerically in correspondence with Table 4.

show the results obtained in terms of key metrics for the TON_IoT dataset, and similarly Table 7 and Table 8 for IoT-23. Besides detection performance metrics, we also consider the throughput, which is relevant when considering large-volume attacks such as DoS and DDoS. This measure is computed by dividing the total number of test instances by total time taken by a model to classify all the test instances. Furthermore, tree-based models were trained on the Raspberry Pi itself, as they are typically more lightweight than NNs, and their training times were measured. This value is useful for hypothesizing possible on-device-training for such models, directly on deployed devices (i.e. Raspberry Pis), with the goal of improving performance over time and user privacy, and without requiring users to update the device software.

Table 5. Results on TON_IoT Dataset - Neural Networks.

Models	Acc	P	R	F_1	ROC-AUC	T
NN small	0.9893	0.9789	0.9904	0.9846	0.9895	2,336
NN	0.9889	0.9826	0.9858	0.9842	0.9882	1,810
CNN small	0.9473	0.9530	0.8937	0.9224	0.9349	2,398
CNN	0.9815	0.9921	0.9545	0.9729	0.9752	2,088
TabNet	0.9868	0.9744	0.9882	0.9813	0.9871	743

Table 5 shows the value of all relevant metrics concerning NNs on the TON_IoT dataset. It is evident from these results that CNNs do not perform as well as the other NNs and TabNet, which achieve almost the same accuracy (98.9%, 98.2% and 98.6% respectively). However, Table 6 shows that tree-based models perform considerably better than NNs using that dataset. We observe that the DT outperforms other classifiers in terms of execution speed and overall performance, as it obtains an almost perfect classification accuracy (99.99%) and F1-score (99.99%). Tree-based ensemble models perform very similarly, with all results hovering around 99.9%.

Table 6. Results on TON_IoT Dataset - DT & Ensamble Models.

Models	Estimators	Acc	P	R	F_1	ROC-AUC	T	Training Time [s]
DT	-	0.9999	0.9998	0.9998	0.9999	0.9998	2,311,528	15.87
RF	20	0.9998	0.9997	0.9998	0.9998	0.9998	122,221	116.81
RF	100	0.9998	0.9997	0.9998	0.9997	0.9998	18,247	573.40
AdaBoost	20	0.9989	0.9986	0.9985	0.9985	0.9988	41,893	110.25
AdaBoost	100	0.9997	0.9996	0.9995	0.9996	0.9996	7,940	561.32
ET	20	0.9998	0.9997	0.9998	0.9997	0.9998	51,809	103.66
ET	80	0.9998	0.9997	0.9998	0.9997	0.9998	19,312	396.65

Furthermore, training and classification speeds vary according to the number of estimators in the various ensembles. The DT also has the best performance for those metrics. In fact, this model is extremely suitable for classifying network traffic with the selected pre-processing. RF, Adaboost, and ET perform slightly worse however, with a noticeable difference in the sample processing speed. Regarding TON_IoT then, the DT clearly prevails, while both CNNs get the worst results. Lastly, we observe that the 1D convolution applied in the context of the TabNet does not obtain the same results as the feed-forward NNs and tree-based models, which seem to be better suited for this classification task.

Table 7. Results on IoT-23 Dataset - Neural Networks.

Models	Acc	P	R	F_1	ROC-AUC	T
NN small	0.9977	0.9954	0.9998	0.9976	0.9977	1,568
NN	0.9984	0.9969	0.9997	0.9983	0.9984	1,250
CNN small	0.9954	0.9941	0.9963	0.9952	0.9953	1,524
CNN	0.9961	0.9955	0.9964	0.9960	0.9961	1,063
TabNet	0.9957	0.9973	0.9939	0.9956	0.9957	258

Table 8. Results on IoT-23 Dataset - DT & Ensamble Models.

Models	Estimators	Acc	P	R	F_1	ROC-AUC	T	Training Time [s]
DT	-	0.9999	0.9999	1.0	0.9999	0.9999	153,991	164.57
RF	20	0.9999	0.9999	0.9999	0.9999	0.9999	72,101	698.52
AdaBoost	20	0.9967	0.9954	0.9979	0.9966	0.9967	36,102	665.36
ET	20	0.9997	0.9994	0.9999	0.9997	0.9997	67,681	540.91

Regarding IoT-23, similar to the TON_IoT results, the largest fully connected NN performs best among the NN-based models with an accuracy of 99.84% as shown in Table 7. Table 8 presents the tree-based models, with the DT and RF as the best performing models. They obtain near-perfect results with an accuracy, precision, recall, F1-score and AUC of at least 99.99%. Our results suggest that the traffic flows in IoT-23 are more easily classified than the traffic captured by TON_IoT. Similar to TON_IoT, the smallest CNN appears to perform worst, while the DT and ensemble models again obtain the best results. Figure 3 and Fig. 4 graphically show the results obtained for both TON_IoT and IoT-23 with regards to the accuracy, F1-score and AUC metrics. These results suggest that the encoded belief over hypothesis carried by the NN characteristic is less effective in this scenario than the piece-wise constant approximation view introduced by tree-like models where decision rules are inferred from the data features.

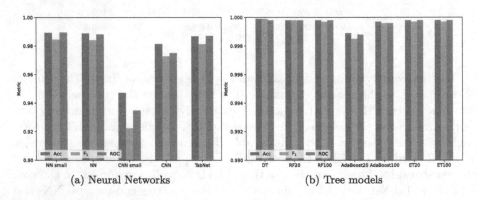

(a) Neural Networks   (b) Tree models

Fig. 3. Comparison of the statistical results of the models on TON_IoT. The left chart includes neural network based models and the right chart the tree-based algorithms. The considered metrics are accuracy, f1-score and AUC-ROC measure. It is clear by the plots that the tree-based models perform much better than the others.

All results up to this point refer to the experiments carried out on the Raspberry Pi 3. Next, the results of the tests carried out by implementing a QNN in the FPGA are exhibited.

Table 9 shows the results of the QNNs trained locally and then implemented on the PYNQ-Z2 FPGA board. As can be seen from Table 10, which exhibits the percentage utilization of the physical components of the FPGA board and the measured values of latency, bandwidth, frequency, and power consumption, this implementation is characterized by extraordinarily fast processing of input data. The difference between the bandwidth measured during the simulation and the bandwidth measured directly on the device can be attributed to overhead in sample transfers. We note that the utilization of LUT, FF and BRAM is relatively low, and combined with a clock frequency of 100 MHz we achieve an extremely low latency. This translates to a generally good accuracy for an 8-bit quantized model, which is 97.47% and 99.81% for TON_IoT and IoT-23, respectively.

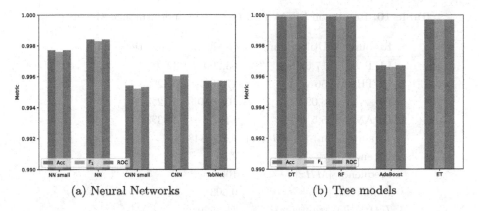

(a) Neural Networks   (b) Tree models

Fig. 4. Comparison of the statistical results of the models on IoT-23 Dataset. The left chart includes NN-based models meanwhile the right chart shows the tree-based algorithms. The considered metrics are accuracy, F1-score and AUC-ROC measure. The charts show the better performance of tree-based models even in this scenario.

Table 9. Results of QNN first tested on PC.

Models	Accuracy	Precision	Recall	F1-score	ROC-AUC
Quant-NN (TON_IoT)	0.9747	0.9798	0.9468	0.9630	0.9682
Quant-NN (IoT-23)	0.9981	0.9964	0.9998	0.9981	0.9981

Overall, the DT seems to outperforms other classifiers for all investigated metrics, but with RF and ET showing similar results, for both TON_IoT and IoT-23. We can firmly state that as tree-based models obtain the best results, they are the best candidates for the IDS system. These results can likely be attributed to the tabular nature of the network traffic alongside the pre-processing applied to the chosen features which favors tree-based algorithms. Furthermore the throughput of these models is significantly higher than the other classifiers considered. The experimental tests demonstrate how the chosen lightweight classifiers obtain excellent result at distinguishing network traffic as benign or malicious within a wide group of different attacks, and how they can be easily integrated into resource-limited devices such as Raspberry Pis and FPGAs. Real-time efficiency of an IDS hardly depends on the dataset used in the training phase. Therefore, to ensure the best security, it is necessary to use a dataset that contains traffic patterns related to recent types of malicious attacks. The datasets we used, TON_IoT and IoT-23, are suitable choices for this purpose and the presented results demonstrate that the chosen models show promising performance.

Table 10. Results on FPGA PYNQ-Z2 using performance Metrics.

Resource	Utilization	Available	Utilization (%)
LUT	17,030	53,200	32.01%
LUTRAM	56	17,400	0.32%
FF	6,090	106,400	5.72%
BRAM	5.5	140	3.93%
T (simulation) [$samples/s$]	1,438,848		
Latency [μs]	2.56		
Frequency [MHz]	100		
Power est. [W]	0.503		
T (PYNQ) [$samples/s$]	717,529		

6   Conclusions and Future Work

In this paper, a study on anomaly-based intrusion detection systems suitable for securing IoT networks against malicious attacks is conducted. We document the performance assessment of different ML classification algorithms, including neural networks, decision tree, random forests, adaboost, extremely randomized trees and TabNet. All the classifiers are benchmarked on recent IoT datasets containing different kinds of attacks, namely TON_IoT and IOT-23. The optimal parameters of the models are obtained using a grid search algorithm combined with a study on the feature importance. The performance of all the classifiers has been measured in terms of accuracy, precision, recall and area under the receiver operating characteristic curve. Moreover, the models are evaluated from the perspective of processing speed.

The experiments are carried out on a Raspberry Pi 3B and a PYNQ-Z2 FPGA board, and the results show that the DT, RF, and ET models show the best trade-off between prominent metrics and processing time. We show how these models achieve excellent results for classifying network traffic processed as tabular data. They are therefore a suitable choice for building IoT specific IDSs. We demonstrate that the combination of Raspberry Pi or FPGA with ML classifiers is capable of achieving excellent results in terms of detection accuracy and response time. As our models are lightweight, the additional overhead on edge devices can be limited. This, alongside the high flexibility of our models, allows for hybrid and distributed deployment of additional security in a resource-constrained IoT setting. The proposed system is trustworthy since even if a centralized IDS or cloud computing fails, the internal security of individual devices is not affected. This property proves useful in industrial IoT, where the consequences of a failure to protect the individual device can have serious consequences. In addition, the versatile design allows ordinary model updates via on-device training, in order to adapt to emerging attacks which implies constant advancement of the network security status.

For future work, we plan on further investigating various models for lightweight implementation on low-powered devices. Additionally, we should explore how our system can be integrated in a real-work networking environment. For this, we plan on integrating our system alongside existing IDS solutions. Furthermore, leveraging incremental learning to extend our heuristics could facilitate more robust online intrusion detection.

A   Model Architectures

- **Neural Network Models**:
  To better understand the behaviour of NNs we experiment with the difference between a small NN and a bigger NN, both for the multilayer perceptron (MLP) using only fully connected layers as well as the CNN.
  - *NN1* (small_NN): fully connected MLP composed of 3 hidden layers, with 64, 256, 64 neurons respectively. There are 14 input features and the output layer has 2 neurons (binary classification). ReLU is used as activation function.
  - *NN2*: smaller fully connected NN composed of one hidden layer of 64 neurons. Input layer has 14 neurons and the output layer 2.
  - *CNN1* (small_CNN): it is composed of 1 convolutional layer characterized by 1 input channel and 16 output channels, kernel size of 2 and stride of 1 and a fully connected layer with 96 input neurons and 2 output neurons with ReLU as activation function.
  - *CNN2*: more advanced CNN composed of 2 convolutional layers and 2 fully connected layers. The first convolutional layer has 1 input channel, 8 output channels, kernel size of 3 and stride of 1. The second convolutional layer has 8 input and 16 output channels, kernel of 3 and stride 1. The fully connect layers have 64 and 2 neurons respectively. ReLU is used as activation function.
  - *Quantized-NN*: is composed of 3 layers. The hidden layer is composed of 64 neurons and the quantization is done with 8 bits using ReLU as activation function. This model is needed for the deployment on the FPGA.
- **Decision Tree (DT)**: for the performance assessment the criterion is set to *entropy*, and the maximum depth of the tree is set to 24, according to the best parameters of the grid search.
- **Random Forest (RF)**: the parameters are 100 estimators, i.e. the number of trees included in the ensemble. The maximum depth of trees is set to 26 and the *gini* impurity is chosen as function to measure the quality of a split.
- **AdaBoost**: We use 100 estimators, with a learning rate of 0.1 and *SAMME.R* as a boosting algorithm [12]. The base estimator is a Decision Tree initialized with a maximum depth of 1.
- **Extremely Random Forest (ET)**: according to the grid search we set the number of estimators equals to 80, *gini* as a criterion and no maximum depth.

- **TabNet**: We set the width of the decision prediction layer and the attention embedding for each mask to 32, in accordance to the authors' instructions [3]. We use 4 as steps in the architecture, with 3 independent Gated Linear Units layers at each step is.

Grid Search: for Decision Trees, RF, AdaBoost, Extremely Randomized Trees we used *GridSearchCV* to find the best hyperparameters.

Tree-based models have the ability to process a large number of samples per second, so we can search for the highest performing hyper parameters (which generally increase model heaviness) even at the cost of sacrificing some classification speed in exchange for higher accuracy. As a result, we prioritize the accuracy over the bandwidth in the determination of the final hyperparameter values.

Optimization Function: on our work we used Adam (Adaptive Moment Estimation) optimizer [16] for all the NNs and for TabNet. The learning rate set for TabNet is 0.02 and 0.01 for all the NNs.

Regularization: we first test the two fully-connected NNs and the two convolutional NNs with different regularisation techniques including Dropout, L1, L2 regularization. Although regularisation is proven effective for preventing overfitting, the classification accuracy of our models did not further improve. The NNs are trained on dataset of millions of samples and they are able to generalize very well on them, this implies our model models do not suffer from overfitting.

B   Metrics

We evaluate our models with conventional ML metrics. Given some classification problem, the true positives (TP) are attack samples that are classified as attack, the false positives (FP) are normal samples that are classified as attack, the true negatives (TN) are normal samples that are classified as normal and the false negatives (FN) are attack samples that are classified as normal. The Accuracy $Acc = \frac{TP+TN}{TP+TN+FP+FN}$ then is the proportion of correction classifications. The Recall $R = \frac{TP}{TP+FP}$ or R monitors how well the classifier can detect attacks. The Precision $P = \frac{TP}{TP+FP}$ or P monitors how well a model can correctly identify attacks, and $F_1 = \frac{2 \cdot Precision \cdot Recall}{Precision + Recall}$ is the harmonic mean of P and R. Finally, the False Positive Rate or $FPR = \frac{FP}{FP+TN}$ monitors the number of false alarms. We also consider the Area under the Curve of the Receiver Operating Characteristics (AUC-ROC), mapping the R in function of the FPR.

Additionally, we define the throughput T of models as the number of samples they are able to process per second. Specifically for FPGA hardware, we also monitor the resource consumption by considering the Lookup Table (LUT), Flip-Flop (FF) and Block RAM (BRAM) utilization.

References

1. RFC 4949: Internet security glossary, version 2 (2007)
2. Almiani, M., AbuGhazleh, A., Al-Rahayfeh, A., Atiewi, S., Razaque, A.: Deep recurrent neural network for IoT intrusion detection system. Simul. Model. Pract. Theory **101**, 102031 (2020)
3. Arik, S.Ö., Pfister, T.: Tabnet: attentive interpretable tabular learning. CoRR **abs/1908.07442** (2019). http://arxiv.org/abs/1908.07442
4. Baron, A.: IMAT: a lightweight IoT network intrusion detection system based on machine learning techniques. Master's thesis, University of Padova (2022)
5. Chaabouni, N., Mosbah, M., Zemmari, A., Sauvignac, C., Faruki, P.: Network intrusion detection for IoT security based on learning techniques. IEEE Commun. Surv. Tutor. **21**(3), 2671–2701 (2019)
6. Doshi, R., Apthorpe, N., Feamster, N.: Machine learning DDoS detection for consumer internet of things devices. In: 2018 IEEE Security and Privacy Workshops (SPW), pp. 29–35. IEEE (2018)
7. Raspberry Pi Foundation: Raspberry pi (2022). https://www.raspberrypi.com
8. Gamage, S., Samarabandu, J.: Deep learning methods in network intrusion detection: a survey and an objective comparison. J. Netw. Comput. Appl. **169**, 1–21 (2020). https://doi.org/10.1016/j.jnca.2020.102767
9. Garcia, S., Parmisano, A., Erquiaga, M.J.: IoT-23: a labeled dataset with malicious and benign IoT network traffic (2020). https://doi.org/10.5281/zenodo.4743746. https://www.stratosphereips.org/datasets-iot23
10. Ge, M., Fu, X., Syed, N., Baig, Z., Teo, G., Robles-Kelly, A.: Deep learning based intrusion detection for IoT networks. In: 2019 IEEE 24th Pacific Rim International Symposium on Dependable Computing (PRDC), pp. 256–25609. IEEE (2019)
11. Hasan, M., Islam, M.M., Zarif, M.I.I., Hashem, M.: Attack and anomaly detection in IoT sensors in IoT sites using machine learning approaches. Internet Things **7**, 100059 (2019)
12. Hastie, T., Rosset, S., Zhu, J., Zou, H.: Multi-class adaboost. Stat. Interface **2**(3), 349–360 (2009)
13. Hodo, E., et al.: Threat analysis of IoT networks using artificial neural network intrusion detection system. In: 2016 International Symposium on Networks, Computers and Communications (ISNCC), pp. 1–6. IEEE (2016)
14. Hosseinpour, F., Vahdani Amoli, P., Plosila, J., Hämäläinen, T., Tenhunen, H.: An intrusion detection system for fog computing and IoT based logistic systems using a smart data approach. Int. J. Digit. Content Technol. Appl. **10**(5) (2016)
15. Hussein, A.Y., Falcarin, P., Sadiq, A.T.: IoT intrusion detection using modified random forest based on double feature selection methods. In: Liatsis, P., Hussain, A., Mostafa, S.A., Al-Jumeily, D. (eds.) TIOTC 2021. CCIS, vol. 1548, pp. 61–78. Springer, Cham (2022). https://doi.org/10.1007/978-3-030-97255-4_5
16. Kingma, D.P., Ba, J.: Adam: a method for stochastic optimization. arXiv preprint arXiv:1412.6980 (2014)
17. Kozik, R., Choraś, M., Ficco, M., Palmieri, F.: A scalable distributed machine learning approach for attack detection in edge computing environments. J. Parallel Distrib. Comput. **119**, 18–26 (2018)
18. Lee, T.-H., Wen, C.-H., Chang, L.-H., Chiang, H.-S., Hsieh, M.-C.: A lightweight intrusion detection scheme based on energy consumption analysis in 6LowPAN. In: Huang, Y.-M., Chao, H.-C., Deng, D.-J., Park, J.J.J.H. (eds.) Advanced Technologies, Embedded and Multimedia for Human-centric Computing. LNEE, vol.

260, pp. 1205–1213. Springer, Dordrecht (2014). https://doi.org/10.1007/978-94-007-7262-5_137

19. Lopez-Martin, M., Carro, B., Sanchez-Esguevillas, A., Lloret, J.: Conditional variational autoencoder for prediction and feature recovery applied to intrusion detection in IoT. Sensors **17**(9), 1967 (2017)

20. Manyika, J., Chui, M., Bisson, P., Jonathan Woetzel, R.D., Bughin, J., Aharon, D.: Unlocking the potential of the internet of things (2015). https://www.mckinsey.com/business-functions/mckinsey-digital/our-insights/the-internet-of-things-the-value-of-digitizing-the-physical-world

21. Mishra, P., Varadharajan, V., Tupakula, U., Pilli, E.S.: A detailed investigation and analysis of using machine learning techniques for intrusion detection. IEEE Commun. Surv. Tutor. **21**(1), 686–728 (2018). https://doi.org/10.1109/COMST.2018.2847722

22. Moustafa, N.: A new distributed architecture for evaluating AI-based security systems at the edge: network ton_iot datasets (2021)

23. Nobakht, M., Sivaraman, V., Boreli, R.: A host-based intrusion detection and mitigation framework for smart home IoT using openflow. In: 2016 11th International Conference on Availability, Reliability and Security (ARES), pp. 147–156. IEEE (2016)

24. Pappalardo, A.: Xilinx/brevitas (2021). https://doi.org/10.5281/zenodo.3333552

25. Paszke, A., et al.: Pytorch: an imperative style, high-performance deep learning library. In: Wallach, H., Larochelle, H., Beygelzimer, A., d'Alché-Buc, F., Fox, E., Garnett, R. (eds.) Advances in Neural Information Processing Systems 32, pp. 8024–8035. Curran Associates, Inc. (2019). http://papers.neurips.cc/paper/9015-pytorch-an-imperative-style-high-performance-deep-learning-library.pdf

26. Pedregosa, F., et al.: Scikit-learn: machine learning in Python. J. Mach. Learn. Res. **12**, 2825–2830 (2011)

27. Project, T.Z.: The zeek network security monitor (2020). https://zeek.org/

28. Sarhan, M., Lo, W.W., Layeghy, S., Portmann, M.: HBFL: a hierarchical blockchain-based federated learning framework for a collaborative IoT intrusion detection. arXiv preprint arXiv:2204.04254 (2022)

29. Shafique, K., Khawaja, B.A., Sabir, F., Qazi, S., Mustaqim, M.: Internet of things (IoT) for next-generation smart systems: a review of current challenges, future trends and prospects for emerging 5G-IoT scenarios. IEEE Access **8**, 23022–23040 (2020). https://doi.org/10.1109/ACCESS.2020.2970118

30. Singh, D., Singh, B.: Investigating the impact of data normalization on classification performance. Appl. Soft Comput. **97**, 105524 (2020)

31. Tsai, C.F., Hsu, Y.F., Lin, C.Y., Lin, W.Y.: Intrusion detection by machine learning: a review. Expert Syst. Appl. **36**(10), 11994–12000 (2009)

32. Wireshark: Wireshark. https://www.wireshark.org/

33. Woolf, N.: DDoS attack that disrupted internet was largest of its kind in history, experts say (2016). https://www.theguardian.com/technology/2016/oct/26/ddos-attack-dyn-mirai-botnet

34. Zhou, W., Jia, Y., Peng, A., Zhang, Y., Liu, P.: The effect of IoT new features on security and privacy: new threats, existing solutions, and challenges yet to be solved. IEEE Internet Things J. **6**(2), 1606–1616 (2018)

Measuring Cyber Resilience of IoT-Enabled Critical National Infrastructures

Adeola Adewumi[1], Mohammad Hammoudeh[2], Tooska Dargahi[3],
and Olamide Jogunola[3(✉)]

[1] School of Science, Engineering and Environment, University of Salford,
Salford M5 4WT, UK
[2] College of Computing and Mathematics, King Fahd University of Petroleum
and Minerals, Dhahran 31261, Kingdom of Saudi Arabia
m.hammoudeh@kfupm.edu.sa
[3] Department of Computing and Mathematics, Manchester Metropolitan University,
Manchester M1 5GD, UK
{t.dargahi,o.jogunola}@mmu.ac.uk

Abstract. Critical National Infrastructure (CNI) is vital and critical to
the delivery of essential services to society and is necessary for a country
to function properly. CNI are increasingly being connected to the internet
to improve operational efficiency and reduce costs. The adoption of the
Industrial Internet of Things (IoT) introduced new attack vectors which
have necessitated a need to build and improve cyber resilience in CNI.
The quantification of cyber resilience via metrics is one of the ways to
improve resilience. However, there is currently no standard methodology
and metrics to quantitatively measure cyber resilience in CNI. This paper
proposes a list of suitable cyber resilience metrics for IoT-enabled CNI.
Smart grid is considered as a CNI case study to measure the effective
ness of the proposed cyber resilience metrics. Evaluation of the systemic
impact metric on smart grid showed that the performance of the system
under an attack is dependent on the recovery time; hence, the higher
the systemic impact, the lower the resilience of the CNI and vice versa.
Quantifying the resilience of CNI is crucial to determining the security
control defenses required to reduce the impact of a cyber attack.

Keywords: Industrial IoT · Critical National Infrastructure · Cyber
Resilience Metrics · Smart Grid

1 Introduction

The advent of Industry 4.0 technologies, and its key enabler, the Internet of
Things (IoT), is shaping the modern world. The Industrial IoT (IIoT) is a network of devices, applications and sensors that facilitate data collection and analysis across various industries, such as manufacturing, power generation and transportation. IIoT has brought huge benefits such as improved efficiency, enhanced
productivity, greater flexibility, cost reduction, and increased profitability [1].

M. Andreoni (Ed.): ACNS 2024 Workshops, LNCS 14586, pp. 265–280, 2024.
https://doi.org/10.1007/978-3-031-61486-6_16

IoT-enabled Critical National Infrastructure (CNI) are increasingly comprising a significant portion of both current and future critical infrastructures [2]. CNI is vital and critical to delivering essential services to society and necessary for a country to function effectively. Due to the adoption of IoT and Artificial Intelligence (AI) in the energy sector, there has been optimization of energy resources, dependence on smart grids, predictive protocols for natural disasters, and a positive impact on climate change. Also, the interconnected elements of smart grid system make it possible to automatically optimize its operations and monitor itself [3].

Despite the benefits derived from its usage, IIoT has also brought forth several risks and cyber threats. The interconnection, interdependence, and complexity of CNI have increased the attack surface which has culminated in a significant increase in cyber attacks. Due to how essential CNIs are to daily life, any cyber disruption or compromise could have a damaging impact on the availability, integrity, and discharge of essential services, cause economic damages, threaten public safety, and even lead to loss of lives. The threat landscape has evolved from traditional to sophisticated cyber attacks. A report by Ponemon Institute gathered that 90% of CNI providers had their Internet-connected critical infrastructure subject to cyber attacks [4], while 56% of organizations in the energy sector that partook in the survey revealed that they had suffered an attack. This invariably means that malicious actors have categorized CNI as a lucrative cyber attack target. The number of threats continues to rise significantly, which also necessitates a need to improve the cyber resilience of Internet-connected CNI.

To proactively ensure the functionality of Internet-connected CNIs during cyber attacks, cyber resilience assessment methods such as checklists, models and metrics are commonly used. Metrics are generally used to make informed decisions which are also valid for improving resilience. However, the lack of standard and comprehensive metrics to measure the resilience of CNI is a unique challenge that will be addressed in this paper. Formal and comprehensive approaches to improving resilience by leveraging metrics are undeveloped. Building or enhancing resilience requires metrics, and if cyber resilience is not measured, there is no way to improve it [5,6].

This paper provides a novel solution to the challenge of IoT-connected CNI cyber resilience by developing metrics that can assess, measure, and improve the cyber resilience of IoT-connected CNI. These metrics are derived by conducting a literature review of related works. We demonstrate the suitability of the proposed metrics for the smart grid network through experimental analysis. The rest of the paper is organized as follows. Section 2 reviews the existing literature and the proposed resilience evaluation metrics in the literature. Section 3 explains our proposed metrics, while Sect. 4 evaluates their efficiency through a smart meter use-case. Section 5 concludes the paper and proposes future research directions.

2   Related Work

CNI refers to systems, resources, information, processes, networks, and people, whose continued operation is essential to ensure the security of a country and upon which daily life depends [7]. The energy sector is among the most sensitive CNIs, noted for its role in energy generation, management, and distribution. It plays a crucial part in maintaining business continuity within a society, affecting both civil and military infrastructures. These CNI sectors are labeled critical due to their significance and daily life importance, prompting the decision to safeguard them. Disruptions such as natural disasters, terrorism, accidental data loss, or cyber attacks, such as Stuxnet, Industroyer, BlackEnergy3, Triton, Havex, and the recent pipedream attack, can severely affect the economy, national public health, and the safety of citizens. Until recently, many organizations within the CNI sectors have deployed and managed industrial control systems (ICS) in isolation and largely disconnected networks. However, the adoption of IoT in CNI has brought interconnection to the fore, and efforts have been made to consider the security of operational technology (OT) alongside information technology (IT).

An appropriate definition for cyber resilience is needed to determine the cyber resilience metrics suitable for CNI. Resilience has been an important term used in different contexts and within multiple disciplines, hence the different definitions of resilience. MITRE describes resilience as the ability of a nation, organisation, mission or business process to anticipate, withstand, recover from, and evolve to improve capabilities in the face of attacks on the supporting cyber resources it needs to function [8]. Cutter et al. [9] defines resilience as the ability to prepare and plan for, absorb, recover from, and more successfully adapt to actual or potential adverse events. These definitions focus on resilience in the context of disaster, especially on how to reduce disaster impacts. The National Institute of Standards and Technology (NIST) [10] defines resilience as the ability to anticipate, withstand, recover from, and adapt to adverse conditions, stresses, attacks, or compromises on systems that use or are enabled by cyber resources.

In this paper, we will adopt the NIST definition and define cyber resilience as the ability of a system to prepare and defend against cyber attacks, minimize damage, maintain functionality level under attack, minimize recovery times from cyberattacks and adapt. Metrics are used to measure, evaluate, and compare processes. Metrics can be quantitative, qualitative, or semi-quantitative, and they can be computed or derived. Cyber resilience metrics are an active research area, especially as related to CNI.

2.1 CNI Most Targeted Industries

Mihalache et al. [11] conducted a review of the cyber resilience trends by analysing the methods for cyber-physical systems (CPS) resilience enhancement. CPS consists of hardware, software and other systems that are integrated and networked as in critical infrastructure operations, and traffic flow management amongst others. The review also showed the authors identified threats in the physical, network and cyber layer. However, no metrics were highlighted to measure the resilience of CPS. Murino et al. [12] proposed a model-free, quantitative, and general-purpose evaluation methodology to extract resilience indexes from system logs, process data and Security Information and Event Management (SIEM) tool logs by simulating attacks against a wastewater treatment plant model. While the analysis was in-depth, the ability of the indexes to differentiate between cyber-attacks and natural event was identified as an issue. Cassottana et al. [13] developed a CPS quantitative resilience assessment framework that measured the resilience of a disruption before and after its occurrence using a power substation as a case study. Fang et al. [14] proposed optimal repair time and resilience reduction worth as metrics to measure the resilience of a network system. These metrics quantify the priority with which a failed component should be repaired and re-installed into the network and the potential loss in the optimal system resilience due to a time delay in the recovery of a failed component. These metrics were computed via mathematical modeling, and they focus on the recovery phase of cyber resilience [14]. "The optimal repair time $T_{ij}{}^{opt}$ is described as the time the arc ij is restored to function properly at a recovery time T," which is mathematically represented as:

$$T_{ij}^{opt} = \Sigma_{t=0}^{T}(1 - s_{ij}(t)) \tag{1}$$

Francis and Bekera [15] proposed resilience metrics and a framework for infrastructure systems. These metrics consolidate the adaptive capacity, absorptive capacity, and recoverability of a resilient system. The adaptive capacity focuses on how the system can adapt to adverse events, while the absorptive capacity is the ability of a system to absorb and overcome adverse impacts. One of the limitations identified with these metrics is their generality and suitability for natural disasters [15]. Their proposed metrics is calculated through the following equation:

$$\rho_i(S_p, F_r, F_d, F_o) = S_p \frac{F_r}{F_o} \frac{F_d}{F_o} \tag{2}$$

where

$$S_p = t_\delta \begin{cases} (t_\delta/t_r^*)EXP[-a(t_r - t_r^*)] & \text{for } t_r \geq t_r^* \\ (t_\delta/t_r^*) & \text{otherwise} \end{cases} \tag{3}$$

S_p is the speed recovery factor, F_o is the original stable system performance level, F_d is the performance level immediately post-disruption, F_r^* is the performance level after post-disruption equilibrium state is achieved, and F_r is the performance at a new stable level after recovery, t_δ is slack time, t_r is time to final recovery, t_r^* is time to complete recovery, and a is the parameter controlling decay in resilience. These metrics are rather too generic and, as such, not the most applicable to evaluate the effectiveness of resilience of IoT-enabled CNI during a cyber attack.

· Hassell et al. [16] identified the percentage of successful and partially successful attacks, the mean number of attack disruptions, defensive efficiency, and attack noise as metrics for evaluating resilience. These metrics focus on the defensive and detective aspects of resilience, and the authors also indicate time as an underlying measurement of effectiveness [16]. Quantified the percentage of successful attack metric as the number of successful attacks observed (NA, success) per the number of total attacks observed (NA, total), and the authors also quantified the mean number of attack disruptions as a summation of the number of disruptions on the ith attack (Ni, disruption) per number of total attacks observed [14]. The metrics are useful in measuring the effectiveness of cyber defense measures within a network, which can also be adopted in an IoT network.

$$P_{A,success} = \frac{N_{A,success}}{N_{A,total}} \times 100\% \tag{4}$$

$$N_{disruption} = \frac{\sum_{i=1}^{N_{A,total}} N_{i,disruption}}{N_{A,total}} \tag{5}$$

Hossain-McKenzie et al. [17] proposed performance-based cyber resilience metrics such as systemic impact, and total recovery effort for analysing power systems against cyber-attacks. A microgrid case study related to ADDSec MTD technology was used to evaluate the metrics. Haque et al. [18] proposed a qualitative cyber resilience framework for the industrial control system. Analytical hierarchy process was used to formulate the metrics based on different individual sub metrics. Redundancy, robustness and rapidity are some of the metrics identified in this paper. The authors also decomposed and categorized further metrics, such as physical redundancy and segmentation, as dimensional and operational metrics, respectively. Even though the authors argued that the metrics are useful in identifying aspects of the network that are non-resilient, one of the shortcomings is that the metrics focus on experts' technical opinions to assess the cyber resilience of the ICS environment. The operational metrics focus on vulnerability scans, insider threat management, training, and awareness. The resilience metrics are mathematically represented as:

$$R_i = W_{phy} \times d_{Ri_{phy}} + W_{org} \times d_{Ri_{org}} + W_{tec} \times d_{Ri_{tec}} \tag{6}$$

Segovia et al. [19] identified stability and performance as metrics that quantify the absorptive and recoverability capability of a system at design time. The absorptive property is the extent to which attacks can be handled, while the recovery capacity describes the ability of a system to restore its operations while undergoing performance degradation. The authors mentioned that these metrics could be used to measure the capacity of a system to absorb and recover from malicious attacks. Also, design and structure metrics were proposed in this paper, and the strength of this metric is assessing situational awareness [19]. These metrics focus on the important aspect of resilience which is the ability of a system to recover. The performance and stability resilience (PR) metric is represented as:

$$PR = \frac{NR - RL}{NR} \tag{7}$$

$$NR = (TS_{sup} - TS_{inf}) \times (KA + KR) \tag{8}$$

where KA represents the absorb time, KR represents the recovery time, RL represents the resilience loss, and TS represents the performance threshold.

In summary, the review of the proposed resilience metrics in the literature indicates a lack of comprehensive standard for measuring CNI resilience.

3   Proposed Metrics for Measuring Cyber Resilience

We will adopt the resilience metrics proposed by Haque et al. [18], and Hossain-McKenzie et al. [17] to address the lack of comprehensive cyber resilience quantification metrics for IoT-enabled CNI and the applicability of these metrics to real-life systems. The metrics are assessed based on the absorptive, adaptive, and recoverability capabilities of a resilient system, which are useful characteristics in improving the resilience of CNI (Fig. 1).

Fig. 1. Cyber Resilience Characteristics

Robustness metric can be defined as the ability of a system to absorb and withstand attacks with a reduced negative impact on the performance of the system [20]. This invariably means that CNI performance is assured even during an unforeseen cyber attack. This metric ensures that the failure of CNI systems is accounted for, which means fail-safes are designed for the CNI components and the network at large. For example, a robust CNI will not fail when design thresholds are exceeded. In addition, robustness reduces the impact of the cyber attacks by preventing the attack from compromising the other part of the CNI network, especially where critical services could be accessed. Cimellaro et al. [21] mathematically represented the robustness metric as:

$$Robustness = 1 - \bar{L}(m_L, \sigma_L); (\%) \tag{9}$$

where $\bar{L}$ represents random variable expressed as a function of the m_L, mean is represented by m_L, and σ_L represents standard deviation.

Redundancy is another metric adapted from [19]. It is one of the metrics used in assessing the maturity of cyber security in an IT environment and can also be adapted in a CNI environment. Redundancy can be described as a system's capability to continue to function due to the provision of alternative resources, which can also be called backup resources or systems. Resilient CNI must always have at least one redundant component which can be used as an alternative in the event of a failure that occurs through a cyber attack. Furthermore, provisioning a redundant system or replicating modules is a function of identifying critical components of the CNI. If non-critical components are provisioned, the purpose of having a resilient system becomes defeated. Redundancy can be quantified as:

$$Redundancy = \frac{\text{Number of critical resources with alternative resource}}{\text{Total number of critical resources}} \times 100$$

Resourcefulness is the ability to adapt to cyber attacks by leveraging on flexible people to prioritize unanticipated challenges and innovate solutions during an attack. Bruneau et al. [20] described resourcefulness as technologies employed to monitor and detect cyber attacks from a technical perspective. This metric is difficult to quantify because it is dependent on employee skills. Rapidity can be described as the ability of a system to recover from a cyber attack in a timely manner while containing the losses and avoiding disruption [17]. Rapidity can also be used to measure the time taken for a system to be restored to pre disruption functionality; the goal is to optimise rapidity, which in turn increases the resilience of a CNI system. Cimellaro et al. [21] mathematically represented the rapidity metric as:

$$Rapidity = \frac{d\delta(t)}{dt}; \quad \text{for} \quad t_{oE} \leq t \leq t_{oE} + T_{RE} \tag{10}$$

$$Rapidity = \frac{L}{T_{RE}} \tag{11}$$

where $\frac{d}{dt}$ is the differential operator, $\delta(t)$ is the functionality of the system, t is the time, and L is the loss functionality.

Systemic Impact (SI) and total recovery effort (TRE) are metrics created by Vugrin et al. [22] for quantifying the resilience of infrastructure systems. However, Hossain-McKenzie et al. [17] made an adjustment to these metrics to accommodate for cyber threats, which will be adopted as metrics in this thesis. Hossain-McKenzie et al. [17] described SI as the ability of a system to mitigate cyber attack and continue operating through adverse conditions. SI is measured by summing the difference between targeted system performance (TSP) and actual system performance (SP) over the period, $d(t)$, the attack commenced till response measures, t_f, are carried out. TSP represents the pre-attack performance level while SP is the performance level during an attack or disruption. SI measures the resilience of the CNI during a disruption and is expressed as:

$$SI = \int_{t_0}^{t_f} [TSP(t) - SP(t)] \, dt \tag{12}$$

Total Recovery Effort (TRE) focuses on the recoverability capacity of the system described as the cumulative effort required for the response measures to overcome the cyber attack and recover the system [17]. This metric can be measured by considering the resources used during the recovery process. TRE is expressed as:

$$TRE = \int_{t_0}^{t_f} \Sigma_k r_k(t)[RE_k(d(t), SP(t), t)] \, dt \tag{13}$$

Fault tolerance is another metric that can be used to measure the resilience of internet-connected CNI. It is defined as the ability of a system to continue to operate at a defined level of performance while the components are failing or malfunctioning. Fault tolerance is an important concept in traditional IT that can also be adopted in CNI. This is due to the adverse impacts of the failure of system components, which could be dangerous or even lead to loss of life. Building fault-tolerant systems are equivalent to creating or having redundant components and systems that can make failover possible in the event of system failure. Hamilton et al. [23] outlined a metric for measuring fault tolerance for Robot systems; however, it can be adapted for CNI.

$$eff = k_1(f)^2 + k_2(P)^2 \tag{14}$$

Based on the CNI cyber attack review conducted, it has been observed that malicious actors usually leverage the network as an attack vector to disrupt the operations of CNI providers. This informs our decision to evaluate the effectiveness of the proposed resilience metrics by considering a smart grid CNI as a case study and set up a network simulation. IEA [24] defined a smart grid as an electricity network that uses digital and other advanced technologies to monitor and manage the transport of electricity from all generation sources to meet the varying electricity demands of end-users. Smart grid components include electric power substations, electric power generators, distribution, and transmission lines, controllers, collector nodes, smart meters, and distribution and transmission control centers [25]. Matey et al. [26] also highlighted some attack surfaces such as data concentrator, SCADA, control system, Communication channel, Remote terminal unit (RTU), Programmable logic controller (PLC), and Advanced meter infrastructure (AMI) which are peculiar to smart grids.

Due to the complexity of the smart grid infrastructure, the communication network of the smart meter component, which is one of the attack surfaces, will be modeled and simulated for cyber resilience evaluation is this paper. Gunduz and Das [3] highlighted some of the common cyber attacks that are prevalent in smart grids, which include phishing, denial of service (DoS), eavesdropping, packet drop attack, false data injection, jamming, a man in the middle and buffer overflow attacks. Research showed that regular servers such as file servers, web and database servers configured in an ideal IT network are also configured in an ICS network on operating systems (OS) such as Windows and Unix to provide support for ICS functions. This shows that the attack surfaces are not only restricted to the ICS components, but cyber attacks can start from the traditional IT servers configured in the ICS network and propagate to the ICS components.

For the performance evaluation of the proposed metrics, we have only simulated a Distributed DoS (DDoS) attack. DDoS is an attack that causes exhaustion of system and/or network resources due to attack and flood a targeted system or network with unwanted service traffic or requests. This leads to unavailability of the resource to its intended users and causes slow network performance. For this simulation, the control server will be flooded with unwanted ping requests, which will impact the server's performance and cause the unavailability of the smart meter control server to provide services such as file transfer and database requests to multiple smart meter clients. This attack will disrupt the smart meter network infrastructure, which will have an overall impact on the resilience of the smart grid network infrastructure. Measuring the network's resilience during the attack depends on the impact of the attack on the server performance.

4   Experimental Analysis

In this section, the metrics proposed above are evaluated using a smart meter network. Various open-source and commercial network simulators are available that can be used to carry out our intended simulation, including GNS3 (Graphical Network Simulator 3), NS2/3 (Network Simulator Version 2/3), OPNET (Optimized Network Engineering Tools) and OMNET++ (Optical Micro-Networks Plus). OPNET modeler version 14.5 is the software application used for network modeling and simulation in this paper. OPNET was chosen because it supports discrete event simulation, which makes it easy to analyze the performance of networks [27]. Also, OPNET was chosen because of some of its unique features, which include its support for the Windows operating system, academic free version, and tutorials on the installation and setup of the environment.

Two network scenarios were modeled: the baseline scenario and the DDoS attack scenario. The smart meter baseline scenario represents the smart meter network infrastructure simulated on OPNET without a cyber attack. The network enables communication between smart meters and the control server. The smart meter is represented as a workstation node as OPNET does not have a node for a smart meter. Twenty smart meters are modeled and connected to Ethernet switches (switch 1 and switch2) with a 100BaseT link which enables data to be sent and received. The smart meter has been modeled to generate packets that are sent through the Ethernet switch to the router and then through the firewall to the control server, as depicted in Fig. 2. Applications such as FTP (file transfer protocol), database, and HTTP have been configured on the control server and within the network. This is to model the real-life smart meter network by generating application traffic as energy data consumed by clients in their homes are usually sent to the control server through a wide area network. Metrics such as throughput and CPU utilization are configured to be measured during the simulation.

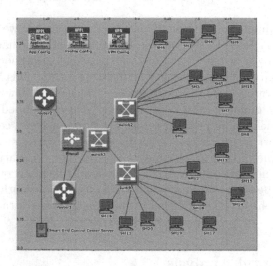

Fig. 2. Considered Smart Meter Network Infrastructure

The smart meter DDoS scenario is simulated with a DDoS attack against the network infrastructure. For the DDoS attack scenario, we created a duplicate of the baseline scenario. We introduced an attacker to the network who compromises some of the smart meters and reprograms them to send unlimited ping traffic to the control server via the switches and routers, as shown in Fig. 3.

The attacker is represented by a workstation node, and DDoS traffic is sent to the server, as seen in Fig. 3, with the attack starting at $t = 0$ s. The DDoS traffic is represented with the dotted lines in red. IP addresses were auto-assigned to the smart meters, control server, and attacker nodes. Also, for both scenarios, the simulation was configured to last 21600 s (6 hrs.) The systemic impact (SI) metric which can measure the impact of the DoS attack on the network is evaluated. For this analysis, SI is defined by Eq. 12 where:

$$TSP_1(t) = \text{throughput of the network before the attack at time } t$$

$$SP_1(t) = \text{throughput of the network during the attack at time } t$$

The time analysis period is from 0 to 18000 (in seconds) i.e., $t_0 = 0$ and $t_f = 18000$. Tables 1 and 2 are the data obtained after the simulation of the DoS attack against the smart meter network. They show the server performance (measured in seconds), CPU utilization (measured in %), throughput (measured

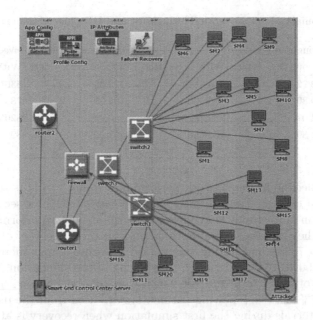

Fig. 3. DDoS Attack Against Control Server

in bits/sec) and the DB query response time (measured in bytes/sec). The base line simulation result shows what the network performance should look like when there is no attack against the network.

Table 1. Smart Meter Network Server Performance and CPU Utilization Simulation Data.

Metric	Server Performance (Sec)		CPU Utilization (%)	
Time(sec)	Without DoS Attack	With DoS Attack	Without DoS Attack	With DoS Attack
t = 0	0.00953	0.0163	0.2838	0.5892
t = 3060	0.01285	0.0169	0.5159	0.8022
t = 8280	0.01286	0.0164	0.5476	0.8332
t = 17820	0.01310	0.0164	0.5534	0.8313

The graph of the throughput metric, was sinusoidal throughout the simulation, as seen in Figs. 4(c) and (d). The throughput of the baseline network never went downward spiral at any time. However, an assumption was made during the simulation which is - the failure of the link between router2 and the control server because of the DDoS attack. This failure caused the control server to become unavailable, and this had an impact on the resilience of the network. Based on the analysis carried out, the attack started at $t = 0$ s with the throughput being 5303.644, which shows that the network was performing optimally. However,

Table 2. Smart Meter Network Throughput and DB Query Simulation Data.

Metric	Throughput (bits/sec)		DB Query Traffic Received (bytes/sec)	
Time(sec)	Without DoS Attack	With DoS Attack	Without DoS Attack	With DoS Attack
t = 0	2842.22	5303.64	2773.33	5361.777778
t = 3060	2769.80	1035.90	5104.99	7857.777778
t = 8280	2454.07	739.18	5440.45	8205.92
t = 17820	2584.89	1648.66	5498.60	8225.71

we noticed a decline in the network performance from $t = 1440$ s to $t = 4680$ s, the throughput decreased significantly from 2071 to 956.625bits/sec respectively. The decrease in throughput is synonymous with an under-performing network which means the network is not at optimal performance. Recovery of the network started at $t = 7380$ s and during this period, the throughput increased gradually from 718.90 to 1648.657bits/sec till the end of the simulation. To calculate the SI metric of cyber resilience, we ran the simulation twice with recovery at t3780 s and t7380 s. The following parameters are used from the data obtained at different intervals during the first simulation when recovery is at t7380:

$$TSP_1(t_2520) = 2283.84, SP_1(t_2520) = 1243.081, SI = 18546325.38$$
$$TSP_1(t_3780) = 2557.273, SP_1(t_3780) = 847.556, SI = 30467156.94$$
$$TSP_1(t_4680) = 2681.478, SP_1(t_4680) = 690.601, SI = 35477428.14$$
$$TSP_1(t_7380) = 2547.85, SP_1(t_7380) = 718.90, SI = 32591889$$

The data shows that at random times t0, t1440, t4680 and t17820, the network metrics; server performance (Fig. 4(B)) and CPU utilization (Fig. 4(A)) are slightly higher during the attack than in the baseline scenario. However, metrics such as throughput are much higher during the attack as seen in Figs. 4(C) and (D). There is a ripple effect of the impact of the DoS attack on the network metrics which serves as a basis for the SI resilience metric. From Table 2, it is observed that there is a 0.3% increase in the CPU utilization of the DoS attack scenario at t3060 and t8280. The increase signifies an increase in the systemic impact on the control server's performance via CPU utilization. Also, based on the peculiarity of DDoS attack against any communication network, legitimate packets from smart meter nodes are either dropped or delayed as is the case during this simulation. Almajali et al. [28] emphasized the characteristics of a resilient network communication infrastructure, the authors mentioned that performance requirements are not compromised even during a cyber attack, and this is true when evaluated against the cyber resilience definition proposed in this paper.

For the systemic impact metric, the performance of the network is dependent on recovery. This means that different recovery times lead to varying network performance after an attack. For example, as seen with the SI calculations with the first simulation where recovery was late (at $t = 7380$ s), the SI was high which signified degradation of the network performance. However, for the second

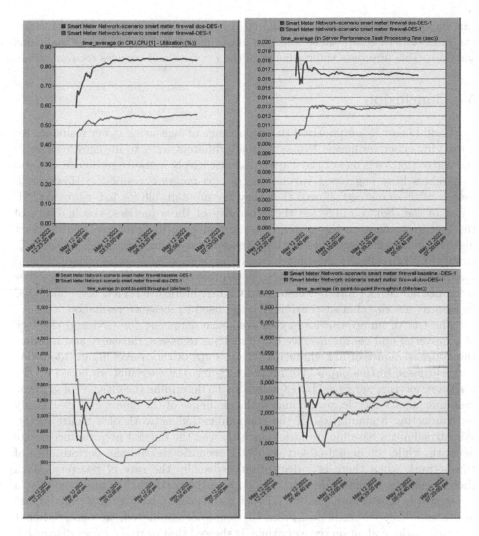

Fig. 4. Average results of DDoS attack and baseline simulation. From top left to bottom right, A) The average time for CPU utilization B) The average time for server performance C) The average time for throughput, late recovery D) The average time for throughput, fast recovery.

simulation, recovery time was early (at $t = 3780$ s), hence the impact of the attack on the network was minimal which showed the network was more resilient. Conclusively, the higher the systemic impact, the lower the resilience. This means that a resilient CNI network is one in which recovery operations are deployed shortly after an attack which reduces the systemic impact significantly.

In addition, in situations where the attack is not prevented at the firewall but impacts the performance of the server, the concepts of resilience namely adaptability and recoverability are leveraged. The redundant servers configured can be spurned up to provide required services to clients while also blocking the indicators of compromise and scanning the network for traces of malicious software. This improves the resilience of the network and reduces recovery time.

5   Conclusion

Kott and Linkov [5] emphasized the importance of measuring cyber resilience for improving cyber resilience. While there are different ways to measure resilience, the use of metrics is one of the ways to quantitatively measure resilience. Several researchers have suggested various metrics to measure resilience. However, a review of these metrics showed that they are not suitable for IoT-enabled CNI. Some of the shortcomings are the generality of these metrics, the inability of the metrics to capture the system's performance during runtime, and abstract mathematical definitions that are hard to apply to evaluate the resilience of IoT-enabled CNI practically. Resilience capacities, such as absorptive, adaptive, and recoverability capacities, were used to determine the suitability of existing cyber resilience metrics for internet-connected CNI. A literature review was conducted to identify metrics that are currently being used to measure resilience.

The lack of an appropriate cyber resilience definition for CNI and the lack of a universal and comprehensive list of metrics to assess, measure, and improve the cyber resilience of IoT-enabled CNI are some of the research gaps identified and addressed in this paper. We proposed cyber resilience metrics based on the resilience metrics suggested in [18] and [17]. To determine the effectiveness of the systemic impact metric, we evaluated the resilience of the smart grid case study by conducting a simulation of the communication network of a smart meter. We carried out a baseline scenario which showed the normal performance of the network, while the denial-of-service attack scenario showed the performance of the network when there is a disruption, especially the rate of recovery. With these scenarios, we measured the resilience of the network. We observed that a low systemic impact indicates high cyber resilience, and a high systemic impact indicates low cyber resilience. From the scenarios simulated, we observed that resilience is dependent on recovery time. It showed that during a cyber disruption to a CNI network, the recovery rate is a function of determining the system's resilience. A high recovery time indicates a highly resilient system, and a low recovery time means a low resilient system.

In the process of carrying out this research work, we identified some challenges and limitations that we encountered which could be considered as future research areas for the cyber resilience of IoT-enabled CNI. One of the challenges is CNI data collection, especially regarding modeling and simulation. Specific datasets, such as the interdependency of CNI components topologies, are needed for detailed CNI modeling. The lack of publicly available precise dataset is a challenge that can impair the correct representation of CNI systems and networks, which can affect the cyber resilience assessment. We noticed that open-source data about different aspects of CNI are not readily available for academic purposes. This can be attributed to privacy and confidentiality issues. However, a standardized data methodology and collection can be proposed for future work. The seconf future research ares on cyber resilience, could be focused on designing tools that can model IoT-enabled CNI and assess cyber resilience. Moreover, the simulation carried out in this research focused on static data analysis, i.e., the DoS attack started at $t0$ and ended at around $t4780$. We aim to focus on the dynamic cyber attack scenarios for future work.

References

1. Hammoudeh, M., et al.: A service-oriented approach for sensing in the internet of things: intelligent transportation systems and privacy use cases. IEEE Sens. J. **21**(14), 15753–15761 (2020)
2. Lloyd's Register Foundation. Foresight review of cyber security for the industrial IoT (2020). Accessed 7 Nov 2023
3. Gunduz, M.Z., Das, R.: Analysis of cyber-attacks on smart grid applications. In: 2018 International Conference on Artificial Intelligence and Data Processing (IDAP), pp. 1–5. IEEE (2018)
4. Muncaster, P.: Nine in 10 CNI providers damaged by cyber-attacks (2019). Accessed 8 Nov 2023
5. Walshe, M., Epiphaniou, G., Al-Khateeb, H., Hammoudeh, M., Katos, V., Dehghantanha, A.: Non-interactive zero knowledge proofs for the authentication of IoT devices in reduced connectivity environments. Ad Hoc Netw. **95**, 101988 (2019)
6. Eplphaniou, G., Mohammad Hammoudeh, H., Yuan, C.M., Ani, U.: Digital twins in cyber effects modelling of IoT/CPS points of low resilience. Simul. Model. Pract. Theory **125**, 102744 (2023)
7. Critical national infrastructure (2023). Accessed 8 Nov 2023
8. Bodeau, D., Graubart, R., Picciotto, J., McQuaid, R.: Cyber resiliency engineering framework. MTR110237, MITRECorporation (2011)
9. Cutter, S.L., et al.: Disaster resilience: a national imperative. Environ. Sci. Policy Sustain. Dev. **55**(2), 25–29 (2013)
10. Ross, R., Pillitteri, V., Graubart, R., Bodeau, D., McQuaid, R.: Developing cyber resilient systems: a systems security engineering approach. Technical report, National Institute of Standards and Technology (2019)
11. Mihalache, S.F., Pricop, E., Fattahi, J.: Resilience enhancement of cyber-physical systems: a review. In: Mahdavi Tabatabaei, N., Najafi Ravadanegh, S., Bizon, N. (eds.) Power Systems Resilience. PS, pp. 269–287. Springer, Cham (2019). https://doi.org/10.1007/978-3-319-94442-5_11
12. Murino, G., Armando, A., Tacchella, A.: Resilience of cyber-physical systems: an experimental appraisal of quantitative measures. In: 11th International Conference on Cyber Conflict (CyCon), vol. 900, pp. 1–19. IEEE (2019)
13. Cassottana, B., Roomi, M.M., Mashima, D., Sansavini, G.: Resilience analysis of cyber-physical systems: a review of models and methods. Risk Anal. **43**(11), 2359–2379 (2023)
14. Fang, Y.-P., Pedroni, N., Zio, E.: Resilience-based component importance measures for critical infrastructure network systems. IEEE Trans. Reliab. **65**(2), 502–512 (2016)
15. Francis, R., Bekera, B.: A metric and frameworks for resilience analysis of engineered and infrastructure systems. Reliab. Eng. Syst. Saf. **121**, 90–103 (2014)

16. Hassell, S., et al.: Evaluating network cyber resiliency methods using cyber threat, vulnerability and defense modeling and simulation. In: MILCOM 2012-2012 IEEE Military Communications Conference, pp. 1–6. IEEE (2012)
17. Hossain-McKenzie, S., Lai, C., Chavez, A., Vugrin, E.: Performance-based cyber resilience metrics: an applied demonstration toward moving target defense. In: IECON 2018-44th Annual Conference of the IEEE Industrial Electronics Society, pp. 766–773. IEEE (2018)
18. Haque, M.A., De Teyou, G.K., Shetty, S., Krishnappa, B.: Cyber resilience framework for industrial control systems: concepts, metrics, and insights. In: 2018 IEEE International Conference on Intelligence and Security Informatics (ISI), pp. 25–30. IEEE (2018)
19. Segovia, M., Rubio-Hernan, J., Cavalli, A.R., Garcia-Alfaro, J.: Cyber-resilience evaluation of cyber-physical systems. In: 2020 IEEE 19th International Symposium on Network Computing and Applications (NCA), pp. 1–8. IEEE (2020)
20. Bruneau, M., et al.: A framework to quantitatively assess and enhance the seismic resilience of communities. Earthq. Spectra **19**(4), 733–752 (2003)
21. Cimellaro, G.P., Reinhorn, A.M., Bruneau, M.: Framework for analytical quantification of disaster resilience. Eng. Struct. **32**(11), 3639–3649 (2010)
22. Vugrin, E.D., Warren, D.E., Ehlen, M.A.: A resilience assessment framework for infrastructure and economic systems: quantitative and qualitative resilience analysis of petrochemical supply chains to a hurricane. Process Saf. Prog. **30**(3), 280–290 (2011)
23. Hamilton, D.L., Walker, I.D., Bennett, J.K.: Fault tolerance versus performance metrics for robot systems. Reliab. Eng. Syst. Saf. **53**(3), 309–318 (1996)
24. Smart grids. Accessed 7 Oct 2023
25. What are the basic components of smart grids (2021). Accessed 7 Oct 2023
26. Matey, A.H., Danquah, P., Koi-Akrofi, G.Y., Asampana, I.: Critical infrastructure cybersecurity challenges: IoT in perspective. Int. J. Netw. Secur. Appl. **13**(4), 41–58 (2021)
27. Zheng, L., Yang, H.: Unlocking the Power of OPNET Modeler. Cambridge University Press, Cambridge (2012)
28. AlMajali, A., Viswanathan, A., Neuman, C.: Analyzing resiliency of the smart grid communication architectures under cyber attack. In: CSET (2012)

SCI – Secure Cryptographic
Implementation

Towards Discovering Quantum-Threats for Applications Using Open-Source Libraries

Xiaodong Ye[1]($\boxtimes$), Teik Guan Tan[2], and Jianying Zhou[1]

[1] Singapore University of Technology and Design, Singapore, Singapore
sgsheldon.ye@gmail.com, jianying_zhou@sutd.edu.sg
[2] pQCee Pte Ltd., Singapore, Singapore

Abstract. The improvement of quantum computing poses a significant threat to cryptographic security. It enables the potential utilization of quantum algorithms to compromise classical cryptographic algorithms, such as public-key cryptosystems including RSA (Rivest-Shamir-Adleman), DH (Diffie-Hellman), and ECC (Elliptic Curve Cryptography). Currently, many applications rely on open-source libraries for various functionalities, including quantum-vulnerable public-key cryptographic implementations to achieve data confidentiality, integrity, and authenticity. So how can we determine the exposure of such applications to quantum attacks? In this paper, we study the use of open-source cryptographic algorithms for the Python programming language. We first identify the most widely used Python cryptographic libraries and then establish a simple keyword-based approach to identify the potential use of vulnerable RSA, ECC, and DH algorithms within Python applications. Notably, the extracted set of 11 keywords demonstrates precision and accuracy exceeding 90%.

Keywords: Quantum Threat · Public Key Cryptography · Vulnerability Detection · Keyword Analysis · Open Source

1 Introduction

In the cryptographic landscape, both asymmetric and symmetric encryption algorithms are pivotal for data security. However, the increasing feasibility of quantum computers poses a significant threat to these classical cryptographic algorithms. Quantum algorithms, such as Shor's algorithm, are known to break widely-used asymmetric encryption schemes like RSA, ECC, and DH, while Grover's algorithm can reduce the security of symmetric encryption methods by speeding up the search for the correct key. This paper focuses on three public key cryptography algorithms and sets the stage for future studies to explore the quantum resilience of a broader spectrum of cryptographic algorithms, including symmetric ones.

Public key (asymmetric) cryptography is considered the anchor of trust in modern cryptographic systems. The use of classical cryptographic algorithms

© The Author(s), under exclusive license to Springer Nature Switzerland AG 2024
M. Andreoni (Ed.): ACNS 2024 Workshops, LNCS 14586, pp. 283–302, 2024.
https://doi.org/10.1007/978-3-031-61486-6_17

like RSA, ECC, and DH has long been relied upon for secure data transmission and protection. This raises concerns about their continued security, as these algorithms may no longer provide the level of protection they once did. The situation is further complicated due to the reliance on open-source libraries used by many applications to implement critical cybersecurity functionality. When called at the API level, it may not be obvious that an underlying vulnerable cryptographic algorithm is used.

Recognizing the urgency of the situation, the industry has made considerable progress in implementing advanced Post-Quantum Cryptography (PQC) techniques [11]. At this point of writing, the NIST post-quantum cryptography standardization process has already identified three digital signing algorithms and one key exchange algorithm to replace the classical algorithms of RSA, ECC, and DH [1]. Despite these developments, the industry still faces challenges with legacy systems and scalability. When implementing PQC, the lack of compatibility between existing system architecture and new technologies, alongside insufficient documentation and code readability, presents challenges for updates and improvements. Moreover, given that these systems typically support critical business functions, replacing or upgrading them can entail risks and costs, impeding timely updates within the industry. Additionally, scalability issues, including hardware limitations, software design constraints, and financial considerations, restrict the comprehensive replacement of originally classical algorithms within the industry.

Therefore, open-source cryptographic libraries containing classical cryptographic algorithms that are vulnerable to quantum attacks will continue to be utilized in the meantime. For users, it may not be apparent whether their applications, which utilize open-source libraries, are exposed to quantum threats. As a consequence, it is vital to initiate the discovery process as early as possible. There is an urgent need to identify these vulnerabilities and conduct a comprehensive analysis of commonly used open-source cryptographic libraries to evaluate their resilience against quantum attacks. This issue falls within the purview of the Common Weakness Enumeration (CWE) framework, specifically under the classifications of CWE-327 (Use of a Broken or Risky Cryptographic Algorithm) and CWE-1395 (Dependency on Vulnerable Third-Party Component).

This paper primarily focuses on Python programming language, due to its widespread usage. According to the PYPL (PopularitY of Programming Language) index as of July 2023, Python holds the top rank with a share of 27.43%, while Java ranks second with a share of 16.19%. Furthermore, we find that applying keyword-based static analysis is an effective way to detect whether there are risky or vulnerable algorithms in the application. The keyword-based method streamlines the detection process by swiftly pinpointing instances where susceptible cryptographic functions are invoked, allowing for timely intervention and mitigation strategies. Also, it offers a cost-effective solution, minimizing the need for extensive code reviews or exhaustive system overhauls. Organizations can effectively bolster their defenses against potential quantum-based intrusions by proactively integrating this approach into the development cycle, preserving security. Early detection of potential vulnerabilities is crucial in implementing preemptive measures to safeguard existing systems against quantum attacks that may be launched by malicious individuals or organizations.

Contributions

In this paper, we conducted a comprehensive analysis of the popularity of open-source asymmetric encryption libraries and identified 14 prominent libraries. The results of the analysis indicate that the "cryptography," "paramiko," and "rsa" libraries emerge as the three most widely used libraries, collectively representing over 80% of the total usage among the top 14 ranked libraries.

We next propose an efficient keyword-based static analysis method for detecting vulnerabilities in applications that utilize potentially risky cryptographic algorithms. By analyzing the invocation methods and key functions within the code and conducting many experiments, we arrive at a carefully selected set of 11 keywords. They are: "65537", "ec", "rsa", "ecc", "ecdsa", "dh", "p256", "p384", "p521", "KexGex" and "KexGroup". This set achieves an accuracy rate of 91.57% and a precision rate of 92.79% in detecting the usage of RSA, ECC, and DH algorithms.

Organization

The structure of the remaining paper is outlined as follows. Section 2 provides background information on the threat posed by quantum algorithms to classical encryption and related work on the detection of API misuses. Section 3 details the methodology, which includes analyzing the popularity of Python libraries and conducting a keyword analysis. Section 4 presents the detection of potential vulnerabilities to quantum attacks, along with experimental results and key findings. Section 5 proposes potential future research directions, while Sect. 6 provides a summary of the study.

2 Background

2.1 Quantum Threat

Beginning with classical algorithms, public key cryptography operates using a pair of keys: the public key, which can be shared with others, and the private key, which must be kept confidential. These keys are generated in a manner that ensures messages encrypted with the public key can only be decrypted using the corresponding private key. The security of these algorithms is grounded in the computational complexity of solving mathematical problems. Take RSA [18], ECC [16] and DH [3,15] algorithms for examples, RSA utilizes the integer factorization problem (IFP), ECC is based on the elliptic curve discrete logarithm problem (ECDLP), and DH relies on the discrete logarithm problem (DLP).

However, with the invention of Shor's algorithm in 1994 [21], a quantum algorithm now exists that can factorize large numbers into their prime factors in polynomial time. Subsequently, Shor's publication in 1999 delves deeper into the quantum algorithms for prime factorization and discrete logarithms [22].

In 2001, a team successfully demonstrated Shor's algorithm [24]. Their paper documented the experimental implementation of Shor's algorithm using seven qubits, resulting in the successful factorization of the number 15.

In a paper by Elie and Nicolas (2021), an advancement in factoring integers is presented, indicating the possibility of factoring a 2048-bit RSA integer in 177 days [8]. This accomplishment was achieved using 3D gauge color codes with a threshold of 0.75% and a processor comprising 13436 physical qubits. This work underscores the ongoing strides in quantum computing, demonstrating the potential of specialized error-correcting techniques and hardware scaling in addressing complex cryptographic challenges.

Additionally, Craig and Martin (2021) conducted research suggesting the potential factorization of 2048-bit RSA integers within 8 h, using 20 million noisy qubits [7]. This research highlights the rapid advancement of quantum hardware and the ongoing development of strategies to mitigate the challenges posed by inherent quantum system noise. Despite the challenges associated with noisy qubits, the promising timeline for factoring 2048-bit RSA integers underscores the potential of quantum computers to revolutionize the fields of encryption and security.

Recently, IBM's "Osprey" has emerged as one of the most advanced quantum computers available, having 433 qubits [2]. This milestone marks a notable technological leap, indicating quantum computers hold the potential to tackle problems previously considered infeasible or computationally intensive.

Not only classical asymmetric encryption algorithms but also symmetric encryption algorithms can be vulnerable to quantum attacks. There are two quantum algorithms used to attack symmetric encryption algorithms. The first is Simon's algorithm [23], which can be used to target the discrete logarithm problem in symmetric cryptographic systems, including block ciphers. In 2017, Thomas Santoli demonstrated two applications of Simon's algorithm for breaking classical symmetric cryptosystems [19]. Another notable algorithm is Grover's algorithm, also known as the quantum search algorithm, which provides a quadratic speedup in breaking symmetric encryption keys [10]. In 2016, Markus Grassl estimated the quantum resources required to carry out an attack on AES using Grover's algorithm [9].

It is also important to note that the successful implementation of quantum algorithms depends on the availability of large-scale, error-corrected quantum computers. Notably, challenges persist due to the limitations and disruptions caused by quantum computing application noise.

2.2 Related Work

A keyword-based detection method to determine the exposure of applications to quantum attacks has not yet been implemented, despite its simplicity and direct approach, which holds the potential for effectiveness in vulnerability detection.

This approach is valuable in component analysis for identifying vulnerabilities in third-party and open-source components.

In 2017, a group of researchers detected the vulnerabilities in IoT firmware by searching keywords in the CVE list [26]. Web applications, such as WordPress and phpMyAdmin, along with web servers like Apache, are primarily susceptible to logical vulnerabilities, including XSS (cross-site scripting), injection attacks, and authentication bypass issues. Clement Elbaz introduced a technique for the automatic extraction of keywords from 0-day vulnerabilities, using updated data from the CVE vulnerability database [4]. The method only relies on the free-form description of vulnerabilities, without using their metadata. As reliable and practical low-noise quantum computers have not yet been developed, the existing dependable encryption algorithms have not been classified as risky in the CVE vulnerability database. This implies that without relevant descriptions of vulnerabilities, analysis becomes unfeasible. Widely used methods for detecting significant keywords from extensive textual data or documents are discussed by Zaffar Ahmed Shaikh [20]. He also analyzed techniques for topic detection and tracking, with a specific emphasis on the automated identification of pivotal terms. These techniques also hold applicability in detecting vulnerabilities in the field of cybersecurity. A review of quantum cybersecurity, published by Faruk MJ in 2022, utilized a keyword-based method to explore the potential intersection between Quantum Computing and Cybersecurity [5]. Researchers conducted the study using specific keywords and provided guidelines for future research.

Apart from keyword detection, current mainstream detection techniques such as taint analysis have been extensively studied. These methods conduct in-depth analysis based on specific rules or protocols. Compared to keyword detection, they are more specific.

To achieve high-precision detection of cryptographic vulnerabilities in Java programs, Sazzadur Rahaman (2019) developed a static analysis tool called "CRYPTOGUARD" [17]. They manually analyzed around one thousand Apache alerts and created 112 test cases based on the results, and the precision reached 98.61%. Another tool developed by Stefan Kruger (2019), "CrySL", allows cryptography experts to specify the secure usage of the cryptographic libraries they provide [13]. It can detect cryptographic misuse in Java and Android applications based on predefined rules with a precision of 92.6%. A paper published by Wenqing Li (2022) also introduced a static analysis detector "CryptoGo" that uses static taint analysis techniques for automated, large-scale analysis of cryptographic API misuses in Go [14]. It has an accuracy of 95.5%. It uniquely integrates cryptographic algorithm classification into cryptographic misuse detection for the first time. The underlying rules of this tool are derived from 12 cryptographic rules, based on an in-depth analysis of API arguments in the latest official Go cryptographic library. Another tool, introduced by Anna Katharina Wickert (2021), known as "LICMA", represents the first multi-language analysis tool designed to detect cryptographic misuses [25]. It includes rules specifically crafted to identify common cryptographic misuses across five different Python libraries as well as the standard Java library. Miles Frantz (2022) also introduced "Cryptolation", a static analysis tool designed to scan Python code [6].

This tool operates in a depth-insensitive and path-insensitive manner, achieving a 98% precision rate. It employs 19 rules to identify several popular attack vectors found within the OWASP top 10. They used Abstract Syntax Trees (ASTs) to check if the imports in the code match the specified rules.

Nevertheless, existing static analysis tools use the rules, to be specific, these tools depend on understanding whether they incorporate vulnerable algorithms or misuses. This verification involves either static or dynamic analysis of particular code repositories or libraries. In the context of quantum threats, algorithms previously deemed safe are now considered vulnerable. Consequently, a targeted reanalysis using these tools is essential. In our approach, we adopted a similar idea for extracting keywords to formulate rules. We derived these rules from the top three most popular libraries and verified them across applications using the top 14 popular libraries. Similar to "Cryptolation", our approach also uses ASTs, but with a different focus. We employed ASTs primarily to create keyword databases and extract sets of keywords. These extracted keywords are then established as rules for detection purposes.

3   Methodology

3.1   Problem Farming

Our objective is to derive an acceptable set of keywords from these libraries to accurately detect the usage of quantum-vulnerable cryptographic algorithms in real-world applications. Considering the diversity in different programming languages, this study concentrates on analyzing applications coded in the widely adopted Python language. Because of the variety and quantity of open-source libraries, we selected the library with high usage for analysis. Specifically, the popularity and community adoption can be determined by analyzing the interesting characteristics of the library. Then, the keywords for detecting the usage of specific algorithms across different applications can be extracted from the source code of libraries.

Our methodology to extract keywords from the source code of cryptographic libraries is rooted in practicality and the understanding of how programmers interact with these resources. Typically, developers engage with open-source cryptographic libraries through their interfaces, which are marked by specific function names, method calls, and other elements. These elements naturally form the "keywords" in our source code analysis. Focusing on these interfaces allows us to target the most probable points of interaction between the application code and the cryptographic algorithms, creating a keyword set that's not only broadly applicable-given the shared interfaces across many libraries for similar functions-but also far more efficient than conducting a line-by-line analysis of entire libraries.

Eventually, the results can be evaluated to demonstrate the performance of the selected keywords. Our methodology for detecting vulnerabilities is shown in Fig. 1.

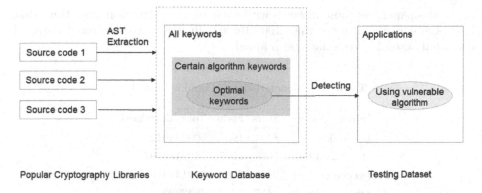

Fig. 1. Methodology for Keywords-based Detection.

3.2 Data Preparation

We first investigated the usage of Python's public key cryptography libraries. However, the retrieved information from Google was limited, lacking specific rankings and reports. To gather more data, we used the Python Package Index (PyPI) to search specifically within the "cryptography" directory under the "security" category. But the data is still unsatisfying. The query returned 1170 projects, with sorting options limited to relevance and date last updated.

Further investigation reveals two useful data sources, Libraries.io and the official Python guides, both of which provide public datasets.

Libraries.io. Libraries.io is a comprehensive platform that facilitates open-source software discovery and dependency management. It acts as a centralized catalog, indexing data from 7,393,803 packages from 32 package managers. Among the statistics it provides, data on stars and forks are particularly interesting, as they contribute to the analysis of a library's popularity.

Python Guides. The Analyzing PyPI package download section provides download statistics of packages. The dataset can be found in Google BigQuery which is a serverless and cost-effective enterprise data warehouse that works across clouds and scales. And it can also be found on "pepy.tech", a website that offers a user-friendly interface. We queried the last 36 months of history for the specific library.

The "Stars" represents the number of times a repository has been liked, indicating the level of recognition and attention it receives from users. A higher number of stars implies a greater degree of endorsement and popularity for the library. On the other hand, "Forks" represents the number of branches created by other users based on the original repository. This quantity also serves as an indicator of the library's popularity and the number of derivative projects built upon it.

In this paper, we chose libraries with asymmetric encryption algorithms that have a star count of more than 100. Table 1 illustrates the collected data. 14 commonly used libraries have been found.

Table 1. Characteristics of Popular Libraries

Library Name	Stars	Forks	Total downloads
paramiko	8404	1934	990944012
cryptography	5668	1577	3823186597
pycrypto	2419	656	272147389
pycryptodome	2417	447	464220244
pycryptodomex	2417	447	690692866
pynacl	949	220	1075460496
ecdsa	831	300	238789509
pyopenssl	808	414	1459994214
rsa	423	100	4378036628
oscrypto	288	46	511899475
asn1crypto	287	128	1212988117
py-ecc	152	81	2372602
python-pkcs11	120	54	301018
pyelliptic	117	59	320220

We utilized a powerful static analysis tool called CodeQL to process the data we obtained and create several databases. The tool is capable of converting code into a database in the form of an Abstract Syntax Tree (AST), which is the foundation for CodeQL's functionality. The created databases, containing all the relevant keywords, are generated from the AST databases. The AST structure provides useful terms like "ImportMember", "Attribute", "Call", "IntegerLiteral", "ClassDef", and "FunctionDef" to build the keyword database. We can extract the relevant keywords by querying each term. It is necessary to extract all keywords according to AST and then remove duplicates to obtain the complete keywords database, as there may be slight variations in the extracted keywords for each item. During the testing phase, a major problem may arise where the extraction of keywords may unintentionally display all files that are dependent on Python. To resolve this issue, a possible solution is to hardcode the file path into the query. By implementing this, only the keywords from the specific project will be displayed during the query, which will effectively filter out any irrelevant results. For example, the query code below shows that "Attribute" can be used to retrieve the attribute name.

```
// CodeQL Query Sample
import python
from Attribute attribute
where
    attribute.getLocation().getFile().toString().matches("D:/testcode/%")
select
    attribute.getParentNode().getParentNode().getAChildNode(),
    attribute.getAChildNode() as attributeChildNode,
    attribute.getName() as attributeName,
    attribute.getLocation().getFile().toString() as fileLocation
```

In our research, we extracted keywords by first placing the target files for keyword extraction into a specific folder. We then used the CodeQL command to generate a database file. Next, in the QL plugin of VS Code, we added the generated database and added the source to the workspace. Taking "test.py" as an example, we could access the full code with a simple left-click. To understand the structure and components of the code more deeply, we utilized the "view AST" feature in the sidebar of QL, which displayed the complete Abstract Syntax Tree (AST) of the code file. The extraction of keywords was then carried out by examining the symbols enclosed in brackets within the AST, in conjunction with the use of specific query statements.

Moving from extracting keywords to creating a complete keywords database, the complete keywords database can be derived in CSV file by executing the CodeQL queries. We used built-in features like "Remove Duplicates" (found under the "Data" tab in Excel) to directly remove duplicates from the selected column.

3.3   Data Analysis

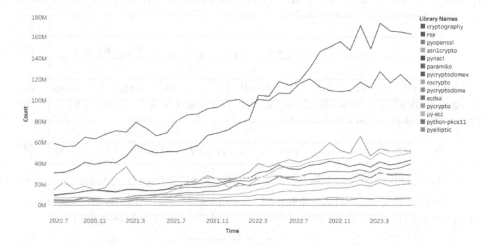

Fig. 2. Trends in Download Statistics Across Different Libraries

Popularity Analysis. Based on the analysis of download counts over the past three years, as depicted in Fig. 2, the "cryptography" library and the "rsa" library have higher download volumes compared to the other libraries. It is worth noting that the remaining libraries consistently maintain download volumes of around 50 million or below per month. Notably, libraries such as "py-ecc", "python-pkcs11", and "pyelliptic" exhibit lower download counts, as depicted by the bottom line in the graph.

However, due to the inconsistent scales of the three dimensions, namely stars, forks, and total downloads, the rankings differ across each dimension. To address this, the TOPSIS (Technique for Order Preference by Similarity to Ideal Solution) method can be applied [12]. It is a multi-criteria decision analysis technique that enables comprehensive evaluation of alternative solutions by simultaneously considering multiple evaluation criteria. Through data standardization, original data is rescaled, and the best and worst indicators for each criterion are identified. Using these as reference points, the method computes the Euclidean distance for each alternative solution, producing a score. Higher scores indicate greater proximity to the ideal solution.

The TOPSIS process involves the following steps. First, we construct a decision matrix A, where each row represents an indicator and each column represents a library.

$$A = (x_{ij})_{m*n}, m = 14, n = 3, i = 1, 2, ..., m, \ j = 1, 2, ..., n \tag{1}$$

Then, we normalize it to obtain a normalized decision matrix B.

$$B = r_{ij} = \frac{x_{ij}}{\sqrt{\sum_{k=1}^{m} x_{kj}^2}} \tag{2}$$

Next, we create a weighted normalized decision matrix C by assigning weights to each indicator based on their relative importance. The sum of the weights assigned to each indicator equals 1.

$$C = (t_{ij})_{m*n} = (r_{ij})_{m*n} * w_j, \ w_j = \frac{W_j}{\sum_{k=1}^{n} W_k}, \ \sum_{i=1}^{n} w_i = 1 \tag{3}$$

After that, we determine the best solution S_b, which is the maximum value of each indicator across all libraries, and the worst solution S_w, which is the minimum value of each indicator.

$$S_b = \{\max(t_{ij}| \ i = 1, 2, ..., m. \ j = 1, 2, ..., n)\} \equiv \{t_{bj}| \ j = 1, 2, ..., n\} \tag{4}$$

$$S_w = \{\min(t_{ij}| \ i = 1, 2, ..., m. \ j = 1, 2, ..., n)\} \equiv \{t_{wj}| \ j = 1, 2, ..., n\} \tag{5}$$

We then calculate the Euclidean distances of each library in the three-dimensional space to the best solution d_{ib} and the worst solution d_{iw}.

$$d_{ib} = \sqrt{\sum_{j=1}^{n} (t_{ij} - t_{bj})^2} \tag{6}$$

$$d_{iw} = \sqrt{\sum_{j=1}^{n}(t_{ij} - t_{wj})^2} \tag{7}$$

Using the distances to the best and worst solutions, we compute the score s_{ib} for each library. This score is obtained by dividing the distance of each library's point in three-dimensional space to the positive ideal solution by the sum of the distances to the positive ideal solution and the negative ideal solution. This step transforms the high-dimensional distance into a two-dimensional score, with higher scores indicating libraries that are closer to the optimal solution and, therefore, indicating higher popularity.

$$s_{ib} = \frac{d_{iw}}{d_{iw} + d_{ib}} \tag{8}$$

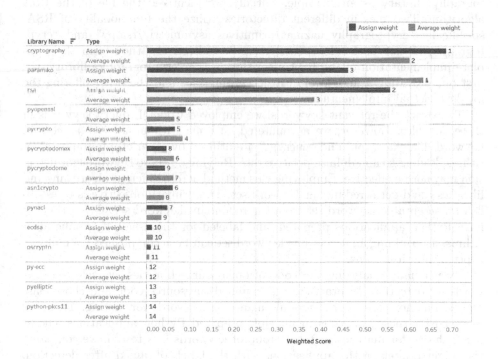

Fig. 3. Library Popularity with Various Weight Assignments

Ranking the scores can determine the popularity of each library. It is important to note that each score represents distances in different two-dimensional spaces, not within the same reference frame. Therefore, the summation of each column does not necessarily equal 1.

Total downloads represent usage more relevantly, followed by the number of forks which also indicates usage, while the quantity of stars primarily reflects popularity but may not directly correspond to actual usage. We first assigned equal weights to the three dimensions for comparative observation. Then, we reassigned weights w_j based on the importance of usage: 0.5 to total downloads, 0.3 to forks, and 0.2 to stars. The results can be presented in Fig. 3. Under both weight configurations, the libraries "cryptography", "paramiko", and "rsa" consistently maintain their positions in the top 3. These three libraries collectively account for over 80% of the total usage among the top 14 ranked libraries.

Keywords Analysis. In open-source cryptography libraries, code related to specific algorithms is often associated with particular keywords. It is because programming practices and standards ensure code readability and maintainability, making it easy to use for developers. Following this, keywords relevant to specific functionalities can be categorized by analyzing the source code.

We analyzed the keywords related to the RSA algorithm in the "cryptography" library as an example. Initially, we identified the file of the RSA algorithm. Two files in different directories utilize the functionality of RSA, specifically "cryptography/hazmat/primitives/asymmetric/rsa.py" and "cryptography/hazmat/backends/openssl/rsa.py". Collectively, they form the complete implementation of the RSA algorithm in the "cryptography" library, the first one providing a high-level abstraction interface and the other offering the low-level actual implementation.

To extract the relevant keywords, we employed CodeQL query keywords in these two files. However, we encountered an issue with broadness, as certain keywords like "decrypt" and "encrypt" are utilized by other cryptography algorithms, leading to a high false positive rate. Relying on these keywords for detection may not be effective. Employing this method across different algorithms and libraries could get a redundant keyword set. The primary objective is to establish an acceptable keyword set from the redundant keyword set. Given that we have Python applications prepared, and labeled for the usage of specific algorithms, determining an acceptable keyword set can be accomplished via multiple experimental iterations.

By manually analyzing the code of open-source libraries, we selected keywords for detection. In practice, we examined the source code and chose class names, function names, and module names as keywords for testing. Then, we searched for these keywords in multiple prepared Python applications, checking each one for matches. After a group of keywords was tested, we compared the original labels of the applications with the labels obtained after detection. This allowed us to calculate precision and accuracy. After each experiment, we reassessed the false positives and false negatives to identify new keywords that might prove useful. Additionally, we conducted experiments to eliminate redundant keywords, thereby streamlining our keyword set for effectiveness.

4   Experiment

In this paper, we used the source code of the top 3 popular libraries as the training set to derive an acceptable keywords set for detection. We next collected over 200 Python applications for testing purposes. The complete testing set consists of three main parts: test cases derived from the library, functionality models for each algorithm, and special cases. The experiments involved the detection of the usage of RSA, ECC, and DH within the top 3 libraries, along with the validation of the selected keywords set. Note the detection method disregards case sensitivity.

4.1   Detecting the Usage of RSA, ECC, DH in Top 1 Library

Taking the "cryptography" library as an initial example, we used 88 keywords extracted from this library, which are relevant to the algorithms, as identifiers. Additionally, we assumed that the three simplest keywords, "rsa", "dh" and "ec" were sufficiently effective.

The results in Table 2 demonstrate the performance of the keyword-based method in detecting the usage of RSA, DH, and ECC algorithms in applications. However, relying on all relevant keywords cannot achieve the goal, solely relying on a single keyword, while more efficient, still appears to be inadequate for detecting the implementation of public key-based algorithms within Python applications. We focused on analyzing the satisfactory keywords set for detecting each algorithm in the following experiments.

Table 2. Performance of Keyword-Based Detection in Top 1 Library

Evaluation Metrics	Identifier: 88 keywords	Identifier: 3 keywords
Accuracy	46.67%	89.77%
Precision	42.86%	90.91%
Recall	100.00%	83.33%
F1 Score	60.00%	86.96%
Specificity	11.11%	94.23%

4.2   Detecting the Usage of RSA in Top 3 Libraries

The results in Table 3 indicate that using a single keyword "rsa" is insufficient. It has been concluded that the keywords "RSAKey" and "65537" are also necessary through analyzing the source code and conducting experiments. The number 65537 is commonly used as the public exponent in RSA encryption due to its efficiency in modular exponentiation and its strong security properties as a prime number. The accuracy has increased from 88.46% to 95.63%, while precision has improved from 88.46% to 90.70%, and recall has risen from 60.53% to 92.86%, and F1 score has increased from 71.88% to 91.76%.

Table 3. RSA Detection in Top 3 Libraries

Evaluation Metrics	Identifier: 1 keyword	Identifier: 3 keywords
Accuracy	88.46%	95.63%
Precision	88.46%	90.70%
Recall	60.53%	92.86%
F1 Score	71.88%	91.76%
Specificity	97.46%	96.61%

4.3   Detecting the Usage of ECC in Top 3 Libraries

The findings indicate that the use of a single keyword "ec" results in an accuracy rate of 92.95%, but the recall rate is only 59.09%. Therefore, we identified five keywords for detection: "ec", "ECDSAKey", "KexNistp256", "KexNistp384", and "KexNistp521". In cryptographic terms, "ec" stands for import modular, whereas "ECDSAKey" refers to the Digital Signature Algorithm that employs elliptic curve cryptography. The keywords beginning with "KexNist" denote key exchange algorithms that utilize the NIST standardized elliptic curves. These curves are particularly designed to ensure secure cryptographic key exchange. With this set of keywords, the accuracy rate improved from 92.95% to 97.44%., precision increased from 86.67% to 90.91%, and recall improved from 59.09% to 90.91%. Moreover, the F1 score increased from 70.27% to 90.91%. See Table 4.

Table 4. ECC Detection in Top 3 Libraries

Evaluation Metrics	Identifier: 1 keyword	Identifier: 5 keywords
Accuracy	92.95%	97.44%
Precision	86.67%	90.91%
Recall	59.09%	90.91%
F1 Score	70.27%	90.91%
Specificity	98.51%	98.51%

4.4   Detecting the Usage of DH in Top 3 Libraries

The results show consistent findings. See Table 5. Using a single keyword "dh" for detection achieves an accuracy of 91.72%. However, the recall is only 47.62%. We next obtained a set of 7 keywords, which improved the accuracy from 91.72% to 96.79%, precision from 83.33% to 89.47%, recall from 47.62% to 85%, and the F1 score from 60.61% to 87.18%. The other 6 keywords are "KexGex", "KexGexSHA256", "KexGroup1", "KexGroup14", "KexGroup14SHA256", and "KexGroup16SHA512". Keywords starting with "KexGex" refer to key exchange algorithms that use the Diffie-Hellman group exchange mechanism. On the other hand, "KexGroup" designates specific Diffie-Hellman algorithms that use predefined prime moduli for secure key exchange between clients and servers.

Table 5. DH Detection in Top 3 Libraries

Evaluation Metrics	Identifier: 1 keyword	Identifier: 7 keywords
Accuracy	91.72%	96.79%
Precision	83.33%	89.47%
Recall	47.62%	85.00%
F1 Score	60.61%	87.18%
Specificity	98.53%	98.53%

4.5   Validation on Selected Keywords Set

By analyzing the algorithms used in each library and summarizing the experimental results, Table 6 is generated with detection metrics. The set of 15 keywords can be used to detect the usage of RSA, ECC, and DH algorithms in the top 3 libraries. Moreover, by optimizing the extraction process for the 15 precise-matched keywords, an extraction of 11 keywords was achieved, refer to Table 7. A combination of exact matching and containment matching techniques was employed for detection.

Table 6. Detection Keywords Set for Top 3 Libraries

Algorithms	Cryptography	Paramiko	RSA
RSA	rsa	RSAKey	65537 rsa
ECC	ec	ECDSAKey KexNistp256 KexNistp384 KexNistp521	
DH	dh	KexGex KexGexSHA256 KexGroup1 KexGroup14 KexGroup14SHA256 KexGroup16SHA512	

Our analysis of the matching rules is as follows. To minimize the occurrence of false positives from the keywords "ec" and "65537" using containment matching, we subjected them to exact matching. We also included the keyword "ecc" to enhance accuracy since it implies "ec". Since both "rsa" and "RSAKey" contain the keyword "rsa", we used a containment relationship for "rsa". For "ECD-SAKey" and "RSAKey", we utilized the extracted features "ecdsa" and "rsa" respectively as keywords. To increase the probability of detection, we transformed the keywords "KexNistp256", "KexNistp384" and "KexNistp521" into the features "p256", "p384" and "p521" respectively. These feature parts are more commonly used, thus increasing the likelihood of detection. We utilized a containment relationship for "KexGex" by extracting the common part from "KexGex" and "KexGexSHA256". Similarly, we condensed "KexGroup1", "KexGroup14", "KexGroup14SHA256," and "KexGroup16SHA512" into the common feature "KexGroup" for containment matching.

Among these keywords, aside from the easily understood simple keywords, there are also "p256", "p384", and "p512". These three keywords refer to the bit lengths of elliptical curves in the NIST's Key Exchange. "KexGex" is a class name found in the code for the DH key exchange algorithm. Similarly, "KexGroup" is also part of a class name within the DH algorithm. These parameters determine the strength and method of the key exchange process.

Table 7. Optimized Keywords Set with 11 keywords

Exact match	65537	ec								
Contain match	rsa		ecc	ecdsa	dh	p256	p384	p521	KexGex	KexGroup

To validate the effectiveness of the 11 optimized keywords extracted from the top 3 public key cryptography libraries, we used 2 sets of keywords to detect applications utilizing algorithms from the top 3 libraries. We first applied exact match using a set of 15 keywords and then applied matching rules using an optimized set of 11 keywords. We manually constructed a new testing set, which includes test files from open-source libraries and some code examples. This set comprised 156 applications, corresponding to 156 Python files, with 70 positive samples and 86 negative samples. The results revealed a total of 69 positive samples, comprising 64 true positive samples and 5 false positive samples. Additionally, there were 87 negative samples, consisting of 81 true negative and 6 false negative samples. The results in Table 8 indicate that the optimized keyword set has a similar performance.

Table 8. Detection on Specific Algorithms in Top 3 Libraries

Evaluation Metrics	Identifier: 15 keywords	Identifier: 11 keywords
Accuracy	92.95%	92.95%
Precision	92.75%	92.75%
Recall	91.43%	91.43%
F1 Score	92.09%	92.09%
Specificity	94.19%	94.19%

We proceeded to test applications that used the 4th to the 14th most popular libraries. Our new testing set comprised 166 applications, out of which 108 used

RSA, ECC, or DH algorithms, while 58 applications used these libraries without utilizing these three algorithms. The experimental results revealed a total of 111 positive cases, including 103 true positives and 8 false positives. Additionally, there were 55 negative cases, consisting of 49 true negatives and 6 false negatives. The results in Table 9 demonstrate the efficacy of the keyword-based detection method.

Table 9. Detection on Specific Algorithms in Top 4 to 14 Libraries

Evaluation Metrics	Identifier: 11 keywords
Accuracy	91.57%
Precision	92.79%
Recall	94.50%
F1 Score	93.64%
Specificity	85.96%

The accuracy of 91.57% indicates that the model can correctly classify the majority of samples overall. With a precision of 92.79%, the model has a high likelihood of being correct when predicting an application involving certain algorithms. A recall of 94.50% signifies that the model can identify most applications containing specific encryption algorithms. An F1 score of 93.64% indicates a balance between precision and recall for the model. A specificity of 85.96% implies that the model also performs relatively well on negative class samples.

The experimental results indicate that the set of keywords extracted from the top 3 popular open-source libraries, when used to detect if applications contain quantum-vulnerable algorithms utilizing the top 14 popular libraries, achieved accuracy and precision of over 90%.

However, Keyword-based detection methods cannot achieve 100% accuracy and precision. In some cases, dynamic code analysis techniques are necessary to make determinations. For example, in cases where a vulnerable algorithm is imported but not used or with self-designed algorithms, keyword-based detection alone is insufficient. Additionally, in some scenarios, when an open-source code repository is forked and substantial modifications are made to function names, it can potentially evade keyword-based detection methods.

5 Future Work

While the current demonstration showcases promising results in identifying cryptography algorithms susceptible to quantum attack, there are several avenues for future research and improvement.

Further investigation into advanced techniques for keyword extraction could yield more comprehensive and accurate sets of keywords. This may involve exploring Natural Language Processing (NLP) methods and Machine Learning (ML) methods to select the optimal set of keywords.

The focus of this paper is on specific algorithms and libraries, but a more comprehensive understanding could be achieved by expanding the scope to include a wider range of cryptography algorithms and programming languages. This would involve analyzing all cryptography algorithms that could potentially be vulnerable to quantum attacks, as well as evaluating commonly used programming languages to create a comprehensive keyword database for detection. This method can be used not only for asymmetric algorithms but also to include specific keywords related to the implementation of symmetric algorithms, with a particular focus on the configuration parameters that define key sizes. By identifying these parameters in the code, we can assess not only the usage of symmetric algorithms but also determine the integer values of the key sizes being used. In addition, the CVE framework could be updated to keep track of and document security vulnerabilities and attacks related to quantum computing.

Ensuring the safety of our systems not only involves detecting potential threats but also implementing effective defense mechanisms. However, there are challenges to this, such as the limitations of legacy applications and situations where using NIST-compliant post-quantum cryptography algorithms may not be practical or efficient. It is crucial to propose workable solutions that strike a balance between security, practicality, and economic considerations. Further research can explore ways to achieve this balance.

6   Conclusion

The paper begins by exploring potential vulnerabilities under quantum attack and the current state of quantum technology from the perspective of quantum cryptography. We discussed potential security vulnerabilities combining CWE-327 and CWE-1395. The usage of classical cryptography algorithms might be vulnerable. We then compared several tools in vulnerability detection, they primarily employ rules for detection purposes. Considering the nature of quantum risks, the prompt and ongoing refinement of detection techniques is essential to effectively address and mitigate potential quantum threats.

Subsequently, we proposed an efficient keyword-based detection scheme for identifying such potential vulnerabilities. We investigated 14 open-source encryption libraries and their popularity by using the TOPSIS method. This investigation identified applications that utilize the "cryptography," "paramiko," and "rsa" libraries as the most widespread. Collectively, they represent 80% of the applications that use the popular cryptography library. These applications are potentially prime targets susceptible to quantum attacks.

Using the classical public key cryptography algorithms RSA, ECC, and DH as examples, the security of these algorithms is based on the complexity of computing the mathematical problems. However, quantum algorithms can accelerate computations, potentially compromising their security. We conducted the static analysis with the CodeQL tool on the top 3 popular libraries to extract keywords for detecting the usage of these three algorithms. This process ultimately yielded a set of 11 keywords. By applying precise and inclusive matching rules, the proposed method efficiently determines the exposure of Python applications to quantum attacks. We tested 166 Python applications, the accuracy rate reached 91.57%, the precision rate achieved 92.79%, and the recall rate reached 94.50%.

The paper presents a practical approach for detecting potential vulnerabilities under quantum attacks in applications that use other programming languages. The comprehensive analysis and data processing workflow highlight the effectiveness of the keyword-based detection method.

References

1. Alagic, G., et al.: Status report on the third round of the nist post-quantum cryptography standardization process. US Department of Commerce, NIST (2022)
2. Choi, C.Q.: Ibm's quantum leap: the company will take quantum tech past the 1,000-qubit mark in 2023. IEEE Spectr. **60**(1), 46–47 (2023)
3. Diffie, W., Hellman, M.: New directions in cryptography. IEEE Trans. Inf. Theor. **22**(6) (1976)
4. Elbaz, C., Rilling, L., Morin, C.: Automated keyword extraction from one-day vulnerabilities at disclosure. In: NOMS 2020-2020 IEEE/IFIP Network Operations and Management Symposium, pp. 1–9. IEEE (2020)
5. Faruk, M.J.H., Tahora, S., Tasnim, M., Shahriar, H., Sakib, N.: A review of quantum cybersecurity: threats, risks and opportunities. In: 2022 1st International Conference on AI in Cybersecurity (ICAIC), pp. 1–8. IEEE (2022)
6. Frantz, M., Xiao, Y., Pias, T.S., Yao, D.D.: Poster: precise detection of unprecedented python cryptographic misuses using on-demand analysis. In: The Network and Distributed System Security (NDSS) Symposium (2022)
7. Gidney, C., Ekerå, M.: How to factor 2048 bit RSA integers in 8 hours using 20 million noisy qubits. Quantum **5**, 433 (2021)
8. Gouzien, É., Sangouard, N.: Factoring 2048-bit RSA integers in 177 days with 13 436 qubits and a multimode memory. Phys. Rev. Lett. **127**(14), 140503 (2021)
9. Grassl, M., Langenberg, B., Roetteler, M., Steinwandt, R.: Applying grover's algorithm to AES: quantum resource estimates. In: Takagi, T. (ed.) PQCrypto 2016. LNCS, vol. 9606, pp. 29–43. Springer, Cham (2016). https://doi.org/10.1007/978-3-319-29360-8_3
10. Grover, L.K.: A fast quantum mechanical algorithm for database search. In: Proceedings of the Twenty-Eighth Annual ACM Symposium on Theory of Computing, pp. 212–219 (1996)
11. Hekkala, J., Muurman, M., Halunen, K., Vallivaara, V.: Implementing postquantum cryptography for developers. SN Comput. Sci. **4**(4), 365 (2023)
12. Hwang, C.L., Lai, Y.J., Liu, T.Y.: A new approach for multiple objective decision making. Comput. Oper. Res. **20**(8), 889–899 (1993)
13. Krüger, S., Späth, J., Ali, K., Bodden, E., Mezini, M.: Crysl: an extensible approach to validating the correct usage of cryptographic apis. IEEE Trans. Software Eng. **47**(11), 2382–2400 (2019)
14. Li, W., Jia, S., Liu, L., Zheng, F., Ma, Y., Lin, J.: Cryptogo: automatic detection of go cryptographic API misuses. In: Proceedings of the 38th Annual Computer Security Applications Conference, pp. 318–331 (2022)

15. Merkle, R.C.: Secure communications over insecure channels. Commun. ACM **21**(4), 294–299 (1978)
16. Miller, V.S.: Use of elliptic curves in cryptography. In: Williams, H.C. (ed.) CRYPTO 1985. LNCS, vol. 218, pp. 417–426. Springer, Heidelberg (1986). https://doi.org/10.1007/3-540-39799-X_31
17. Rahaman, S., et al.: Cryptoguard: high precision detection of cryptographic vulnerabilities in massive-sized java projects. In: Proceedings of the 2019 ACM SIGSAC Conference on Computer and Communications Security, pp. 2455–2472 (2019)
18. Rivest, R.L., Shamir, A., Adleman, L.: A method for obtaining digital signatures and public-key cryptosystems. Commun. ACM **21**(2), 120–126 (1978)
19. Santoli, T., Schaffner, C.: Using simon's algorithm to attack symmetric-key cryptographic primitives. arXiv preprint arXiv:1603.07856 (2016)
20. Shaikh, Z.A.: Keyword detection techniques: a comprehensive study. Eng. Technol. Appl. Sci. Res. **8**(1), 2590–2594 (2018)
21. Shor, P.W.: Algorithms for quantum computation: discrete logarithms and factoring. In: Proceedings 35th Annual Symposium on Foundations of Computer Science, pp. 124–134. IEEE (1994)
22. Shor, P.W.: Polynomial-time algorithms for prime factorization and discrete logarithms on a quantum computer. SIAM Rev. **41**(2), 303–332 (1999)
23. Simon, D.R.: On the power of quantum computation. SIAM J. Comput. **26**(5), 1474–1483 (1997)
24. Vandersypen, L.M., Steffen, M., Breyta, G., Yannoni, C.S., Sherwood, M.H., Chuang, I.L.: Experimental realization of shor's quantum factoring algorithm using nuclear magnetic resonance. Nature **414**(6866), 883–887 (2001)
25. Wickert, A.K., Baumgärtner, L., Breitfelder, F., Mezini, M.: Python crypto misuses in the wild. In: Proceedings of the 15th ACM/IEEE International Symposium on Empirical Software Engineering and Measurement (ESEM), pp. 1–6 (2021)
26. Xie, W., Jiang, Y., Tang, Y., Ding, N., Gao, Y.: Vulnerability detection in IoT firmware: a survey. In: 2017 IEEE 23rd International Conference on Parallel and Distributed Systems (ICPADS), pp. 769–772. IEEE (2017)

Pushing AES-256-GCM to Limits: Design, Implementation and Real FPGA Tests

Peter Cibik[iD], Patrik Dobias[iD], Sara Ricci[iD], Jan Hajny[(✉)][iD], Lukas Malina[iD], Petr Jedlicka[iD], and David Smekal[iD]

Department of Telecommunications, Brno University of Technology, Technicka 12, Brno, Czech Republic
{xcibik00,xdobia13,ricci,hajny,malina,xjedli23,smekald}@vutbr.cz

Abstract. In this paper, we present the optimization of the AES-256-GCM encryption algorithm for high-speed security solutions based on Field Programmable Gate Arrays (FPGA). We discuss strategies and techniques to achieve the perfect balance between compactness and high throughput, aiming at applications with data rates over 100 Gbps. Using the presented optimizations, we were able to reduce the number of LUTs by 50% and FFs by 85% compared to reference implementation without any effect on security. Moreover, our resulting implementation achieves a frequency of only 200 MHz, which is very practical for a real deployment on existing chips, compared to many purely theoretical solutions that already exist in the literature. Besides the description of optimization techniques, we also present results from implementation on real hardware in a real IP network. All components were not only simulated but also deployed on real FPGA-enabled network cards based on Xilinx UltraScale+ chips. In particular, the performance of network packet encryption was measured in a real physical network, with high-speed data generators and network components. Therefore, we consider our results highly relevant not only for designers but also practitioners seeking cutting-edge solutions for fast networks.

Keywords: Acceleration · AES-256 · GCM · Cryptography · FPGA · Hardware implementation · Quantum-Resistant Cryptography · Optimization

1 Introduction

AES-256-GCM offers a powerful combination of authenticated encryption and high-performance throughput, making it an essential encryption standard for secure data transmission and storage. It is worth mentioning that with the threat of a quantum computer, the quantum-safe AES-256-GCM strengthens its importance. However, integrating AES-256-GCM into complex FPGA solutions presents challenges in terms of size and throughput optimization.

This work is supported by the Ministry of the Interior of the Czech Republic under Grant VJ01010008.

The main bottleneck in AES-GCM implementations is usually the computation of the authentication tag. This prompted several authors to focus on the optimization of this part. For instance, Zhou *et al.* [12] proposed to improve the throughput of Galois field multiplication by using pipelined Karatsuba multipliers. Using this approach, the authors removed all critical paths during tag computation, and the bottleneck moved to the AES. On the other hand, Henzen and Fichtner [2] aimed to achieve a throughput of 100 Gb/s for ethernet applications. To the best of our knowledge, they were the first to propose the use of 4 parallel cores instead of a single core in architecture design which are needed for the expected results.

This article explores the optimization of AES-256-GCM for FPGA implementations to meet the requirements of compactness and high-throughput data processing. By addressing these challenges, we enable the seamless integration of AES-256-GCM into secure solutions that demand real-time data handling while maintaining the necessary security levels, for example, in more complex quantum-safe solutions.

2   Related Work

Hardware-accelerated AES-GCM implementation has been explored in several research papers and documents. In addition to the FPGA-based hardware implementations, there are also a few works focusing on hardware-acceleration using Application Specific Integrated Circuits (ASIC). For the sake of completeness, we summarize previous hardware implementations on both of these digital design platforms even though these two technologies differ in some aspects. In general, ASIC offers more room for optimization and its elementary hardware units are logical gates instead of LookUp Tables (LUTs), FlipFlops (FFs), Block Random Access Memory (BRAM) and Digital Signal Processing (DSP) blocks in FPGA. The above implies that a comparison of two implementations each from another platform cannot be accurate.

Table 1. Comparison of existing AES measurements on FPGA.

Paper	HW Platform	Network	IL	LBT	LBP
[4]	Virtex-4	Not Tested	✓	NA	NA
[12]	Virtex-5	Not Tested	NA	✓	NA
[2]	Virtex-5	Not Tested	NA	✓	NA
[1]	UltraScale	Not Tested	NA	✓	NA
[9]	Virtex-7	Not Tested	✓	✓	NA
Our work	UltraScale+	Tested	✓	✓	✓

states for "initial latency", LBT for "latency before tag", LBP for "latency between packets" - you can find more about latency in Sect. 6.1

In Table 1, we highlight the main differences among the existing AES measurements on FPGAs. In 2005, Yang *et al.* [10] presented a high-speed hardware architecture for GCM mode. Their throughput-optimized ASIC implementation of AES-GCM achieves a throughput of 34 Gb/s, running at a frequency of 271 MHz. It is important to note that their implementation has an initial latency that impacts the throughput. In 2006, Hodjat and Verbauwhede [3] explored the area-throughput trade-off for an ASIC implementation of the AES scheme. In particular, they concentrate on the optimization of the critical path of the AES cipher to optimize the throughput achieving 30 to 70 Gb/s in a 0.18 μm standard cell library. In this case, the initial delay is not considered.

In 2007, Lemsitzer *et al.* [4] explored a design-space pipelined AES-GCM implementation optimized for FPGA. They described 4 implementations with different degrees of parallelism. Using the highest degree of parallelism, they reached a theoretical throughput of 15.3 Gb/s at the maximum frequency of 140 MHz on a Virtex-4 FPGA. Their theoretical throughput is lower than in our proposal and has lower throughput to utilisation ratio. In fact, if we consider a multiple instances implementation as in our case, they would reach 175k LUTs rather than 80k LUTs in our implementation. In the same year, Zhou *et al.* [11] presented an AES architecture implementation that was then improved in a follow-up article [12] in 2009. In the latter, they address high-throughput implementations with a focus on the AES engine and the modular multiplication and their complexity on FPGA platforms. They achieve a throughput of 31 Gb/s at 243 MHz and 39 Gb/s at 305 MHz on Virtex-4 and Virtex-5 FPGAs. They use only one instance of AES-GCM compared to other works, with a loss of parallelization. Moreover, the latency between the last ciphertext transaction and the tag is of 11 cycles. For instance, if we consider a plaintext of 1024b that requires 8 cycles to be processed, their implementation would have a throughput reduced by 55% with respect to the theoretical, that they report. In 2010, Henzen and Fichtner [2] presented four pipelined AES-GCM cores parallelization that reached the speed required for the new Ethernet standard. Their implementation has a throughput of 119.3 Gb/s at 233 MHz on Virtex-5 FPGA. The authors do not consider the latency during the key changes with a loss of performance for real package size data.

In 2015, Buhrow *et al.* [1] proposed a scalable AES-GCM architecture for highly parallel implementations on FPGAs. Their implementation can process multiple separately-keyed packets simultaneously every clock cycle. They achieve a throughput of 482 Gb/s at 314 MHz on Xilinx Virtex Ultrascale FPGA and 800 Gb/s in a system comprising multiple FPGAs, respectively. Although they presented a theoretical throughput, they took into account the latency. With respect to our implementation, they need a higher power of h for large data. For instance, for 1500B of data, their implementation computes h^{93} instead of h^9 as in our case. In 2017, Vliegen *et al.* [9] maximize the throughput of side-channel-protected AES-GCM implementations on an FPGA. They obtain a throughput of 15.24 Gb/s on a high-end Virtex-7 device. The only drawback of this implementation is a big initial latency of 71 cycles.

Note that all of the works above present only theoretically computed throughput derived from the maximum frequency reported after implementation and the data interface's bit size. However, as noted in [1], these computations typically overlook crucial delays (such as initial delay, delays between the last ciphertext and tag, and delays between packets) that can significantly affect the actual throughput. To address this, we decided to implement the full system and perform tests on physical devices to demonstrate the real-world throughput achieved by our implementation.

2.1 Contribution

In this article, we present three AES-256-GCM implementations all suitable for post-quantum deployment due to the quantum-safe size of the key. Our implementation is specifically optimized to reach the highest performance which means achieving the wire-speed processing of packets with allocate appropriate hardware resources, based on limited resources on board and necessity to fit in with other parts of whole solution, and low initial latency. To do so, we propose a new architecture with parallelization on the GCM level with only one AES-256-GCM pipeline.

In short, to compare with competitors, we built an effective AES-256-GCM to fit in a more complex encryptor solution based on FPGA, due to achieved low utilization, reaching up to 100 Gbps throughput running on 200 MHz frequency able to adapt to the fluctuation of data flow thanks to low initial latency as described in details following sections.

The rest of this article is organized as follows. Section 3 reviews the original implementation of an AES-256-GCM, and Sect. 4 states the design goals of our optimization and describes the proposed architecture. Section 5 describes our experimental setup and Sect. 6 reports the results. The final section contains the conclusions.

3   Preliminary

Our entry point was an implementation of AES-256-GCM that follows the articles [5, 7]. The original implementation had six parallel pipelines of the AES-256-GCM and the distributional logic. Parallelization was done at the packet level, which means that each packet goes to a specific pipeline and is processed as a whole. The architecture of the parallel pipelines is shown in Fig. 9 and the inner structure of the AES_GCM_ENCRYPTION component is shown in Figure 10 of Appendix 7.

The original architecture used six standalone parallel pipelines of AES-256-GCM, each of them consisting of one separate key-expansion component, one Galois Multiplication (GM) component, one AES encryption core component, and FIFO components. So, in total, we have:

- Key expansion component - six times.
- AES encryption core component - six times.
- Galois Multiplication component - six times,

in six separate standalone processing pipelines. There is no parallelization on the GCM level.

4   Proposed Architecture

Our AES-256-GCM implementation needs to be suitable for the post-quantum environment. Therefore, to easily fit on a chip with the other primitives of the system and achieve the expected throughput of the whole solution, we focused on refactoring and its optimization. There are three main goals to be achieved:

- **Initial latency** - how many clock cycles does it take from the first valid input to the first valid output.
- **Utilization (size)** - how many resources does the implementation consume, especially LUTs, FFs, and BRAM.
- **Throughput** - how fast can we process (encrypt/decrypt) network data. We would like to achieve wire speed (100 Gbps).

Achieving better results in all of these three domains can be challenging because they are mutually exclusive in certain matters.

All components are written in VHDL (2008) language. Synthesis and FW generation were provided by Vivado 2019.1 targeting a frequency of 200 MHz for Xilinx FPGA chip xcvu9p-flgb2104-2-i.

Since GCM mode uses AES encryption only, components can be used for both AES-256-GCM Encryption and Decryption only by switching one generic input. The presented results are the same for both of them.

By applying different optimisation techniques like pipelining, resource sharing, effective implementation, pre-computing of the values etc., described it the following sections, there is an ability to achieve better results without the impact on security of the implementation.

4.1   Core Components

To achieve our goals, we had to first implement core components, that are used in the AES-GCM, namely AES encryption, key expansion, and Galois field multiplication, efficiently. We have implemented fully-pipelined key expansion and AES components that enable encryption in each cycle even when encryption key changes. Moreover, by setting generic parameter on these components, it is possible to modify number of registered rounds, to allow changes in area vs timing costs. Implementation of most processes during round is straightforward on the hardware, as it requires mostly permutation and XOR operations. The critical process is SubBytes, that represents nonlinear operation. We have implemented it using the substitution S-BOX table, that is stored in block RAM. For Galois Field multiplication, we have implemented also pipelined digit-parallel multiplier that uses four parallel multipliers with 32 bit digit size and their output is concatenated and reduced to 128 bits.

4.2 Plain Implementation

In this stage, we redesigned the whole implementation of the AES-256-GCM (published in [5,7]) from parallelization per packet to parallelization inside GCM mode [8]. We decided to use four AES core components for data encryption, when at the beginning of packet processing, two of them are also used for `initial block` and `h` computation. The new component architecture is shown in Fig. 11 of Appendix 7. In comparison with the original one (see Sect. 3 for more details), only one processing pipeline is used instead of six.

The main idea behind this new implementation is to allow for the processing of all 512 bit transactions in each cycle. To achieve this, four parallel branches are used inside of the `gcm` component, as one `AES core component` can process 128 bits at a time. The branches can be additionally divided into two parts, encryption, and tag computation. Parallelization of the encryption phase is straightforward due to the fact that AES-256 is in counter mode. A challenge lies in generating the tag. We decided to use eight tag parts, which are `XOR`ed at the end, resulting in the GCM tag. This is done using `GM` components in the parallel branches. These components have one clock cycle delay; so to permit continuous processing of all four branches we had to use eight tag parts. To allow this, we needed higher powers of h, particularly h^8 in the middle of the packet and $h^9, h^8, \ldots, h^3, h^2$ for the last two 512 bits transactions. If the packet is shorter than 1024 bits, we only need lower powers.

This design can process 512 bits of input and, respectively, produce 512 bits of output each clock cycle after an initial latency and pipeline filling.

Cumulatively, plain `gcm` implementation consists of the following parts:

- Key expansion component - once,
- AES encryption core component - four times,
- Galois Multiplication component - five times.

The AES encryption core components are set as `ENC_PIPELINE = 1`, which means that after each AES round is registered. Four GM components are used for the tag computation, and the last one is used for `h` powers computation.

For this design, we are using a fixed order of how and which `h` powers are computed, and compute all of them before starting the tag computation data processing, respectively. Based on that, the highest power of h needed is h^9.

Table 2 shows the order and delay of the output produced by the GM component. If a similar value is on both inputs, the output is ready after one clock cycle. On the contrary, different inputs require two clock cycles. Figure 1 shows how the data are processed. Incoming data are processed by four parallel AES encryption core components followed by four parallel GM components to ensure the processing of whole input data with each clock cycle. Only one key expansion component is used.

4.3 Opt1 Implementation

To speed up powers generation of h and reduce the initial latency, in the opt1 implementation, we added two more AES encryption core components. One is

Table 2. h powers generation

Clock cycle	1	2	3	4	5	6	7	8	9	10
GM input a	h	h^2	h^4	h^2	h	h	h	h		
GM input b	h	h^2	h^4	h^4	h^4	h^2	h^6	h^8		
GM output		h^2	h^4	h^8		h^6	h^5	h^3	h^7	h^9

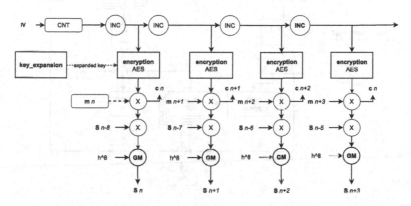

Fig. 1. Abstract scheme of data-processing by gcm plain component

responsible for h computation, and the second one computes the initial block. So the other four components are only used for data processing. We also updated the settings of ENC_PIPELINE = 2 for all AES encryption core components. This means that two rounds are performed each clock cycle. Before that, the data are stored in pipelining register. Moreover, since all AES encryption core components use the same setting, only one key expansion component is used with the same round key, respectively, at the same time. The extended component architecture and how the whole flow works is shown in Fig. 2.

In total, for opt1 implementation, there are:

- Key expansion component - once,
- AES encryption core component - six times,
- Galois Multiplication component - five times.

4.4 Opt2 Implementation

Since h to the power of 9 is not needed for short data, i.e., under 128 B in length, and for starting the data processing, one more optimization could be developed. In particular, we reordered the h powers generation. The new order is shown in Table 3, and also updated the logic to be able to start processing data as soon

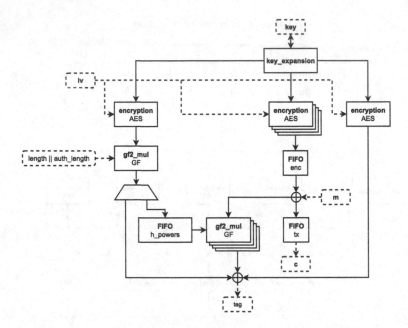

Fig. 2. Gcm internal component interconnection and flow of opt1 and opt2 implementation

Table 3. Updated h powers generation

Clock cycle	1	2	3	4	5	6	7	8	9	10
GM input a	h	h^2	h^4	h	h	h^2	h^5	h		
GM input b	h	h^2	h^4	h^2	h^4	h^4	h^2	h^8		
GM output		h^2	h^4	h^8		h^3	h^5	h^6	h^7	h^9

as the sufficient h power is ready without waiting for the last one. In this way, h powers computed are based on the data length, stopping on the needed one. This leads to an initial latency reduction and a higher throughput for shorter data.

Opt2 implementation is an extension of opt1 implementation, which is described in Sect. 4.3. Note that the amount of internally used components is the same in both implementations, i.e., *Opt1* and *Opt2*.

5   Experimental Setup

To test and benchmark our implementations, we implement the full system - production-like post-quantum encryptor solution which dmeonstrate the use-case where whole communication between client and server, over high-speed network, is secured.

As you can see in Fig. 3, it is based on server with two high-speed smart NICs with the FPGA chip. Each card has one physical Ethernet interface to communicate with the end device, one interface to exchange encrypted data, and one interface to exchange keys for encryption and decryption. Firmware loaded in both FPGAs on the smart NICs consists of subcores for encryption and decryption using AES-256-GCM, key exchange scheme powered by Kyber, ECDH, and (optional) QKD.

The system ensures the exchange and synchronization of the key and subsequently secure communication between end devices.

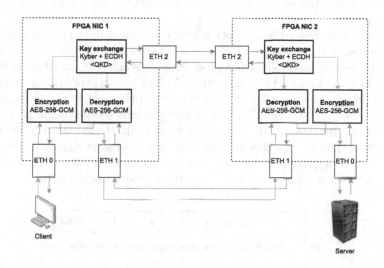

Fig. 3. Block scheme of physical setup during testing and benchmarking.

5.1 Implementation Details

AES encryption core component processes 128 bit data blocks. All our implementations were verified against NIST test vectors[1], with many thousands of test inputs compared against the software golden model implementation in verification and in our demo environment as described above.

6 Experimental Results

There are three main domains where we would like to achieve better results with these re-implementations and optimizations. Each of them has a different measurement setup.

---

[1] https://csrc.nist.gov/Projects/cryptographic-algorithm-validation-program/cavp-testing-block-cipher-modes.

6.1 Latency

The first domain is the Initial Latency (IL). It reflects the number of clock cycles from the first input valid block of data (also with metadata in the same cycle) to the first processed block of data on the output. Therefore, in the lower level of perspective, it is clock cycles amount from metadata_ready and rx_src_rdy=' 1' in the same clock cycle to first tx_src_rdy=' 1'. It is important because the data flow is not constant, there are gaps between packets, etc. so this quantity tells us how flexibly the component can react from state when no data are transmitted, to fill all the internal pipelines and process data from input to output interface. In Fig. 4 compares the results of all four implementations, the original one and our three proposals.

As there is only one AES encryption core component in the original architecture, the initial delay increases for small packet sizes up to 384 b. This is because fewer 128 bit blocks need to be encrypted. From this size, the initial delay is then constant. In plain architecture, the whole 512 b transactions are encrypted, so the initial delay is the same for all packet sizes. In the opt1 implementation, we reduced the initial delay as described in the previous section, so it is still constant for all packet sizes. In the opt2 implementation, the initial delay increases at the start since bigger packets need more h powers to start computing but then drop to a constant delay of 21 cycles. This is because from packet size 1408 b we need to wait only until h^8 is computed to start processing the data.

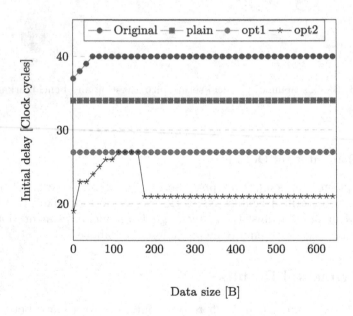

Fig. 4. Comparison of initial delay.

Note that the metadata can be ready sooner than the transferred data. Figure 5 depicts the results in this specific aforementioned situation. This is a between-transactions delay (LBP) with one specific condition. It can be perceived as a period, in clock cycles, between the first and second processed packet resp. from `tag_rdy` of packet n to first `tx_src_rdy` of packet $n + 1$.

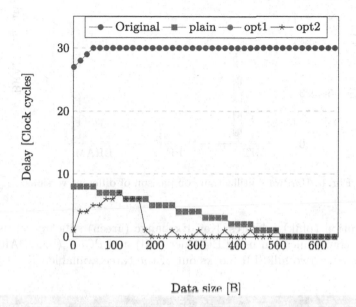

Fig. 5. Comparison of delay after metadata change.

For both latency measurement types, the lowest is for the opt2 implementation. You can see the improvement caused by h powers generation optimization in opt2 compared to opt1.

Additionally, in most related works the latency between the last ciphertext and tag (LBT), together with between-transactions delay, was reported, as it has the biggest impact on throughput when keys are not changed per packet. In all our implementations the latency is 1 clock cycle for the first packet and 0 for all the following packets, as the FIFOs get filled.

6.2   Utilization

The second domain we try to optimize is utilization. A comparison of the after-synthesis results is shown in Fig. 6.

In all our proposed implementations, the number of used LUTs is half in comparison to the original implementation. For FFs, it is seven times less. The amount of used BRAM is affected by the setting of the ENC_PIPELINE for plain, opt1, and opt2 implementations since a higher value leads to the usage of less BRAM resp. moving it to LUTs.

Moreover, in Figure 7, we present the placement of all components in our final system with the gcm op2 architecture. The system consists of Encryption (yellow)

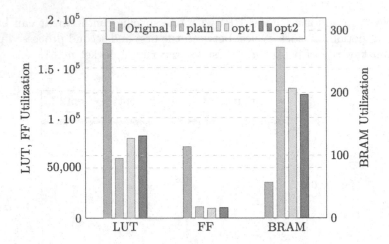

Fig. 6. Hardware utilization comparison of different versions.

and Decryption (pink) subcores, Key Exchange (green) subcore, and subcores to support communication using Ethernet (red) and PCI-E (blue). Altogether, it utilizes almost two full SLR blocks out of the three available.

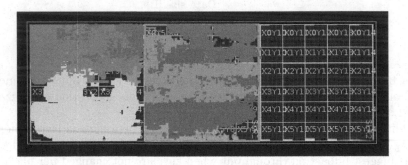

Fig. 7. Components placement after the implementation phase.

6.3 Throughput

The last but most important domain is throughput. We used two methods to measure the throughput in our experimental setup. First, we used the `iperf3` tool, to measure the throughput of real network traffic, then we used network traffic generator firmware. Using the `iperf3` method, we achieved the throughput of 70 Gbps, which was the maximum speed of the given setup without any influence of encryption, as we achieved also the same speed with the client and server directly connected. While using the network traffic generator, the throughput was even higher, with values up to 100 Gbps for bigger packets. The comparison of the measured throughput for all four implementations using the second method is shown in Fig. 8.

In the encryption setup, the packet payload is encrypted, and an authentication tag is appended to it. The packet size in the results is also with an Ethernet header, which is not encrypted. The graph also shows an enhancement for shorter packets caused by opt2. For packets over ∼350 B we achieve a wire speed of 100 Gbps. We can therefore state that for normal distribution and standard Ethernet MTU 1500 B we achieve wire speed.

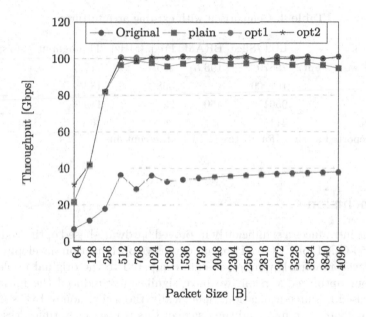

Fig. 8. Throughput comparison of different versions for different packet sizes.

As listed in article [6], based on available resources, a final, opt2 implementation of AES-256-GCM is also suitable for mid-size resp. small FPGA Xilinx boards.

6.4 Comparison

The comparison with other high-speed architectures is shown in Table 4. In this article we present several implementations that gradually apply different optimization steps. The most effective one, opt2 implementation, applying all the optimization parts, achieves maximum theoretical frequency after implementation of 229 MHz, which corresponds to a throughput of 117.3 Gbps. opt2 implementation is comparable with the implementation of [2], with the difference that our implementation uses more LUTs, but less BRAMs. When compared to [12], our implementation has three times higher throughput, so to catch up, they would need to use 3 parallel cores. Compared to [1], our implementation has a lower resource use, but at the cost of lower throughput. It is worth noting that our implementation was optimized to achieve a frequency of 200 MHz as the remaining modules work at that frequency. It should not be difficult to increase the frequency to achieve even higher throughput by using registers on critical paths, but it will lead to increasing the initial latency, and our goal was to achieve wire-speed throughput on 200 MHz frequency with as lowest initial latency and utilization as possible.

Table 4. Comparison with existing architectures.

Work	LUT/Slice	BRAM	Freq. [MHz]	Throughput [Gb/s]
our work - opt2	79879	196,5	229	117.3
[1]	109000	-	358	183.3
[2]	9561*	450	233	119.3
[12]	4115*	59	287	36.7

* Reported as slices for Virtex 5, each slice contains 4 LUTs.

7   Conclusion

Our article introduces a significantly improved hardware-based optimized version of AES-256-GCM for FPGA. Through extensive optimization developments, we have achieved remarkable improvements compared to the original implementation. In our optimized version, we have significantly reduced the initial delay and decreased resource utilization. Specifically, the utilization of LUTs has been reduced by more than half, and the usage of FFs is now seven times less than in the original implementation. With our optimized solution, we have achieved a wire speed of 100 Gbps at a frequency of 200 MHz. This impressive throughput enables the efficient processing of high-volume data in real-time. Additionally, our solution's versatility allows for deployment on mid-size FPGAs, expanding its applicability across a range of systems. These substantial improvements in performance and resource utilization demonstrate the practicality and potential of our optimization for delivering secure and high-performance cryptographic solutions in FPGA-based systems. By enhancing AES-256-GCM, we address the demands of modern secure applications, particularly quantum-resistant ones. In our future work, we will focus on the integration of optimized AES-256-GCM into a post-quantum encryptor that also enables hybrid key establishment based on Crystals-Kyber, ECDH or QKD systems.

Acknowledgement. This work is supported by the Ministry of the Interior of the Czech Republic under Grant VJ01010008.

Appendix A

AES and gcm Component Internal Schemes

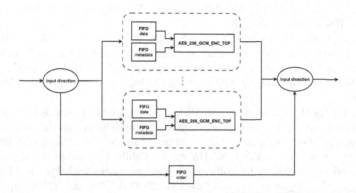

Fig. 9. parallel_top component architecture scheme

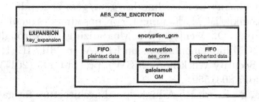

Fig. 10. AES_GCM_ENCRYPTION component architecture scheme

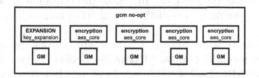

Fig. 11. gcm plain component architecture scheme

References

1. Buhrow, B., Fritz, K., Gilbert, B., Daniel, E.: A highly parallel AES-GCM core for authenticated encryption of 400 GB/s network protocols. In: 2015 International Conference on ReConFigurable Computing and FPGAs (ReConFig), pp. 1–7 (2015). https://doi.org/10.1109/ReConFig.2015.7393321
2. Henzen, L., Fichtner, W.: FPGA parallel-pipelined AES-GCM core for 100g ethernet applications. In: 2010 Proceedings of ESSCIRC, pp. 202–205 (2010). https://doi.org/10.1109/ESSCIRC.2010.5619894

3. Hodjat, A., Verbauwhede, I.: Area-throughput trade-offs for fully pipelined 30 to 70 Gbits/s AES processors. IEEE Trans. Comput. **55**(4), 366–372 (2006). https://doi.org/10.1109/TC.2006.49

4. Lemsitzer, S., Wolkerstorfer, J., Felber, N., Braendli, M.: Multi-gigabit GCM-AES architecture optimized for FPGAs. In: Paillier, P., Verbauwhede, I. (eds.) CHES 2007. LNCS, vol. 4727, pp. 227–238. Springer, Heidelberg (2007). https://doi.org/10.1007/978-3-540-74735-2_16

5. Malina, L., Cibik, P., Jedlicka, P., Smekal, D., Ricci, S., Hrabovsky, J.: Hardware-based cryptographic accelerator for post quantum era. In: 2021 13th International Congress on Ultra Modern Telecommunications and Control Systems and Workshops (ICUMT), pp. 149–155 (2021). https://doi.org/10.1109/ICUMT54235.2021.9631686

6. Malina, L., Ricci, S., Dobias, P., Jedlicka, P., Hajny, J., Choo, K.K.: On the efficiency and security of quantum-resistant key establishment mechanisms on FPGA Platforms, pp. 605–613, January 2022. https://doi.org/10.5220/0011294200003283

7. Malina, L., Smekal, D., Ricci, S., Hajny, J., Cíbik, P., Hrabovsky, J.: Hardware-accelerated cryptography for software-defined networks with P4. In: Maimut, D., Oprina, A.-G., Sauveron, D. (eds.) SecITC 2020. LNCS, vol. 12596, pp. 271–287. Springer, Cham (2021). https://doi.org/10.1007/978-3-030-69255-1_18

8. McGrew, D., Viega, J.: The galois/counter mode of operation (GCM). submission to NIST Modes of Operation Process (2004), https://csrc.nist.rip/groups/ST/toolkit/BCM/documents/proposedmodes/gcm/gcm-spec.pdf, https://csrc.nist.rip/groups/ST/toolkit/BCM/documents/proposedmodes/gcm/gcm-spec.pdf

9. Vliegen, J., Reparaz, O., Mentens, N.: Maximizing the throughput of threshold-protected AES-GCM implementations on FPGA. In: 2017 IEEE 2nd International Verification and Security Workshop (IVSW), pp. 140–145 (2017). https://doi.org/10.1109/IVSW.2017.8031559

10. Yang, B., Mishra, S., Karri, R.: A high speed architecture for galois/counter mode of operation (gcm). Cryptology ePrint Archive, Paper 2005/146 (2005). https://eprint.iacr.org/2005/146, https://eprint.iacr.org/2005/146

11. Zhou, G., Michalik, H., Hinsenkamp, L.: Efficient and high-throughput implementations of AES-GCM on FPGAS. In: 2007 International Conference on Field-Programmable Technology, pp. 185 102 (2007). https://doi.org/10.1109/FPT.2007.4439248

12. Zhou, G., Michalik, H., Hinsenkamp, L.: Improving throughput of AES-GCM with pipelined Karatsuba multipliers on FPGAs. In: Becker, J., Woods, R., Athanas, P., Morgan, F. (eds.) ARC 2009. LNCS, vol. 5453, pp. 193–203. Springer, Heidelberg (2009). https://doi.org/10.1007/978-3-642-00641-8_20

Automated Generation of Masked Nonlinear Components:
From Lookup Tables to Private Circuits

Lixuan Wu[1,2], Yanhong Fan[3(✉)], Bart Preneel[4], Weijia Wang[1,2,3],
and Meiqin Wang[1,2,3]

[1] School of Cyber Science and Technology, Shandong University, Qingdao, China
{mqwang,weijiawang}@sdu.edu.cn, lixuanwu@mail.sdu.edu.cn
[2] Key Laboratory of Cryptologic Technology and Information Security,
Ministry of Education, Shandong University, Jinan, China
[3] Quan Cheng Shandong Laboratory, Jinan, China
yanhongfan@sdu.edu.cn
[4] imec-COSIC, KU Leuven, Leuven, Belgium
bart.preneel@esat.kuleuven.be

Abstract. Masking is considered to be an essential defense mechanism against side-channel attacks, but it is challenging to be adopted for hardware cryptographic implementations, especially for high-security orders. Recently, Knichel et al. (CHES 2022) proposed an automated tool called AGEMA that enables the generation of masked implementations in hardware for arbitrary security orders using composable gadgets. This accelerates the construction and practical application of masking schemes. This paper proposes a new automated tool named AGMNC that can generate masked nonlinear components with much better performance. The effectiveness of AGMNC is evaluated in several case studies. The evaluation results show a significant performance improvement, particularly for the first-order secure SKINNY S-box: saving 41% area, 25% latency, and 49% dynamic power. We achieve such a good result by integrating three key techniques: a new composable AND-XOR gadget, an optimization strategy based on the latency asymmetry feature of the AND-XOR gadget, and an implementation optimization for synchronization. Besides, we use the formal verification tool SILVER and FPGA-based practical experiments to confirm the security of the masked implementations.

Keywords: Side-Channel Analysis · Masking · Composable Gadget

1 Introduction

With the rapid growth of the Internet of Things (IoT), the number of connected devices has increased significantly. IoT devices are attractive targets for a range of attacks; in particular, the easy access to these devices renders them vulnerable to physical attacks. Among these physical attacks, Side-Channel Analysis (SCA) attacks [20,21] have gained significant attention from researchers and

© The Author(s), under exclusive license to Springer Nature Switzerland AG 2024
M. Andreoni (Ed.): ACNS 2024 Workshops, LNCS 14586, pp. 319–339, 2024.
https://doi.org/10.1007/978-3-031-61486-6_19

practitioners due to their ability to extract secret information from the devices without the need for direct access to the internal components. SCA attacks can exploit various physical properties, such as timing [21] and power consumption [20], to extract secret information processed by the device. In response to the severe threat posed by SCA attacks, numerous approaches have been proposed to mitigate this risk. Among approaches, masking [10] has emerged as the most widely studied and deployed countermeasure due to its sound theoretical foundations. For example, the first necessary requirement of a masking scheme is the Ishai-Sahai-Wagner (ISW) d-probing model [17] that ensures that any d internal variables are independently distributed from the secret input.

However, it is still non-trivial to adopt masking in practice, since d-probing security is invalid in the presence of many known physical defaults. For instance, many masking schemes (see, e.g., [15,17] for an incomplete list) were shown to be insecure in hardware. It is mainly because they fall short in resisting glitches that are known to be the most challenging hardware physical default to overcome. In this respect, the glitch-extended probing model [13] has been proposed to formalize glitches.

Although introducing some simple, practical, and formal adversary models has facilitated the design and security verification of masking schemes, designing masking schemes with high-security orders for complex circuits remains challenging due to the high computational cost. Following a divide-and-conquer strategy, researchers have defined some composable security notions that allow large circuits to be constructed by sub-circuits satisfying composability, also known as gadgets. In this way, constructing large circuits is reduced to the construction of small ones satisfying composability. Those security notions include NI [2], SNI [3], PINI [9], and so on. Also, the glitch-extended probing model and composable security notions are also combined. To further promote the practical application of composability, an automation tool called AGEMA was introduced by Knichel et al. [18], which allows designers to generate hardware masked implementation from an unprotected implementation using composable gadgets.

We note that, albeit AGEMA can easily generate masked hardware circuit from a simple but unprotected design, there still exists a large hardware performance gap between masked circuits generated from AGEMA and manually designed ones. In this paper, based on the fact that nonlinear components of the whole circuit are the most complex and difficult part of masking, we propose a software tool AGMNC that takes some architecture-level optimizations into account to reduce the gap.

Major Contributions. This paper has three major contributions:

A New Composable AND-XOR Gadget. There are usually XOR operations between the quadratic terms and linear terms in the Boolean expressions of an S-box. Consider, for example, the Boolean function $f = ab + c$: this function is realized in AGEMA by trivially combining an HPC-AND gadget and XOR operations. The implementation in AGEMA requires the insertion of additional registers in the input path of each share of primary input c to synchronize the output shares. To overcome this disadvantage, we propose an AND-XOR gadget, which considers the HPC-AND gadget and XOR operations jointly. Compared to the trivial combination, the AND-XOR gadget saves $d+1$ registers, where d is the security order: a circuit is secure against attacks or order d if it can resist an attacker that combines d measurements for each trace.

Two Optimizations. In addition to the AND-XOR gadget, AGMNC integrates two key techniques to improve the hardware performance of the masked implementation, namely latency asymmetry and implementation optimization. The latency asymmetry means that the latency from each input port to the output port is different in a gadget. The HPC-AND gadget, for example, has a latency from the input port to the output port of 1 cycle and 2 cycles, respectively. By using the properties of AND-XOR and HPC-AND gadgets, this technique significantly reduces the latency and area of the final implementation. Based on the observation and analysis, we describe a new optimization technique to synchronize the latency of the final implementation. This technique requires fewer registers than synchronization without optimization.

An Automation Tool AGMNC. Based on the previous gadget and key techniques, we have developed a new automation tool AGMNC. The tool takes a look-up table as input and automatically generates the masked circuit. To illustrate the effectiveness of this tool, we apply AGMNC to several S-boxes. The results show a significant improvement in the hardware performance of the masked implementations. More specifically, for the first-order secure SKINNY S-box, AGMNC achieves a maximum reduction of 41%, 25%, and 49% in area, latency, and dynamic power, respectively, compared to AGEMA. Further, we apply the formal verification tool SILVER [19] and FPGA-based practical experiments to confirm the security of the masked implementations.

Paper Organization. We first present some necessary notions in Sect. 2. In Sect. 3, we highlight a new gadget and two key techniques applied in AGMNC, including the AND-XOR gadget, the latency asymmetry feature and the implementation optimization. To further evaluate the efficiency of AGMNC, Sect. 4 instantiates several S-boxes and full ciphers as case studies. In Sect. 5, we offer theoretical and experimental security analysis for the final masked implementations generated by AGMNC. We conclude our work in Sect. 6.

2 Preliminaries

2.1 Boolean Masking

We denote a binary random variable with lower-case italic x, the i-th share of a variable with x_i. A capital $X(\in \mathbb{F}_2^n, n > 1)$ represents a binary random vector, while X_j denotes the j-th shares of a vector X.

Boolean masking based on secret sharing has gained significant attention in hardware security as an essential defense against SCA attacks. The Boolean masking of a secret vector $X \in \mathbb{F}_2^n$ consists of s independent and random shares, denoted as $(X_0, X_1, \cdots, X_{s-1})$. It is necessary to ensure correctness by satisfying the condition $X = \bigoplus_{i=0}^{s-1} X_i$. Usually, the process of obtaining the above s

shares involves two steps. Firstly, the X_i ($0 \leq i \leq s - 2$) are initialized with uniformly random strings. Secondly, X_{s-1} is derived as $X_{s-1} = (\bigoplus_{i=0}^{s-2} X_i) \oplus X$. Rather than performing leaking computations on the vector X, computations are performed on the shares X_i.

2.2 Probing Security

There are various models available to characterize and evaluate the security of masking schemes. Among them, the d-probing model [17] has gained significant popularity and is widely used. In this model, the number d of probes reflects the order of the attack. Since the d-probing model cannot characterize physical effects in hardware implementations, such as glitches, the model is limited to software implementations. Specifically, glitches are switching activities of wires in a circuit due to different delays of signals contributing to their intended values. To account for the impact of glitches, Faust et al. [13] adapted the d-probing model and introduced the glitch-extended probing model. This model assumes that each probe placed on a combinatorial circuit propagates backward to the last synchronization point (e.g., registers). Since this paper is related to hardware implementations, our evaluations and assessments are conducted under the glitch-extended probing model.

2.3 Composable Masking Schemes

The design of masking schemes that enables high order security remains a highly challenging task, even for an experienced designer. This encourages the development of composable gadgets, which are considered to be an efficient approach to designing masking schemes. Specifically, composable gadgets are modules that realize atomic logic operations with specific properties. Since these gadgets achieve particular properties, combining these gadgets to construct masking schemes for large circuits is possible. Therefore, this approach of using composable gadgets simplifies the construction of masking schemes, as the focus is on finding gadgets realizing logic operations with specific properties rather than dealing with the whole complex circuits.

To achieve the composability of gadgets, Barthe et al. proposed the concept of Strong Non-Interferene (SNI) [3]. Under the concept of SNI, each probe placed on the output of the SNI-secure gadget is restricted to be perfectly simulatable without any information captured by this probe. Although SNI satisfies the composability of gadgets, it will lead to a large overhead with respect to fresh entropy and circuit area, especially for high-security orders. As a more efficient solution than SNI, Probe-Isolating Non-Interference (PINI) was introduced by Cassiers et al. in [9]. Based on the concept of share domain [16], any probe was restricted to only propagate within its own share domain under the PINI. Formally, the concept of PINI can be described through Definition 1.

Definition 1 (d-Probe-Isolating Non-interference). *Given a gadget G with secret input X, $X \in \mathbb{F}_2^n$, let t_i denotes probes placed on internal wires* *of G and t_o denotes probes placed on output wires of G, such that $t_i + t_o \le d$. The gadget G is d-PINI if and only if for all possible t_i and t_o, there exists a set of primary input indexes PI_i, with $|PI_i \le t_i|$, primary output indexes PI_o, with $|PI_o \le t_o|$, such that the observations of t_i and t_o can be perfectly simulated by $X_{PI_i \cup PI_o}$.*

2.4   Hardware Private Circuits

Since PINI enables the trivial composition of gadgets, several concrete implementations of composable gadgets have been proposed. The HPC1 gadget introduced in [8] realizes the function of a 2-input AND gate and can be simply extended to arbitrary security orders. Specifically, HPC1 consists of a DOM-AND and a refresh gadget, where the sharing of one input of DOM-AND is refreshed through the refresh gadget. The number of fresh masks required by HPC1 is $d(d+1)/2 + [1, 2, 4, 5, 7, 9, 11, 12, 15, 17]^1$ for security order $d \le 10$. Further, another composable gadget HPC2 was introduced in the same work. The HPC2 is another construction for a 2-input AND gate that can be extended to arbitrary security orders. Compared to HPC1, HPC2 requires less fresh randomness, i.e., $d(d+1)/2$. Both HPC1 and HPC2 exhibit latency asymmetry feature: this means that if the first input sharing enters the HPC1 or HPC2 gadget at cycle k and another input sharing enters the gadget at cycle $k+1$, then the output can be generated at cycle $k+2$.

2.5   AGEMA

Knichel et al. [18] proposed an open-source software tool AGEMA, which makes it easy for designers to generate hardware masked circuits based on the unprotected HDL implementations. Based on the PINI concept, AGEMA supports several composable gadgets, including HPC1 and HPC2. Pipelining and clock gating are two synchronization techniques applied in AGEMA. Pipelining inserts additional registers to synchronize the input signals of each composable gadget, and clock gating modulates the clock signals of registers to achieve the same goal. Although pipelining requires a larger area overhead, it achieves better throughput than clock gating. Pipelining is more efficient than clock gating when large amounts of information are processed. In order to provide a fair comparison, the hardware performance below related to AGEMA is generated using the pipelining synchronization technique.

3   Key Techniques of AGMNC

In this section, we explain how AGMNC can generate more efficient masked implementations of S-boxes. The key techniques include a new AND-XOR gadget, latency asymmetry of the AND-XOR gadget, and implementation optimization.

---

[1] This is a compact notation indicates that for security order $d = 1$, 1 additional mask is required; for security order $d = 2$, 2 additional masks are required, and so on.

3.1   AND-XOR Gadget

Cassiers et al. [8] introduced HPC1 and HPC2 to realize 2-input composable AND gadgets under the PINI notion in the glitch-extended probing model. As they can achieve arbitrary security orders, HPC1 and HPC2 are essential gadgets used in AGEMA to generate masked implementations. To facilitate the explanation and analysis, we utilize the term HPC-AND gadget to generally represent the implementation of a 2-input AND gadget using HPC1 or HPC2.

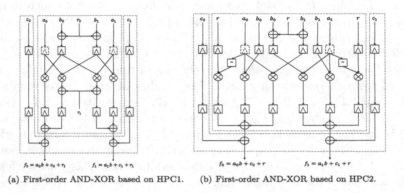

(a) First-order AND-XOR based on HPC1.   (b) First-order AND-XOR based on HPC2.

Fig. 1. AND-XOR in AGEMA.

There are usually XOR operations between the quadratic terms and linear terms in the Boolean expressions of nonlinear components, such as an S-box. The scenario can be denoted as the Boolean function $f = ab + c$, where $a \in \mathbb{F}_2, b \in \mathbb{F}_2, c \in \mathbb{F}_2$. In AGEMA, the Boolean function above is realized using the HPC-AND gadget and XOR operations. The implementation for the first order security is depicted in Figs. 1(a) and 1(b), where the red dashed line is the HPC-AND gadget, and the blue dashed line is the XOR operations. Since the latency of a single HPC-AND is 2 cycles, it is necessary to insert two layers of registers in the shared path of primary input c (i.e., c_0, c_1) to synchronize the latency before performing the XOR operations.

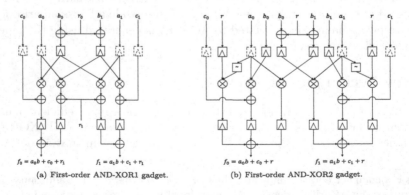

(a) First-order AND-XOR1 gadget.   (b) First-order AND-XOR2 gadget.

Fig. 2. AND-XOR gadget.

After careful analysis, we construct two new compact designs for the two cases in Figs. 1(a) and 1(b). As an example, we provide a schematic overview of our designs for the first security order in Figs. 2(a) and 2(b), respectively. Although the dashed line registers (denoted as $Reg_{pipe}[]$ in Algorithms 1 and 2) are essential for a pipelined architecture, they do not impact the security of the statement. Both designs integrate the above HPC-AND gadget and XOR operations into a new gadget (called AND-XOR1 and AND-XOR2 gadget, respectively). Our new gadgets can achieve PINI security under the glitch-extended probing model and are generic for arbitrary security orders. From Fig. 2, it can be seen our new gadgets save a layer of registers in the path of the shares of primary input c. Since the c consists of at least $d + 1$ shares, our designs generally reduce the number of registers by $d + 1$ than AGEMA, where d is the security order. The construction principle and security analysis of new gadgets are shown below.

Algorithm 1. AND-XOR1 gadget

Input: shares $(a_i)_{0 \leq i \leq d}$, $(b_i)_{0 \leq i \leq d}$ and $(c_i)_{0 \leq i \leq d}$, such that $\bigoplus_{i=0}^{d} a_i = a$, $\bigoplus_{i=0}^{d} b_i = b$
     and $\bigoplus_{i=0}^{d} c_i = c$.
Output: shares $(f_i)_{0 \leq i \leq d}$, such that $\bigoplus_{i=0}^{d} f_i = ab + c$.
 1: **if** $d = 1$ **then**
 2:      $M[b_0] = Reg[b_0 \oplus r_0]$, r_0 denotes a random bit.
 3:      $M[b_1] = Reg[b_1 \oplus r_0]$
 4: **else if** $d = 2$ **then**
 5:      $r_2 = Reg[r_0 \oplus r_1]$, r_0, r_1 and r_2 denote a random bit, respectively.
 6:      $M[b_0] = Reg[b_0 \oplus r_0]$
 7:      $M[b_1] = Reg[b_1 \oplus r_1]$
 8:      $M[b_2] = Reg[b_2 \oplus r_2]$
 9: **else if** $d \geq 3$ **then**
10:      refer to the appendix of [8].
11: **for** $i = 0$ to d **do**
12:      **for** $j = i + 1$ to d **do**
13:          $r_{ij} = r_{ji}$, denotes a random bit.
14: **for** $i = 0$ to d **do**
15:      **for** $j = 0$ to $d, j \neq i$ **do**
16:          $u_{ij} = Reg[Reg_{pipe}[a_i] \otimes M[b_j] \oplus r_{ij}]$
17: **for** $i = 0$ to d **do**
18:      $f_i = Reg[Reg_{pipe}[a_i] \otimes M[b_i] \oplus Reg_{pipe}[c_i]] \oplus \bigoplus_{j=0, j \neq i}^{d} u_{ij}$

Construction Principle. Algorithm 1 describes the generic algorithm-level of the AND-XOR1 gadget. The first-order case is depicted in Fig. 2(a). At the start of AND-XOR1 gadget (lines 1 to 10), a refresh gadget is essential to provide the desired security. The details of the refresh gadget are only provided for the cases of the first security order (lines 2 to 3) and the second security order (lines 5 to 8). The cases of security order $d \geq 3$ are given in the appendix of [8]. Then, some randomness is generated in lines 11 to 13. Lines 14 to 16 describe the cross-domain multiplications, i.e., the multiplications of two signals from different domains, the results of which are XOR-ed with randomness and then stored in registers. Lines 17 to 18 delineate three functionalities. Firstly, it multiplies signals that belong to the same domain. Subsequently, the results of the multiplications above are combined with the shares of primary input c utilizing XOR operations. Finally, the XOR operations are utilized once more in combination with the results of the cross-domain multiplications (lines 14 to 16).

The AND-XOR2 gadget is the other design, shown in Algorithm 2. In addition, the first-order secure AND-XOR2 gadget is illustrated in Fig. 2(b). The first three lines of Algorithm 2 generate some randomness that will be used in the following operations. From lines 4 to 9, four signals, namely u_{ij}, v_{ij}, q_{ij} and t_{ij}, are defined. The signal u_{ij} is used to represent the results of $\overline{a_i} \otimes r_{ij}$. The signal v_{ij} masks the shares of the primary input b with randomness r_{ij}. The multiplications of two signals from different domains are computed by q_{ij}. The t_{ij} represents the combination of the results of $\overline{a_i} \otimes r_{ij}$ with the cross-domain multiplications (i.e., q_{ij}) using XOR operations. Lines 10 to 11 correspond to two parts, one is the multiplications of two signals from the same domain and the combination of the above multiplications with the shares of primary input c using XOR operations, and the other one is the combination of the cross-domain multiplications q_{ij} with u_{ij}. These final output shares of the AND-XOR2 gadget are generated by XORing the results of these two parts.

Algorithm 2. AND-XOR2 gadget

Input: shares $(a_i)_{0 \leq i \leq d}$, $(b_i)_{0 \leq i \leq d}$ and $(c_i)_{0 \leq i \leq d}$, such that $\bigoplus_{i=0}^{d} a_i = a$, $\bigoplus_{i=0}^{d} b_i = b$ and $\bigoplus_{i=0}^{d} c_i = c$.

Output: shares $(f_i)_{0 \leq i \leq d}$, such that $f = \bigoplus_{i=0}^{d} f_i = ab + c$.

1: **for** $i = 0$ to d **do**
2:     **for** $j = i + 1$ to d **do**
3:         $r_{ij} = r_{ji}$, denotes a random bit.
4: **for** $i = 0$ to d **do**
5:     **for** $j = 0$ to d, $j \neq i$ **do**
6:         $u_{ij} = Reg[\overline{Reg_{pipe}[a_i]} \otimes Reg[r_{ij}]]$
7:         $v_{ij} = Reg[b_j \oplus r_{ij}]$
8:         $q_{ij} = Reg[Reg_{pipe}[a_i] \otimes v_{ij}]$
9:         $t_{ij} = u_{ij} \oplus q_{ij}$
10: **for** $i = 0$ to d **do**
11:     $f_i = Reg[Reg_{pipe}[a_i] \otimes Reg[b_i] \oplus Reg_{pipe}[c_i]] \oplus \bigoplus_{j=0, j \neq i}^{d}(t_{ij})$

Security Analysis. Below, we provide Theorems 1 and 2 to prove the PINI security of AND-XOR1 and AND-XOR2 gadgets under the glitch-extended probing model.

Theorem 1. *Assuming that all randomness bits used in the AND-XOR1 gadget are statistically independent of each share of the primary inputs a, b and c, then the AND-XOR1 gadget is glitch-robust PINI.*

Proof.

i. When a probe placed on the input to $M[b_i], 0 \leq i \leq d$, we can observe the variables b_i and its responding 1-bit randomness r_i. This case can be denoted as $P_{b_i} = [b_i, r_i]$, which can be perfectly simulated by b_i and r_i.

ii. When a probe placed on the input to u_{ij}, this case can be represented as $P_{u_{ij}} = [a_i, b_j \oplus r_j, r_{ij}]$, which can be perfectly simulated by a_i and randomness r_j and r_{ij}. If the additional variable u_{ji} is probed, this can be simulated by adding a_j to the simulation set. This is because the randomness r_i and r_j (used to mask b_i and b_j, respectively) are independent of each other. All other probes can be categorized into the above two cases, one with a single probe (i.e., u_{ij}) and the other one with a pair of probes whose subscripts are rotated (i.e., u_{ij} and u_{ji}). This is in line with the concept of PINI.

iii. The probe on f_i, i.e., $P_{f_i} = [a_i, b_i \oplus r_i, c_i] \cup \{\bigcup_{j=0, j \neq i}^{d} u_{ij}\}$ can be simulated by a_i, c_i and $b_i \oplus r_i$, which can be seen as a new random bit. If additionally P_{f_j} needs to be simulated, this can be done by following step ii, i.e., adding the share a_j and c_j to the simulation set. This is because two output shares have at most one common cross-domain. This is in line with the PINI notion.

Theorem 2. *Assuming that all randomness bits used in the AND-XOR2 gadget are statistically independent of each share of the primary inputs a, b and c, then the AND-XOR2 gadget is glitch robust PINI.*

Proof.

i. When a probe placed on the input to u_{ij}, we can observe the variables a_i and r_{ij}. It can be represented as $P_{u_{ij}} = [a_i, r_{ij}]$, which can be perfectly simulated by a_i and randomness r_{ij}.

ii. When a probe placed on the input to v_{ij}, this case can be represented as $P_{v_{ij}} = [b_j, r_{ij}]$, which can be perfectly simulated by b_j and randomness r_{ij}.

iii. The probe on q_{ij}, i.e., $P_{q_{ij}} = [a_i, b_j \oplus r_{ij}]$ can be simulated by $[a_i, r_{ij}]$. When an additional variable q_{ji} is probed, this can be achieved by adding a_j, b_i and b_j to the simulation set. All other probes can be done based on the above two cases, one is a single probe (i.e., q_{ij}) and the other one is a pair of probes whose subscripts are rotated (i.e., q_{ij} and q_{ji}).

iv. The probe on t_{ij}, i.e., $P_{t_{ij}} = [\overline{a_i} \otimes r_{ij}, a_i \otimes (b_j \oplus r_{ij})]$ can be simulated by a_i, r_{ij} and $b_j \oplus r_{ij}$, which can be seen as a new random bit. If additionally $P_{t_{ji}}$ needs to be simulated, this can be done by adding a_j, b_i, and b_j to the simulation set. The above case of considering two probes is in line with the notion of PINI. All other probes can be processed using the above two cases, one with a single probe (i.e., t_{ij}) and the other one with a pair of probes whose subscripts are rotated (i.e., t_{ij} and t_{ji}).

v. The probe on the output share, i.e., $P_{f_i} = [a_i, b_i, c_i] \cup \{\bigcup_{j=0, j \neq i}^{d} t_{ij}\}$ can be simulated by a_i, b_i, c_i and processing d times the random bit r_{ij} to simulate t_{ij}. From the expression of f_i, it can be seen two output shares have at most one cross-domain in common, and using the same argument as step iv, i.e., adding some input shares from only one other domain and some additional randomness to the simulation set. This is in line with the notion of PINI.

Compared with the implementations in AGEMA (as shown in Fig. 1), the two new gadgets have $d+1$ fewer registers while maintaining the same requirements of randomness and latency, where d is the security order. More specifically, a single AND-XOR1 gadget requires $d(d+1)/2 + [1, 2, 4, 5, 7, 9, 11, 12, 15, 17]$ bits of randomness and 2 cycles of latency. Similarly, a single AND-XOR2 gadget requires $d(d+1)/2$ bits of randomness and 2 cycles of latency. Due to the fewer registers, our new gadgets require a lower area than AGEMA for the Boolean function $f = ab + c$. It is worth mentioning that, in addition to the area advantages of the Boolean function mentioned above, we believe that these two new gadgets can yield comparable results as two standalone gadgets in the S-box implementations. To facilitate the analysis of the common features of these two new gadgets, we typically use the term AND-XOR gadget to represent both the AND-XOR1 and AND-XOR2 gadgets in the remainder of this paper.

3.2   Latency Asymmetry of AND-XOR Gadget

To further enhance the latency of the AND-XOR gadget, we conduct a detailed analysis of its latency asymmetry and integrate this feature into the automation tool AGMNC. Latency asymmetry is a peculiar feature supported by the HPC-AND gadget. This feature arises because only the shares from one primary input of the HPC-AND gadget need to be refreshed. In other words, the HPC-AND gadget has two sorts of shares from primary input, one of which has 1 cycle of latency and the other has 2 cycles of latency. Interestingly, the AND-XOR gadget also exhibits this feature for the following reason: as shown in Algorithms 1 and 2, only the shares from primary input b need to be refreshed, while the shares from primary input a and c use $Reg_{pipe}[]$ to compensate for the latency asymmetry caused by the refresh of the shares from b. In other words, the AND-XOR gadget has three sorts of input ports, one with a latency of 2 cycles (marked as 'b') and the remaining two with a latency of 1 cycle (marked as 'a' and 'c'). In the following, we demonstrate the impact of the latency asymmetric feature with several concrete examples.

To demonstrate the impact of utilizing the latency asymmetry, Fig. 3 presents two implementations with the Boolean function $f = xyz$ as an example. Note that Fig. 3 is a general schematic, where each signal is actually composed of $d+1$ shares and d is the security order of the masked implementation. Figure 3(a) emulates the AGEMA implementation without considering the latency asymmetry, which requires $4(d+1)$ additional registers to synchronize the latency and yields an implementation with a latency of 4 cycles. On the other hand, Fig. 3(b) emulates the AGMNC implementation, which takes into account the latency asymmetry. This results in an implementation with only $2(d+1)$ additional registers and a latency of 3 cycles. Comparing these two implementations reveals that Fig. 3(b) requires 50% fewer registers and 25% less latency than Fig. 3(a). It can be seen that utilizing the latency asymmetry feature can lead to significant improvements in terms of both area and latency.

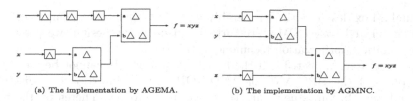

(a) The implementation by AGEMA.   (b) The implementation by AGMNC.

Fig. 3. Functionality xyz implementations using HPC-AND.

The latency asymmetry feature can be effectively utilized in the implementation of a Boolean function, as demonstrated by the following example using $f = (xy + z)t + m$. Firstly, we connect the later arriving signal to the input port of the gadget with the shorter latency, i.e., connecting the output of the AND-XOR gadget (marked as α) to the input port 'a' of the other AND-XOR gadget (marked as β), instead of the input port 'b' in Fig. 4(a). However, since the AND-XOR gadget has multiple input ports, there are inevitably some input ports that do not satisfy the latency requirements, i.e., ports 'a' and 'c' of the AND-XOR gadget (marked as α) and port 'b' and 'c' of the AND-XOR gadget (marked as β) in Fig. 4(a). In such scenarios, inserting registers in the input path is a viable solution to satisfy the latency constraints. Therefore, Fig. 4(b) presents the final implementation of this example using the solution above, i.e., $5(d + 1)$ registers are inserted in the input path, where d is the security order.

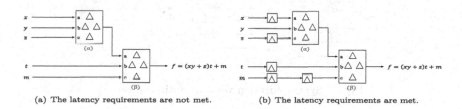

(a) The latency requirements are not met.   (b) The latency requirements are met.

Fig. 4. The latency asymmetry of AND-XOR gadget.

To the best of our knowledge, we are the first to integrate the latency asymmetry feature into an automated tool for generating masking schemes. Although a tool was also developed to exploit this feature, [8] focused on finding a circuit representation and did not automatically translate the circuit representation into a masked circuit. In addition to supporting the new AND-XOR gadget and implementation optimization to be described below, AGMNC has developed an automated procedure to generate masked circuit integrating the latency asymmetry feature.

3.3 Implementation Optimization

Until now, we have presented two key techniques employed by AGMNC, namely the AND-XOR gadget and its latency asymmetry, which result in most cases in a final S-box design with considerably lower area or latency compared to the design generated by AGEMA. To further optimize our design, we present an implementation optimization technique in this section.

As elaborated in Sect. 3.2, if the latency requirements cannot be met by all input ports of the HPC-AND or AND-XOR gadget, insertion of registers in the input path becomes necessary to synchronize latency. Therefore, the number of registers inserted to synchronize latency directly impacts the area of the final S-box design. Further, we propose an efficient implementation technique for optimizing the number of registers required for synchronization. We present two synchronization methods below using the representation of SKINNY S-box[2] as an example. In this example, there are three layers, where $\mathcal{N}_0$ and $\mathcal{N}_1$ are nonlinear and $\mathcal{L}$ is linear. The t_0, t_1, t_2 and t_3 are the outputs of AND-XOR gadgets, while l_0, l_1, l_2, l_3 and l_4 are the outputs of linear operations.

As shown in Fig. 5, we depict the common implementation without optimization, where six, four, and zero different registers inserted in the $\mathcal{N}_0, \mathcal{N}_1$ and $\mathcal{L}$ layers, respectively, to synchronize latency. Note that since there are two registers to store the value of $x_1 + 1$ in the $\mathcal{N}_0$, only six registers are needed instead of seven.

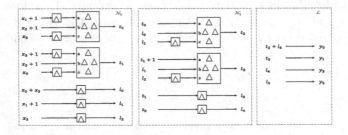

Fig. 5. Synchronization without optimization.

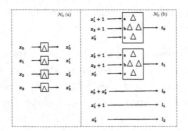

Fig. 6. Synchronization with optimization.

After observing and analyzing the above implementation, we note that in layer $\mathcal{N}_0$, the signals that do not satisfy the latency requirements are generated

---

[2] The detail of the representation for SKINNY S-box is shown in the Eq. (1) below.

using linear operations of four primary inputs (i.e., x_0, x_1, x_2 and x_3). Since the number of these unsynchronized signals is larger than the number of primary inputs (i.e., $6 > 4$), we propose a synchronization method that involves the insertion of registers in the path of the primary inputs. By doing so, we can ensure that the latency requirements of these primary inputs are met. Once this is achieved, we can use these already synchronized primary inputs to generate those unsynchronized signals yet. This approach allows us to realize the synchronization correctly with fewer registers. Specifically, in the example of the SKINNY S-box, we insert registers in the path of each primary input (i.e., x_0, x_1, x_2 and x_3) until the latency constraints are satisfied, obtaining signals x_0', x_1', x_2' and x_3' at layer $\mathcal{L}_0(a)$ of Fig. 6. Then, at layer $\mathcal{L}_0(b)$, we assign x_0', x_1', x_2' and x_3' to signals, the latency of which does not meet the requirements yet. At layer $\mathcal{L}_0$, this new approach requires only four registers to synchronize latency, saving two registers compared to the approach of AGEMA shown in Fig. 5. Since the $\mathcal{L}_1$ layer in the example exhibits a one-to-one correspondence between the unsynchronized signals and the primary inputs to that layer (i.e., l_1, l_2, t_1 and t_0), this layer behaves the same as Fig. 5. It should be noted that due to the masking scheme, i.e., each signal in Figs. 5 and 6 consists of at least $d + 1$ shares, our implementation technique actually saves $2(d + 1)$ registers in the above example.

3.4   Automation Tool AGMNC

Figure 7 shows the implementation principle of the automation tool AGMNC. The input of AGMNC is the look-up table description of nonlinear component (e.g., an S-box), and the output is a hardware masked implementation. The operation process of AGMNC consists of two phases: one is the pre-processing and the other one is the implementation-processing.

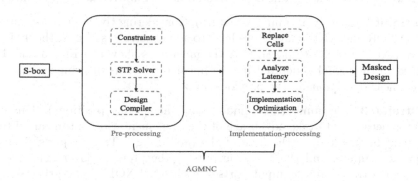

Fig. 7. The operation process of automation tool AGMNC.

In the pre-processing phase, AGMNC first finds a circuit representation suitable for our techniques and tool above for a given S-box using several constraints and the STP solver described in the next paragraph. Then, this circuit representation is synthesized into the corresponding netlist through the Design Compiler. The unprotected netlist is fed to the implementation-processing module. For the implementation-processing phase, the first step is to extract and replace cells. This involves replacing the AND-XOR and AND gates in the netlist with the AND-XOR and HPC-AND gadgets, respectively. The next step is calculating the latency for each input and output port of each AND-XOR and HPC-AND gadget. The latency asymmetry feature is checked and confirmed in this step. Subsequently, the implementation optimization technique is executed to synchronize the internal and output signals, the latency of which does not meet the requirements. The key techniques in the implementation-processing phase have been detailed in Sects. 3.1 to 3.3, hence this section focuses on the pre-processing phase.

Given the inherent complexity of searching for the circuit representation of a particular S-box, we utilize a solver based on the Boolean satisfiability (SAT) problem, namely STP, to find the circuit representation. As mentioned above, in the pre-processing phase, we should add several constraints to the STP solver to find the circuit representation suitable for our techniques and tool. The meaning and necessity of each constraint are described below.

Constraint 1 (the depth and number of AND-XOR and HPC-AND gadgets). Since the latency of a single AND-XOR or HPC-AND gadget is two cycles, while the linear operations can be executed without latency, we control the latency of the final design by constraining the depth of AND-XOR and HPC-AND gadgets. Since the area of a single AND-XOR or HPC-AND gadget is significantly higher than that of a linear operation, especially for high-security orders, it is crucial to constrain the number of AND-XOR and HPC-AND gadgets to find a final design with excellent area. The depth and number of above gadgets are optional.

Constraint 2 (latency asymmetry feature). Considering the latency asymmetry of AND-XOR and AND gadgets, we have to add constraints so that the 'b' input port of each AND-XOR and HPC-AND gadget (as shown in Figs. 3 and 4) is assigned to the signal generated by the linear operations of primary inputs or by the linear operations in the previous layer.

Constraint 3 (the number of unique signals at specific positions). This constraint is necessary to take advantage of the implementation optimization technique and further reduce the area of the final design. The unique signals are the primary inputs and the linear outputs in the previous layer. The specific positions are the 'a' and 'c' input ports of each AND-XOR gadget, the 'a' input port of each HPC-AND gadget, each linear output, and the final output.

More specifically, Eq. (1) is a circuit representation of SKINNY S-box found by the STP solver. Equation (1) consists of two layers of AND-XOR gadget and one final output layer. Two AND-XOR gadgets are in each AND-XOR gadget layer (i.e., t_0, t_1, t_2 and t_3), respectively. There are three, two linear outputs in each AND-XOR gadget layer (i.e., l_0, l_1, l_2, l_3 and l_4), respectively. The underlined terms are exactly the specific positions in each layer, with 8 unique variables (i.e., $x_0, x_1, x_2, x_3, l_1, l_2, l_3$ and l_4). In other words, at least $8(d+1)$ registers need to be inserted to synchronize the latency, where d is the security order.

$$
\begin{aligned}
S &= \mathcal{L} \circ \mathcal{N}_1 \circ \mathcal{N}_0 \\
\mathcal{N}_0 : t_0 &= \underline{(x_1 + 1)}(x_2 + 1) + \underline{x_3}, \quad t_1 = \underline{(x_3 + 1)}(x_2 + 1) + \underline{x_0}, \\
l_0 &= \underline{x_0 + x_3}, \quad l_1 = \underline{x_1 + 1}, \quad l_2 = \underline{x_2} \\
\mathcal{N}_1 : t_2 &= \underline{t_0}l_0 + \underline{l_1}, \quad t_3 = \underline{(t_1 + 1)}l_1 + \underline{l_2}, \quad l_3 = \underline{t_1}, \quad l_4 = \underline{t_0} \\
\mathcal{L} : y_0 &= \underline{t_2 + l_3}, \quad y_1 = \underline{t_3}, \quad y_2 = \underline{l_4}, \quad y_3 = \underline{l_3}.
\end{aligned}
\tag{1}
$$

4 Performance Evaluations

This section provides several S-box and full cipher implementations to highlight the benefits of applying our techniques and tool from Sect. 3.

4.1 S-Boxes

Following [24], we encode the constraints above described in Sect. 3.4 into the STP solver. As a result, we find several circuit representations for the 4-bit S-boxes of SKINNY [4], PRESENT [5] and PRINCE [6]. Further, we also adapt the design in [7] to reconstruct the 8-bit S-box of AES [12], in which two parts are modified, one is the inversion in $GF(2^4)$ (seen as a 4-bit S-box by the STP solver), and the other one is the generation of the inputs signals for the inversion in $GF(2^4)$. In particular, we reduce an AND gate in the inversion in $GF(2^4)$ compared to the design from [7], further reducing some randomness and hardware area required by the masked AND gadget.

To our knowledge, AGEMA is the most related work with our paper. To compare our work to state of the art, we provide two different masking schemes, one is generated by AGMNC, and the other one is generated by AGEMA, referring to [7,8]. We use Synopsys Design Compiler R-2020.09-SP4 and NanGate 45 nm standard cell library to synthesize these implementations of different S-boxes. Tables 1 and 2 list the synthesized results of the SKINNY S-box and AES S-box. Regarding synchronization techniques, since pipelining can achieve better throughput than clock gating when large amount of information are processed, our work is focused on pipelining and the results of AGEMA is also based on pipelining.

From the results, our work significantly reduces the area overhead compared to AGEMA. Specifically, we achieve an area reduction of about 21%–41% using AND-XOR1 gadgets and about 13%–34% using AND-XOR2 gadgets. Notably, for the first-order secure SKINNY S-box, the reduction is approximately 41% and 34% using AND-XOR1 and AND-XOR2 gadgets, respectively. The area reduction can be attributed to the utilization of AND-XOR gadgets and to two key techniques, i.e., the latency asymmetry and implementation optimization. Regarding latency, our work outperforms AGEMA by 25%, and specifically, for the AES Sbox, we reduce the latency from eight cycles to six cycles. The latency asymmetry feature of AND-XOR and HPC-AND gadgets leads to a latency reduction. In addition, compared to AGEMA, our work reduces the dynamic power of about 16%–49% and about 23%–47% using AND-XOR1 and AND-XOR2 gadgets, respectively. In particular, the dynamic power reduction for the first-order secure SKINNY S-box is approximately 49% and 47% using AND-XOR1 and AND-XOR2 gadgets, respectively. These results demonstrate that our proposed techniques and tool not only greatly reduce the area and latency overhead, but also significantly reduce the dynamic power.

4.2   Full Ciphers

For the full ciphers, we provide two case studies: SKINNY, which is round-based encryption and AES, which is byte-serial encryption. The above cases refer to designs from [4, 11], respectively.

To ensure a fair comparison, we initially employ AGEMA to generate the masking scheme of the above ciphers and then replace its S-boxes with our constructions. Tables 3 and 4 list the hardware performance of SKINNY and AES. Although our work focuses on S-box implementations, we have also made comparable performance in the full ciphers. Specifically, we achieve approximately 18%–27% (resp., 17%–24%), 20%–22% (resp., 20%–22%) and 18%–32% (resp., 19%–31%) reduction in area, latency and dynamic power using AND-XOR1 gadgets (resp., AND-XOR2 gadgets), respectively. It is worth mentioning that compared to the current automated tool AGEMA, for the first order masking schemes of the SKINNY cipher, we achieve a reduction of approximately 27% (resp., 24%) in the area and 20% (resp., 20%) in latency using AND-XOR1 gadgets (resp., AND-XOR2 gadgets), respectively. Due to the reduction of an AND gate in the representation of the AES S-box, we reduce the randomness by 2 (resp., 1), 5 (resp., 3), and 10 (resp., 6) bits in the AES with security order 1, 2 and 3 using AND-XOR1 gadgets (resp., AND-XOR2 gadgets), respectively. Whether the security order is 1, 2, or 3, and whether using AND-XOR1 or AND-XOR2 gadgets, we achieve the reduction of approximately 20% in the area and 22% in latency, respectively. The results significantly reduce the gap between the hand-crafted implementation [22] and the current automation tool AGEMA.

Table 1. Hardware performance of the SKINNY S-box.

Masking Scheme	Order	Area [GE]	Latency [cycle]	Power [uW]	Rand. [bit]	Delay [ns]	Ref.
HPC1	1	658	4	5.39	8	0.34	AGEMA [18]
	2	1156	4	10.00	20	0.39	AGEMA [18]
	3	1733	4	15.90	40	0.39	AGEMA [18]
	4	2379	4	22.52	60	0.45	AGEMA [18]
HPC2	1	785	4	6.79	4	0.39	AGEMA [18]
	2	1552	4	14.17	12	0.45	AGEMA [18]
	3	2570	4	24.08	24	0.50	AGEMA [18]
	4	3839	4	36.56	40	0.54	AGEMA [18]
AND-XOR1	1	385 (↓41%)	3 (↓25%)	2.75 (↓49%)	8	0.30	This Work
	2	747	3	5.81	20	0.36	This Work
	3	1187	3	10.10	40	0.37	This Work
	4	1696	3	15.20	60	0.44	This Work
AND-XOR2	1	517 (↓34%)	3 (↓25%)	3.61 (↓47%)	4	0.36	This Work
	2	1151	3	8.65	12	0.43	This Work
	3	2035	3	15.74	24	0.48	This Work
	4	3169	3	15.74	40	0.54	This Work

Table 2. Hardware performance of the AES S-box.

Masking Scheme	Order	Area [GE]	Latency [cycle]	Power [uW]	Rand. [bit]	Delay [ns]	Ref.
HPC1	1	4263	8	47.28	68	0.49	AGEMA [18]
	2	7840	8	85.81	170	0.54	AGEMA [18]
	3	12085	8	133.05	340	0.54	AGEMA [18]
	4	16920	8	188.31	510	0.60	AGEMA [18]
HPC2	1	5340	8	61.43	34	0.60	AGEMA [18]
	2	11206	8	133.96	102	0.76	AGEMA [18]
	3	19203	8	231.31	204	0.91	AGEMA [18]
	4	29330	8	358.36	340	1.04	AGEMA [18]
AND-XOR1	1	2895 (↓32%)	6 (↓25%)	31.28 (↓34%)	66 (↓3%)	0.49	This Work
	2	5745	6	63.54	165	0.57	This Work
	3	9243	6	106.06	330	0.64	This Work
	4	13314	6	157.48	495	0.74	This Work
AND-XOR2	1	3967 (↓26%)	6 (↓25%)	42.90 (↓30%)	33 (↓3%)	0.55	This Work
	2	9078	6	97.33	99	0.69	This Work
	3	16239	6	173.77	198	0.78	This Work
	4	25469	6	274.26	330	0.91	This Work

Table 3. Hardware performance of the SKINNY round-based encryption function.

Masking Scheme	Order	Area [GE]	Latency [cycle]	Power [uW]	Rand. [bit]	Delay [ns]	Ref.
HPC1	1	18855	165	191.98	128	0.57	AGEMA [18]
	2	30759	165	323.93	320	0.62	AGEMA [18]
	3	43931	165	459.97	640	0.62	AGEMA [18]
HPC2	1	20881	165	221.47	64	0.62	AGEMA [18]
	2	37095	165	409.09	192	0.67	AGEMA [18]
	3	57328	165	646.12	384	0.72	AGEMA [18]
AND-XOR1	1	13694 (↓27%)	132 (↓20%)	129.83 (↓32%)	128	0.45	This Work
	2	23049	132	228.17	320	0.50	This Work
	3	33663	132	334.16	640	0.50	This Work
AND-XOR2	1	15806 (↓24%)	132 (↓20%)	151.74 (↓31%)	64	0.50	This Work
	2	29513	132	292.81	192	0.56	This Work
	3	47231	132	476.81	384	0.60	This Work

Table 4. Hardware performance of the AES byte-serial encryption function.

Masking Scheme	Order	Area [GE]	Latency [cycle]	Power [uW]	Rand. [bit]	Delay [ns]	Ref.
HPC1	1	39318	2043	396.84	68	1.24	AGEMA [18]
	2	59794	2043	600.98	170	1.42	AGEMA [18]
	3	80946	2043	820.55	340	1.94	AGEMA [18]
HPC2	1	40395	2043	409.65	34	1.29	AGEMA [18]
	2	63161	2043	662.63	102	1.42	AGEMA [18]
	3	88050	2043	930.67	204	1.48	AGEMA [18]
AND-XOR1	1	30969 (↓21%)	1589 (↓22%)	306.53 (↓23%)	66 (↓3%)	1.22	This Work
	2	47362	1589	477.11	165	1.49	This Work
	3	64393	1589	651.54	330	1.60	This Work
AND-XOR2	1	32041 (↓21%)	1589 (↓22%)	324.74 (↓21%)	33 (↓3%)	1.33	This Work
	2	50695	1589	521.34	99	1.49	This Work
	3	71409	1589	732.92	198	1.88	This Work

5   Security Analysis

5.1   Theoretical Analysis

To ensure the sub-circuits are PINI secure under the glitch-extended probing model, we have examined the implementations of all sub-circuits with the SILVER tool [19], including HPC1, HPC2, AND-XOR1, AND-XOR2, NOT_ masked, XOR_masked and XNOR_masked. Further, the validity of the connections between sub-circuits is guaranteed because AGMNC uses deterministic procedures to realize the connections between sub-circuits. In addition to the above analysis, for the masked S-boxes described in this paper, we confirm the security of all 4-bit S-boxes and some AES S-boxes under the glitch-extended probing model using SILVER. Given that the SILVER is currently incapable of analyzing full cipher implementations, we opted to perform experimental analysis.

5.2   Experimental Analysis

We implement full ciphers on a SAKURA-G [23] board, where a Spartan-6 FPGA is embedded. Our designs are supplied with a stable clock signal at the frequency of 24 MHz. The power consumption traces are monitored with a PicoScope 5244D oscilloscope at a sampling frequency of 250 MS/s. Each randomness bit is dynamically generated during runtime with the use of a 31-bit maximum length Linear Feedback Shift Register (LFSR) presented in [1]. Then, each LFSR is initialized with an independent random seed. As the leakage assessment scheme, we perform fixed-versus-random t-test [14], which is widely used to evaluate the security of masked implementations. In each design, we keep the key constant and collect 1 million traces to conduct the t-test analysis.

Figures 8 and 9 depict the t-test results of SKINNY based on AND-XOR2 for the first-order and second-order masking schemes, respectively. The results in Figs. 8(a), 9(a) and 9(b) confirm the first-order security for the first-order design, as well as the first- and second-order security for the second-order design. For comparison, we also provide the results in Figs. 8(b) and 9(c) for the two designs when PRNG OFF to check our measurement setup.

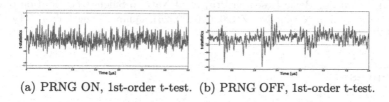

(a) PRNG ON, 1st-order t-test. (b) PRNG OFF, 1st-order t-test.

Fig. 8. SKINNY round-based encryption, first-order based on AND-XOR2.

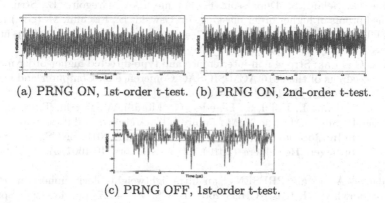

(a) PRNG ON, 1st-order t-test. (b) PRNG ON, 2nd-order t-test.

(c) PRNG OFF, 1st-order t-test.

Fig. 9. SKINNY round-based encryption, second-order based on AND-XOR2.

6 Conclusion

In this paper, we developed a user-friendly tool for the automated generation of masked nonlinear components (AGMNC), which enables hardware designers, regardless of their experience level, to elegantly and efficiently create secure masked hardware S-box circuits starting from the look-up table description.

AGMNC utilizes the AND-XOR gadget, latency asymmetry feature, and implementation optimization to generate efficient masked circuits. Furthermore, we show how to find implementations of given S-boxes that satisfy our techniques using the STP solver. We use AGMNC to generate a masked implementation of several S-boxes and evaluate the hardware performance from the perspective of the individual S-box and the full cipher. The evaluation shows that our designs require less area, latency, dynamic power, and even randomness, with a reduction of up to 41%, 25%, 49%, and 3% than AGEMA, respectively. Finally, we use the SILVER tool and FPGA-based practical experiments to verify the security of our designs. As an open problem, to bridge the gap between PINI-based designs and hand-crafted ones in terms of hardware performance, it is essential to propose additional gadgets and optimization techniques.

Acknowledgments. The authors would like to thank the anonymous reviewers for their valuable comments and suggestions on the paper. This work is supported by the National Key Research and Development Program of China (Grant No. 2018YFA0704702), the National Natural Science Foundation of China (Grant No. 62032014), the Major Basic Research Project of Natural Science Foundation of Shandong Province, China (Grant No. ZR202010220025), Quan Cheng Laboratory (Grant No. QCLZD202306).

References

1. Alfke, P.: Efficient shift registers, LFSR counters, and long pseudo-random sequence generators (1998). https://docs.xilinx.com/v/u/en-US/xapp052
2. Barthe, G., Belaïd, S., Dupressoir, F., Fouque, P.-A., Grégoire, B., Strub, P.-Y.: Verified proofs of higher-order masking. In: Oswald, E., Fischlin, M. (eds.) EURO-CRYPT 2015. LNCS, vol. 9056, pp. 457–485. Springer, Heidelberg (2015). https://doi.org/10.1007/978-3-662-46800-5_18
3. Barthe, G., et al.: Strong non-interference and type-directed higher-order masking. In: Proceedings of the 2016 ACM SIGSAC Conference on Computer and Communications Security, pp. 116–129 (2016)
4. Beierle, C., Jean, J., Kölbl, S., Leander, G., Moradi, A., Peyrin, T., Sasaki, Yu., Sasdrich, P., Sim, S.M.: The SKINNY family of block ciphers and its low-latency variant MANTIS. In: Robshaw, M., Katz, J. (eds.) CRYPTO 2016. LNCS, vol. 9815, pp. 123–153. Springer, Heidelberg (2016). https://doi.org/10.1007/978-3-662-53008-5_5
5. Bogdanov, A., et al.: PRESENT: an ultra-lightweight block cipher. In: Paillier, P., Verbauwhede, I. (eds.) CHES 2007. LNCS, vol. 4727, pp. 450–466. Springer, Heidelberg (2007). https://doi.org/10.1007/978-3-540-74735-2_31
6. Borghoff, J., et al.: PRINCE – a low-latency block cipher for pervasive computing applications. In: Wang, X., Sako, K. (eds.) ASIACRYPT 2012. LNCS, vol. 7658, pp. 208–225. Springer, Heidelberg (2012). https://doi.org/10.1007/978-3-642-34961-4_14
7. Boyar, J., Peralta, R.: A small depth-16 circuit for the AES S-box. In: Gritzalis, D., Furnell, S., Theoharidou, M. (eds.) SEC 2012. IAICT, vol. 376, pp. 287–298. Springer, Heidelberg (2012). https://doi.org/10.1007/978-3-642-30436-1_24
8. Cassiers, G., Grégoire, B., Levi, I., Standaert, F.X.: Hardware private circuits: from trivial composition to full verification. IEEE Trans. Comput. **70**(10), 1677–1690 (2020)
9. Cassiers, G., Standaert, F.X.: Trivially and efficiently composing masked gadgets with probe isolating non-interference. IEEE Trans. Inf. Forensics Secur. **15**, 2542–2555 (2020)
10. Chari, S., Jutla, C.S., Rao, J.R., Rohatgi, P.: Towards sound approaches to counteract power-analysis attacks. In: Wiener, M. (ed.) CRYPTO 1999. LNCS, vol. 1666, pp. 398–412. Springer, Heidelberg (1999). https://doi.org/10.1007/3-540-48405-1_26
11. Daemen, J., Rijmen, V.: The design of Rijndael. In: 2nd edition. Springer, Cham (2002)
12. Daemen, J., Rijmen, V.: AES proposal: Rijndael (1999)
13. Faust, S., Grosso, V., Pozo, S., Paglialonga, C., Standaert, F.X.: Composable masking schemes in the presence of physical defaults & the robust probing model (2018)

14. Gilbert Goodwill, B.J., Jaffe, J., Rohatgi, P., et al.: A testing methodology for side-channel resistance validation. In: NIST Non-invasive Attack Testing Workshop, vol. 7, pp. 115–136 (2011)
15. Groß, H., Mangard, S.: A unified masking approach. J. Cryptogr. Eng. 8, 109–124 (2018)
16. Groß, H., Mangard, S., Korak, T.: Domain-oriented masking: compact masked hardware implementations with arbitrary protection order. Cryptology ePrint Archive (2016)
17. Ishai, Y., Sahai, A., Wagner, D.: Private circuits: securing hardware against probing attacks. In: Boneh, D. (ed.) CRYPTO 2003. LNCS, vol. 2729, pp. 463–481. Springer, Heidelberg (2003). https://doi.org/10.1007/978-3-540-45146-4_27
18. Knichel, D., Moradi, A., Müller, N., Sasdrich, P.: Automated generation of masked hardware. Cryptology ePrint Archive (2021)
19. Knichel, D., Sasdrich, P., Moradi, A.: SILVER – statistical independence and leakage verification. In: Moriai, S., Wang, H. (eds.) ASIACRYPT 2020, Part I. LNCS, vol. 12491, pp. 787–816. Springer, Cham (2020). https://doi.org/10.1007/978-3-030-64837-4_26
20. Kocher, P., Jaffe, J., Jun, B.: Differential power analysis. In: Wiener, M. (ed.) CRYPTO 1999. LNCS, vol. 1666, pp. 388–397. Springer, Heidelberg (1999). https://doi.org/10.1007/3-540-48405-1_25
21. Kocher, P.C.: Timing attacks on implementations of Diffie-Hellman, RSA, DSS, and other systems. In: Koblitz, N. (ed.) CRYPTO 1996. LNCS, vol. 1109, pp. 104–113. Springer, Heidelberg (1996). https://doi.org/10.1007/3-540-68697-5_0
22. Moulin, C., Cassiers, G., Standaert, F.-X.: Handcrafting: improving automated masking in hardware with manual optimizations. In: Balasch, J., O'Flynn, C. (eds.) COSADE 2022. LNCS, vol. 13211, pp. 257–275. Springer, Cham (2022). https://doi.org/10.1007/978-3-030-99766-3_12
23. SAKURA: side-channel attack user reference architecture. http://satoh.cs.uec.ac.jp/SAKURA/index.html
24. Stoffelen, K.: Optimizing s-box implementations for several criteria using SAT solvers. In: Peyrin, T. (ed.) FSE 2016. LNCS, vol. 9783, pp. 140–160. Springer, Heidelberg (2016). https://doi.org/10.1007/978-3-662-52993-5_8

A Command-Activated Hardware Trojan Detection Method Based on LUNAR Framework

Xue Yang[1], Congming Wei[2,3]([✉]), Yaoling Ding[2], Shaofei Sun[2], An Wang[2], and Jiazhe Chen[4]

[1] School of Computer Science and Technology, Beijing Institute of Technology, Beijing 100081, China
[2] School of Cyberspace Science and Technology, Beijing Institute of Technology, Beijing 100081, China
weicm@bit.edu.cn
[3] Advanced Cryptography and System Security Key Laboratory of Sichuan Province, Chengdu 610054, China
[4] China Information Technology Security Evaluation Center, Beijing, China

Abstract. Hardware Trojans have become a major challenge to ICs due to their serious damage to the reliability and security. However, hardware Trojans can be activated in a variety of ways, making accurate activation of hidden hardware Trojans extremely difficult. In this paper, we propose an automatic anomaly detection method based on LUNAR (Learnable Unified Neighborhood-based Anomaly Ranking) based on graph neural networks to efficiently, quickly, accurately, and automatically detect unknown commands secretly inserted by untrusted parties. This method could effectively detect the command-activated hardware Trojans, which are the most frequently used activation mode. While retaining the linear time complexity advantage of PBCS (Pruning Bytes Command Search), we try to use neighbor information in a trainable way to find anomalies in each node, which could effectively reduce manual intervention in unsupervised conditions. Our experiments mainly focus on the preprocessed waveform sets with obvious features, Gaussian noise waveform sets with weak features, and original waveform sets without any obvious features. The results show that the LUNAR framework can detect anomalies significantly better than One-Class SVM, Isolation Forest and Local Outlier Factor, which are easily affected by parameter adjustment, especially in scenarios with no preprocessing and no obvious features.

Keywords: Hardware Trojan Detection · Graph Neural Network · Side Channel Analysis

1 Introduction

In recent years, with the rapid development of information technology and processors, integrated circuits, as key basic equipment, have been widely used in

M. Andreoni (Ed.): ACNS 2024 Workshops, LNCS 14586, pp. 340–358, 2024.
https://doi.org/10.1007/978-3-031-61486-6_20

various fields such as aerospace, industrial Internet, finance, and medical treatment [1,2]. At the same time of the development of integrated circuit technology, the structure and function of electronic information system tend to be complex, which directly leads to a significant increase in the difficulty of security detection [3]. Figure 1 shows the level of trust at different stages of a typical integrated circuit's life cycle [4]. Each party involved in ICs design and manufacturing can insert malicious circuits that compromise the security and trust of the underlying hardware, known as hardware Trojans [5]. Hardware Trojans can independently complete the attack function, such as leaking information to the at-tacker, changing the circuit function, and directly destroying the circuit.

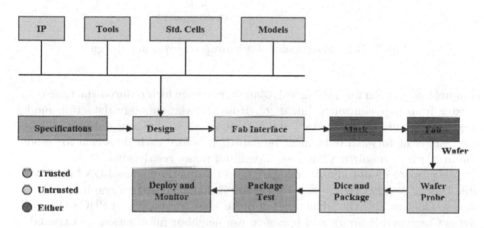

Fig. 1. Vulnerable steps of a modern IC life cycle [6]

Attackers often create a stealth Trojan that evades detection through routine post-testing, but becomes apparent during prolonged field operations. For ICs of moderate complexity, the number of possible Trojans can be very large and have different activation mechanisms (called triggers) and effects (called payloads) [1]. Figure 2 shows a simplified block diagram of a hardware Trojan that causes a failure when triggered (by modifying the signal S to S'). The activation condition that triggers the logic implementation is true. Such malicious inclusions effectively play the role of "spy or terrorist" on the chip and can be very powerful, potentially leading to disastrous consequences in a variety of applications [7].

Trojans in hardware usually require a trigger to activate, which means finding the trigger is key to detecting hardware Trojans. The object of our research is a hardware Trojan whose trigger type is command-activated, which aims to efficiently, quickly, accurately and automatically detect unknown commands secretly inserted by untrusted parties. The traditional method for command-activated hardware Trojans is to check whether the device returns the expected response value. This inefficient search strategy requires searching the entire command space, resulting in extremely high time complexity. Shang et al. proposed an command search algorithm based on byte pruning and combined with side

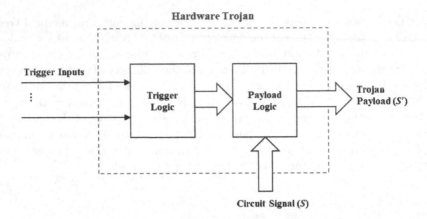

Fig. 2. General structure of a hardware Trojan in a design

channel information for hardware Trojan detection, which reduced the time complexity from exponential to linear [8]. However, the anomaly detection model used lacks trainable parameters and cannot adapt to different datasets. Therefore, sufficient forward data must be captured before each detection for model training, which requires a large workload and many restrictions.

We propose an automated anomaly detection method using LUNAR (Learnable Unified Neighborhood-based Anomaly Ranking) based on graph neural networks, which retains the advantages of linear time complexity of PBCS (Pruning Bytes Command Search), and learns to use neighbor information in a trainable way to find anomalies of each node. The unsupervised detection method can effectively reduce the workload of manual intervention in the anomaly detection stage:

1. No need to use gold chips, nor to manual capture a large number of side channel information of invalid commands byte by byte as a training set.
2. The LUNAR framework makes up for the lack of other methods' ability to learn optimization or adapt to specific datasets, and can maintain high accuracy in scenarios with low signal-to-noise ratio, such as power waveforms without any preprocessing and scenes with little Gaussian noise.
3. The output of LUNAR-PBCS is not affected by different communication protocols, and the k that defines the neighborhood range has very little influence on the final exception.

With the help of LUNAR-PBCS, we can accurately recover the executable commands of the 8051 MCU in a short time according to the side channel information when the chip parses the commands.

The rest of this article is organized as follows. In Sect. 2, we give a preliminary look at APDU (Application Protocol Data Units) and parsing paths. Then we summarize the relevant work in this field in Sect. 3. Sections 4 and 5 describe model design and system design, respectively, and explain the core algorithms used in our approach. In addition, in Sect. 6, we design three scenarios to validate our method and compare the effect of our method with the original three anomaly detection methods. Finally, we conclude the paper in Sect. 7.

2   Preliminaries

2.1   Application Protocol Data Unit

APDU is a communication data unit between the host computer and the chip that conforms to a specific communication protocol, and is often used for data interaction and smart card control. In the smart card control scenario, APDU is the data unit between the smart card and the card reader. The APDU used in this paper is defined by the ISO/IEC 7816-4 protocol [9].

In the ISO/IEC 7816-4 protocol, there are two types of APDU: C-APDU (Command APDU) and R-APDU (Response APDU). The command APDU is sent by the card reader to the smart card and contains the required 5-byte header (CLA, INS, P1, P2, Lc) and 0 to 255 bytes of data. The response APDU is sent by the smart card to the card reader and contains the mandatory 2-byte status word and 0 to 256 bytes of data. Standard smart cards judge APDU bytes sequentially, so the parsing path for C-APDU is CLA-INS-P1-P2-Le.

2.2   Parsing Path and Valid Bytes

Commands received by hardware interworking are parses in a specified sequence. This sequence is called the parsing path. For example, the C-APDU parsing path in ISO/IEC 7816-4 is CLA-INS-P1-P2-Le in byte order.

The judgment process of command parsing is usually pruned. Only when the currently judged byte matches the valid command set, the validity of the next byte will continue to be judged according to the parsing path. At this time, the byte is recognized as a valid byte. Otherwise, the byte is an invalid byte, and the validity of the next byte is no longer judged according to the parsing path. The chip returns the response value of the empty command and the chip enters the idle state.

The chip's parsing behavior and discrimination process for each byte of different data are different, and the change of CMOS in the circuit is also different, which will lead to differences in the captured side channel information, so that we have the opportunity to make a successful outlier detection.

3   Related Works

3.1   Hardware Trojan Detection

Integrated circuits are widely used in aerospace, industrial Internet, medical treatment, finance and other fields. The security of integrated circuits directly affects the normal operation of various systems and the security of confidential information, so hardware Trojans are a serious and valuable security problem

[10]. The implant forms and activation methods of hardware Trojans are complicated, and the conventional detection methods mainly include destructive detection, logical test, side channel analysis and so on.

The destructive detection method is based on the failure analysis technique. It reverses the packaged integrated circuit, scans the circuit layer by layer, and reconstructs the circuit structure diagram to find out whether there is a hardware Trojan in the circuit [11]; Logical testing was proposed by Wolff et al. [12]. Automatic Test Pattern Generation (ATPG) testing technology based on VLSI fault testing mainly adopts different test vector generation methods [13,14]. The hardware Trojan is detected by observing the effect of the hardware Trojan on the circuit value at the output port. This detection method is extremely costly and requires the generation of an extremely large number of test vectors for execution and monitoring. In addition, the generated vectors are often difficult to cover the entire command set; Side channel analysis realizes hardware Trojan detection through the change of side channel information during chip running. If there is a hardware Trojan implanted, it will inevitably cause effects such as reduced performance and changed power consumption. This article mainly discusses the method, so it will be explained in more detail below.

3.2   Hardware Trojan Detection Based on SCA

When a chip is working, it will cause changes in the side channel information such as thermal signal, electromagnetic radiation signal or power consumption signal [4]. Although the hardware Trojan is in the inactive state most of the time, the implantation of the hardware Trojan and the behavior of constantly detecting trigger conditions will have some impact on the side channel information, making it a breakthrough for detection.

Power-based and path-delay based channel analysis are two basic schemes of hardware Trojans. Power-based bypass analysis is often based on gold chips to detect hardware Trojans by comparing the target device with a trusted device with the same specifications as the target device and without hidden Trojan circuits. Such trusted devices are called gold chips, and researchers often use machine learning classification or clustering algorithms to complete detection based on data labels [15]. Bypass analysis based on path delay detects Trojans by comparing and measuring the delay difference of circuits. This is because the implantation of hardware Trojans can lead to changes in the number of gates in the circuit, which will change the delay characteristics of the circuit [16–19], such as signal flipping delay and signal transmission delay. Trojans in the circuit can be detected based on power consumption and path delay information. However, due to the existence of process noise, the detection effect is often not very satisfactory, especially the bypass detection based on delay information. Therefore, researchers propose the bypass analysis by measuring multiple parameters and combining them [20,21]. For example, Narasimhan et al. proposed to calculate the maximum operating frequency of the circuit with the two parameters of static current and dynamic current, which can reduce the influence of process noise [20] and improve the Trojan detection effect.

In this paper, a new method to avoid the use of gold chips is proposed, which combines the unified local outlier anomaly detection method based on graph neural network with the anomaly detection of side channel information and applies it to hardware Trojan detection.

3.3 Pruning Bytes Command Searching

Hardware usually completes data interaction and chip control by receiving and parsing commands and returning response values. Different types of hardware follow different command and response value protocols, and APDU is one of the communication data units between the host computer and the chip that conforms to a specific communication protocol. The APDU used in this article is defined by the ISO/IEC 7816-4 protocol.

For hardware Trojans triggered by specific commands, exhaustive testing can theoretically be performed. As shown in Fig. 3, first of all, the executable command set composed of valid commands and the empty command set composed of invalid commands are obtained by analyzing whether the response value or the side channel information during chip execution has significant characteristics. Comparing the executable command set with the official command-list, the executable command set can be divided into user commands published by the manufacturer and hidden commands not disclosed by the manufacturer, and then possible Trojan commands can be targeted in the hidden commands. This exhaustive based functional testing technology has simple principle, high stability, and is not affected by process variables and test noise, but the number of test vectors is large, the time complexity is high, and because the function may require a specific context, the executable commands are likely to be lost [22].

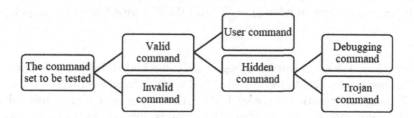

Fig. 3. The process of inferring Trojan command

4   Valid Command Detection Algorithm Based on Power Analysis

4.1 LUNAR Framework

Goodge et al. proposed a unified Anomaly detection framework LUNAR based on the idea of graph neural network and local outlier detection [23]. Anomalies can be detected by learning features based on nearest neighbor nodes. This approach uses the messaging framework of single-layer GNN to represent a set of data as a graph. Where the node corresponds to each sample data, and the directed edge connects the target node to a set of source nodes that are the nearest neighbors of the sample. For a given target node, the network uses information from its neighbors to learn to calculate its outlier score. It differs from the GNN implementation in that:

a. Use any feature-based tabular dataset to build k-NN graphs, without being limited to graph datasets.
b. Using the distance from a node to its k nearest neighbors as input is more general than using eigenvectors.
c. A learnable message aggregation function is used, whereas most GNNs use fixed aggregation functions.

Nearest Neighborhood Graph: For a sample data x_i, we define it as a target node and use edge (j, i) to connect target node x_i, to source node j, where j is a group of k nearest neighbors of x_i. The eigenvector of an edge is equal to the distance between two points x_i, to j in Euclidean space.

$$e_{j,i} = \begin{cases} dist(x_i, x_j) \text{ if } j \in \mathcal{N}_i \\ 0 \text{ otherwise} \end{cases} \tag{1}$$

Since all training samples are assumed to be normal, we only need to look for the nearest neighbor in the training sample, so the anomaly does not affect the neighborhood.

Then, we need to define the message function, the aggregation function, and the update function.

Message: The message passed from source node j to destination node i via edge (j, i) is the eigenvector of edge (j, i). That's the distance between two points.

$$\phi^{(1)} := e_{j,i}. \tag{2}$$

Aggregation: We use a learnable aggregation method suitable for dealing with neighbor nodes of a fixed size k. Instead of using a fixed average or maximum pool. Message aggregation involves joining them to give a K-dimensional vector $e(i)$, where each entry represents the distance from x_i to its corresponding neighbor node.

$$e^{(i)} := [e_{1,i}, \ldots, e_{k,i}] \in \mathbb{R}^k. \tag{3}$$

This vector is mapped through the neural network to a single scalar value representing the anomaly of node i:

$$h_{\mathcal{N}_i}^{(1)} := \mathcal{F}\left(e^{(i)}, \Theta\right). \tag{4}$$

Update: Update the learned aggregate information output:

$$\gamma^{(1)} := h_{\mathcal{N}_i}^{(1)}. \tag{5}$$

4.2   PBCS Combined with LUNAR

Hardware Trojan detection based on side channel information requires us to capture the corresponding side channel information in real time when the chip receives and analyzes the commands, that is, on the one hand, the PC controls the chip to send and receive commands, and on the other hand, the oscilloscope is controlled to capture the side channel information when the chip is working. The side channel information mentioned in this paper is all power signals. Next, we introduce the implementation flow of the hardware Trojan side channel detection based on LUNAR.

In general, LUNAR uses a graph neural network to construct a dataset into a graph. A single sample data is regarded as a point in the graph, the sample point is defined as the target node, and the nearest neighbor node is defined as the source node. Treat the distance between the edges as information (eigenvalue). A target node is described by k source nodes. LUNAR then uses a learnable aggregation method for dealing with neighbor nodes of a fixed size, which attenuates the effect of k. This vector in turn is mapped by the neural network into a scalar that can represent the node outliers.

In the experiment implementation process of this paper, the traversal command i is sent to the chip and the corresponding side channel information x_i is captured in real time to obtain the side channel information dataset X to be detected. Based on the unified framework of the LUNAR model, the abnormal scores of different transformations are obtained, and the valid commands are determined. LUNAR avoids directly training high-dimensional input features when training, instead using the distance between two points.

Since abnormal samples occupy a significantly lower proportion in datasets, during the detection process, it is first assumed that all side channel information samples are normal, and then the anomalies are located through the neighborhood based on the actual distribution of the data. This anomaly detection scheme driven by data distribution has the advantage of not requiring the use of golden chips, nor the need to manually capture side channel information of a large number of invalid commands byte by byte as a training set.

5   System Design

5.1   Assumptions

Before describing the implementation method of hardware Trojan detection, the experimental hypothesis of this paper is described first.

Assumption 1. There are power leaks when chips perform operations, and the hardware power leaks obey the same probability distribution when the operations are the same.

Common internal chips are usually based on CMOS processes, in which all operations of the chip will be completed by changing the state of the logic gate circuit. When the chip performs different operations, it will cause changes in the logic gate circuit of different parts. This change may be reflected in the physical level of the overall current change of the chip, which can also be called power consumption change. Assumption 1 is the physical basis and core concern of power consumption analysis during side channel analysis.

Assumption 2. When the hardware performs an operation, the power leak can be captured by some means.

Generally speaking, the inspector has absolute control over the device that has hardware Trojan detection requirements. Most hardware devices without special protection can be modified by circuit using some side channel technology to capture power leakage. This is the basic condition for side channel analysis, so Assumption 2 is also easy to implement.

Assumption 3. Executable commands are sparse in the possible command space.

This is not an unrealistic assumption, because the command space is extremely large, and the operations that the chip needs to perform are limited. In fact, in most devices, executable commands occupy only a very small part of the command space. When designing Trojan commands, it is necessary to ensure their concealment, and the functions that usually need to be performed are relatively limited, so Assumption 3 can also be achieved.

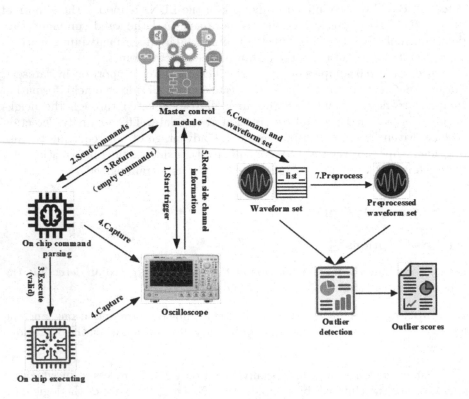

Fig. 4. System design

5.2   Detection System

The detection system of this paper is shown in Fig. 4. In the process of detection, the master control module on the computer firstly sets the trigger conditions of the oscilloscope, and the oscilloscope enters the state of preparation for sampling. The master control module sends traversal commands to the chip, and the chip command parsing module analyzes the commands. At the same time, the oscilloscope captures the power, electromagnetic and other information of the chip. The oscilloscope sends the captured power or electromagnetic waveform to the master control module on the computer. The master control module organizes the commands and waveforms as the side channel information dataset X to be detected.

After obtaining the side channel information dataset X, the validity of current byte will be detected through the LUNAR framework combined with PBCS. If the current byte is valid, we will continue to traverse the next byte, and detect the valid bytes byte by byte until the executable command set is obtained. Then we compare it with the official command-list published by the manufacturer to confirm whether there are hidden executable commands in the chip, which are possible Trojan commands.

6   Evaluation and Findings

6.1   Evaluation Method

For the calculation of outlier scores, we similarly follow the framework of LUNAR proposed by Goodge et al. The loss function is used to train GNN to output "0" points for a normal node and "1" points for an abnormal node. Since all the training points belong to the normal class, the network can output "0" scores regardless of the input, thus achieving perfect training accuracy. To avoid such trivial solutions, we generate negative samples as artificial exceptions and train the model to output "1" point for negative sample nodes. Negative samples can be generated by uniform distribution and subspace perturbation.

The first method is to generate negative samples through uniform distribution:

$$x^{(negative)} \sim \mathcal{U}\left(-\varepsilon,\ 1+\varepsilon\right) \in \mathbb{R}^d \qquad (6)$$

where ε is a small and positive constant. The value of ε in all experiments is set to 0.1 for simplicity. The training data will be normalized to the range $[0, 1]$. Considering that abnormal samples may be too far away from normal samples, making it difficult for the model to learn the decision boundary, it is necessary to generate some abnormal samples that are closer to and more difficult to distinguish from normal samples.

The second method is to select a subspace among all the feature dimensions of the normal sample and generate a negative sample by adding Gaussian noise to the features in the subspace:

$$z \sim \mathcal{N}\left(0,\ I\right) \in \mathbb{R}^d, \qquad (7)$$

$$x^{(negative)} = x_i^{(train)} + M \circ \varepsilon z \tag{8}$$

where ε is a minimal positive integer, $M \in R^d$ is a vector of binary random variables, every element of M has p, p has probability 1, and $(1-p)$ has probability 0. Each dimension set to 1 will be disturbed by noise. The value of p is set to 0.2 in all experiments.

Based on the above information, our purpose is to learn the decision boundary between normal and negative samples, which can be generalized to real exceptions in the test set. In this paper, the generation of negative samples is mixed with the above two methods.

6.2   Experiment and Result

Next, three different experimental scenarios are introduced, which are microcontroller unit following ISO/IEC 7816-4 with filter, microcontroller unit following ISO/IEC 7816-4 with Gaussian noise and microcontroller unit following ISO/IEC 7816-4 without filter.

In order to better reflect the byte-based experimental effect of PBCS, the second byte called INS is iterated in the following scenario in a microcontroller following the ISO/IEC 7816-4 protocol, where the first byte CLA = 00 is a valid byte, and other bytes are added to 00 according to the protocol. That is, the command set I traversed is [00 00 00 00 00, 00 01 00 00 00, 00 02 00 00 00 00, ..., 00 FF 00 00 00 00], and the side channel information of each command execution is captured at the same time to obtain the side channel information dataset X to be detected.

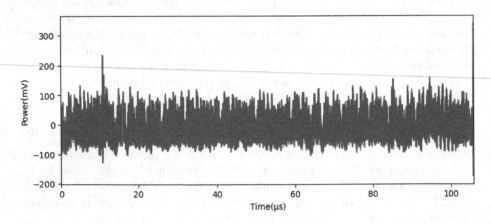

Fig. 5. Power waveforms with low-pass filter when the INS byte is invalid (four waveforms are overlaid).

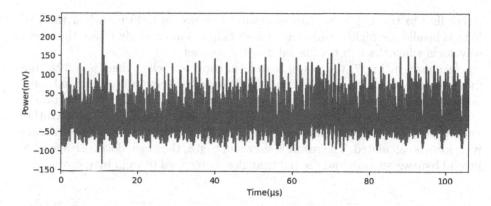

Fig. 6. Power waveform with low-pass filter when the INS byte is valid

Scenario 1: Microcontroller Unit Following ISO/IEC 7816-4 with Pre-processing. In actual scenarios, since the behavior of capturing power signals is acquired and the packaged chips need to be processed, various noises inevitably exist in the environment. Directly captured side channel information datasets usually have a low signal-to-noise ratio, so certain preprocessing is required.

In the power waveforms, features can be extracted by external filter, digital filter, sliding window average and other methods. When the external filter is connected or the low-pass filter is used for preprocessing, the signal-to-noise ratio can be effectively improved and the points of interest with significant features can be better located. The preprocessed power waveforms are shown above, where Fig. 5 is the power waveform when INS byte is invalid, and Fig. 6 is the power waveform when INS byte is valid. The power waveform when an INS byte is invalid is overlaid with the power waveform when an INS byte is valid.

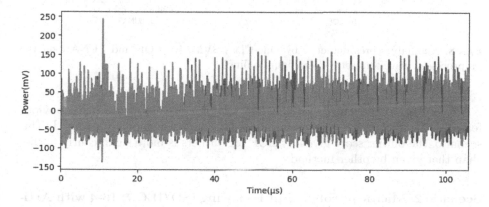

Fig. 7. Overlay the power waveform corresponding to the invalid INS byte (yellow) with the power waveform corresponding to the valid INS byte (blue) in the preprocessed waveform set. (Color figure online)

According to the Fig. 5, we can see that the power waveforms when the INS byte is invalid are highly consistent, which helps us more easily locate the power waveform when the INS byte is valid in the dataset.

As shown in Fig. 7, the power waveform captured when there is a filter has many significant characteristics, and the anomaly detection is easier and more accurate at this time. The waveform set containing both valid bytes and invalid bytes is detected by One-Class SVM, IF (Isolation Forest), LOF (Local Outlier Factor) and LUNAR four methods respectively, and the outlier score of each waveform is calculated. The result is shown in Fig. 8, the green dots correspond to invalid byte waveforms, and the red triangles correspond to valid byte waveforms.

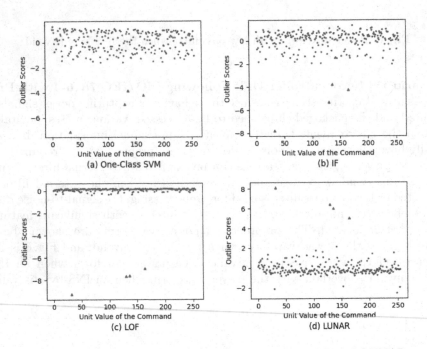

Fig. 8. Anomaly scores detected by One-Class SVM, IF, LOF and LUNAR on the preprocessed waveform set. (Color figure online)

According to the Fig. 8, we can find that for waveform sets with obvious features, the four methods can accurately determine the anomaly points. In this scenario, the outlier score given by LOF for outliers is more significantly outlier than that given by other methods.

Scenario 2: Microcontroller Unit Following ISO/IEC 7816-4 with Artificial Gaussian Noise. There may be various noises in the real experiment environment. Based on the above experiments, we added Gaussian noise with Xmean = 0 and sigma = 0.05 to the power waveform to verify the detection

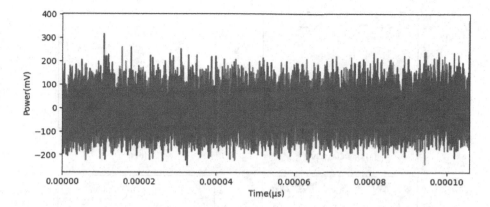

Fig. 9. Power waveforms with Gaussian noise when the INS byte is invalid (four wave-forms are overlaid).

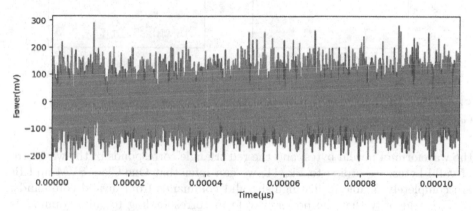

Fig. 10. Overlay the power waveform corresponding to the invalid INS byte (yellow) with the power waveform corresponding to the valid INS byte (blue) in the Gaussian noise waveform set. (Color figure online)

capabilities of each detection method in a noisy environment. Figure 9 shows the power waveforms when four INS invalid bytes are overlaid. Different from the preprocessed waveform, we can see that the power waveform when the INS byte is invalid is no longer highly consistent at this time, which makes it more challenging for us to locate the power waveform when the INS byte is valid in the dataset.

When Gaussian noise is added, the power waveform (yellow) corresponding to invalid INS byte and the waveform (blue) corresponding to valid INS byte are shown in Fig. 10. Different from the waveforms with low-pass filter, we can see that the difference between the two types of power waveforms is no longer stable, which also brings more severe challenges to unsupervised detection.

Use One-Class SVM, IF, LOF, and LUNAR methods to detect waveform sets containing valid bytes and invalid bytes, and calculate the anomaly score of each waveform. The results are as shown in Fig. 11. The green dots correspond to

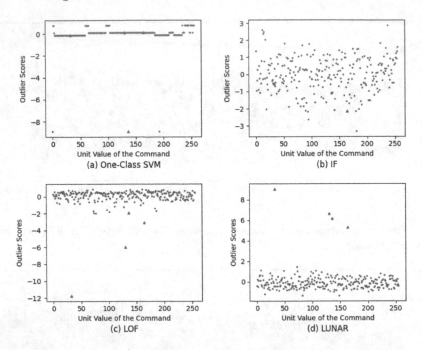

Fig. 11. Anomaly scores detected by One-Class SVM, IF, LOF and LUNAR on the Gaussian noise waveform set. (Color figure online)

the waveform of invalid bytes, and the red triangle corresponds to the waveform of valid bytes. According to Fig. 11, we can infer that One-Class SVM and IF are completely unable to distinguish valid commands from invalid commands. LOF can identify that the power waveform corresponding to valid commands has a relatively high degree of abnormality but cannot be an absolute outlier. Only LUNAR can accurately The determination of valid commands, that is, for waveform sets with more complex feature differences, LUNAR-based detection has the best detection ability among the above methods.

Scenario 3: Microcontroller Unit Following ISO/IEC 7816-4 Without Preprocessing. The detector's behavior of capturing signals is acquired. Therefore, in actual scenarios, it is usually necessary to reprocess the packaged chips. This inevitably leads to the fact that directly captured side channel information datasets usually have a low signal-to-noise ratio. However, inspectors are not always able to explore the most appropriate preprocessing methods in less time to capture points of interest and amplify features in the raw data. Therefore, the following challenge is to perform anomaly detection on the power waveform without preprocessing.

The following Fig. 12 shows the power waveform corresponding to the invalid INS byte (yellow) and the power waveform corresponding to the valid INS byte (blue) without preprocessing. Different from the preprocessing, it is difficult for us to see the difference between the two types of power waveforms, which also brings more severe challenges to unsupervised detection. For waveform sets con-

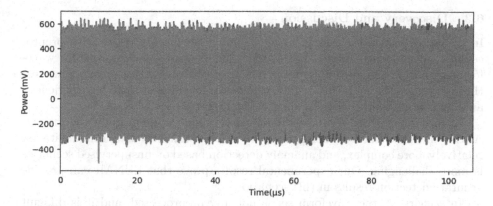

Fig. 12. Overlay the power waveform corresponding to the invalid INS byte (yellow) with the power waveform corresponding to the valid INS byte (blue) without preprocessing. (Color figure online)

taining both valid bytes and invalid bytes, we still use four methods: one-class SVM, IF, LOF, and LUNAR. And we calculate the outlier score of each waveform. The results are shown in Fig. 13, the green dots correspond to invalid byte waveforms, and the red triangles correspond to valid byte waveforms. According to Fig. 13, it can be inferred that only the detection-based LUNAR can accurately detect the correct results for the waveform sets with not obvious features.

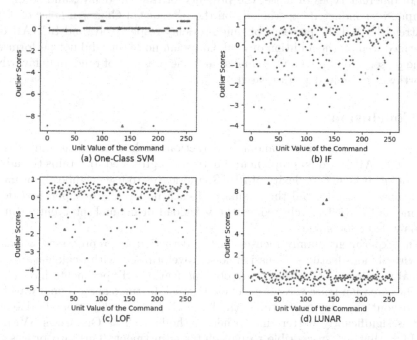

Fig. 13. Anomaly scores detected by One-Class SVM, IF, LOF and LUNAR on the original waveform set. (Color figure online)

6.3   Discovery and Discussion

In scenario 1, when the waveform set has obvious characteristics with preprocessing, anomaly detection is not a very difficult problem. However, for waveforms with a low signal-to-noise ratio, how to effectively extract points of interest through preprocessing is challenging, which requires inspectors to be experienced and have an in-depth understanding of the target device.

In scenario 2, there is artificially added Gaussian noise in the waveform set. At this time, the feature differences between abnormal data and normal data are relatively more complex, and anomaly detection based on unsupervised scenarios is more challenging. Our experimental results prove that LUNAR can provide accurate detection results in this scenario.

In scenario 3, the waveform set is not any preprocessed, and it is difficult to find the characteristics corresponding to the abnormal waveform, and it is difficult to directly detect the anomaly at this time. Our experimental results show that the LUNAR also has a good effect in this scenario. We suspect that this is because LUNAR improves the ability to learn optimizations or adapt to specific datasets that other methods lack. Moreover, significantly better than other methods, k defined in the LUNAR framework has little influence on the final anomaly. It is difficult for One-Class SVM, IF and LOF to adjust the parameters in the true "correct" direction without supervision, which has a great negative impact on the correctness of the results.

In addition, there are still many scenarios worth exploring, such as the presence of different types of noise, the presence of random delays, and so on. For example, we conducted experiments on the presence of Gaussian noise of different strengths and the presence of random delay respectively, and LUNAR only performed well on the addition of weak Gaussian noise, but did not perform well on the presence of more Gaussian noise and the presence of random delay, which is worthy of more in-depth research.

7   Conclusion

In this paper, an automatic anomaly detection method using the unified local outlier LUNAR based on graph neural network is proposed. It retains the advantages of linear time complexity of PBCS, and learns to use neighbor information in a trainable way to find the anomaly of each node. The unsupervised detection method can effectively reduce the workload of manual intervention in the anomaly detection stage.

The experiment mainly focuses on the detection of preprocessed waveform sets with obvious features, Gaussian noise waveform sets with weak features, and original waveform sets without any obvious features. Experiments have shown that for Gaussian noise waveform sets with weak features and original waveform sets without any obvious features, the LUNAR framework's anomaly detection effect is significantly better than other methods such as One-Class SVM, IF, and LOF that are susceptible to parameter adjustment. This also proves that our method can achieve highly automated and accurate detection even in the environment with low signal-to-noise ratio.

Acknowledgement. This work was supported by the National Key R&D Plan of China (2022YFB3103800), The Open Fund of Advanced Cryptography and System Security Key Laboratory of Sichuan Province (SKLACSS-202207), National Natural Science Foundation of China (62302036, 62272047), and Henan Key Laboratory of Network Cryptography Technology (LNCT2022-A24).

References

1. Bhunia, S., Hsiao, M.S., Banga, M., et al.: Hardware trojan attacks: threat analysis and countermeasures. Proc. IEEE **102**(8), 1229–1247 (2014)
2. Lv, Y.Q., Zhou, Q., Cai, Y.C., et al.: Trusted integrated circuits: the problem and challenges. J. Comput. Sci. Technol. **29**(5), 918–928 (2014)
3. Sumathi, G., Srivani, L., Thirugnana Murthy, D., et al.: A review on HT attacks in PLD and ASIC designs with potential defence solutions. IETE Tech. Rev. **35**(1), 64–77 (2018)
4. Chakraborty, R.S., Narasimhan, S., Bhunia, S.: Hardware trojan: threats and emerging solutions. In: 2009 IEEE International High Level Design Validation and Test Workshop, pp. 166–171. IEEE (2009)
5. Adee, S.: The hunt for the kill switch. IEEE SpEctrum **45**(5), 34–39 (2008)
6. DARPA, TRUST in Integrated Circuits (TIC) - Proposer Information Pamphlet, 2007
7. Bhunia, S., Abramovici, M., Agrawal, D., et al.: Protection against hardware trojan attacks: towards a comprehensive solution. IEEE Des. Test **30**(3), 6–17 (2013)
8. Shang, N., Wang, A., Ding, Y., et al.: A machine learning based golden-free detection method for command-activated hardware Trojan. Inf. Sci. **540**, 292–307 (2020)
9. ISO/IEC 7816-4:2005 Identification cards - Integrated circuit cards - Part 4: Organization, security and commands for interchange. Iso.org. 2008-10-03
10. Skorobogatov, S., Woods, C.: Breakthrough silicon scanning discovers backdoor in military chip. In: Prouff, E., Schaumont, P. (eds.) CHES 2012. LNCS, vol. 7428, pp. 23–40. Springer, Heidelberg (2012). https://doi.org/10.1007/978-3-642-33027-8_2
11. Wang, X., Tehranipoor, M., Plusquellic, J.: Detecting malicious inclusions in secure hardware: challenges and solutions. In: 2008 IEEE International Workshop on Hardware-Oriented Security and Trust, pp. 15–19. IEEE (2008)
12. Wolff, F., Papachristou, C., Bhunia, S., et al.: Towards Trojan-free trusted ICs: problem analysis and detection scheme. In: Proceedings of the Conference on Design, Automation and Test in Europe, pp. 1362–1365 (2008)
13. Banga, M., Hsiao, M.S.: A region based approach for the identification of hardware Trojans. In: 2008 IEEE International Workshop on Hardware-Oriented Security and Trust, pp. 40–47. IEEE (2008)
14. Banga, M., Hsiao, M.S.: A novel sustained vector technique for the detection of hardware Trojans. In: 2009 22nd International Conference on VLSI Design, pp. 327–332. IEEE (2009)
15. Liakos, K.G., Georgakilas, G.K., Moustakidis, S., et al.: Machine learning for hardware Trojan detection: a review. In: 2019 Panhellenic Conference on Electronics & Telecommunications (PACET), 1–6. IEEE (2019)
16. Jin, Y., Makris, Y.: Hardware Trojan detection using path delay fingerprint. In: 2008 IEEE International Workshop on Hardware-Oriented Security and Trust, pp. 51–57. IEEE (2008)

17. Rai, D., Lach, J.: Performance of delay-based Trojan detection techniques under parameter variations. In:2009 IEEE International Workshop on Hardware-Oriented Security and Trust, pp. 58–65. IEEE (2009)
18. Li, J., Lach, J.: At-speed delay characterization for IC authentication and Trojan horse detection. In: 2008 IEEE International Workshop on Hardware-Oriented Security and Trust, pp. 8–14. IEEE (2008)
19. Tehranipoor, M., Koushanfar, F.: A survey of hardware trojan taxonomy and detection. IEEE Des. Test Comput. **27**(1), 10–25 (2010)
20. Narasimhan, S., Du, D., Chakraborty, R.S., et al.: Multiple-parameter side-channel analysis: a non-invasive hardware Trojan detection approach. In: 2010 IEEE International Symposium on Hardware-Oriented Security and Trust (HOST), pp. 13–18. IEEE (2010)
21. Koushanfar, F., Mirhoseini, A.: A unified framework for multimodal submodular integrated circuits trojan detection. IEEE Trans. Inf. Forensics Secur. **6**(1), 162–174 (2010)
22. Ma, X., Wang, H., Li, B., et al.: A power analysis method against backdoor instruction in chips. ACTA Electron. Sin. **47**(3), 686 (2019)
23. Goodge, A., Hooi, B., Ng, S.K., et al.: Lunar: unifying local outlier detection methods via graph neural networks. In: Proceedings of the AAAI Conference on Artificial Intelligence, vol. 36, no. 6, pp. 6737–6745 (2022)

Cross-Correlation Based Trace Segmentation for Clustering Power Analysis on Public Key Cryptosystems

Yaoyuan Hu[1], An Wang[1(✉)], Weiping Gong[2(✉)], Jingjie Wu[2(✉)], Ziyu Wang[1], Shiming Zhang[3], and Shufan Ma[3]

[1] School of Cyberspace Science and Technology, Beijing Institute of Technology, Beijing, China
wangan@bit.edu.cn
[2] Guizhou Police College, Guiyang 550005, China
457615678@qq.com, wjj972@163.com
[3] AVIC (CHENGDU) UAS CO., LTD., Chengdu 610000, China

Abstract. Simple Power Analysis (SPA) is a technique that directly analyzes the power consumption information collected during the execution of cryptographic algorithms. It is primarily based on the fact that different key values in public key cryptosystems (PKC) correspond to distinct operations, reflected in the power traces, allowing for key recovery. Effective segmentation of the power trace significantly enhances the efficiency of SPA, reducing the difficulty of key retrieval. This paper introduces a semi automated Cross-Correlation Based Trace Segmentation method. We experimentally validated the segmentation method in scenarios involving smart cards, USB keys, and microcontrollers simulating unmanned aerial vehicle cryptographic modules. The results demonstrate the method's high effectiveness in segmenting power traces of PKC.

Keywords: Side-channel analysis · Simple power analysis · Public key cryptosystems · Power trace segmentation

1 Introduction and Related Work

In 1999, Kocher et al. first proposed an power analysis method for cryptographic systems, successfully recovering the DES algorithm key using Simple Power Analysis (SPA) and Differential Power Analysis (DPA) [11]. In the following years, power analysis experienced rapid development, witnessing the emergence of various novel power attacks, such as template attacks [4], collision attacks [2], correlation power analysis [3], Mutual Information Analysis [5], and more.

In 2000, Mayer-Sommer et al. asserted that SPA constitutes an effective and easily implementable attack. Due to its inherent simplicity, SPA may pose a more serious threat in numerous practical applications compared to DPA [13]. In 2002, Mangard et al. utilized SPA through the observation of power consumption patterns in the AES key expansion process, revealing information leakage

© The Author(s), under exclusive license to Springer Nature Switzerland AG 2024
M. Andreoni (Ed.): ACNS 2024 Workshops, LNCS 14586, pp. 359–375, 2024.
https://doi.org/10.1007/978-3-031-61486-6_21

on a significant portion of smart card processors. This disclosure unveiled the secret keys employed in the AES software implementations on smart cards [12]. Furthermore, SPA has evolved into a critical metric for evaluating the security of cryptographic devices [7–9].

In SPA, attackers infer key information by monitoring the power consumption variations of the target device during the execution of cryptographic algorithms. In public key cryptosystems (PKC), different keys correspond to different operations, and these operations manifest differently in the power trace. Therefore, if we can effectively segment the trace based on different operations, we can efficiently classify the trace and subsequently recover the key. In the case of an unknown encryption interval, IO trigger signals can be employed to locate the encryption interval [1]. At the current stage, the general process of SPA involves segmentation, dimensionality reduction, and clustering [6]. Among these, clustering methods find extensive application in the side-channel analysis domain. Chmielewski et al. employed clustering algorithms to attack the electromagnetic (EM) leakage of a protected ECC algorithm, achieving an accuracy of over 97% [15]. Additionally, Mesterharm et al. automated EM leakage analysis using clustering algorithms [14]. Combining clustering algorithms with Convolutional Neural Networks (CNN) can effectively reduce errors in side-channel analysis [17]. Indeed, clustering algorithms have even been applied in template attacks [10].

In 2022, Jens Trautmann and colleagues proposed a semi-automated segmentation method for the traces of block cipher algorithms [16]. However, when applied to PKC, this method may encounter the following three issues:

- In block cipher algorithms, the same operation is executed between different rounds, whereas in PKC. Taking RSA as an example, when the key bit is 0, a square operation is performed, and when the key bit is 1, one square operation and one multiplication operation are executed. Therefore, when constructing the CO template, it is not possible to determine whether to build the CO template for key 0 or key 1. In such cases, the aforementioned segmentation method may become ineffective.
- The above-mentioned segmentation method struggles to effectively find the CO template when dealing with issues related to random delays, leading to suboptimal segmentation results. In the case of AES, AES-128 consists of 10 rounds of encryption operations. The method mentioned earlier uses one or several fixed interval lengths to estimate the length of each round in the AES algorithm. However, due to the presence of random delays in the power trace, there are significant time variations between each round. Therefore, calculating the correlation coefficient using a fixed length of continuous segments for 10 rounds will not exhibit any sharp peaks, thus making it difficult to effectively highlight the segmentation positions amidst other locations.
- The number of rounds in block cipher algorithms is fixed, allowing for the effective utilization of these rounds to construct the entire encryption interval's CO template. However, the number of rounds in PKC is uncertain. In

situations where the number of rounds is uncertain, the segmentation method mentioned above is unable to construct the CO template effectively.

1.1 Our Contributions

We proposes a Cross-Correlation Based Trace Segmentation method that accomplishes effective segmentation of power traces in PKC.

- We provide detailed steps for each operation in the proposed method and offer comprehensive explanations of the algorithms employed in each step.
- We validated our method using a publicly available dataset [18] containing power traces collected from different platform software and hardware implementations of RSA and SM2 algorithms. This method achieves a segmentation accuracy of 100% on the dataset. We conducted a comparative analysis of various existing trace segmentation methods in several aspects.
- We provided explicit assumptions, discussed the strengths and weaknesses of our method and introduced specific fine-tuning mechanisms.

1.2 Paper Organization

In Sect. 2, we provide a concise overview of the application of correlation coefficients in side-channel analysis and introduce the concept of simple power analysis in PKC. Section 3 offers a detailed exposition of our segmentation method. Moving on to Sect. 4, we demonstrated the effectiveness of our trace segmentation method on the dataset [18] and conducted comparative analyses with other segmentation techniques. Finally, in Sect. 5, we summarized the entire content of the paper.

2 Preliminary

2.1 Correlation Coefficients for Power Analysis

In side-channel power analysis, attackers typically observe the power consumption variations of a cryptographic system under different input states to infer the key or other sensitive information. Correlation coefficients can be used to quantify the degree of correlation between input and power consumption, assisting attackers in identifying power patterns associated with the key.

$$\rho_{X,Y} = \frac{\text{cov}(X,Y)}{\sigma_X \sigma_Y}. \tag{1}$$

2.2 Simple Power Analysis on PKC

SPA is a technique that enables direct analysis of power consumption information collected during the execution of cryptographic algorithms. Typically, attackers can recover sensitive security parameters or key information in a cryptographic device based on just one or a few given power traces. In the implementation of PKC, conditional branches are generated based on the values of the key. When the corresponding power traces also differ, the key values differ. Attackers can directly extract key information by analyzing the power consumption shapes on the power trace. Therefore, unprotected implementations of PKC are common targets for SPA attacks.

Taking the RSA algorithm as an example, modular exponentiation is used in both RSA encryption and decryption, often accelerated using the square-and-multiply algorithm. The specific implementation process of the square-and-multiply algorithm is shown in Algorithm 1: a 1024-bit integer d is utilized as the RSA encryption key. When the key bit involved in the operation is 1, a square operation followed by a multiply operation is performed. When the key bit is 0, only a square operation is executed. We can capture the power trace during the RSA decryption phase, as depicted in Fig. 1. It is evident that the shapes of the power traces correspond to the square and multiply operations. Thus, by analyzing just one power trace, we can sequentially recover the square and multiply operations, leveraging the differences between key bits 0 and 1 associated with square and multiply operations. This enables the complete recovery of the RSA encryption algorithm key.

Algorithm 1: Squaring-Multiplication Algorithm for RSA Encryption.

Input: 1024-bit integer $d = d_{1023}d_{1022}\ldots d_2 d_1 d_0$.
Output: $x^d \bmod N$.

1 $Q = 1$;
2 **for** $j = 1023$ **down to** 0 **do**
3     $Q = Q^2 \bmod N$;
4   **if** $d_j = 1$ **then**
5        $\mid$ $Q = Q \cdot x \bmod N$;
6   **end**
7 **end**
8 **return** Q;

---

3   Cross-Correlation Based Trace Segmentation

3.1   Assumptions

To achieve effective trace segmentation, we make the following assumptions regarding the power traces during the encryption and decryption of PKC:

- During the execution of cryptographic algorithms, we assume that when the same operation is performed, the corresponding shapes of the power traces are similar.
- During the execution of cryptographic algorithms, we assume that when different operations are performed, the corresponding shapes of the power traces

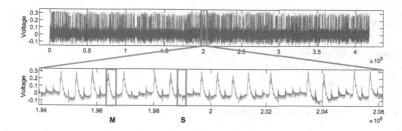

Fig. 1. Power trace of RSA decryption on STM32F429.

are distinct. However, due to influences such as the cryptographic device, operands, registers, etc., there remains a certain degree of similarity in the power trace shapes.

3.2 The Method Steps

Based on the aforementioned assumptions, the steps of the method for trace segmentation are as follows:

1. Select a segment of the original power trace representing the power trace of a single operation as the template.
2. Use the length of this template as the sliding window size and slide the window point by point along the original power trace.
3. Calculate the correlation coefficient between the power trace within the sliding window and the template trace with each slide.
4. Choose an appropriate filtering parameter to filter the correlation coefficient curve, enhancing the appearance of prominent peaks in the curve.
5. Record the peak positions of the filtered correlation coefficient curve and set a tolerance interval. Within this tolerance interval, the maximum value of the original correlation coefficient curve is identified as the desired point for trace segmentation.

Algorithm 2 is a pseudocode for calculating correlation coefficients using a sliding window. The input to the algorithm includes the original power trace T, the starting position of the template pos, the sliding stride s, and the length l of the sliding window. Based on the trace length, sliding window length, and step size, the number of sliding steps n can be determined. The algorithm computes correlation between the selected template $Temp$ and the traces within the sliding window W. The output is the calculated correlations Cor. In the experiments of this paper, the s is selected as 1, indicating that correlation calculations are performed on each trace within a sliding window. Increasing the s value slightly improves computational speed while sacrificing a marginal precision. However, it should be noted that when the s value is not equal to 1, the resulting segmentation points need to undergo iterative computations related to the s variable in order to obtain the final segmentation points.

Algorithm 2: Cross-Correlation Based Trace Segmentation.

Input: Trace T, length of the sliding window l, stride s, start position pos.
Output: Correlations Cor.
1 $Temp = T[pos : pos + l]$;
2 **for** $i = 0$ **to** n **do**
3 | $W = T[i * s : i * s + l]$;
4 | $Cor[i] = \textbf{CalculateCorrelation}(T, W)$;
5 **end**
6 **return** Cor;

3.3 Advantages of the Method

The method proposed in this paper has several advantages. Firstly, it effectively addresses the issue of random delays, allowing for accurate trace segmentation. Additionally, the method incorporates a fine-tuning mechanism that enables efficient and precise segmentation. The specific descriptions are as follows:

- The method is also effective in addressing the issue of random delays during the encryption process. When the power trace is protected with random delays, during the sliding process of the window over this portion of the power trace, relatively high correlation coefficients will be computed between the random delay and the selected template trace, resulting in several small peaks on the correlation coefficient curve. These small peaks can be eliminated by applying a simple filtering operation to the correlation coefficient curve, consolidating them into a single peak, which corresponds to the desired point for trace segmentation.
- The method provides a certain tolerance interval, reducing the potential impact of segment point offsets caused by filtering the correlation curve. As mentioned earlier, when calculating the correlation coefficient between the template trace and the trace containing random delays, multiple peaks may occur. Filtering all these peaks together may result in a potential offset in the final peak. Therefore, we introduce a fault-tolerant interval to address this issue. The obtained segmentation points are allowed to slide within the fault-tolerant interval on the unfiltered trace. By locating the maximum value on the unfiltered correlation coefficient curve, the impact of potential offsets caused by filtering can be mitigated. Algorithm 3 is pseudocode for the fine-tuning mechanism we designed. The input to the algorithm includes the unfiltered correlation Cor, the peak segmentation points P obtained from the filtered correlation coefficients, the sliding window length l, and the fine-tuning factor f. For each segmentation point p_i, the final segmented point FP after fine-tuning is determined by selecting the index of the maximum value within the range $Cor[p - f \cdot l : p + f \cdot l]$. The fine-tuning factor f refers to the ratio of the interval within which the computed segmentation points can be shifted. By allowing movement within this interval, the segmentation point with the maximum correlation coefficient is selected, effectively enhancing the experimental

precision. In the experiments of this paper, a range of 0.2 to 0.4 is chosen for the fine-tuning factor f.

Algorithm 3: Fine-Tuning Mechanism for Correlation.

Input: Unfiltered correlation Cor, Segmentation points before fine-tuning P,
sliding window length l, Fine-tuning factor f.

Output: Final segmentation points FP.

1 **for** $p_i \in P$ **do**
2     $SubCor = Cor[p - f \cdot l : p + f \cdot l]$;
3     $FP[i] = $ **GetMaxIndex**$(SubCor)$;
4 **end**
5 **return** FP;

---

4 Experiments and Comparisons

We experimentally validated the segmentation method in scenarios involving smart cards, USB keys, and microcontrollers simulating unmanned aerial vehicle cryptographic modules. The results demonstrate the method's high effectiveness in segmenting power traces of PKC. Below, we will showcase the segmentation results of this method on different power traces.

4.1 Experimental Results

SM2 on AT89S52. Figure 2 represents the original power trace of the SM2 decryption algorithm implemented in software on AT89S52. We can clearly observe power traces corresponding to two different operations, highlighted with orange rectangles in the figure. However, in actual segmentation, there is no need to differentiate which power trace corresponds to which operation. We randomly select a trace segment corresponding to one operation in the power trace as the template, marked with a red rectangle in the figure. Then, using the size of this template as the sliding window size, we slide along the power trace from the starting point to the endpoint, calculating the correlation coefficient between the template and the trace within the sliding window at each point.

Figure 3 depicts the computed correlation coefficient curve. We selected a suitable filtering parameter to filter the correlation coefficient curve, ensuring that prominent peaks appear in the curve. Figure 4 displays the correlation coefficient curve after filtering. The red dots in the figure represent the trace segmentation points selected from the filtered correlation coefficient curve. These segmentation points are not precisely at the peak positions due to the fine-tuning introduced by the tolerance interval provided in our method. Upon closer observation of the filtered correlation coefficient curve, we can discern the possibility of distinguishing different operations based on the height of the curve peaks. Combined with algorithm characteristics, there is an opportunity to directly recover the algorithm key based on the heights of the curve peaks. Figure 5 illustrates the specific trace segmentation results achieved by the method. This method demonstrates excellent robustness. Segmentation success rate of 100%.

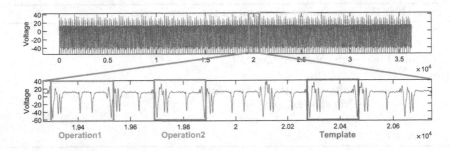

Fig. 2. Power trace of SM2 decryption on AT89S52.

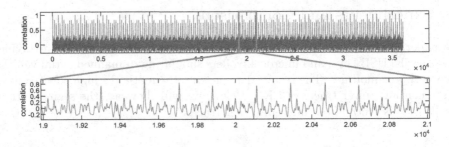

Fig. 3. Correlation trace of SM2 decryption on AT89S52.

RSA on STM32F429. Figure 6 represents the original power trace of the RSA decryption algorithm implemented in software on STM32F429. We can clearly observe from the power trace that one type of operation corresponds to a significant drop, while the other type of operation corresponds to a smaller drop. Following the method steps outlined in Sect. 3.2, specific trace segmentation results are obtained as shown in Fig. 7. Segmentation success rate of 100%.

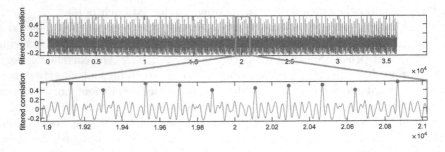

Fig. 4. Filtered correlation trace of SM2 decryption on AT89S52.

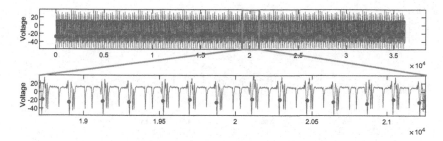

Fig. 5. Power trace segmentation result of SM2 decryption on AT89S52.

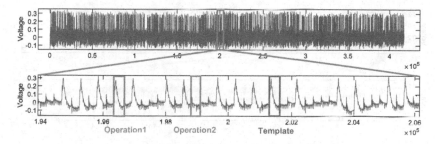

Fig. 6. Power trace of RSA decryption on STM32F429.

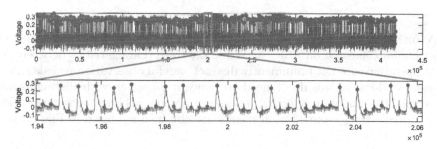

Fig. 7. Power trace segmentation result of RSA decryption on STM32F429.

SM2 on Smart Card. Figure 8 represents the original power trace of the SM2 algorithm implemented on smart card. The number of peaks between different operation intervals varies. We randomly select one type of operation as a template. Following the method steps outlined in Sect. 3.2, specific trace segmentation results are obtained as shown in Fig. 9. Segmentation success rate of 100%.

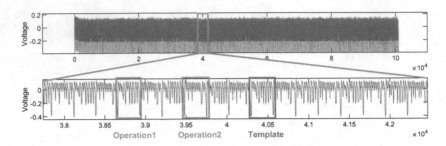

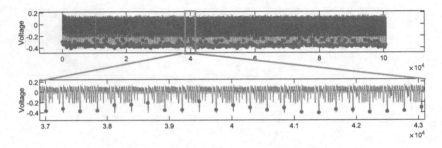

Fig. 8. Power trace of SM2 decryption on smart card.

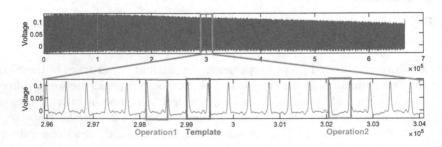

Fig. 9. Power trace segmentation result of SM2 decryption on smart card.

RSA on ASIC X. Figure 10 represents the original power trace of the RSA algorithm implemented on ASIC X. While the trace characteristics between different operations are not prominently distinct, careful observation reveals subtle differences. However, we don't need to concern ourselves with distinguishing operations. By randomly selecting a segment, we can achieve the segmentation effect. Specific trace segmentation results are obtained as shown in Fig. 11.

Fig. 10. Power trace of RSA decryption on ASIC X.

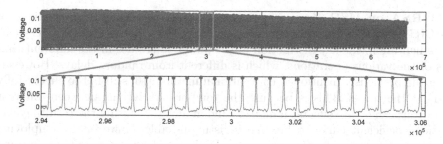

Fig. 11. Power trace segmentation result of RSA decryption on ASIC X.

RSA on Smart Card. Figure 12 represents the original power trace of the RSA algorithm implemented on smart card. From the zoomed-in plot of the original trace, it is not immediately apparent that there are significant differences between the different operations. However, upon closer observation, it can be noticed that one of the operations exhibits a distinct downward spike in the trace, while the other operation does not. Although we needn't to understand the internal differences between these operations, we can randomly select one operation as the template and apply the methodology described in Sect. 3.2 to obtain the segmentation results. The segmentation results are illustrated in Fig. 13.

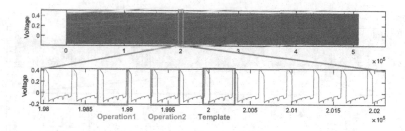

Fig. 12. Power trace of RSA decryption on smart card.

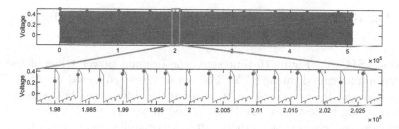

Fig. 13. Power trace segmentation result of RSA decryption on smart card.

CRT-RSA on USB Key. Figure 14 represents the original power trace of the CRT-RSA signature implemented on USB Key. In the case of CRT-RSA implementation, the key distinction in the power traces lies in the different timings of the various operations, which is different from random delays. However, using the previously mentioned conventional method [16] still fail to successfully segment the traces. This is because the temporal variations between different operations can create effects similar to random delays, causing the resulting correlation coefficient curve to become indistinguishable. However, by employing the method described in this paper, randomly selecting a segment, performing sliding computations, and applying relevant adjustments, effective segmentation points can be obtained. The segmentation results are illustrated in Fig. 15.

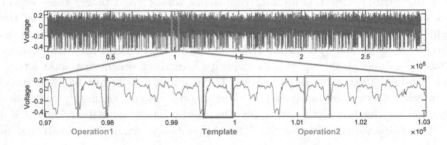

Fig. 14. Power trace of CRT-RSA on USB Key.

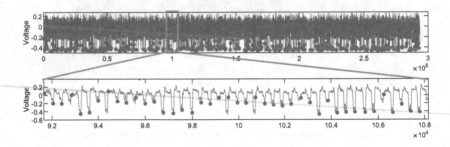

Fig. 15. Power trace segmentation result of CRT-RSA on USB Key.

RSA on ASIC Y. Figure 16 represents the original power trace of the RSA algorithm implemented on ASIC Y. The power traces collected on ASIC Y has dense points and it is challenging to observe the differences between different operations using basic techniques. It is indeed necessary to utilize dimensionality reduction and clustering methods after successful segmentation to identify specific differences. In this case, we can randomly select one segment as the template and slide it over the original trace to calculate the final segmentation points. Even with a relatively large number of data points in the trace, our method remains effective. The segmentation results are illustrated in Fig. 17.

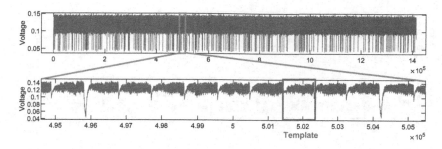

Fig. 16. Power trace of RSA on ASIC Y.

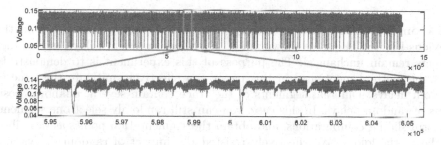

Fig. 17. Power trace segmentation result of RSA decryption on ASIC Y

RSA on SAKURA-G. Figure 18 represents the original power trace of the RSA algorithm implemented on SAKURA-G. For this trace, we are aware of its characteristics and distinguishing features. The significant power consumption in the depicted portion corresponds to RSA decryption, while the less significant power consumption represents redundancy. After zooming in on the trace during the decryption phase, we observed periodic spikes with regular patterns. Each cryptographic operation corresponds to the interval between two prominent peaks. The trace itself exhibits clear distinctions between different operations. The segmentation results are illustrated in Fig. 19.

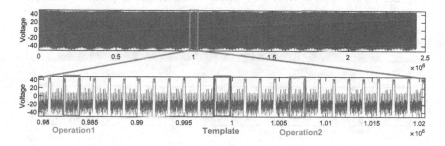

Fig. 18. Power trace of RSA decryption on SAKURA-G.

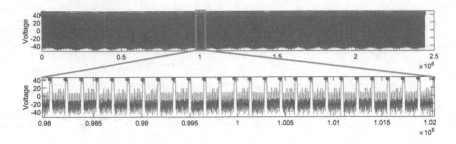

Fig. 19. Power trace segmentation result of RSA decryption on SAKURA-G.

RSA on SAKURA-G Containing Random Delays. Differing from the previous Fig. 18. The trace shown in Fig. 20 includes random delays, while other aspects remain unchanged. The purpose of this experiment is to demonstrate that the method mentioned in this paper can effectively mitigate the issue of random delays. Different segments of the trace contain several unknown positions of random delays. In this case, you can still randomly select one segment, perform sliding computations, and obtain the segmentation points as described in the methodology. We effectively resisted the impact of random delays and successfully carried out trace segmentation, as shown in the results in Fig. 21.

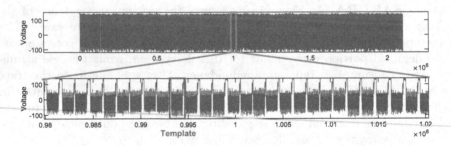

Fig. 20. Power trace of RSA decryption on SAKURA-G (random delay).

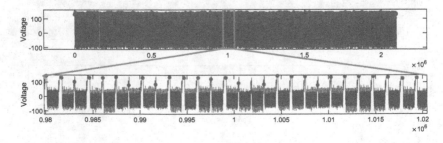

Fig. 21. Power trace segmentation result of RSA decryption on SAKURA-G (random delay).

4.2   Experimental Summary

Our segmentation method has effectively implemented trace segmentation on the public datasets [18], demonstrating the feasibility of applying our segmentation method to the power trace of PKC. In some cases, we can even directly discern the differences between different operations through the correlation coefficient curves calculated and even possess some potential for key recovery.

4.3   Comparison and Summary of Different Methods

We conducted a series of comparisons between the segmentation methods mentioned in this paper and the segmentation method proposed in this paper. In terms of the automation level of different methods, only SPA-GPT achieved the automatic segmentation of power traces, while other methods were semi-automated. Regarding the computation time of different methods, both the Findpeak and This paper had computation times within 3 min, while SPA-GPT required 10–30 min, and the computation time for the Semi-Auto CO Location in public key segmentation was not available. As for the ability to resist random delays, Semi-Auto CO Location method was unable to resist the impact of random delays on power traces, while other methods effectively resisted random delays in power segmentation. Comparing the power trace segmentation of PKC, except for Semi-Auto CO Location, all other methods demonstrated the capability to segment power traces of PKC. Regarding the key recovery capability, both SPA-GPT and This paper have the potential for key recovery, while the other two methods lack such potential (Table 1).

Table 1. Comparison of Different Methods

	Findpeak	SPA-GPT [19]	Semi-Auto CO Location [16]	This Paper
Automatic	Semi	Fully	Semi	Semi
Time (mins)	<=3	10–30	NULL	<= 3
Random Delay	Yes	Yes	No	Yes
Attack on PKC	Yes	Yes	No	Yes
Key Recovery	No	Yes	No	Yes

5   Conclusions

At the current stage, the automation of SPA primarily involves three steps: segmentation, dimensionality reduction, and clustering. Among them, effective segmentation of the power trace is particularly crucial. In this paper, we introduce a semi-automated, simple and effective method tailored for PKC, successfully achieving the efficient segmentation of power traces. We address challenges related to diverse operations, random delays, and uncertain rounds. The experiments demonstrate promising results for PKC implemented on different devices.

Acknowledgement. This work was supported by National Key R&D Program of China (No. 2022YFB3103800), Guizhou Provincial Key Technology R&D Program (No. [2023]442), Foundation of Guizhou Educational Committee (Nos. [2021]053, [2023]080), Project for High Quality Development of Manufacturing Industry (No. TC220A04X-2).

References

1. Beckers, A., Balasch, J., Gierlichs, B., Verbauwhede, I.: Design and implementation of a waveform-matching based triggering system. In: Standaert, F.-X., Oswald, E. (eds.) COSADE 2016. LNCS, vol. 9689, pp. 184–198. Springer, Cham (2016). https://doi.org/10.1007/978-3-319-43283-0_11
2. Bogdanov, A.: Improved side-channel collision attacks on AES. In: Adams, C., Miri, A., Wiener, M. (eds.) SAC 2007. LNCS, vol. 4876, pp. 84–95. Springer, Heidelberg (2007). https://doi.org/10.1007/978-3-540-77360-3_6
3. Brier, E., Clavier, C., Olivier, F.: Correlation power analysis with a leakage model. In: Joye, M., Quisquater, J.-J. (eds.) CHES 2004. LNCS, vol. 3156, pp. 16–29. Springer, Heidelberg (2004). https://doi.org/10.1007/978-3-540-28632-5_2
4. Chari, S., Rao, J.R., Rohatgi, P.: Template attacks. In: Kaliski, B.S., Koç, K., Paar, C. (eds.) CHES 2002. LNCS, vol. 2523, pp. 13–28. Springer, Heidelberg (2003). https://doi.org/10.1007/3-540-36400-5_3
5. Gierlichs, B., Batina, L., Tuyls, P., Preneel, B.: Mutual information analysis. In: Oswald, E., Rohatgi, P. (eds.) CHES 2008. LNCS, vol. 5154, pp. 426–442. Springer, Heidelberg (2008). https://doi.org/10.1007/978-3-540-85053-3_27
6. Heyszl, J., Ibing, A., Mangard, S., De Santis, F., Sigl, G.: Clustering algorithms for non-profiled single-execution attacks on exponentiations. In: Francillon, A., Rohatgi, P. (eds.) CARDIS 2013. LNCS, vol. 8419, pp. 79–93. Springer, Cham (2014). https://doi.org/10.1007/978-3-319-08302-5_6
7. ISO: ISO/IEC 19790: Information Security Management Systems – Requirements. ISO/IEC Standard 19790, International Organization for Standardization (2012)
8. ISO: ISO/IEC 30104: Information technology - Security techniques - Security requirements for cryptographic modules. ISO/IEC Standard 30104, International Organization for Standardization (2015)
9. ISO: ISO/IEC 17825: Information technology - Security techniques - Testing methods for the mitigation of non-invasive attack classes against cryptographic modulese. ISO/IEC Standard 1782590, International Organization for Standardization (2016)
10. Kim, T.: A study of template clustering in the side channel template analysis. In: 2018 International Conference on Information and Communication Technology Convergence (ICTC), pp. 1295–1297. IEEE (2018)
11. Kocher, P., Jaffe, J., Jun, B.: Differential power analysis. In: Wiener, M. (ed.) CRYPTO 1999. LNCS, vol. 1666, pp. 388–397. Springer, Heidelberg (1999). https://doi.org/10.1007/3-540-48405-1_25
12. Mangard, S.: A simple power-analysis (SPA) attack on implementations of the AES key expansion. In: Lee, P.J., Lim, C.H. (eds.) ICISC 2002. LNCS, vol. 2587, pp. 343–358. Springer, Heidelberg (2003). https://doi.org/10.1007/3-540-36552-4_24
13. Mayer-Sommer, R.: Smartly analyzing the simplicity and the power of simple power analysis on smartcards. In: Koç, Ç.K., Paar, C. (eds.) CHES 2000. LNCS, vol. 1965, pp. 78–92. Springer, Heidelberg (2000). https://doi.org/10.1007/3-540-44499-8_6

14. Mesterharm, C., Izmailov, R., Alexander, S., Tsang, S.: Automated clustering of EM side-channel emissions to detect anomalous device behavior. In: Cyber Sensing 2020, vol. 11417, pp. 59–68. SPIE (2020)
15. Nascimento, E., Chmielewski, Ł: Applying horizontal clustering side-channel attacks on embedded ECC implementations. In: Eisenbarth, T., Teglia, Y. (eds.) CARDIS 2017. LNCS, vol. 10728, pp. 213–231. Springer, Cham (2018). https://doi.org/10.1007/978-3-319-75208-2_13
16. Trautmann, J., Beckers, A., Wouters, L., Wildermann, S., Verbauwhede, I., Teich, J.: Semi-automatic locating of cryptographic operations in side-channel traces. IACR Transactions on Cryptographic Hardware and Embedded Systems, pp. 345–366 (2022)
17. Wang, A., He, S., Wei, C., Sun, S., Ding, Y., Wang, J.: Using convolutional neural network to redress outliers in clustering based side-channel analysis on cryptosystem. In: Qiu, M., Lu, Z., Zhang, C. (eds.) Smart Computing and Communication. SmartCom 2022. LNCS, vol. 13828, pp. 360–370. Springer, Cham (2023). https://doi.org/10.1007/978-3-031-28124-2_34
18. Wang, Z.: Traces for SPA-GPT (2023). https://github.com/pilipili520/SPA-GPT. Accessed 01 Dec 2023
19. Wang, Z., et al.: SPA-GPT: general pulse tailor for simple power analysis based on reinforcement learning. Cryptology ePrint Archive (2023)

Fully Hybrid TLSv1.3 in WolfSSL
on Cortex-M4

Mila Anastasova[1]([✉]), Reza Azarderakhsh[1], and Mehran Mozaffari Kermani[2]

[1] Computer and Electrical Engineering and Computer Science Department
and I-SENSE at Florida Atlantic University, Boca Raton, FL, USA
{manastasova2017,razarderakhsh}@fau.edu
[2] Computer Engineering and Science Department at University of South Florida,
Tampa, FL, USA
mehran2@usf.edu

Abstract. To provide safe communication across an unprotected medium such as the internet, network protocols are being established. These protocols employ public key techniques to perform key exchange and authentication. Transport Layer Security (TLS) is a widely used network protocol that enables secure communication between a server and a client. TLS is employed in billions of transactions per second. Contemporary protocols depend on traditional methods that utilize the computational complexity of factorization or (elliptic curve) logarithm mathematics problems. The ongoing advancement in the processing power of classical computers requires an ongoing increase in the security level of the underlying cryptographic algorithms. This study focuses on the analysis of Curve448 and Edwards curve Ed448, renowned for their superior security features that offer a 224-bit level of security as part of the TLSv1.3 protocol. The exponential advancement of quantum computers, however, presents a substantial threat to secure network communication that depends on classical crypto schemes, irrespective of their degree of security. Quantum computers have the capability to resolve these challenges within a feasible timeframe. In order to successfully transition to Post-Quantum secure network protocols, it is imperative to concurrently deploy both classical and post-quantum algorithms. This is done to fulfill the requirements of both enterprises and governments, while also instilling more assurance in the reliability of the post-quantum systems. This paper presents a detailed hybrid implementation architecture of the TLSv1.3 network protocol. We showcase the first deployment of Curve448 and Crystals-Kyber for the purpose of key exchanging, and Ed448 and Crystals-Dilithium for verifying the authenticity of entities and for X.509 Public Key Infrastructure (PKI). We rely upon the widely used OpenSSL library and the specific wolfSSL library for embedded devices to provide our results for server and client applications.

Keywords: Network Protocols · TLSv1.3 · PKI · X.509, Elliptic Curve Cryptography (ECC) · Post-Quantum Cryptography (PQC) · Cortex-M4

© The Author(s), under exclusive license to Springer Nature Switzerland AG 2024
M. Andreoni (Ed.): ACNS 2024 Workshops, LNCS 14586, pp. 376–395, 2024.
https://doi.org/10.1007/978-3-031-61486-6_22

1   Introduction

In the era of digital technology, where information is easily transmitted worldwide, the foundation of interconnected systems is formed by complex network protocols ensuring reliability and interoperability of communication networks. Security protocols, such as the most world wide SSL/TLS, relays on cryptographical algorithms, to ensure data integrity, confidentiality, authentication and non-repudiation. Public Key Cryptography (PKC) allows the secure communication establishment between entities through insecure channel, such as the Internet, and is a fundamental component of security network protocols. Transport Security Layer (TLS), also knows by the name of its predecessor Socket Security Layer (SSL), integrates PKC algorithms for key exchange and digital signature to allow secure data exchange across communication parties. It enables them to transition their application data exchange to a Symmetric Key Cryptographic scheme, which guarantees significantly improved computation time. Throughout the years, the SSL/TLS protocol specification has been going through changes, in order to eliminate vulnerabilities, improve timing and increase security of the performed communication. In 2016, the latest version, TLSv1.3 [1], was released, included many revisions, along with the deprecation of weak algorithms that were supported in earlier versions of TLS, as well as the addition of new algorithms.

The Elliptic Curve Cryptography (ECC) family of algorithms is one of the most widely deployed cryptographic PKC schemes, owing to their small key and signature sizes, which allow them to be used in bandwidth-constrained scenarios, as well as their relatively low computational cost, which allows them to be used in both high- and low-end devices. Curve448, used for Elliptic Curve Diffie-Hellman (ECDH) based key derivation, and its birationally equivalent Ed448, forming Edwards curve Digital Signature Algorithm (EdDSA), have become of interest among multiple ECC primitive instantiations, based on eliminating several cryptographic security concerns inherent in NIST curves while offering high security level.

The progressive development of Quantum Computers, marked by the continuous increase in q-bit quantities, presents a significant challenge to conventional cryptographic methods that form the basis of network communication. Shor [2] demonstrates that classical cryptographic primitives are vulnerable to quantum computer attacks once a sufficiently powerful computer is constructed. This would enable the solving of Factorization and Discrete Logarithm problems, which form the core of classical cryptographic primitives.

In 2016, the National Institute of Standards and Technology [3] (NIST) began evaluating the efficacy and efficiency of a list of recently submitted cryptographic algorithms that are resistant to attacks by quantum computers. Following three rounds of evaluation and enhancements, NIST has announced four algorithms that will ultimately be standardized thereafter used in a broad variety of security protocols. Among six families of post-quantum robust cryptographic algorithms, lattice-based schemes show to be one of the most promising based on their relatively compact key sizes and the extremely efficient computational cost. Based on Module-Learning With Errors (M-LWE), Crystals-Kyber Key Encapsulation Mechanism (KEM), based on Public Key Encryption (PKE) along with a variation of the Fujisaki–Okamoto (FO) transform to ensure $IND - CCA2$-security, is the only PQ key exchange finalists of the NIST PQ Standardization process. Similarly, M-LWE-based Crystals-Dilithium Digital Signature Algorithms (DSA) form part of the three PQ secure finalists for DSA along with Falcon and SPHINCS+, showing on average (key generation + sign + verify) performance advantage among its competitors and *reasonably* compact keys and signature sizes.

Given that the PQ algorithms are relatively new, they fail to fulfill the security criteria set by the government and industry. Therefore, a hybrid instantiation is necessary to provide a seamless transition to PQ network protocols. In this work, we present, to the best of our knowledge, the first entirely hybrid instantiation of the widely deployed TLSv1.3 protocols, integrating classical high security Curve448 ECDH and Crystals-Kyber1024 PQ KEM algorithms for key derivation among client and server and Edwards curve Ed448 traditional digital signature algorithm along with Crystals-Dilithium5, in order to ensure data privacy, integrity, authentication, and non-repudiation in the presence of classical and PQ adversary. We perform hybrid key derivation and enhance the Public Key Infrastructure (PKI) defined by the X.509 certificate standard by integrating hybrid keys, certificate (signature) generation and signature verification.

Ensuring the deployment of cryptographic algorithms and security protocols on resource-constrained devices and bandwidth-limited scenarios is crucial due to the increasing integration of small embedded systems in everyday life, driven by the Internet of Things (IoT) and the desire to enhance lifestyle and comfort. This study aims to assess the performance of the hybrid TLSv1.3 protocol using Curve448 with Kyber1024 and Ed448 with Dilithium5 algorithms. The evaluation is conducted on the NIST approved ARMv7-based Cortex-M4 processor, specifically on the WiFi enabled STM32F413 Discovery Board. We base our work on the widely deployed OpenSSL library in order to generate the hybrid X.509 keys and signatures and wolfSSL embedded-focused library for performance evaluation.

1.1   Related Work

The widespread use of Internet of Things (IoT) devices, embedded systems, and various other low-end computer platforms has brought about an epoch of remarkable connectivity via the deployment of network protocols. Yet, the inherent characteristics of these devices, featuring restricted processing capabilities and limitations in power and energy supply, provide a significant obstacle in the implementation of resilient cryptographic protocols. Elliptic Curve Cryptography is considered a fundamental aspect of secure communication because of its simplicity and robust security promises. Nevertheless, the use of this technology on low-end devices requires a careful and sophisticated strategy to overcome the underlying constraints.

Curve448, introduced by *Hamburg* in [4], is meticulously designed to strike a balance between strength and computational efficiency, making it a compelling choice for secure key exchange and digital signatures. The high security level, in comparison to other NIST curves or Curve2551 and Ed25519 proposed in [5] and

[6], comes at the cost of computational overhead based on the larger length of the field arithmetics. This challenge is significantly important when it comes to IoT devices with limited computational resources and bounded battery life. This is the reason for exhaustive effort in the optimal implementation of the cryptographic schemes aiming at optimal execution on embedded devices. The nature of ECC allows optimizations on the field arithmetic layer, where different research teams have shown efficient implementation for Curve448 and Ed448 targeting 8-bit AVR and 16-bit MSP, and 32-bit Cortex-M4 devices [7–12]. The higher-layer group operation may also introduce implementation optimizations based on applying optimal strategies for point addition and multiplication, the core of ECC schemes. Several works have been performed, applying different point multiplication architectures, such as low execution latency (Sliding Window [13] method, Signed Comb [14] method), compact code side (Double-and-Add [15]) or constant time performance (Double-and-Always-Add, Montgomery Ladder [16]). The optimal implementation of Curve448 and Ed448 is further being evaluated as part of network protocols [17].

Deploying post-quantum cryptography primitives on low-end devices is particularly problematic because to the increased resources needed for its implementation. Lattice-based post-quantum primitives, such as Kyber and Dilithium, rely on computationally easy problems and do not need intricate multi-precision field arithmetic due to the tiny modulus used in operations. Both methods rely on two computationally intensive algorithms: the Secure Hash Algorithm 3 (SHA-3) and the Number Theoretic Transform (NTT), which is essentially equivalent to the Fast Fourier Transform (FFT) function applied over finite fields. Various studies in the literature have offered distinct approaches, demonstrating the most effective techniques for executing certain procedures.

Several researchers focus on optimizing the design of ARMv8-based devices to demonstrate the effectiveness of NTT transform function and modular reduction in enabling the use of NEON-specific Single Instruction Multiple Data (SIMD) instructions. This optimization leads to significant improvements in the runtime performance of the lattice-based Kyber and Dilithium PQ primitives [18–22]. Targeting Advanced Vector Extension (AVX) ISA (AVX2 and AVX-512) was presented in [23,24]. Other writers focus on exploiting the computational capabilities of more advanced devices, such as GPUs, which are known for their high processing power [25–27]. *Botros et al.* have provided an implementation design for low-end IoT devices that focuses on optimizing the RAM use of Kyber while enhancing its speed performance [28]. *Alkim et al.* [29] demonstrate superior outcomes of NTT calculations by utilizing an improved modular reduction architecture, which enables the adoption of an efficient Instruction Set Architecture (ISA) in combination with lazy-reduction deployment. *Abdulrahman et al.* present several ways for implementing NTT, enhancing register use management, and achieving vector-matrix accumulation outcomes in their study [30].

The extensively improved classical and post-quantum public-key cryptography (PKC) primitives serve as the fundamental mathematical components of security network protocols, particularly the SSL/TLS network protocol, which is the most extensively utilized. It employed several cryptographic techniques to provide safe and dependable communication between server and client entities within the Internet network. While extensive research has been conducted on the performance outcomes of cryptographic primitives, there has been a lack of sufficient research on the complete integration of classical and hybrid systems into network protocols, which is the focus of this study.

The incorporation of post-quantum (PQ) and hybrid operating modes into the TLSv1.3 network protocol necessitates substantial effort due to the utilization of numerous cryptographic methods. Several studies in the literature have explored the development of a PQ operational mode for the TLSv1.3 protocol and its predecessor, TLSv1.2, as well as other network protocols [31,32]. *Kampanakis et al.* [33] examine the utilization of PQ signatures inside X.509 PKI certificates, specifically in relation to the package fragmentation mechanism. *Crockett et al.* [31] present a study of hybrid key exchange within the context of TLS and SSH network protocols. They examine several classical and post-quantum cryptographic primitives and explore ways for deploying hybrid authentication and X.509 PKI. *Campagna et al.* [34] describes the inclusion of hybrid key exchange in the TLSv1.2 network protocol, which incorporates SIKE and BIKE post-quantum key encapsulation mechanisms (PQ KEMs) in addition to elliptic curve Diffie-Hellman (ECDH) methods. *Sikeridis et al.* [35] improve the OQS and OpenSSL library by incorporating a PQ-standalone message signature and modifying the X.509 PKI with post-quantum capabilities. The authors also evaluate the impact of the PQ message signature `CertificateVerify` execution cost in TLSv1.3. [36]. *Marchsreiter et al.* [37] present an assessment of the post-quantum and hybrid operating mode of TLSv1.3, utilizing a hybrid key agreement and hybrid digital signature technique for server authentication via message signature `CertificateVerify`. Nevertheless, the authors provide their findings derived from the deployment of PQ-standalone X.509 PKI. Furthermore, the assessment solely relies on NIST curves, neglecting the assessment of TLSv1.3 integrated Curve448 and Ed448.

In our research, we focus on the deficiencies in the existing literature by conducting an assessment of hybrid TLSv1.3. Specifically, we provide the first evaluation of a fully hybrid TLSv1.3 implementation that utilizes Curve448 with Kyber1024 as classical and post-quantum key exchange methods, and Ed448 with Dilithium5 as classical and post-quantum digital signature algorithms, respectively.

1.2 Contributions

In this work, we present, to the best of our knowledge, the first fully hybrid TLSv1.3 based on Curve448 and Crystals-Kyber1024 for key exchange and Ed448 and Crystals-Dilithium5 for authentication and certificate verification. Our contributions include the following:

1. We provide the entirely hybrid version of the TLSv1.3 network protocol, including Curve448 and Ed448 to guarantee resilience against classical computer adversaries, as well as Crystals-Kyber1024 and Crystals-Dilithium5 to provide protection against quantum computer attacks.

2. We enhance the widely deployed OpenSSL library by including the capability to generate the X.509 hybrid Ed448_Dilithium5-based keys and certificates in PEM file format, where the certificate hybrid key and signature are both based on classical Ed448 and PQ Dilithium5 algorithms.
3. We implement hybrid key exchange based on emerging high-security level Curve448 and the PQ Kyber1024 algorithms, where both communication parties issue a symmetric key value based on a classical and PQ shared secret derivation.
4. We upgrade the embedded-specific wolfSSL cryptographic library to sign a message using both classical and PQ signature algorithms and to verify hybrid signatures based on Ed448_Dilithium5.
5. We deploy functions to process hybrid certificates Ed448_Dilithium5 certificates, including classical Ed448 and PQ Dilithium5 public key and signature values. We also enable verification of Ed448_Dilithium5 hybrid certificate signatures.
6. We evaluate the proposed hybrid TLSv1.3 based on Curve448_Kyber1024 for key agreement and Ed448_Dilithium5 for authentication and certificate validation on the NIST recommended ARMv7 Cortex-M4 STM32F413 WiFi equipped microcontroller and report the execution timing for the entire TLSv1.3 transmitting a 15B short message both directions, and for the pure TLSv1.3 handshake, neglecting the AEAD scheme overhead.

The subsequent sections of the paper are structured in the following manner. In Sect. 2 we provide a comprehensive explanation of the mathematical principles that form the foundation of Curve448 and Ed448 ECC algorithms. Additionally, we analyze the distinctive features of Crystals-Kyber and Crystals-Dilithium PQ algorithms. Section 3 provides an introduction to the TLS1.3 network protocol and the X.509 PKI architecture. It also emphasizes the improvements made in the design to achieve a completely hybrid TLSv1.3. In Sect. 4 we present an evaluation of the execution latency of the TLSv1.3 protocol, as part of the wolfSSL embedded cryptographic library. Ultimately, we bring our effort to a close in Sect. 5.

2 Preliminaries

This section offers a concise explanation of the mathematical concepts that form the foundation of the classical Curve448 and Ed448 key exchange and digital signature algorithms. We discuss the mathematical base of PQ Crystals-Kyber and Crystals-Dilithium algorithms. Finally, we present the X.509 PKI structure denoting the required changes for hybrid PQ transition.

2.1 ECC Mathematical Background

Elliptic Curve cryptography stands as one of the most optimal asymmetric key encryption scheme due to the compact key sizes and minimal computation latency, converting it in suitable scheme in scenarios of limited bandwidth or processing power, which is often the case of low-end embedded devices.

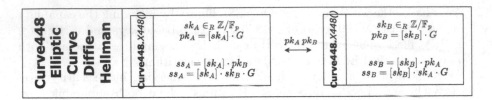

Fig. 1. X448 algorithm. G represents the value of the base point

Ed448-Goldilocks Edwards curve is denoted by the equation:

$$E_{Ed}/\mathbb{F}_p : ax^2 + y^2 = 1 + dx^2 y^2$$

Given that $d = -39081$ and $a = 1$ the curve operations for cryptographic purposes are defined over a finite field denoted as $\mathbb{F}_p$ where p is equal to $2^{448} - 2^{224} - 1$. The curve elements of Curve448 are represented by coordinate pairs $(x, y) \in \mathbb{F}_p \times \mathbb{F}_p$. A birational map exists to project a point from Edwards curve representation to the Montgomery curve representation.

$$(x, y) = (sqrt(156324) * u/v, (1 + u)/(1 - u))$$

The use of Montgomery curves representation often guarantees an ideal design for implementation, since it allows for efficient execution of group operations. The fundamental operation of ECC involves performing integer-point multiplications such that $P = k \cdot Q$ results in point Q being added to itself k times. Among the various point multiplication techniques is the so-called Montgomery Ladder, which ensures execution latency benefits based on the unified point doubling and addition formula, in addition to the constant time execution ensuring Simple Power Analysis (SPA) resistance, and the well-defined Differential Power Analysis countermeasure integration techniques. Furthermore, Montgomery ladder provides $X-$only coordinate operations when curve elements are presented in projective representation with three coordinates (X, Y, Z). The affine coordinates are retrieved at the end the of Montgomery Ladder execution as $(x, y) = (\frac{X}{Z}, \frac{Y}{Z})$.

ECC provides resilience against classic computer adversaries because to the challenging nature of solving the Elliptic Curve Discrete Logarithm problem. It is employed for both key exchange and authentication, making it a desirable choice in cryptographic network protocols like TLSv1.3, which is the main subject of this study.

2.2   X448

The implementation of key agreement with Curve448 is achieved by the Elliptic Curve Diffie-Hellman-like algorithm (ECDH). Similar to other techniques based on elliptic curve cryptography (ECC), Curve448 depends on performing scalar-point multiplication.

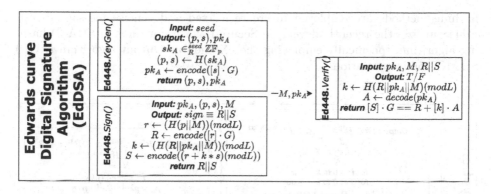

Fig. 2. Ed448 algorithm [38]. H denotes $SHAKE256$. L represents the order of Ed448 curve. G represents the value of the base point

During the execution of the Elliptic Curve Diffie-Hellman (ECDH) protocol, both parties involved generate a scalar secret key sk. They then perform a scalar-point multiplication operation, known as X448 for Curve448, using a parameter base point G. This operation results in a new point on the curve, which is used as their public key information pk as $pk = sk \cdot G$. The parties exchange the calculated public keys. Both parties currently possess their own private keys as well as the public key of the other party. By utilizing the obtained public key and their own secret key, each participant engages in an additional scalar point multiplication operation X448. As a consequence, a shared secret value ss is obtained, which is denoted by a point on the elliptic curve. The ECDH technique based on Curve448 is visually represented in Fig. 1, with the subindex value A, B indicating the computation parties as Alice and Bob.

Alice and Bob apply a Key Derivation Function (KDF) to extract a symmetric key value from their shared secret. This enables them to transition to a computationally efficient symmetric encryption method, guaranteeing that their data flow is secured and safeguarded from eavesdropping.

2.3 Ed448

The Digital Signature Algorithm (DSA) enables the recipient of a message to verify the sender's identity (authentication), guarantees the integrity of the data by preventing any unauthorized modifications during transmission (data integrity), and eliminates the sender's ability to deny delivering the message (non-repudiation). In order to uphold these cryptographic principles, one can employ ECC techniques, which rely on either EC Digital Signature Algorithms (ECDSA) or Edwards Curve Digital Signature Algorithms (EdDSA), depending on the specific elliptic curve being deployed.

Ed448 is an EdDSA method that utilizes the scalar-point multiplication operation X448, similar to the ECDH algorithm based on Curve448. In order to deal with the arbitrary length of messages conveyed across the Internet, extra hashing methods are employed to create a fixed and concise message digest. Ed448 utilizes the recently developed Secure Hash Algorithms 3 (SHA-3) hashing algorithm, specifically employing the eXtendable Output algorithm (XOF) SHAKE256 instantiation.

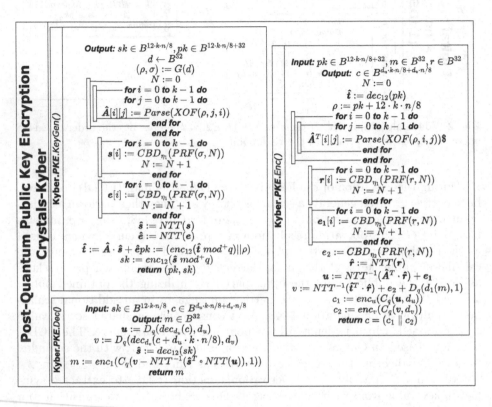

Fig. 3. Crystals-Kyber algorithm [39]. Each variable represents (the coefficients of) a polynomial, bold text style denotes vector of polynomials, capital letter notation denotes a matrix. *enc* and *dec* represents encode/decode, C and D present Compress/Decompress, respectively

The signature entity performs key generation and signing functions using the two fundamental operations of point multiplication and hashing, as illustrated in Fig. 2. Like Curve448 ECDH, a key pair (sk, pk) is created, where the secret key value is then utilized to acquire the signature of the message M, $R\|S$. After receiving the message and the signature, the recipient can authenticate the sender's identity by utilizing the public key value. The verification function determines whether to accept or reject the signature on the message value.

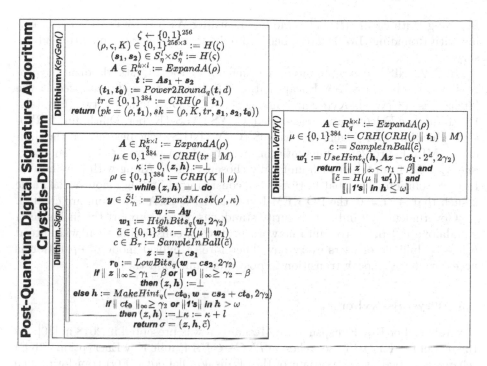

Fig. 4. CRYSTALS-Dilithium algorithm [40]. Each variable represents a polynomial, bold text style denotes vector of polynomials, capital letter notation denotes a matrix

Within the realm of network protocols, digital signature algorithms play a vital role in verifying the identity of communication parties and are an integral component of the Public Key Infrastructure, namely in certificate verification procedures. The integration of elliptic curve algorithms into TLSv1.3 is gaining popularity, although it is vulnerable to attacks in the age of quantum computing. This necessitates the switch to post-quantum key agreement and digital signature techniques.

2.4   Lattices Mathematical Background

Post Quantum Cryptographic Algorithms promise resistance against an adversary with a quantum computing power. Based on complex mathematical problems, PQ schemes promise to upgrade the cryptographic strength of the security network protocols. Among different families of PQ primitives, such as Code-, Hash-, Multivariate-, and Isogeny-based schemes, Lattice-based cryptographic primitive ensure relatively compact key sizes, compared to other PQ schemes, with the main advantage the limited computational requirements. Lattices are used to define both - public key encryption schemes and digital signature algorithms, relying on the Shortest Vector Problem (SVP), Closest Vector Problem (CVP) and Learning With Errors (LWE) (and it variations such as Ring-

Learning With Errors (RLWE), Module-Learning With Errors (MLWE), Learning with Rounding (LWR), etc.), believed to be resistant against quantum adversary.

In 2022 NIST has announced the finalists of the PQ standardization process, where the only Key Encapsulation Mechanics *to-be-standardized* is the lattice-based Crystals-Kyber and among three PQ DSA finalists, two (Crystals-Dilithium and Falcon) are lattice-based. CRYSTALS-{Kyber, Dilithium} CRYptographic SuiTe for Algebraic LatticeS (CRYSTALS) schemes rely on the difficulty (MLWE problem) differentiating $(A, As_1 + s_2)$ with $A \in Z_q^{n \times l}$, $s_1 \in Z_q^l$, and $s_2 \in Z_q^n$ from (A, b) with uniformly chosen value b. Along with the Shortest Integer Solution (SIS) that lattices pose, consisting of finding a non-trivial value x such that $A \cdot x = 0$, the PQ KEM Kyber and PQ DSA Dilithium are created.

Government and industry security standards do not support the inclusion of standalone PQ primitives into network protocols, considering their widespread usage by billions of users every day. Therefore, a hybrid mode of operation is necessary for a smooth transition to post-quantum robustness.

2.5   Crystals-Kyber

Crystals-Kyber Key Encapsulation Mechanism was presented in 2018 in [39]. As the rest of PQ KEMs Kyber relies on $INC - CPA$ Public Key Encryption (PKE) scheme wrapped by the (variant of the) Fujisaki-Okamoto (FO) transform. The Kyber.PKE method consists of key generation, encryption and decryption, represented as Kyber.PKE.KeyGen(), Kyber.PKE.En(), and Kyber.PKE.Dec() in Fig. 3, respectively. The Key Encapsulation Mechanism (KEM) algorithm wraps this functions in key generation, encapsulation and decapsulation, via some additional hash and XOF functions, in order to provide $IND - CCA2$ security of the underlying scheme.

Crystals-Kyber is instantiated with different set of parameters to offer distinct levels of security. Specifically, Kyber512, Kyber768, and Kyber1024 correspond to NIST Security Level 2, 3, and 5, respectively. Based on the security level of Curve448 and Ed448, providing 224-bit security, and the nature of the PQ primitives lacking trust, we consider the highest security level, in particular, Kyber1024, to integrate in the TLSv1.3 protocol in the scope of this work. We should note that Crystals-Kyber768 is the recommended security level to be used. The least recommended security level to be utilized is Crystals-Kyber768. Despite its high security level, Kyber1024 remains appealing due to its low latency, which is equivalent to that provided by traditional cryptographic public key methods.

2.6   Crystals-Dilithium

The Crystals-Dilithium lattice-based DSA method is derived from the mathematical issue of Module Learning With Error (MLWE), similar to the Crystals-Kyber algorithm. It was suggested in the publication by *Ducas et al.* [40] and

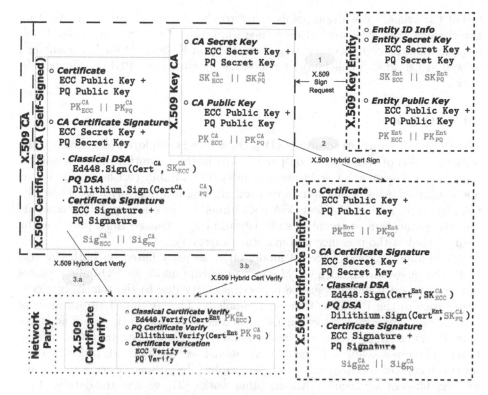

Fig. 5. The Public Key Infrastructure (PKI) built using classical (Ed448) and post-quantum (Dilithium5) Digital Signature Algorithm (DSA) techniques. The gray data refers to the information fields found in the X.509 files. Superscript indicates the owner of the data, while subscript indicates the type of information (Color figure online)

has been selected as one of the three DSA finalists for the NIST PQ standardization process. Like Kyber, this system provides many levels of security. In our study, we specifically concentrate on Dilithium5, which guarantees a high level of security comparable to Ed448. The specifics of the PQ signature algorithm are presented in Fig. 4, where the details about the three underlying functions Dilithium.KeyGen(), Dilithium.Sign(), and Dilithium.Verify() are presented.

The application of DSA in the scope of TLSv1.3 involves the signing of a TLSv1.3 handshake message for server authentication and its incorporation into the PKI framework, where trusted authorities issue signatures to verify the authenticity of information for a specific entity. This work specifically addresses both aspects.

3   Hybrid Network Protocol Deployment

This section provides a comprehensive explanation of the TLSv1.3 network protocols and the underlying X.509 Public Key Infrastructure architecture. We represent the primary execution points using graphical representation, highlighting the changes that were made to enhance the protocol's execution mode. These modifications involve incorporating Curve448 and Kyber1024 for key exchange, as well as Ed448 and Dilithium5 for message signature and PKI certificate validation.

3.1   PQ X.509

The Public Key Infrastructure (PKI) architecture is employed to guarantee the authentication of communication participants in the network through a reliable organization known as a Certificate Authority (CA). Public certificates are issued and confirmed using X.509 standards via digital signature algorithms. Typically, CA signatures rely on classical DSA algorithms. In the era of quantum computing, the verification of an entity's identification by a trusted third party can be easily forged in the presence of a quantum adversary.

The entirely hybrid TLSv1.3 model offers security based on both classical and post quantum algorithms. Making an abrupt move to PQ-only protocol implementation would jeopardize network security due to the relatively recent application of the PQ algorithms in technology. The continued employment of traditional cryptographic techniques poses a concern due to the rapid advancements in quantum computing technology and the expanding computational capabilities of these machines. Thus, a hybrid model, secures network traffic relaying on two independent categories of cryptographic algorithms, offering robustness against different adversaries. Among other works, [31], go into the details of the security and performance implications of the hybrid execution model of widely deployed network protocols, and define the motivation behind hybrid operation mode as guaranteeing the security of the system as long as one of the underlying cryptographic algorithms remains uncompromised.

As shown in Fig. 5, a Certificate Authority (CA), denoted as X.509 CA, owns a key file that contains both secret and public key values. By employing the confidential key data, the CA generates a signature, first, for its own certificate. The certificate includes the public key information of the CA for the purpose of validating issued signatures. It is important to note that real-world scenarios frequently involve a chain of CA certificates, which is not addressed in this study. After obtaining its own key and certificate files, the CA proceeds to distribute the certificate to third-parties for further verification reasons.

We outline, in Fig. 5, the sequential steps involved in acquiring a validated entity certificate. After an entity creates a key file, it sends identifying information and the public key as a Signature Request to the CA for validation (1. X.509 Sign Request in Fig. 5) and verification of its identity. The CA verifies the data of the entity and affixes its signature to the information, therefore generating a certificate for the specified entity (2. X.509 (Hybrid) Cert Sign in Fig. 5).

Finally, when any communication network party initializes a connection with the given entity, the certificate information is used (3.a X.509 (Hybrid) Cert Verify in Fig. 5). To verify the identity of the entity, the public key, part of the CA certificate, is being used (3.b X.509 (Hybrid) Cert Verify in Fig. 5).

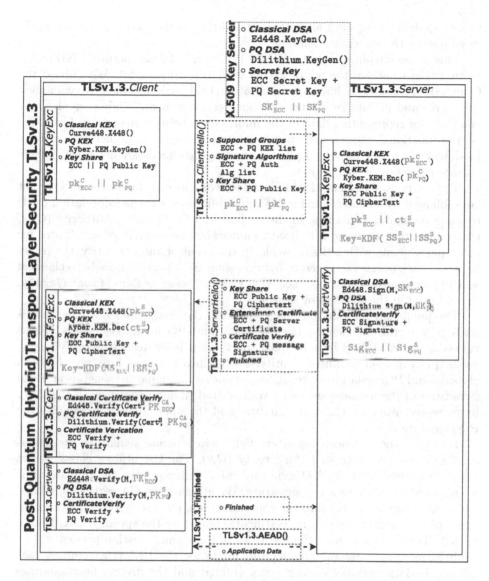

Fig. 6. TLSv1.3 execution flow graphical representation. Gray data refers to the information fields included in X.509 files, where superscript indicates the owner of the data and subscript indicates the type of information. The compute stages are represented by solid box lines, the message flow is represented by discontinuous lines, and the certificate file is represented by scattered box lines (Color figure online)

The implementation of Public Key Infrastructure (PKI) includes the use of Digital Signature Algorithm (DSA) processes, which are susceptible to attacks from adversaries with quantum computing capabilities. This study proposes a way of applying a PQ DSA algorithm, in addition to the conventional approach, to guarantee the system's reliability.

This paper introduces a novel hybrid Public Key Infrastructure (PKI) architecture that combines the use of Ed448 with Dilithium5 DSA. We utilized the OpenSSL cryptography library to generate hybrid PEM key files. We combined the secret and private key values by concatenating them. While several methods exist for representing data in the information fields, our primary focus was on the functional aspects and effectiveness of the system. Implementing more modifications to the data field placements may be effortlessly done, yet, it falls outside the scope of this project.

The entity owner of a key PEM file, which consists of a classical and PQ secret keys followed by a classical and a PQ key public keys, uses its information fields to generate digital signatures. In the context of a Certification Authority (CA), the confidential key value is utilized to authorize the issuance of certificates for other participants within the network. In the event of another entity, the secret key values are utilized to generate hybrid signatures. This includes both classical and PQ signatures of, for instance, the TLSv1.3 message `CertificateVerify`, as explained in the subsequent section.

The public key information is stored within the certificate PEM files. In this context, a certificate includes both classical and PQ public key values. These values are then utilized by a recipient party that is interested in verifying the authenticity of the transmitting entity. The verification procedure relies on both classical and PQ signature systems, analogous to the signature generation. Both signatures of the message are being transmitted simultaneously, with the lower bytes representing the classical signature and the upper bytes representing the PQ signature value.

Lastly, in the certificate signature field, two separate signatures are generated and saved by a trusted third party (CA). The CA utilizes classic secret key data to produce a classical signature value. Subsequently, the PQ key value is employed to generate a PQ signature. By utilizing the CA certificate's keys, which are often integrated into the communication parties' systems, the authenticity of both signatures on any certificate, issued by the specified CA, is confirmed, therefore confirming the identities of the communication parties.

Implementing a hybrid architecture mode for the PKI is a complex task due to the large number of files being created and the diverse functionalities required to process these files and extract their value. This work introduces the first version of hybrid Ed448 and Dilithium5 PEM keys and certificates. The creation and processing of these keys and certificates are performed using the OpenSSL general crypto library and the wolfSSL embedded device-specific library.

3.2   PQ TLSv1.3

TLSv1.3 guarantees a secure connection setup with a single roundtrip communications. The client and server establish a shared secret using key agreement

Table 1. Performance of the entirely hybrid TLSv1.3 handshake and the overall TLSv1.3 protocol when a short 15B message is delivered between communication parties. The values are expressed in terms of clock cycles [CC]

Work	KEX	Auth	Cert Verify	TLS1.3 handshake	TLS1.3 with AEAD
wolfSSL [41]	X448	Ed448	Ed448	–	44,358,855
Anastasova et al. [17]	X448	Ed448	Ed448	–	46,310,749
This work	X448 & Kyber1024	Ed448 & Dil5	–	97,624,103	106,735,300
	X448 & Kyber1024	Ed448 & Dil5	Ed448 & Dil5	114,017,313	123,139,034

cryptographic mechanisms like ECDH or PQ KEMs. Both communication parties utilize a key derivation function (KDF) to create a symmetric key value. This key value is then utilized to encrypt their application data traffic using an Authenticated Encryption with Additional Data (AEAD) cipher (Table 1).

The simplified graphical representation of TLSv1.3 is depicted in Fig. 6. The server and client exchange their respective certificate files, which contain a signature created by a trusted third party (CA) to authenticate the certificate's legitimacy. After obtaining the certificate, the client confirms its genuineness by verifying the signature using the public key information of the CA, which is incorporated on the client's side. The server's authentication step entails creating a signature of the message. After receiving the message, the user authenticates the signature by utilizing the server's public key value acquired from the server's certificate. Ultimately, the server sends an HMAC (Hash-based Message Authentication Code) of the entire message using the predetermined symmetric key value. Upon the successful completion of the TLSv1.3 protocol handshake, both communicating entities have the ability to securely transmit data across the established channel.

Within the present work, we enhance the design of the TLSv1.3 network protocol by integrating fully hybrid version of the protocol. For key exchange, we use the Curve448 ECDH method in conjunction with the Kyber1024 PQ scheme. Specifically, as indicated in Fig. 6, the cipher key for TLSv1.3 is obtained by utilizing the shared secret information from both Curve448 and Kyber1024. The session data is produced by combining the classical and PQ values and utilizing them as input to a Key Derivation Function (KDF).

In order to carry out message signature, we utilize a hybrid technique by using both Ed448 and Dilithium5. Like the Key Exchange (KEX) methods, both the traditional and PQ DSA are performed simultaneously. The server's PEM key file has a classical secret key value, which is stored at the most significant bytes of the secret key field. This value is utilized to generate a classical signature. The PQ signature is generated using the least significant bytes from the secret key field, which contains the PQ secret key data. After generating both the classical and PQ signatures, they are combined and sent as a component of the Certificate Verify message.

The hybrid Public Key Infrastructure (PKI), which is a component of TLSv1.3, is also included in this project. In this work, the PEM key and certificate fields have been altered to include the classical and Post-Quantum (PQ) values, as explained in the previous section. Our hybrid TLSv1.3 architecture now includes the complete integration of the hybrid PKI.

4   Performance Evaluation

The next section examines the obtained results in relation to performance. We provide information on the latency of our design when it is run on the STM32F413 discovery board. This board is equipped with a Cortex-M4 CPU and is built on the ARMv7 architecture, which has been selected by NIST for evaluating post-quantum primitives on low-end embedded devices. We execute our experiments at a frequency of 76.6MHz, simulating a real-world scenario. The findings are presented in terms of clock cycles. Multiple scenarios are considered in relation to verification processes. We provide the complete implementation of the TLSv1.3 protocol, including the exchange of brief messages between the client and server. Additionally, we demonstrate the independent execution of the TLSv1.3 handshake, showcasing the modifications made throughout this project.

The generation of the X.509 key and certificate files is based on modification deployed on the OpenSSL cryptographic library. Since keys and certificates are being generated outside the scope of the TLSv1.3 protocol, we do not report performance results. However, it is important to note, that for the X.509 key generation and certificate verification (signature), again a hybrid approach involving Ed448 and Dilithium5 was used.

We report the performance of TLSv1.3 protocol after integrating Curve448 and Crystal-Kyber, and Ed448 and Crystals-Dilithium for key generation, entity authentication and certificate verification. The client computes ECC key generation and PQ KEM key generation and decapsulation routines in order to derive a session key with the server. On the server side, the X.509 hybrid certificate is being transmitted to the client along with a signature over the entire footprint of the TLSv1.3 message value. The client uses the CA public key value to verify the validity of the server certificate, thus executes hybrid signature verification.

The communication parties transmit data through a UART serial connection based on 115200bps transmission speed. It is important to note that, based on the large sizes of the transmitted certificate values, the performance results show significant drop. However, the communication latency forms a large part of the protocol execution time in a real-world scenario where data is transmitted all over the worlds and should not be neglected when evaluating the impact of PQ protocol transition.

We report around 114 million clock cycles for the execution of the fully hybrid TLSv1.3 handshake based on Curve448 and Kyber1024 and Ed4448 and Dilithium5 cryptographic primitives. The implementation of the whole TLSv1.3 protocol, including the transmission of a brief message encrypted using an AEAD cipher, leads to an additional computational cost of around 20.3 million clock cycles. By excluding the verification of the server certificate, which is based on the CA signature, we observe an approximate improvement of 17.5% and

16% for the TLSv1.3 handshake and the fully hybrid TLSv1.3 handshake with AEAD encrypted message transmission, respectively. However, it is important to note that this scenario is not typical in real-world network communication. Therefore, our focus is on the statistics related to the complete execution of the TLSv1.3 protocol on the STM32F413 board. Enabling TLSv1.3 in entirely hybrid mode leads to a ×2.77 the execution of the original wolfSSL classical-only implementation and ×2.67 the latency of the optimal and side-channel robust Curve448 and Ed448 design as part of wolfSSL [17].

5   Conclusion

This work introduces the initial fully hybrid operating mode of the widely used TLSv1.3 network security protocol. The mode is based on Curve448 and Crystals-Kyber for key exchange, and Ed448 and Crystals-Dilithium for the digital signature method. Within our approach, the client and server engage in the exchange of information, encompassing public key data for both classical and post-quantum (PQ) primitives. Our solution offers an architectural framework where the involved parties engage in message signing and verification using a combination of traditional and post-quantum methods. In addition, we offer hybrid Public Key Infrastructure (PKI) by making changes to the commonly used OpenSSL software. This allows us to create hybrid keys and certificates that comply with the X.509 standard. We add the ability to process the hybrid data within these keys and certificates, transforming the Certification Authority (CA) into a hybrid entity that possesses both classical and Post-Quantum (PQ) key values. To present performance results on the full hybrid TLSv1.3 protocol, we utilize the wolfSSL cryptography library specifically designed for embedded devices.

Acknowledgements. The authors would like to thank the reviewers for their comments. This work is supported by NSF 214796 grant.

References

1. Rescorla, E.: The Transport Layer Security (TLS) Protocol Version 1.3. RFC 8446, August 2018
2. Shor, P.W.: Polynomial-time algorithms for prime factorization and discrete logarithms on a quantum computer. SIAM Rev. **41**(2), 303–332 (1999)
3. T. N. I. of Standards and T. (NIST)., Post-quantum cryptography standardization, 2017-2018. Accessed 20 May 2021
4. Hamburg, M.: Ed448-Goldilocks, a new elliptic curve, Cryptology ePrint Archive (2015)
5. Bernstein, D.J.: Curve25519: new Diffie-Hellman speed records. In: Yung, M., Dodis, Y., Kiayias, A., Malkin, T. (eds.) PKC 2006. LNCS, vol. 3958, pp. 207–228. Springer, Heidelberg (2006). https://doi.org/10.1007/11745853_14
6. Bernstein, D.J., Duif, N., Lange, T., Schwabe, P., Yang, B.Y.: High-speed high-security signatures. In: International Workshop on Cryptographic Hardware and Embedded Systems, pp. 124–142. Springer (2011)

7. Seo, H.: Compact implementations of Curve Ed448 on low-end IoT platforms. ETRI J. **41**(6), 863–872 (2019)

8. Faz-Hernández, A., López, J., Dahab, R.: High-performance implementation of elliptic curve cryptography using vector instructions. ACM Trans. Math. Softw. (TOMS) **45**(3), 1–35 (2019)

9. Seo, H., Azarderakhsh, R.: Curve448 on 32-bit ARM Cortex-M4. In: Hong, D. (ed.) ICISC 2020. LNCS, vol. 12593, pp. 125–139. Springer, Cham (2021). https://doi.org/10.1007/978-3-030-68890-5_7

10. Anastasova, M., Bisheh-Niasar, M., Seo, H., Azarderakhsh, R., Kermani, M.M.: Efficient and side-channel resistant design of high-security Ed448 on ARM Cortex-M4. In: 2022 IEEE International Symposium on Hardware Oriented Security and Trust (HOST), pp. 93–96. IEEE (2022)

11. Anastasova, M., Azarderakhsh, R., Kermani, M.M., Beshaj, L. Time-efficient finite field microarchitecture design for Curve448 and Ed448 on Cortex-M4. In: Seo, S.H., Seo, H. (eds.) Information Security and Cryptology – ICISC 2022. ICISC 2022. LNCS, vol. 13849, pp. 292–314. Springer, Cham (2023). https://doi.org/10.1007/978-3-031-29371-9_15

12. Bisheh-Niasar, M., Anastasova, M., Abdulgadir, A., Seo, H., Azarderakhsh, R.: Side-channel analysis and countermeasure design for implementation of Curve448 on Cortex-M4. In: Proceedings of the 11th International Workshop on Hardware and Architectural Support for Security and Privacy, pp. 10–17 (2022)

13. Blake, I., Seroussi, G., Seroussi, G., Smart, N.: Elliptic Curves in Cryptography, vol. 265. Cambridge University Press, Cambridge (1999)

14. Hamburg, M.: Fast and compact elliptic-curve cryptography, Cryptology ePrint Archive, 2012

15. Meloni, N.: New point addition formulae for ECC applications. In: Carlet, C., Sunar, B. (eds.) WAIFI 2007. LNCS, vol. 4547, pp. 189–201. Springer, Heidelberg (2007). https://doi.org/10.1007/978-3-540-73074-3_15

16. Montgomery, P.L.: Speeding the Pollard and elliptic curve methods of factorization. Math. Comput. **48**(177), 243–264 (1987)

17. Anastasova, M., El Khatib, R., Laclaustra, A., Azarderakhsh, R., Kermani, M.M.: Highly optimized Curve448 and Ed448 design in wolfSSL and side-channel evaluation on Cortex-M4. In: 2023 IEEE Conference on Dependable and Secure Computing (DSC), pp. 1–8. IEEE (2023)

18. Becker, H., Hwang, V., Kannwischer, M.J., Yang, B.Y., Yang, S.Y.: Neon NTT: faster dilithium, kyber, and saber on cortex-a72 and apple m1, Cryptology ePrint Archive (2021)

19. Nguyen, D.T., Gaj, K.: Optimized software implementations of CRYSTALS-Kyber, NTRU, and Saber using NEON-based special instructions of ARMv8. In: Proceedings of the NIST 3rd PQC Standardization Conference (NIST PQC 2021) (2021)

20. Zhao, L., Zhang, J., Huang, J., Liu, Z., Hancke, G.: Efficient implementation of kyber on mobile devices. In: 2021 IEEE 27th International Conference on Parallel and Distributed Systems (ICPADS), pp. 506–513. IEEE (2021)

21. Kim, Y., Song, J., Youn, T.-Y., Seo, S.C., et al.: Crystals-dilithium on armv8. Secur. Commun. Netw. **2022** (2022)

22. Zheng, J., He, F., Shen, S., Xue, C., Zhao, Y.: Parallel small polynomial multiplication for dilithium: a faster design and implementation. In: Proceedings of the 38th Annual Computer Security Applications Conference, pp. 304–317 (2022)

23. Seiler, G.: Faster AVX2 optimized NTT multiplication for Ring-LWE lattice cryptography, Cryptology ePrint Archive (2018)

24. Zheng, J., Zhu, H., Song, Z., Wang, Z., Zhao, Y.: Optimized Vectorization Implementation of CRYSTALS-Dilithium, arXiv preprint arXiv:2306.01989 (2023)
25. Wright, J., Gowanlock, M., Philabaum, C., Cambou, B.: A crystals-dilithium response-based cryptography engine using GPGPU. In: Arai, K. (ed.) FTC 2021. LNNS, vol. 360, pp. 32–45. Springer, Cham (2022). https://doi.org/10.1007/978-3-030-89912-7_3
26. Zhao, X., Wang, B., Zhao, Z., Qu, Q., Wang, L.: Highly efficient parallel design of Dilithium on GPUs, 2022
27. Shen, S., Yang, H., Dai, W., Zhang, H., Liu, Z., Zhao, Y.: High-throughput gpu implementation of dilithium post-quantum digital signature, arXiv preprint arXiv:2211.12265 (2022)
28. Botros, L., Kannwischer, M.J., Schwabe, P.: Memory-efficient high-speed implementation of Kyber on Cortex-M4. In: Buchmann, J., Nitaj, A., Rachidi, T. (eds.) AFRICACRYPT 2019. LNCS, vol. 11627, pp. 209–228. Springer, Cham (2019). https://doi.org/10.1007/978-3-030-23696-0_11
29. Alkim, E., Bilgin, Y.A., Cenk, M., Gérard, F.: Cortex-M4 optimizations for {R, M} LWE schemes. IACR Transactions on Cryptographic Hardware and Embedded Systems, pp. 336–357 (2020)
30. Abdulrahman, A., Hwang, V., Kannwischer, M.J., Sprenkels, A.: Faster kyber and dilithium on the Cortex-M4. In: Ateniese, G., Venturi, D (eds.) Applied Cryptography and Network Security. ACNS 2022. LNCS, vol. 13269, pp. 853–871. Springer, Cham (2022). https://doi.org/10.1007/978-3-031-09234-3_42
31. Crockett, E., Paquin, C., Stebila, D.: Prototyping post-quantum and hybrid key exchange and authentication in TLS and SSH, Cryptology ePrint Archive (2019)
32. Anastasova, M., Kampanakis, P., Massimo, J.: PQ-HPKE: post-quantum hybrid public key encryption, Cryptology ePrint Archive (2022)
33. Kampanakis, P., Panburana, P., Daw, E., Van Geest, D.:The viability of post-quantum X. 509 certificates, Cryptology ePrint Archive (2018)
34. Campagna, M., Crockett, E.: Hybrid post-quantum key encapsulation methods (PQ KEM) for transport layer security 1.2 (TLS). In: Internet Engineering Task Force, Internet-Draft draft-campagna-tls-bike-sike-hybrid, vol. 1 (2019)
35. Sikeridis, D., Kampanakis, P., Devetsikiotis, M.: Post-quantum authentication in TLS 1.3: a performance study, Cryptology ePrint Archive (2020)
36. Sikeridis, D., Kampanakis, P., Devetsikiotis, M.: Assessing the overhead of post-quantum cryptography in TLS 1.3 and SSH. In: Proceedings of the 16th International Conference on emerging Networking EXperiments and Technologies, pp. 149–156 (2020)
37. Marchsreiter, D., Sepúlveda, J.: Hybrid post-quantum enhanced TLS 1.3 on embedded devices. In: 2022 25th Euromicro Conference on Digital System Design (DSD), pp. 905–912. IEEE (2022)
38. Josefsson, S., Liusvaara, I.: Edwards-Curve Digital Signature Algorithm (EdDSA). RFC 8032, January 2017
39. Bos, J., et al.: CRYSTALS-Kyber: a CCA-secure module-lattice-based KEM. In: 2018 IEEE European Symposium on Security and Privacy (EuroS&P), pp. 353–367. IEEE (2018)
40. Ducas, L., et al.: Crystals-dilithium: a lattice-based digital signature scheme. IACR Transactions on Cryptographic Hardware and Embedded Systems, pp. 238–268 (2018)
41. wolfSSL, wolfSSL. https://www.wolfssl.com/. Accessed 23 Jan 2023

Author Index

Printed in the United States
by Baker & Taylor Publisher Services

Printed in the United States
by Baker & Taylor Publisher Services